W9-DAP-278

ПORTHLAПDERS

BOOK FOUR: THE PLAGUE WIDOW

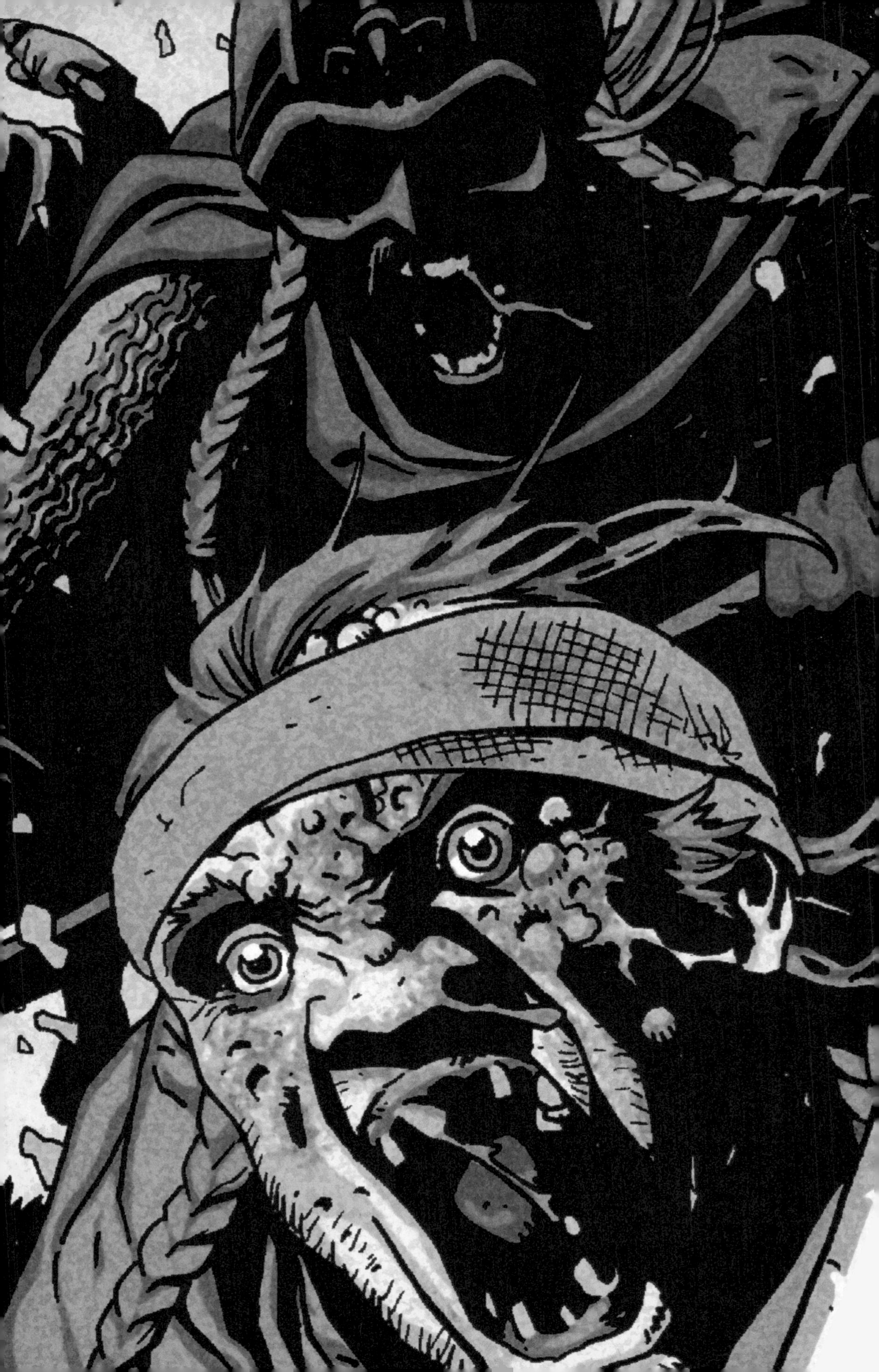

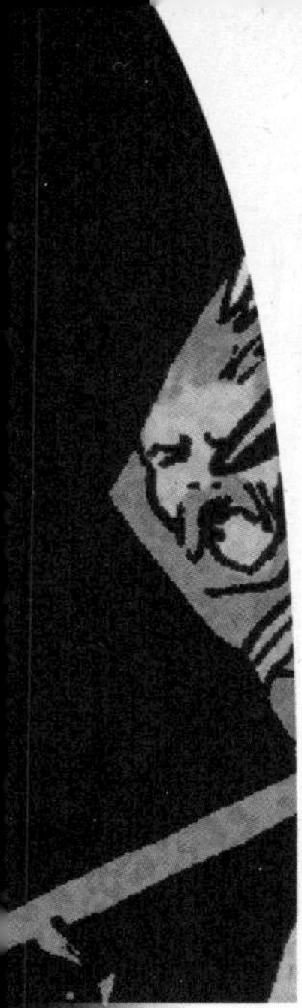
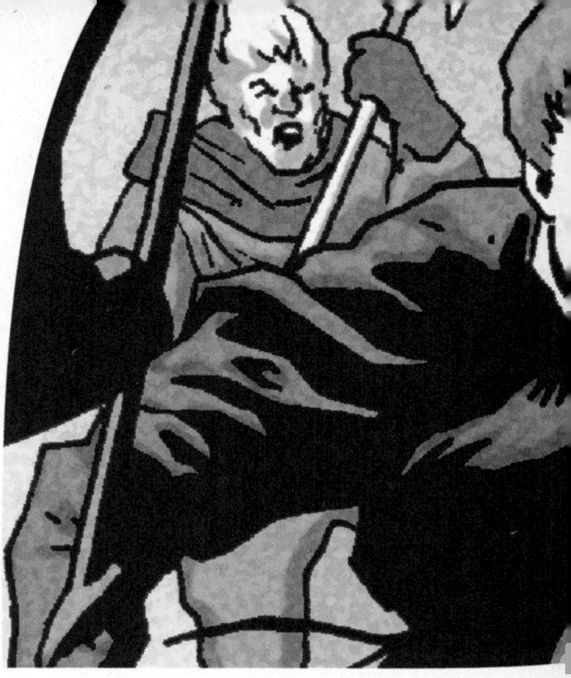

NORTHLANDERS

BOOK FOUR: THE PLAGUE WIDOW

Brian Wood Writer

Leandro Fernandez Artist

Dave McCaig Colorist

Travis Lanham Letterer

Original series covers by
Massimo Carnevale

Cover illustration by
Massimo Carnevale
and design by **Brian Wood**

Northlanders created by
Brian Wood

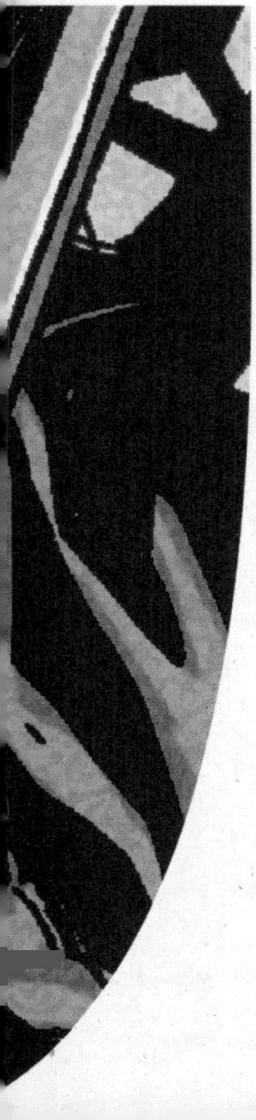
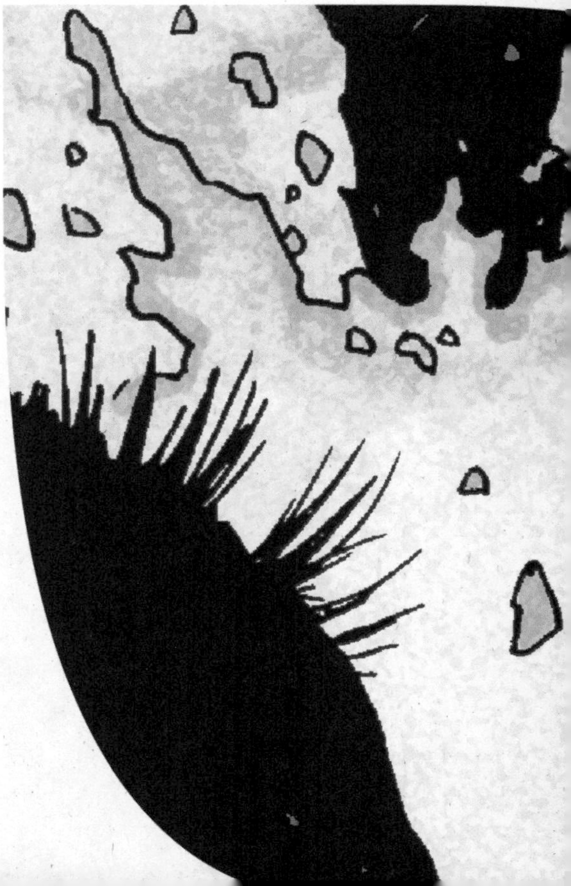

Karen Berger SVP – Executive Editor
Mark Doyle Editor – Original Series
Bob Harras Group Editor – Collected Editions
Robbin Brosterman Design Director – Books

DC COMICS
Diane Nelson President
Dan DiDio and **Jim Lee** Co-Publishers
Geoff Johns Chief Creative Officer
Patrick Caldon EVP-Finance and Administration
John Rood EVP-Sales, Marketing and Business Development
Amy Genkins SVP-Business and Legal Affairs
Steve Rotterdam SVP-Sales and Marketing
John Cunningham VP-Marketing
Terri Cunningham VP-Managing Editor
Alison Gill VP-Manufacturing
David Hyde VP-Publicity
Sue Pohja VP-Advertising and Custom Publishing
Bob Wayne VP-Sales
Mark Chiarello Art Director

NORTHLANDERS: THE PLAGUE WIDOW
Published by DC Comics. Cover and compilation
© 2010 Brian Wood and DC Comics. All Rights
Reserved. Originally published as NORTHLANDERS
21-28. Copyright © 2009, 2010 Brian Wood and
DC Comics. All Rights Reserved. VERTIGO and
all characters, their distinctive likenesses and related elements featured in this
publication are trademarks of DC Comics. The stories, characters and incidents
featured in this publication are entirely fictional. DC Comics does not read or
accept unsolicited submissions of ideas, stories or artwork. DC Comics,
1700 Broadway, New York, NY 10019. A Warner Bros. Entertainment Company
Printed in USA. First Printing. ISBN: 978-1-4012-2850-7

SUSTAINABLE
FORESTRY
INITIATIVE
Certified Chain of Custody
Promoting Sustainable
Forest Management
www.sfiprogram.org
Fiber used in this product line meets the
sourcing requirements of the SFI program.
www.sfiprogram.org PWC-SFICOC-260

Part 1: Seven Hundred on the Volga

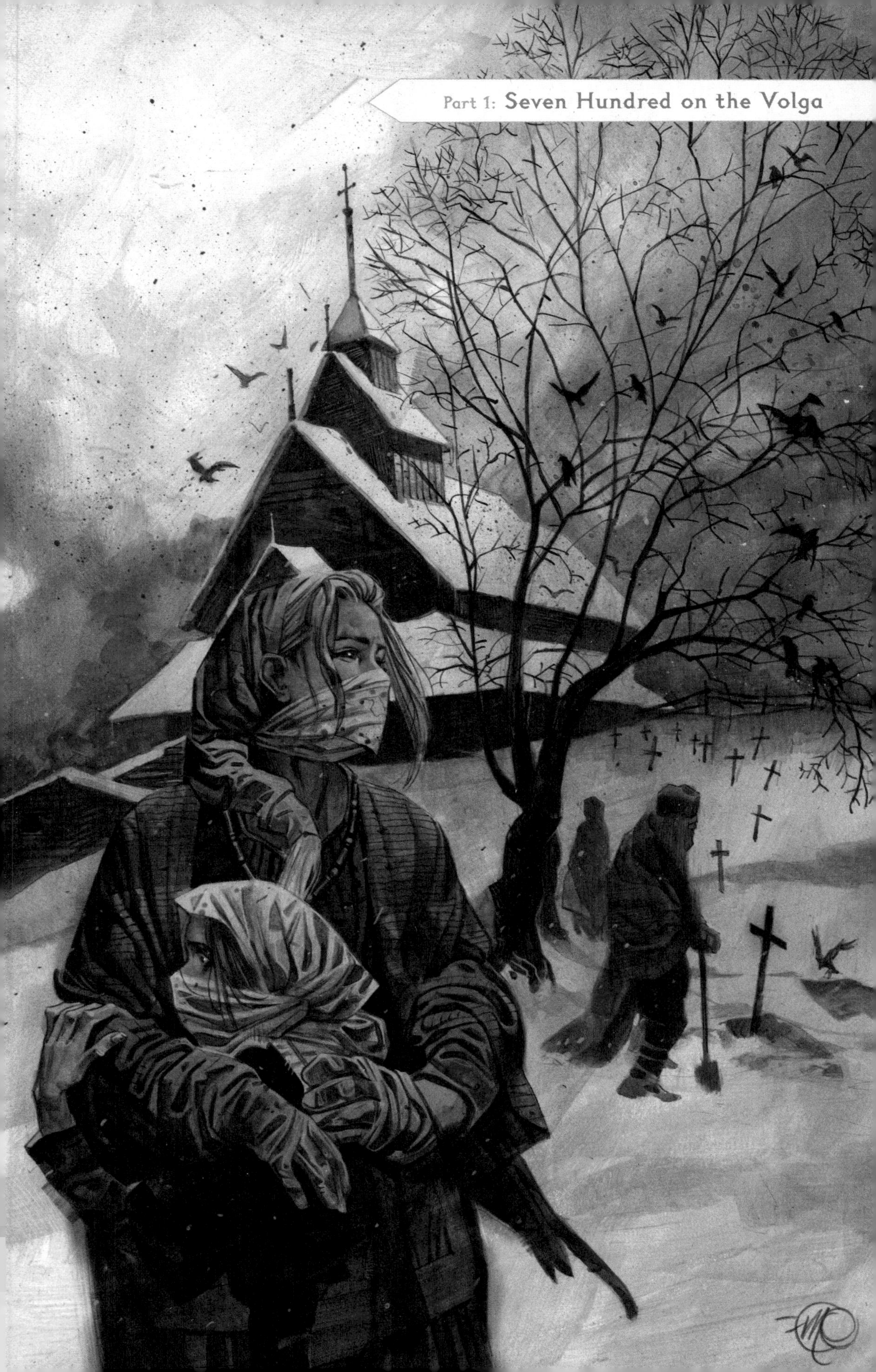

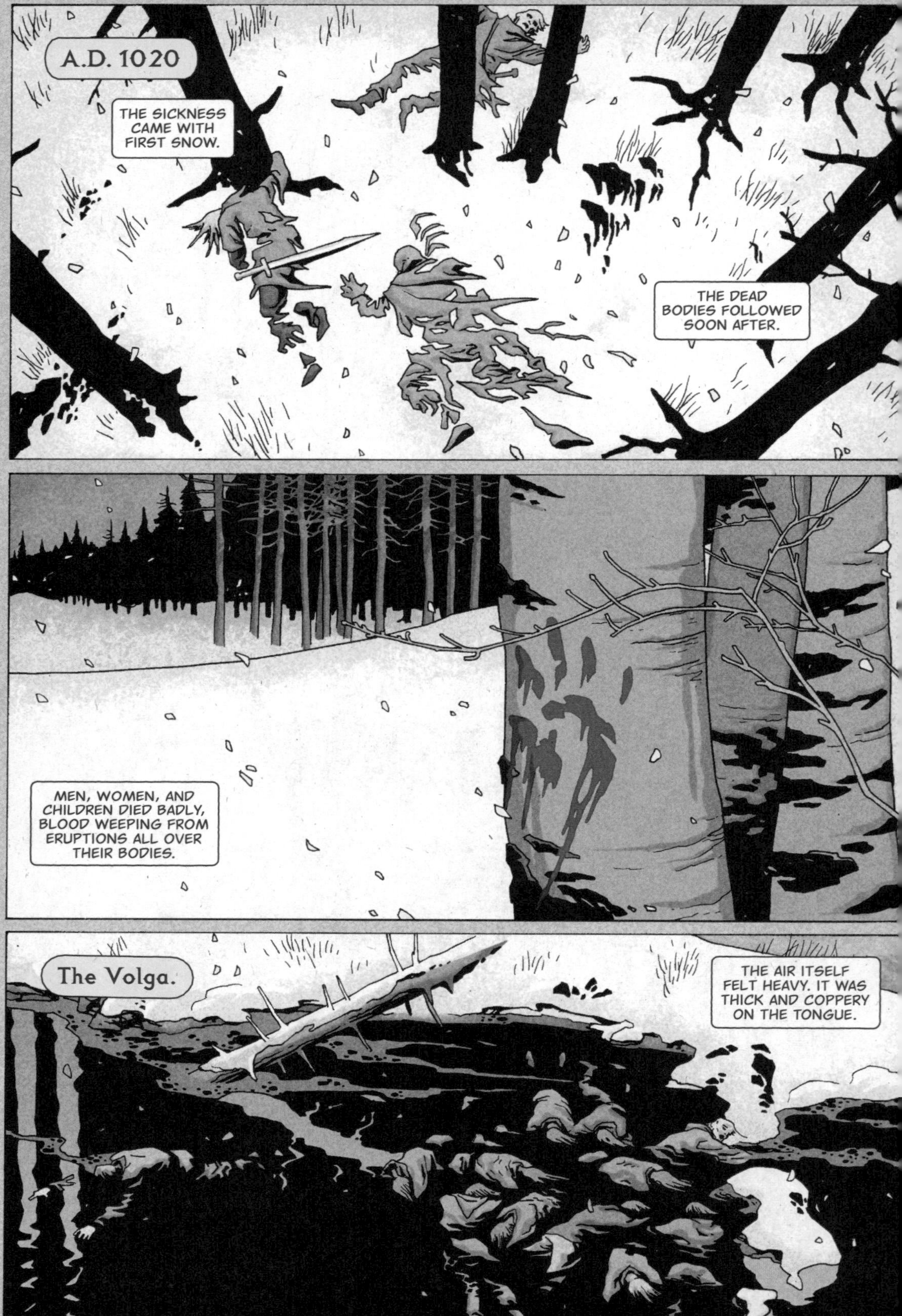
A.D. 1020
THE SICKNESS CAME WITH FIRST SNOW.
THE DEAD BODIES FOLLOWED SOON AFTER.
MEN, WOMEN, AND CHILDREN DIED BADLY, BLOOD WEEPING FROM ERUPTIONS ALL OVER THEIR BODIES.
The Volga.
THE AIR ITSELF FELT HEAVY. IT WAS THICK AND COPPERY ON THE TONGUE.

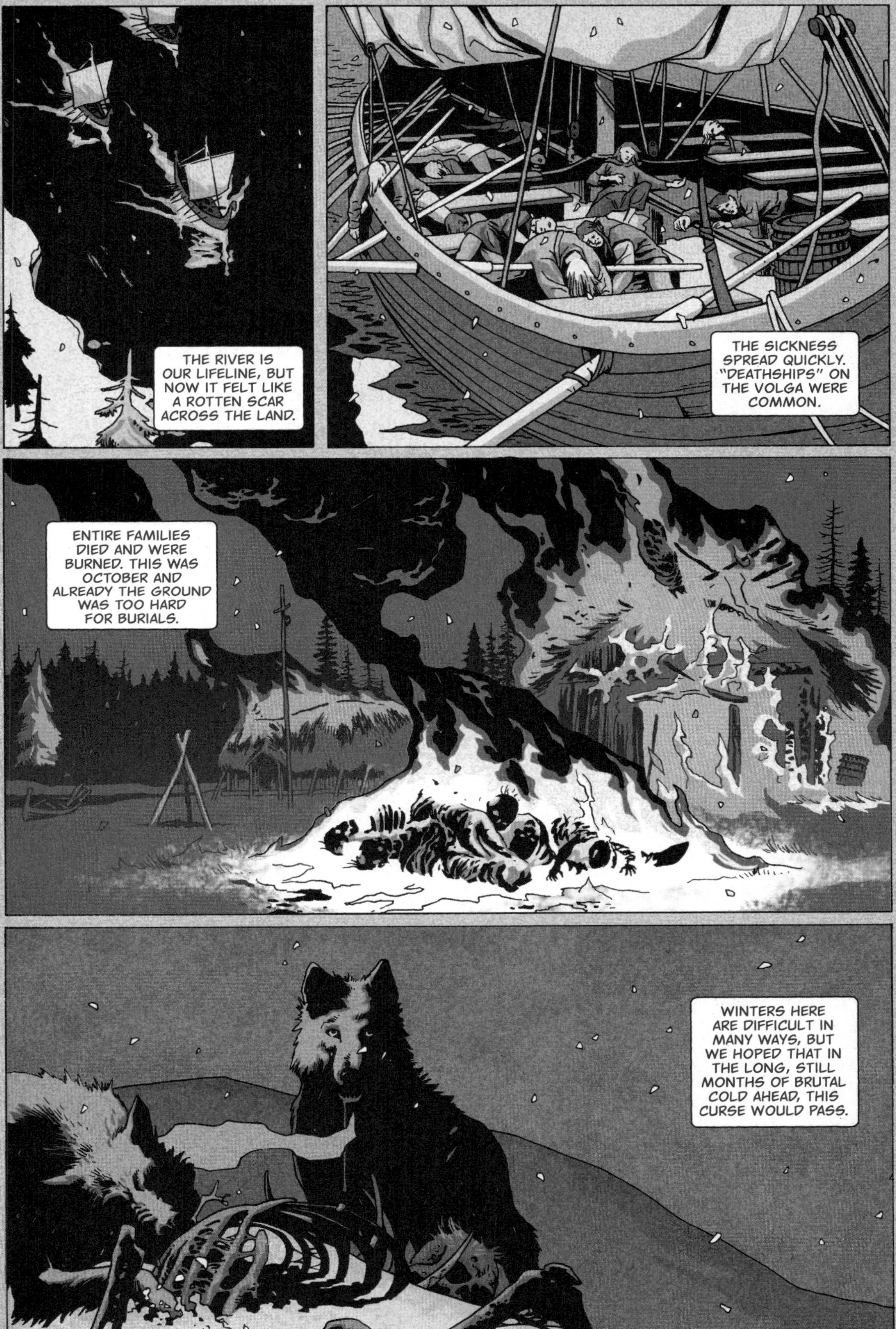
THE RIVER IS OUR LIFELINE, BUT NOW IT FELT LIKE A ROTTEN SCAR ACROSS THE LAND.
THE SICKNESS SPREAD QUICKLY. "DEATHSHIPS" ON THE VOLGA WERE COMMON.
ENTIRE FAMILIES DIED AND WERE BURNED. THIS WAS OCTOBER AND ALREADY THE GROUND WAS TOO HARD FOR BURIALS.
WINTERS HERE ARE DIFFICULT IN MANY WAYS, BUT WE HOPED THAT IN THE LONG, STILL MONTHS OF BRUTAL COLD AHEAD, THIS CURSE WOULD PASS.

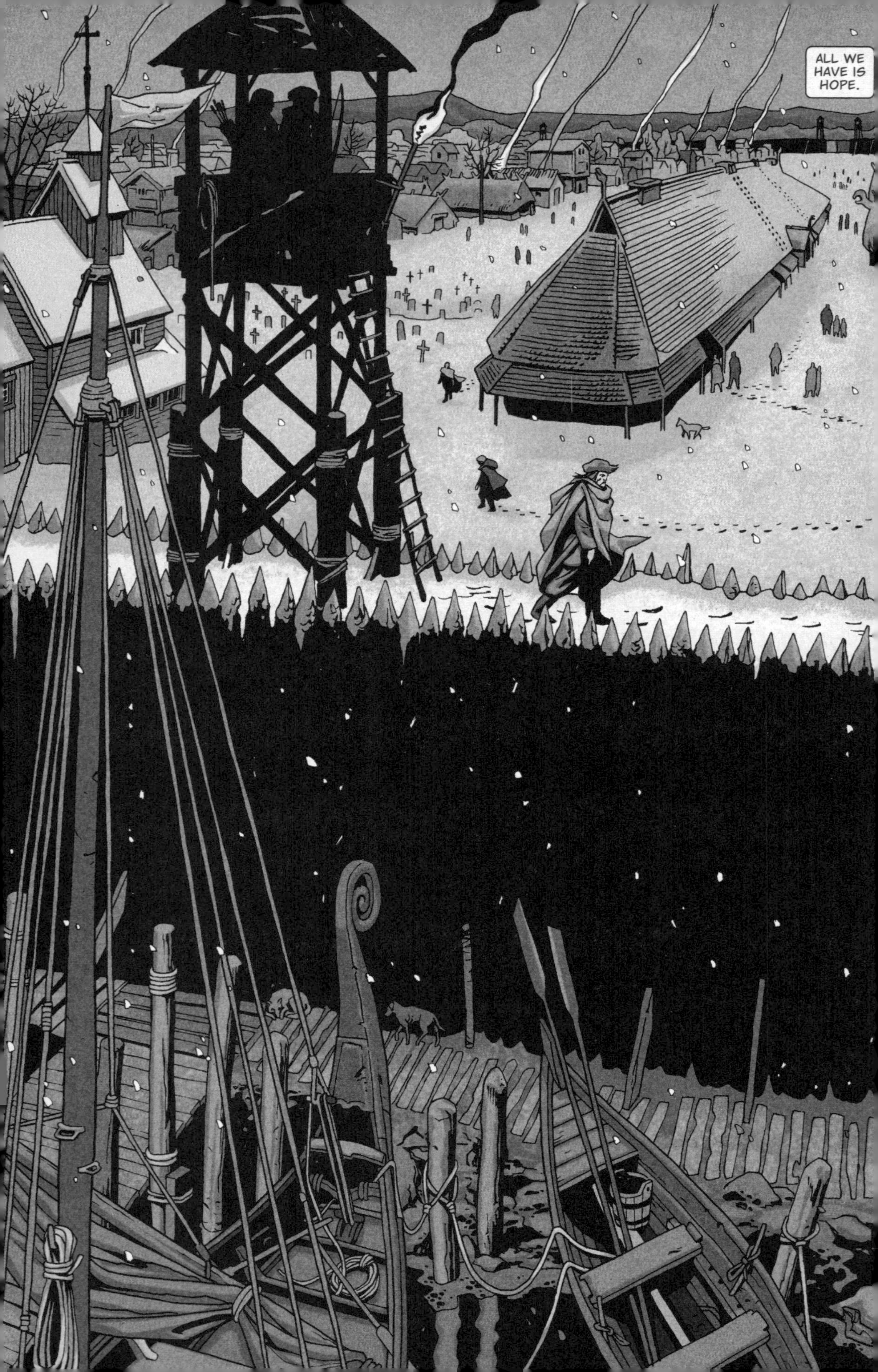
ALL WE HAVE IS HOPE.

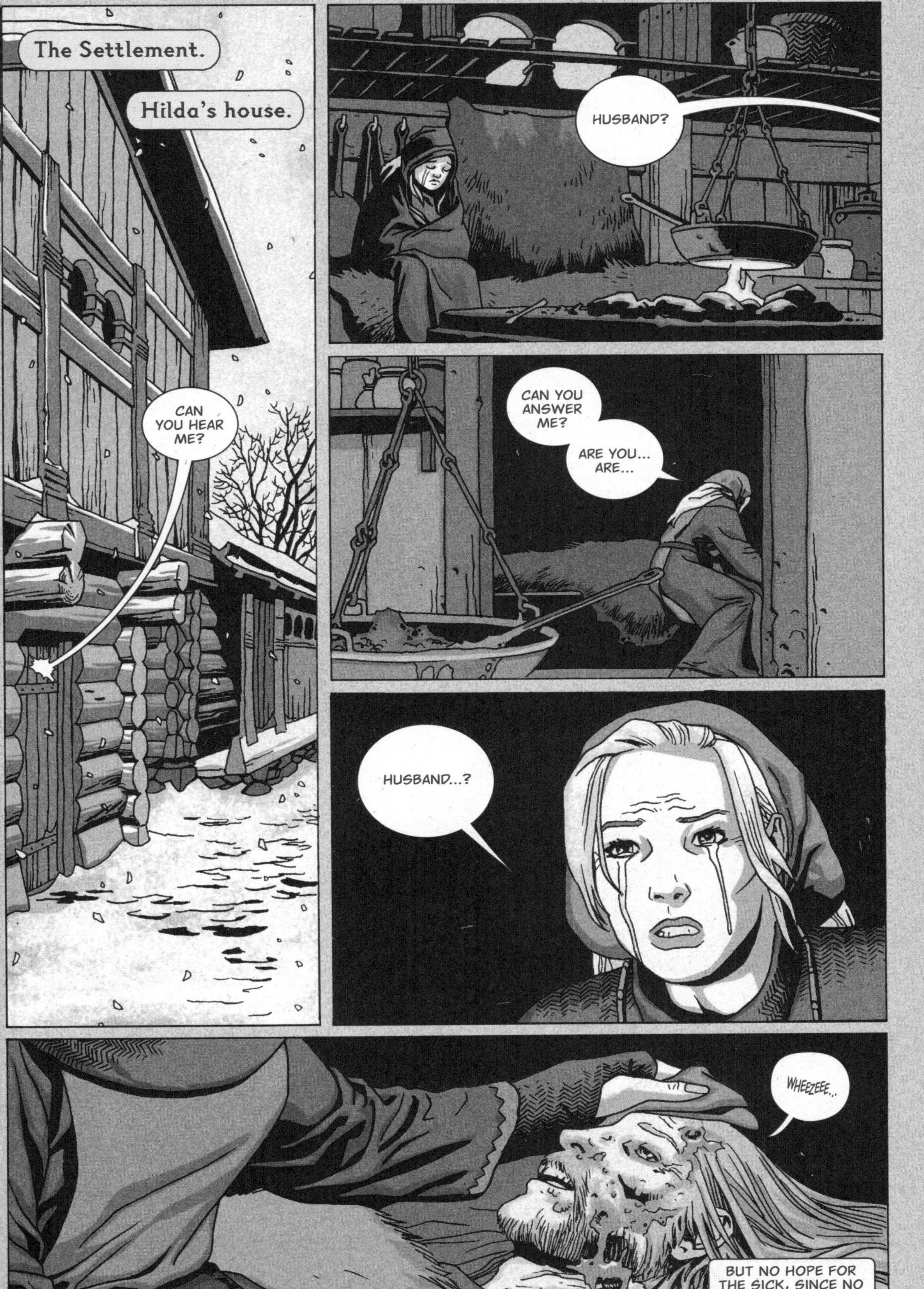
The Settlement.
Hilda's house.
CAN YOU HEAR ME?
HUSBAND?
CAN YOU ANSWER ME?
ARE YOU... ARE...
HUSBAND...?
WHEEZEEE...
BUT NO HOPE FOR THE SICK, SINCE NO ONE WAS SURVIVING THIS PLAGUE.

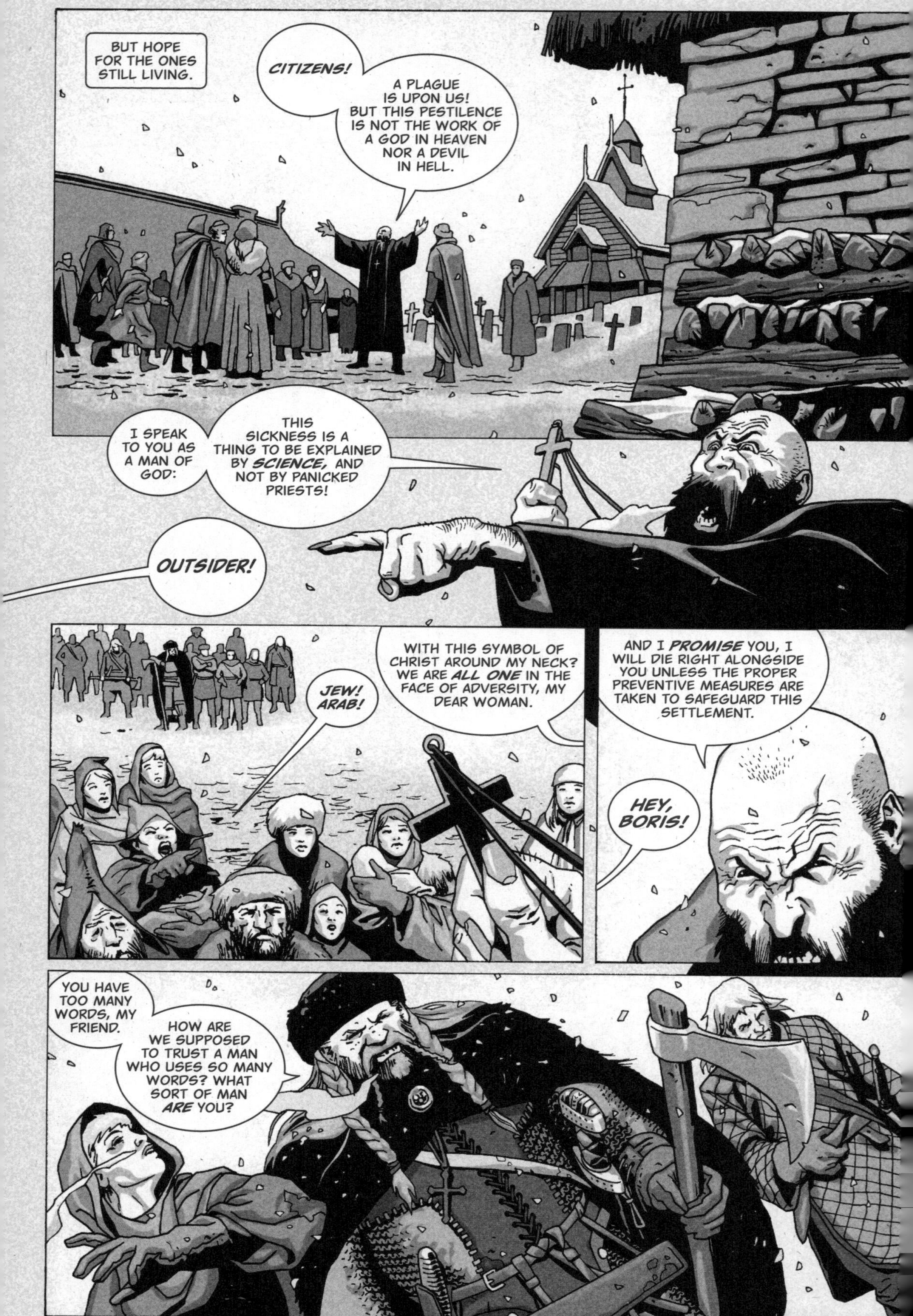
BUT HOPE FOR THE ONES STILL LIVING.
CITIZENS!
A PLAGUE IS UPON US! BUT THIS PESTILENCE IS NOT THE WORK OF A GOD IN HEAVEN NOR A DEVIL IN HELL.
I SPEAK TO YOU AS A MAN OF GOD:
THIS SICKNESS IS A THING TO BE EXPLAINED BY SCIENCE, AND NOT BY PANICKED PRIESTS!
OUTSIDER!
JEW! ARAB!
WITH THIS SYMBOL OF CHRIST AROUND MY NECK? WE ARE ALL ONE IN THE FACE OF ADVERSITY, MY DEAR WOMAN.
AND I PROMISE YOU, I WILL DIE RIGHT ALONGSIDE YOU UNLESS THE PROPER PREVENTIVE MEASURES ARE TAKEN TO SAFEGUARD THIS SETTLEMENT.
HEY, BORIS!
YOU HAVE TOO MANY WORDS, MY FRIEND.
HOW ARE WE SUPPOSED TO TRUST A MAN WHO USES SO MANY WORDS? WHAT SORT OF MAN ARE YOU?

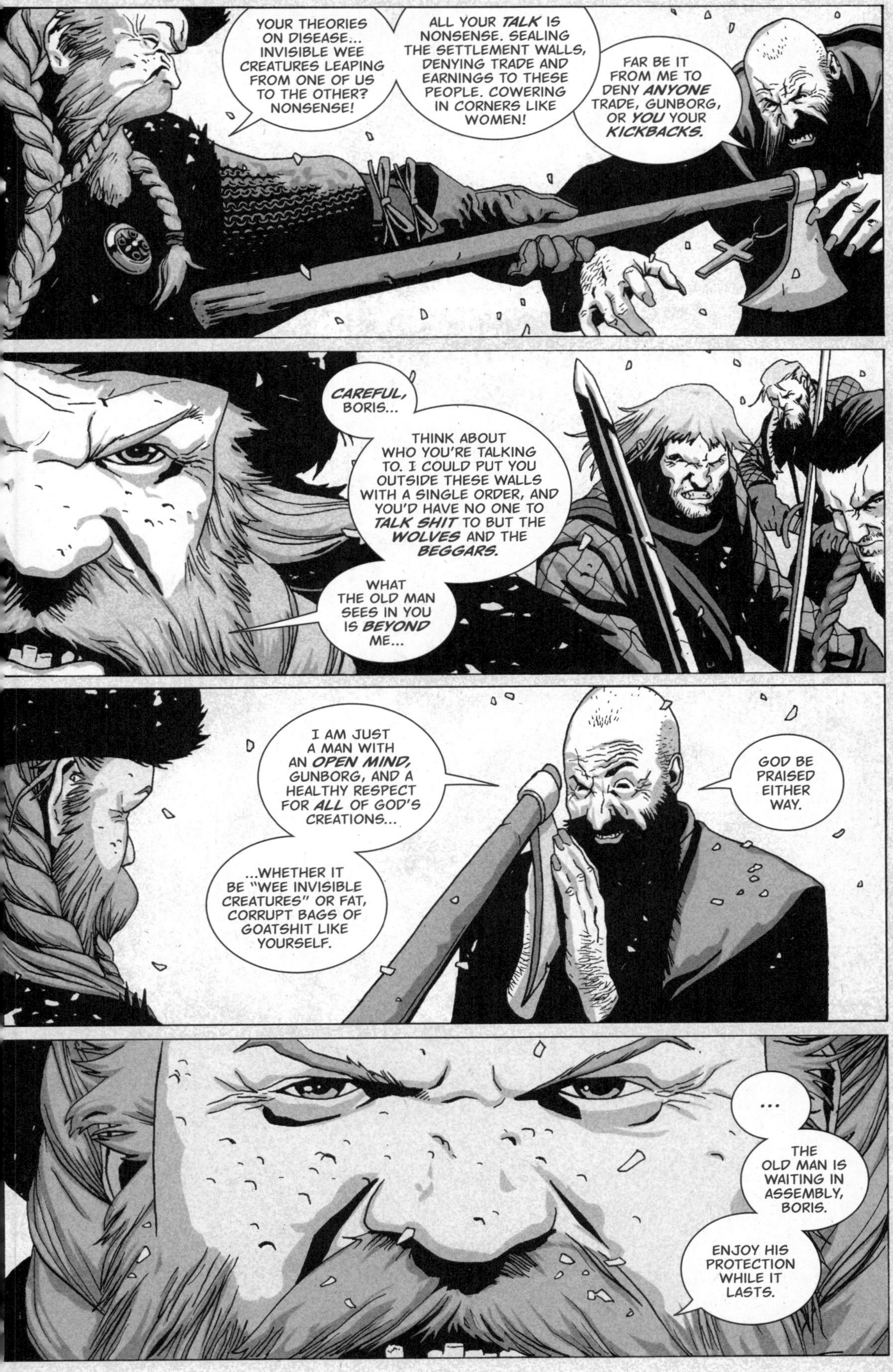
YOUR THEORIES ON DISEASE... INVISIBLE WEE CREATURES LEAPING FROM ONE OF US TO THE OTHER? NONSENSE!
ALL YOUR TALK IS NONSENSE. SEALING THE SETTLEMENT WALLS, DENYING TRADE AND EARNINGS TO THESE PEOPLE. COWERING IN CORNERS LIKE WOMEN!
FAR BE IT FROM ME TO DENY ANYONE TRADE, GUNBORG, OR YOU YOUR KICKBACKS.
CAREFUL, BORIS...
THINK ABOUT WHO YOU'RE TALKING TO. I COULD PUT YOU OUTSIDE THESE WALLS WITH A SINGLE ORDER, AND YOU'D HAVE NO ONE TO TALK SHIT TO BUT THE WOLVES AND THE BEGGARS.
WHAT THE OLD MAN SEES IN YOU IS BEYOND ME...
I AM JUST A MAN WITH AN OPEN MIND, GUNBORG, AND A HEALTHY RESPECT FOR ALL OF GOD'S CREATIONS...
...WHETHER IT BE "WEE INVISIBLE CREATURES" OR FAT, CORRUPT BAGS OF GOATSHIT LIKE YOURSELF.
GOD BE PRAISED EITHER WAY.
...
THE OLD MAN IS WAITING IN ASSEMBLY, BORIS.
ENJOY HIS PROTECTION WHILE IT LASTS.

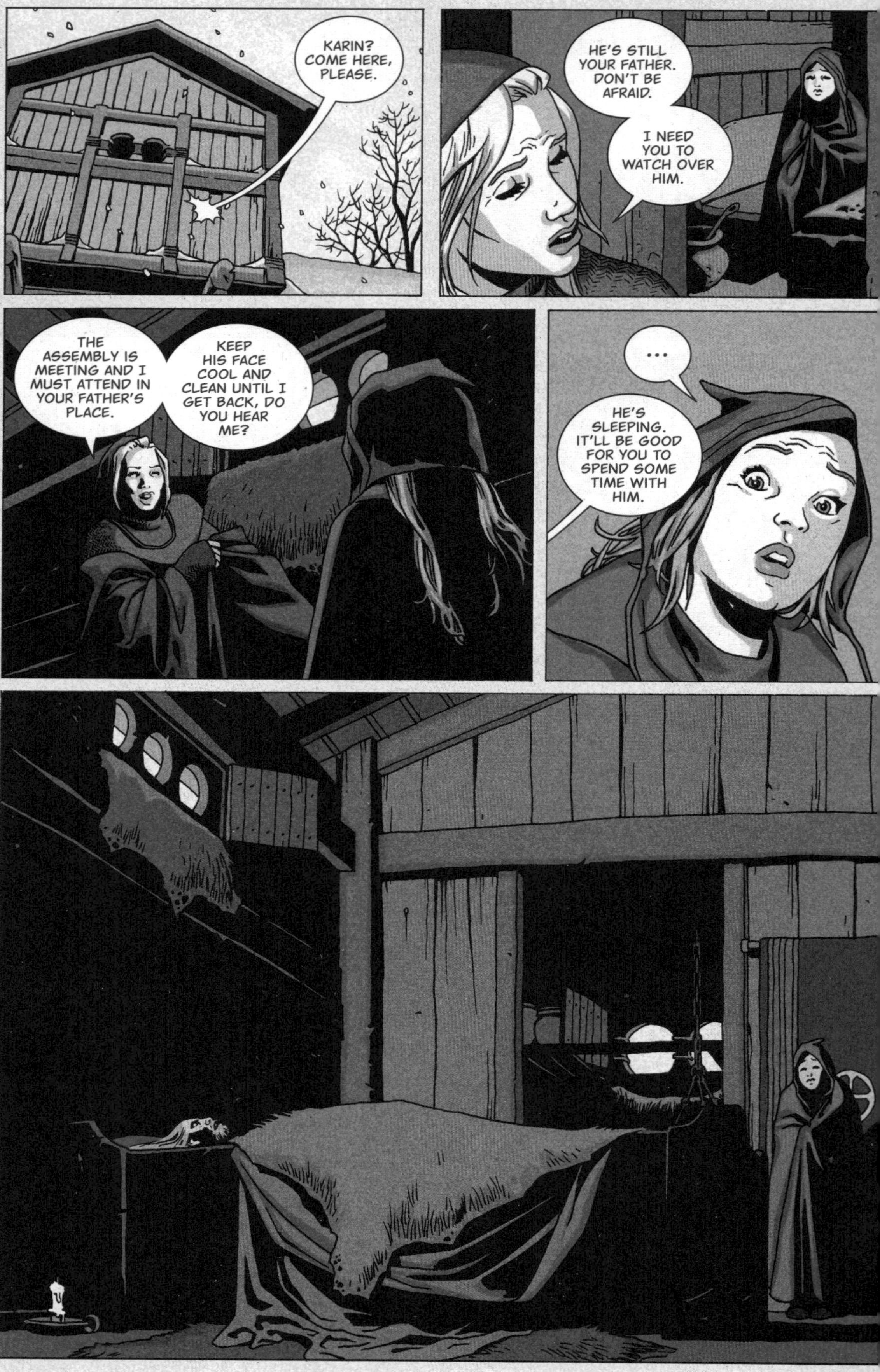
KARIN? COME HERE, PLEASE.
HE'S STILL YOUR FATHER. DON'T BE AFRAID.
I NEED YOU TO WATCH OVER HIM.
THE ASSEMBLY IS MEETING AND I MUST ATTEND IN YOUR FATHER'S PLACE.
KEEP HIS FACE COOL AND CLEAN UNTIL I GET BACK, DO YOU HEAR ME?
...
HE'S SLEEPING. IT'LL BE GOOD FOR YOU TO SPEND SOME TIME WITH HIM.

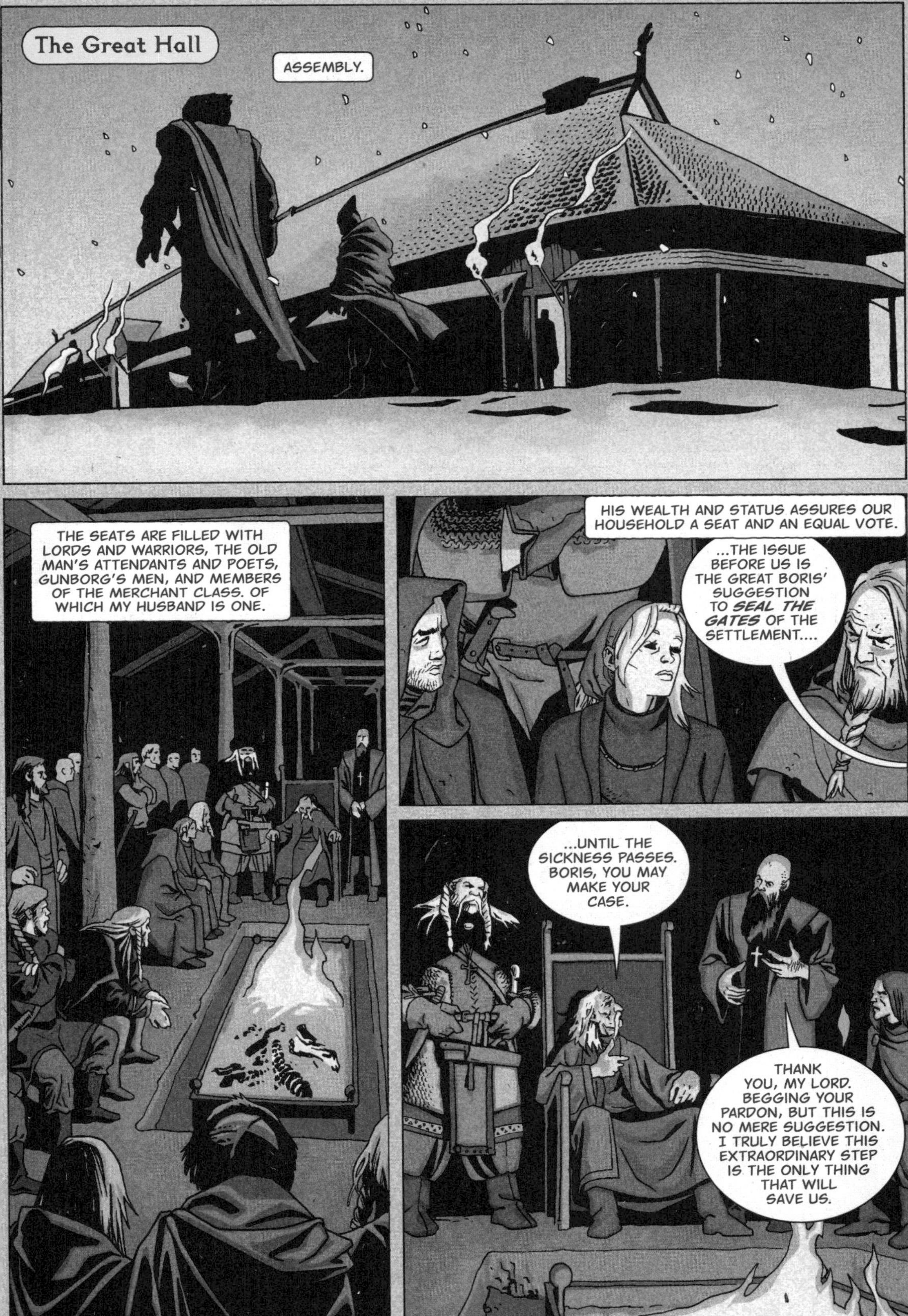
The Great Hall
ASSEMBLY.
THE SEATS ARE FILLED WITH LORDS AND WARRIORS, THE OLD MAN'S ATTENDANTS AND POETS, GUNBORG'S MEN, AND MEMBERS OF THE MERCHANT CLASS. OF WHICH MY HUSBAND IS ONE.
HIS WEALTH AND STATUS ASSURES OUR HOUSEHOLD A SEAT AND AN EQUAL VOTE.
...THE ISSUE BEFORE US IS THE GREAT BORIS' SUGGESTION TO SEAL THE GATES OF THE SETTLEMENT....
...UNTIL THE SICKNESS PASSES. BORIS, YOU MAY MAKE YOUR CASE.
THANK YOU, MY LORD. BEGGING YOUR PARDON, BUT THIS IS NO MERE SUGGESTION. I TRULY BELIEVE THIS EXTRAORDINARY STEP IS THE ONLY THING THAT WILL SAVE US.

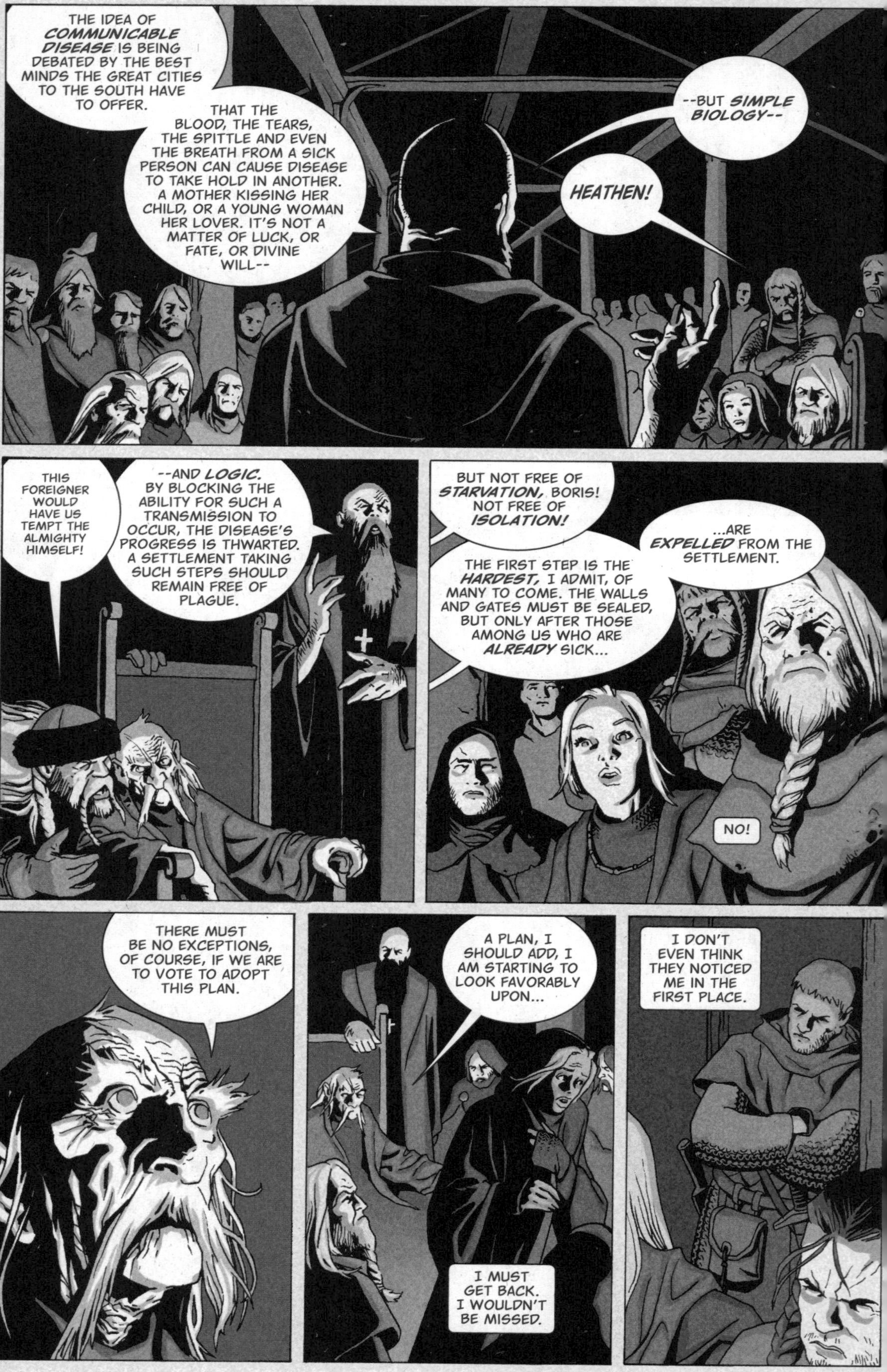
THE IDEA OF COMMUNICABLE DISEASE IS BEING DEBATED BY THE BEST MINDS THE GREAT CITIES TO THE SOUTH HAVE TO OFFER.
THAT THE BLOOD, THE TEARS, THE SPITTLE AND EVEN THE BREATH FROM A SICK PERSON CAN CAUSE DISEASE TO TAKE HOLD IN ANOTHER. A MOTHER KISSING HER CHILD, OR A YOUNG WOMAN HER LOVER. IT'S NOT A MATTER OF LUCK, OR FATE, OR DIVINE WILL--
HEATHEN!
--BUT SIMPLE BIOLOGY--
THIS FOREIGNER WOULD HAVE US TEMPT THE ALMIGHTY HIMSELF!
--AND LOGIC. BY BLOCKING THE ABILITY FOR SUCH A TRANSMISSION TO OCCUR, THE DISEASE'S PROGRESS IS THWARTED. A SETTLEMENT TAKING SUCH STEPS SHOULD REMAIN FREE OF PLAGUE.
BUT NOT FREE OF STARVATION, BORIS! NOT FREE OF ISOLATION!
THE FIRST STEP IS THE HARDEST, I ADMIT, OF MANY TO COME. THE WALLS AND GATES MUST BE SEALED, BUT ONLY AFTER THOSE AMONG US WHO ARE ALREADY SICK...
...ARE EXPELLED FROM THE SETTLEMENT.
NO!
THERE MUST BE NO EXCEPTIONS, OF COURSE, IF WE ARE TO VOTE TO ADOPT THIS PLAN.
A PLAN, I SHOULD ADD, I AM STARTING TO LOOK FAVORABLY UPON...
I MUST GET BACK. I WOULDN'T BE MISSED.
I DON'T EVEN THINK THEY NOTICED ME IN THE FIRST PLACE.

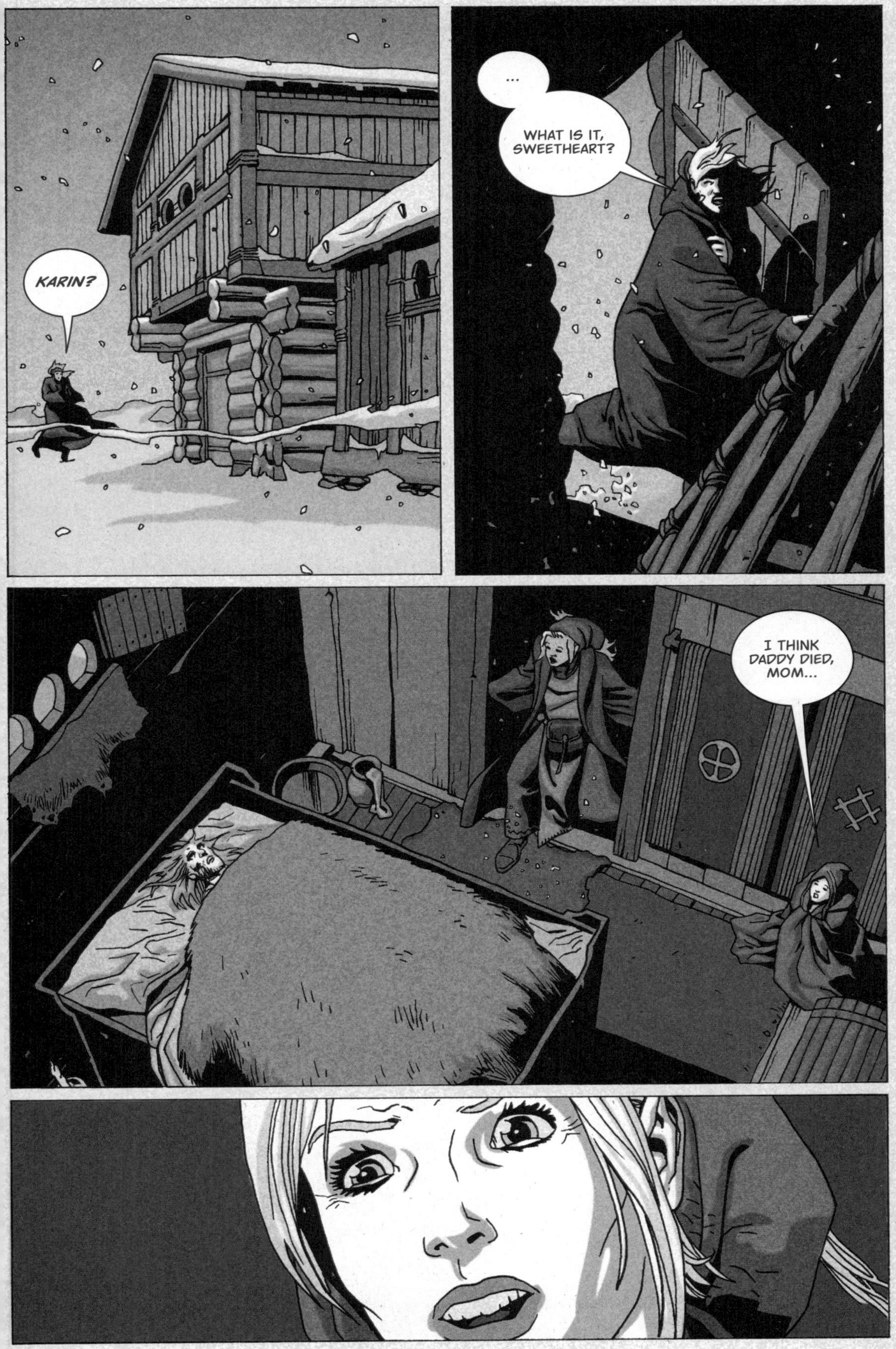
KARIN?
...
WHAT IS IT, SWEETHEART?
I THINK DADDY DIED, MOM...

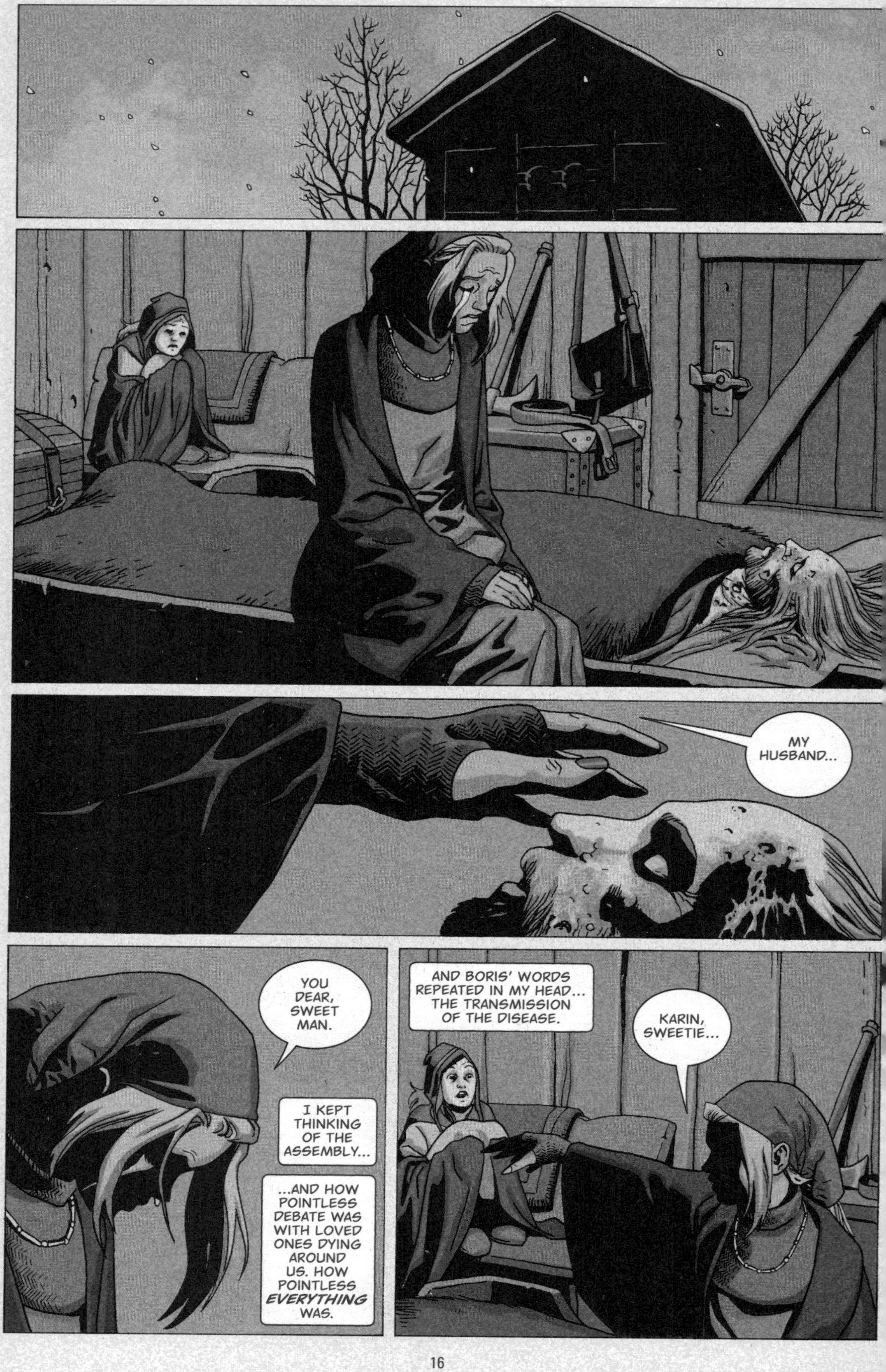
MY HUSBAND...
YOU DEAR, SWEET MAN.
I KEPT THINKING OF THE ASSEMBLY...
...AND HOW POINTLESS DEBATE WAS WITH LOVED ONES DYING AROUND US. HOW POINTLESS *EVERYTHING* WAS.
AND BORIS' WORDS REPEATED IN MY HEAD... THE TRANSMISSION OF THE DISEASE.
KARIN, SWEETIE...

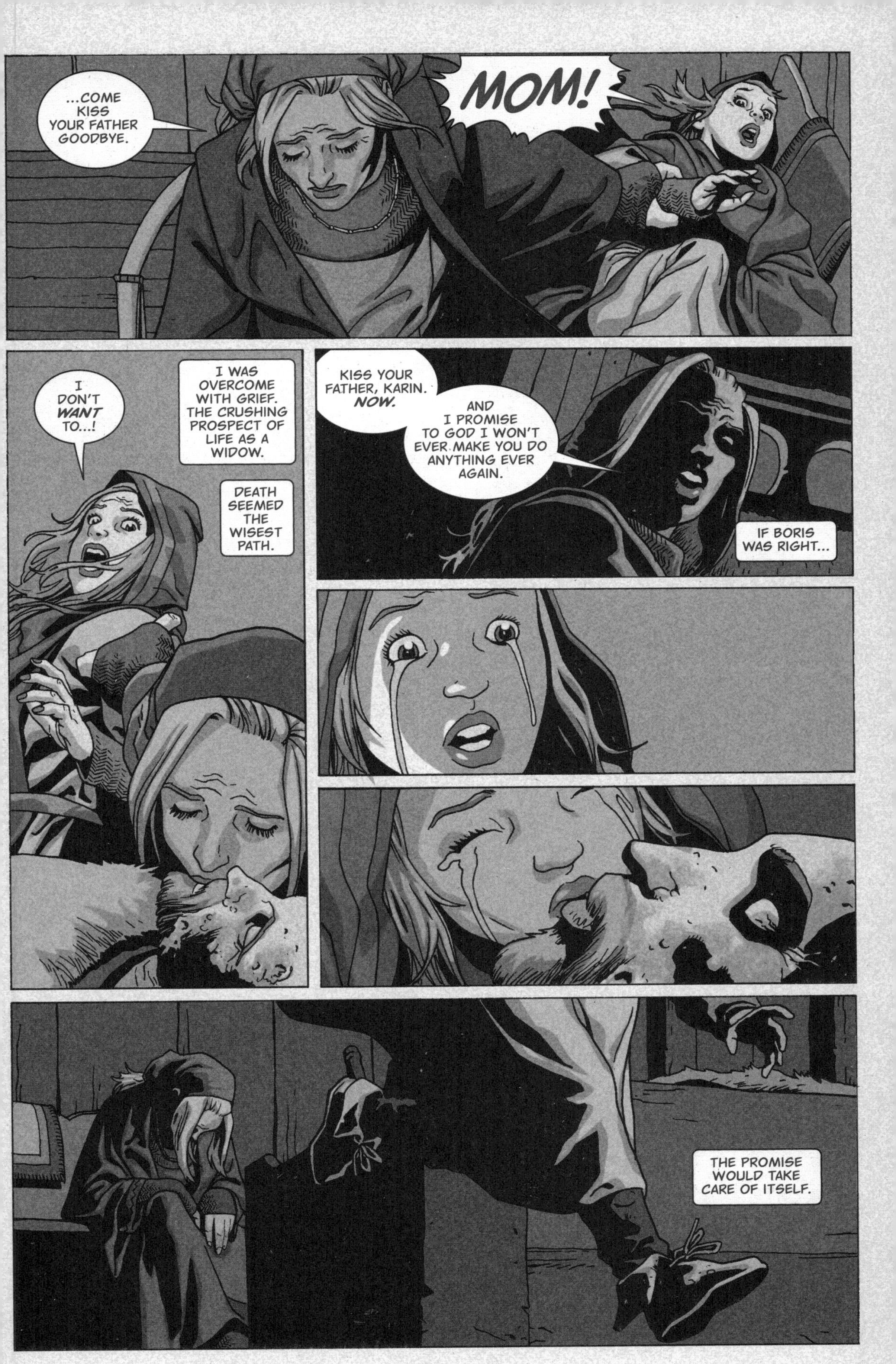

...COME KISS YOUR FATHER GOODBYE.
MOM!
I DON'T *WANT* TO...!
I WAS OVERCOME WITH GRIEF. THE CRUSHING PROSPECT OF LIFE AS A WIDOW.
DEATH SEEMED THE WISEST PATH.
KISS YOUR FATHER, KARIN. *NOW.*
AND I PROMISE TO GOD I WON'T EVER MAKE YOU DO ANYTHING EVER AGAIN.
IF BORIS WAS RIGHT...
THE PROMISE WOULD TAKE CARE OF ITSELF.

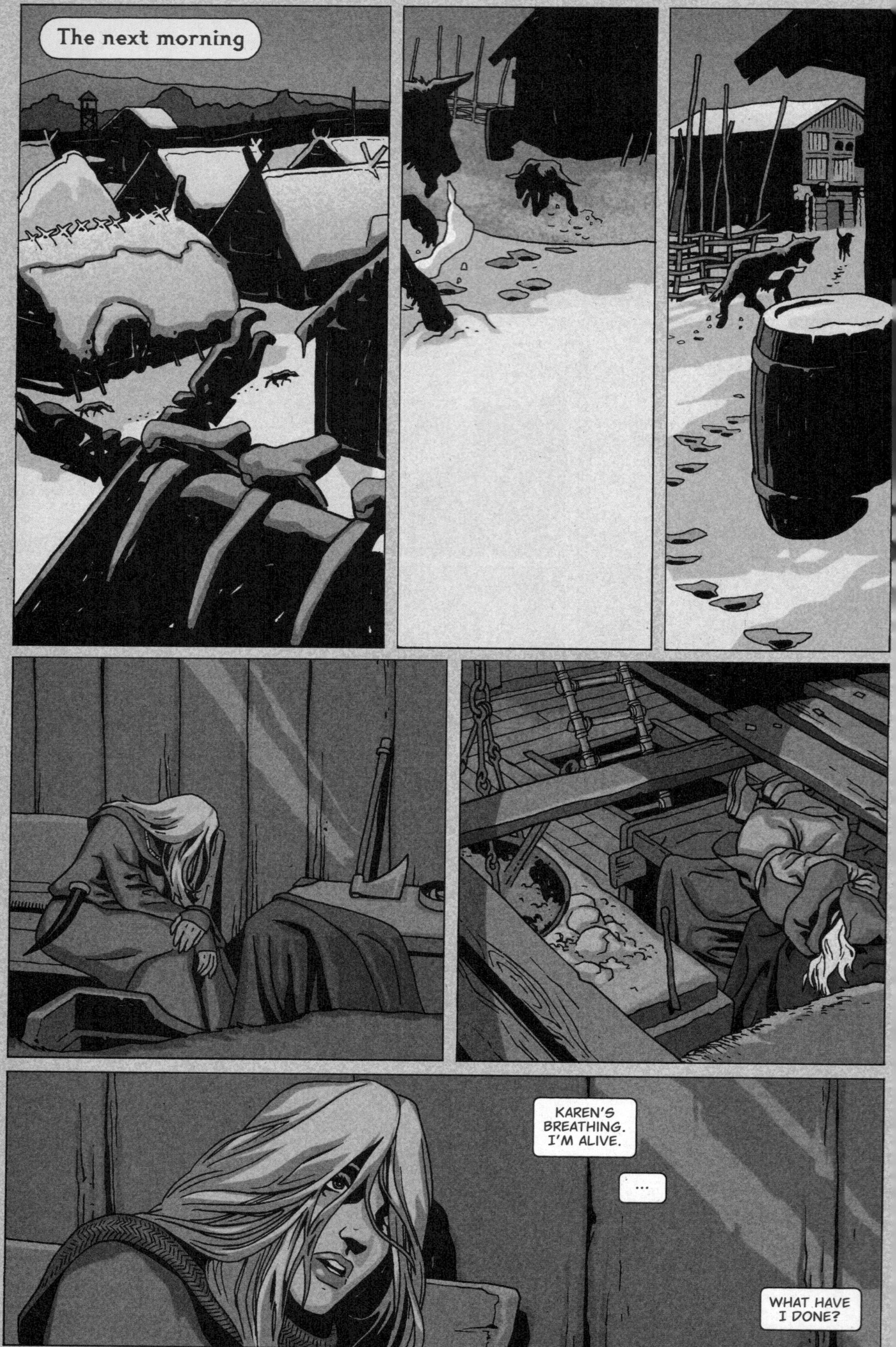
The next morning
KAREN'S BREATHING. I'M ALIVE.
...
WHAT HAVE I DONE?

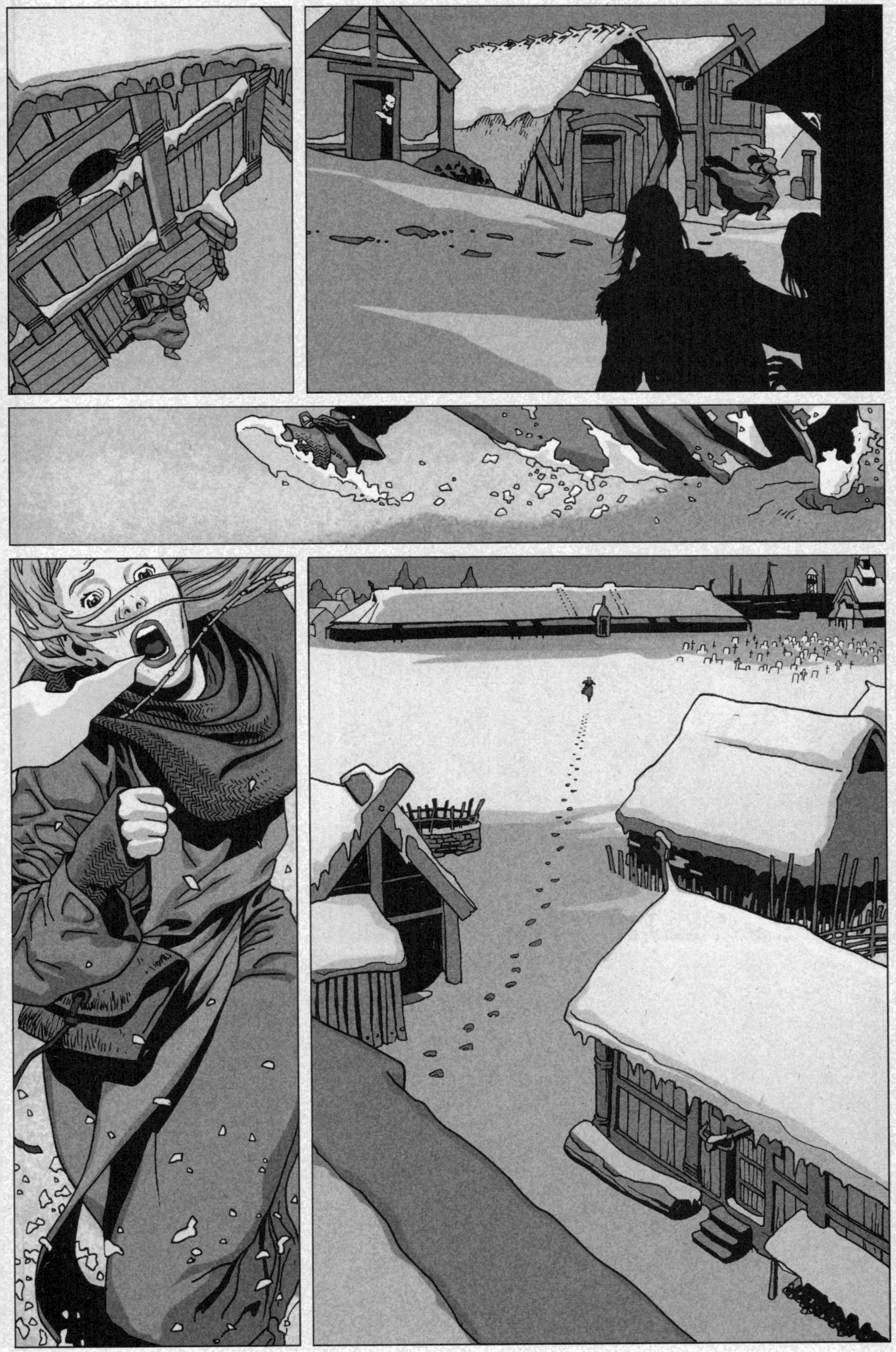

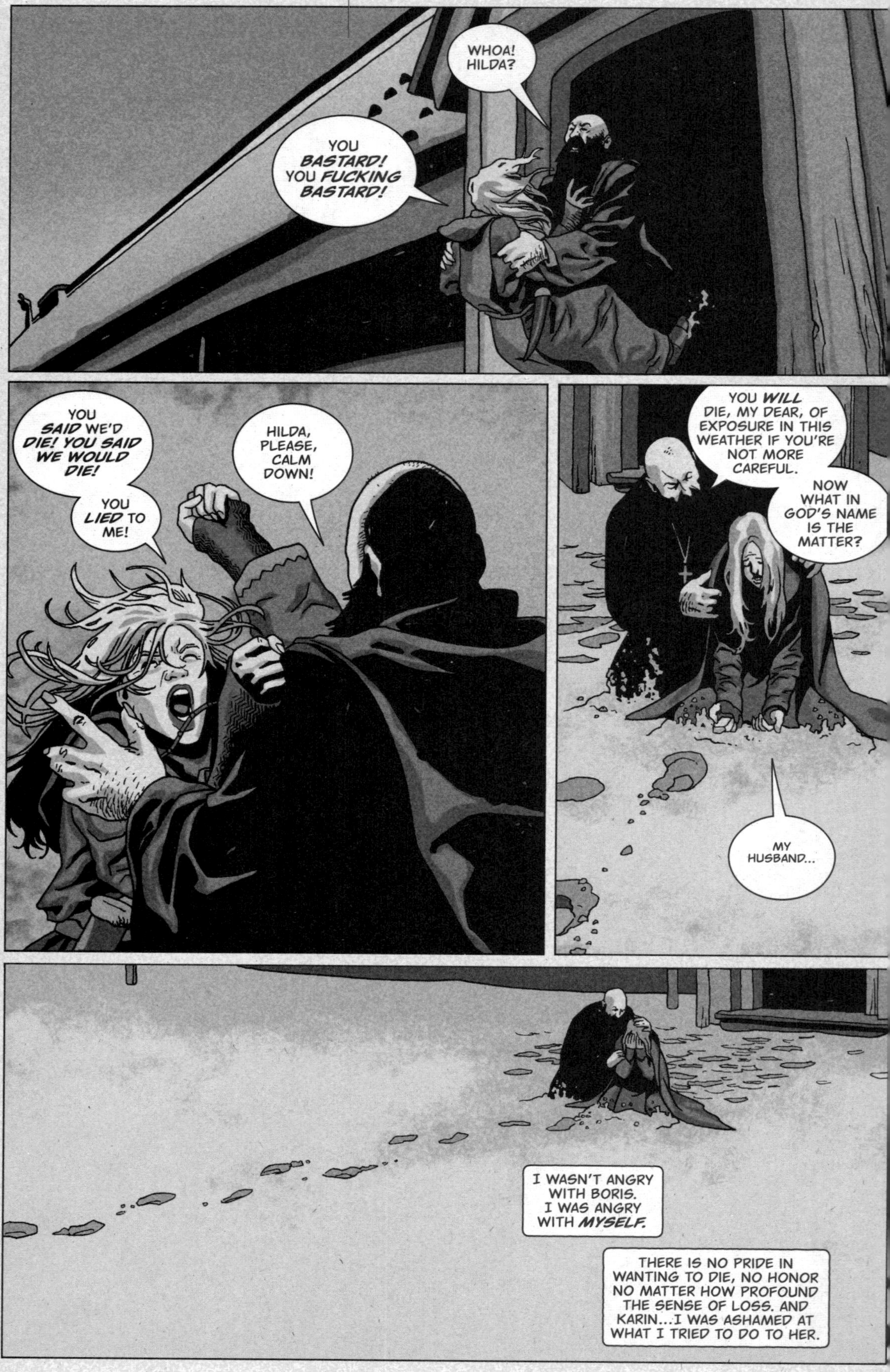
WHOA! HILDA?
YOU BASTARD! YOU FUCKING BASTARD!
YOU SAID WE'D DIE! YOU SAID WE WOULD DIE!
YOU LIED TO ME!
HILDA, PLEASE, CALM DOWN!
YOU WILL DIE, MY DEAR, OF EXPOSURE IN THIS WEATHER IF YOU'RE NOT MORE CAREFUL.
NOW WHAT IN GOD'S NAME IS THE MATTER?
MY HUSBAND...
I WASN'T ANGRY WITH BORIS. I WAS ANGRY WITH MYSELF.
THERE IS NO PRIDE IN WANTING TO DIE, NO HONOR NO MATTER HOW PROFOUND THE SENSE OF LOSS. AND KARIN...I WAS ASHAMED AT WHAT I TRIED TO DO TO HER.

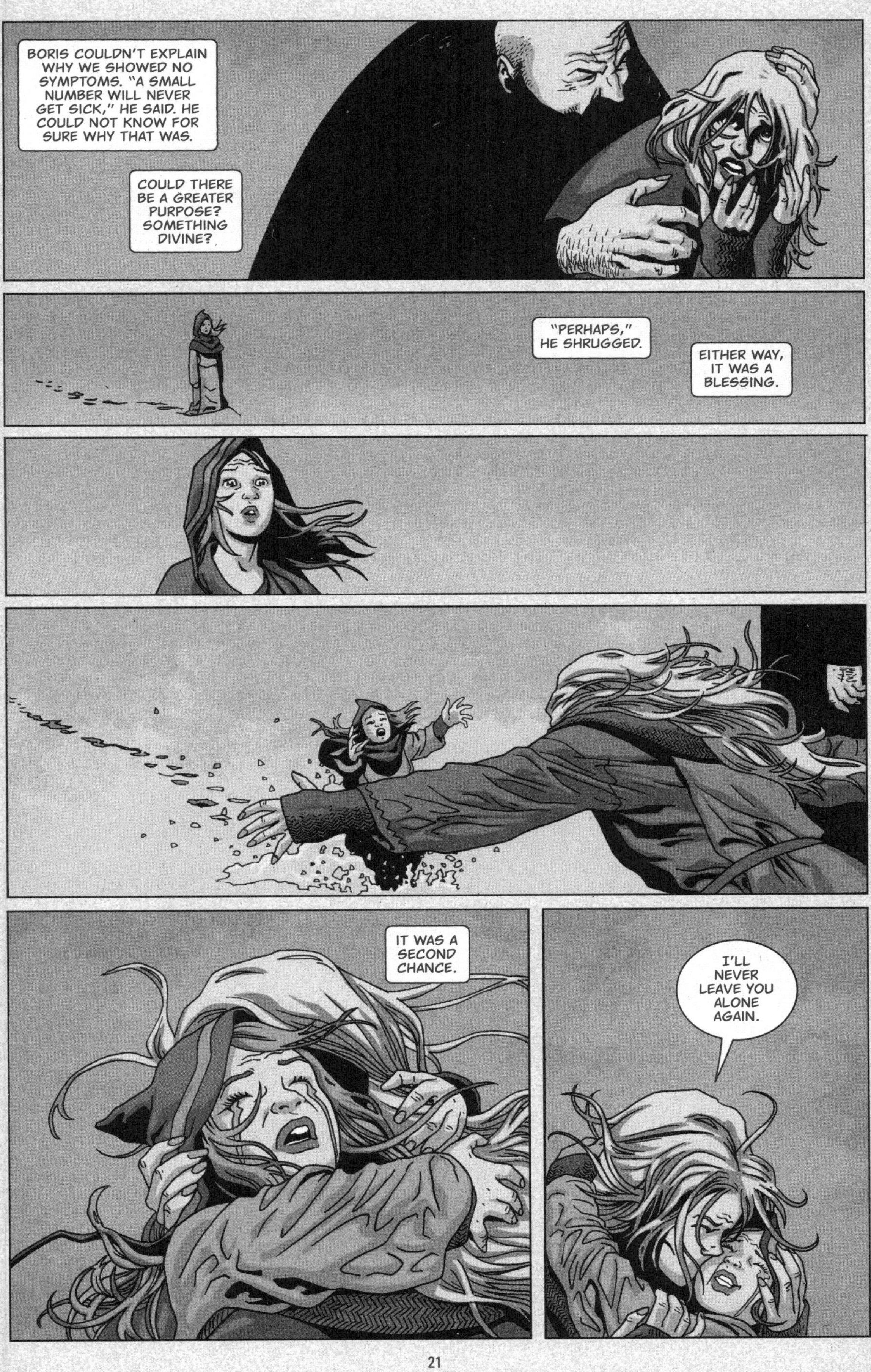
BORIS COULDN'T EXPLAIN WHY WE SHOWED NO SYMPTOMS. "A SMALL NUMBER WILL NEVER GET SICK," HE SAID. HE COULD NOT KNOW FOR SURE WHY THAT WAS.
COULD THERE BE A GREATER PURPOSE? SOMETHING DIVINE?
"PERHAPS," HE SHRUGGED.
EITHER WAY, IT WAS A BLESSING.
IT WAS A SECOND CHANCE.
I'LL NEVER LEAVE YOU ALONE AGAIN.

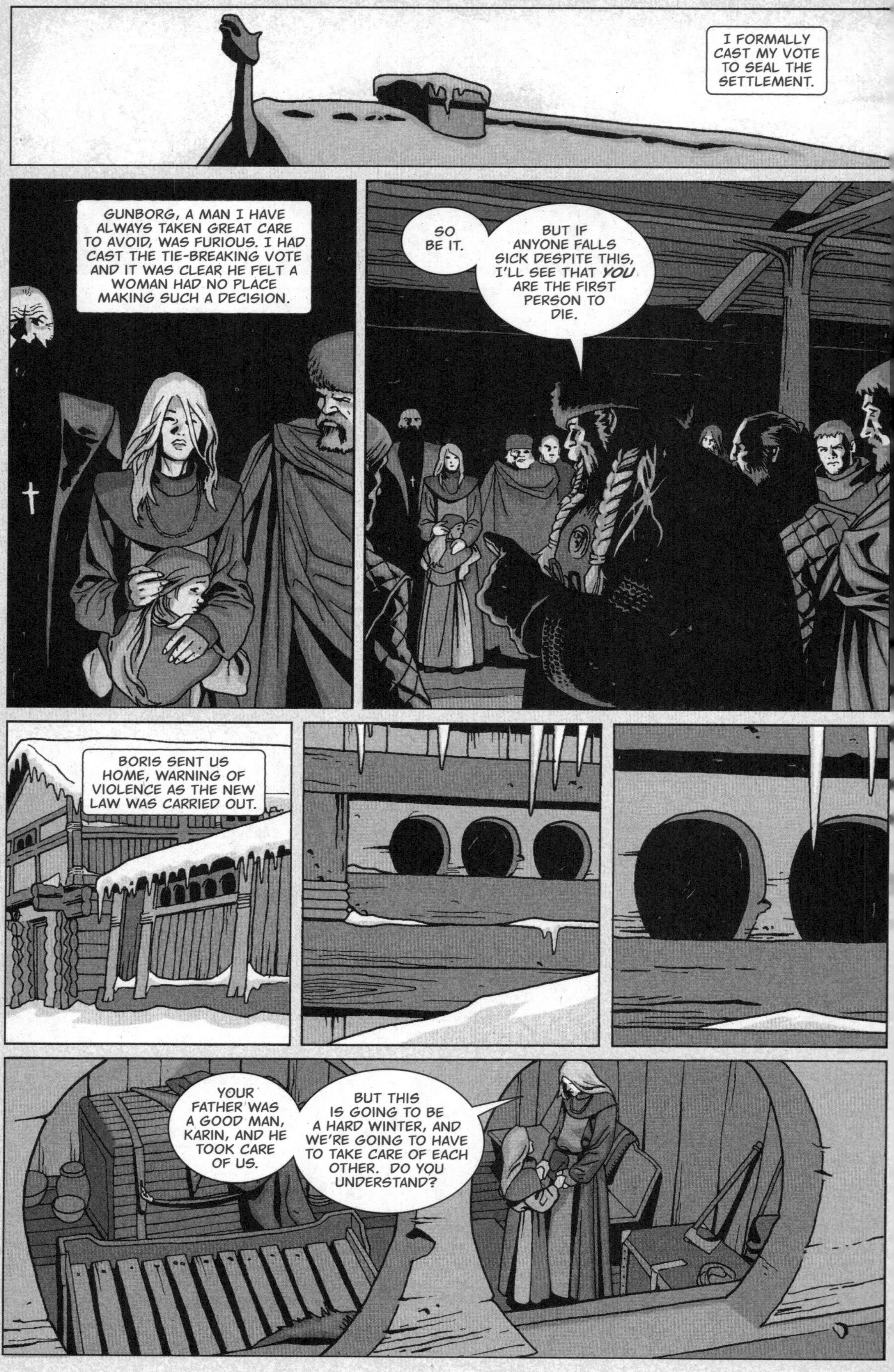
I FORMALLY CAST MY VOTE TO SEAL THE SETTLEMENT.
GUNBORG, A MAN I HAVE ALWAYS TAKEN GREAT CARE TO AVOID, WAS FURIOUS. I HAD CAST THE TIE-BREAKING VOTE AND IT WAS CLEAR HE FELT A WOMAN HAD NO PLACE MAKING SUCH A DECISION.
SO BE IT.
BUT IF ANYONE FALLS SICK DESPITE THIS, I'LL SEE THAT *YOU* ARE THE FIRST PERSON TO DIE.
BORIS SENT US HOME, WARNING OF VIOLENCE AS THE NEW LAW WAS CARRIED OUT.
YOUR FATHER WAS A GOOD MAN, KARIN, AND HE TOOK CARE OF US.
BUT THIS IS GOING TO BE A HARD WINTER, AND WE'RE GOING TO HAVE TO TAKE CARE OF EACH OTHER. DO YOU UNDERSTAND?

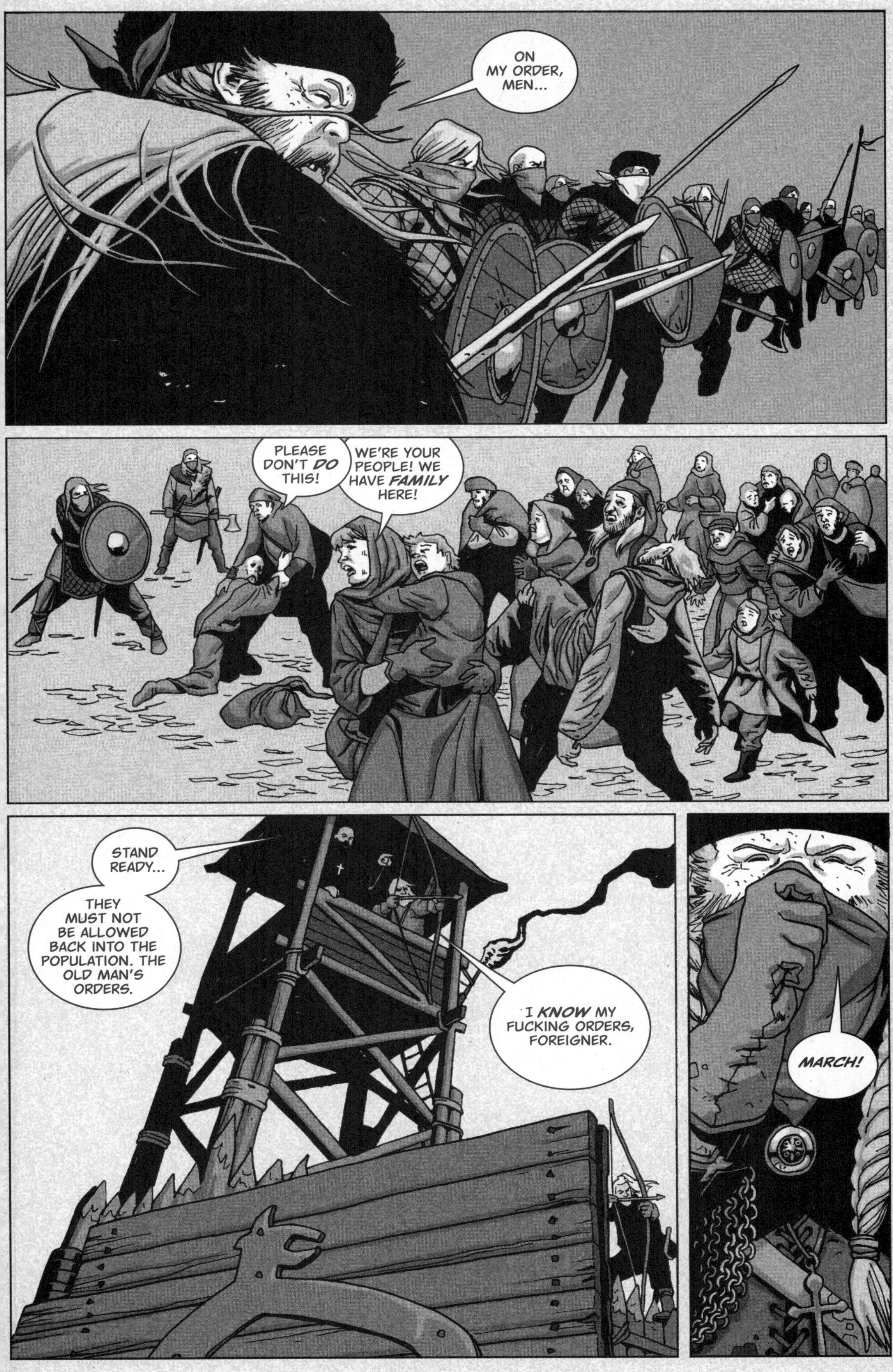
ON MY ORDER, MEN...
PLEASE DON'T *DO* THIS!
WE'RE YOUR PEOPLE! WE HAVE *FAMILY* HERE!
STAND READY...
THEY MUST NOT BE ALLOWED BACK INTO THE POPULATION. THE OLD MAN'S ORDERS.
I *KNOW* MY FUCKING ORDERS, FOREIGNER.
MARCH!

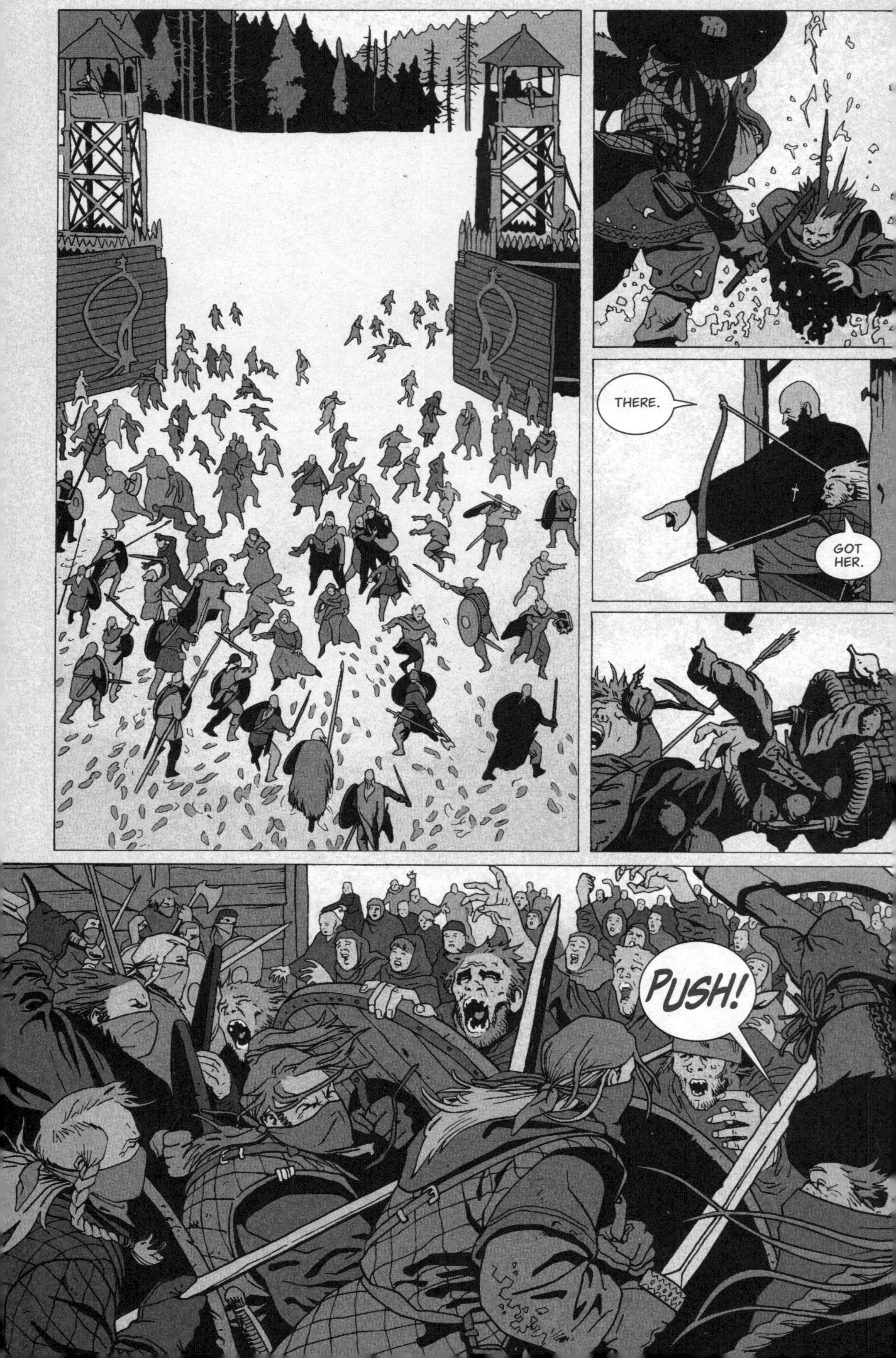
THERE.
GOT HER.
PUSH!

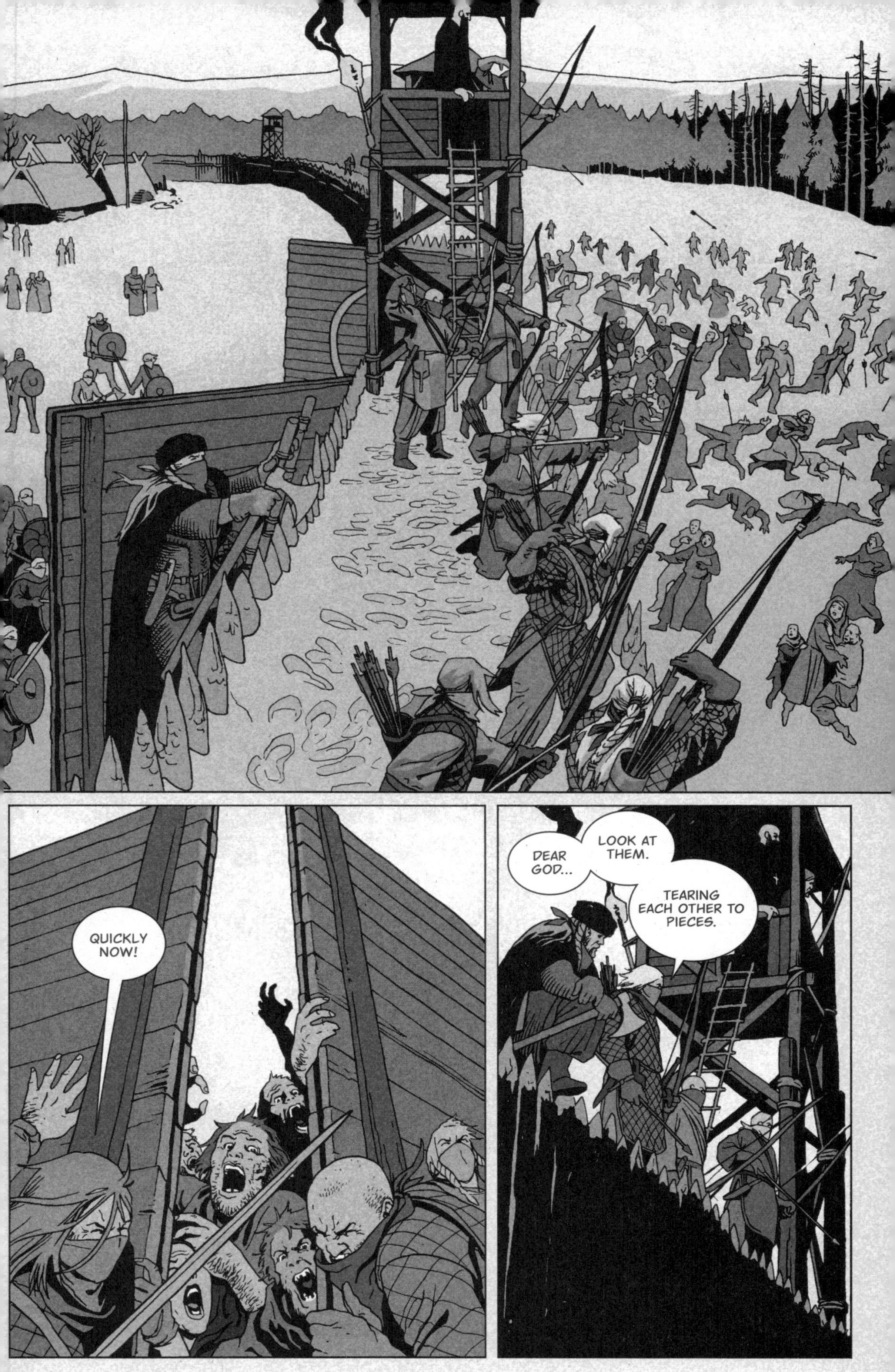
QUICKLY NOW!
DEAR GOD...
LOOK AT THEM.
TEARING EACH OTHER TO PIECES.

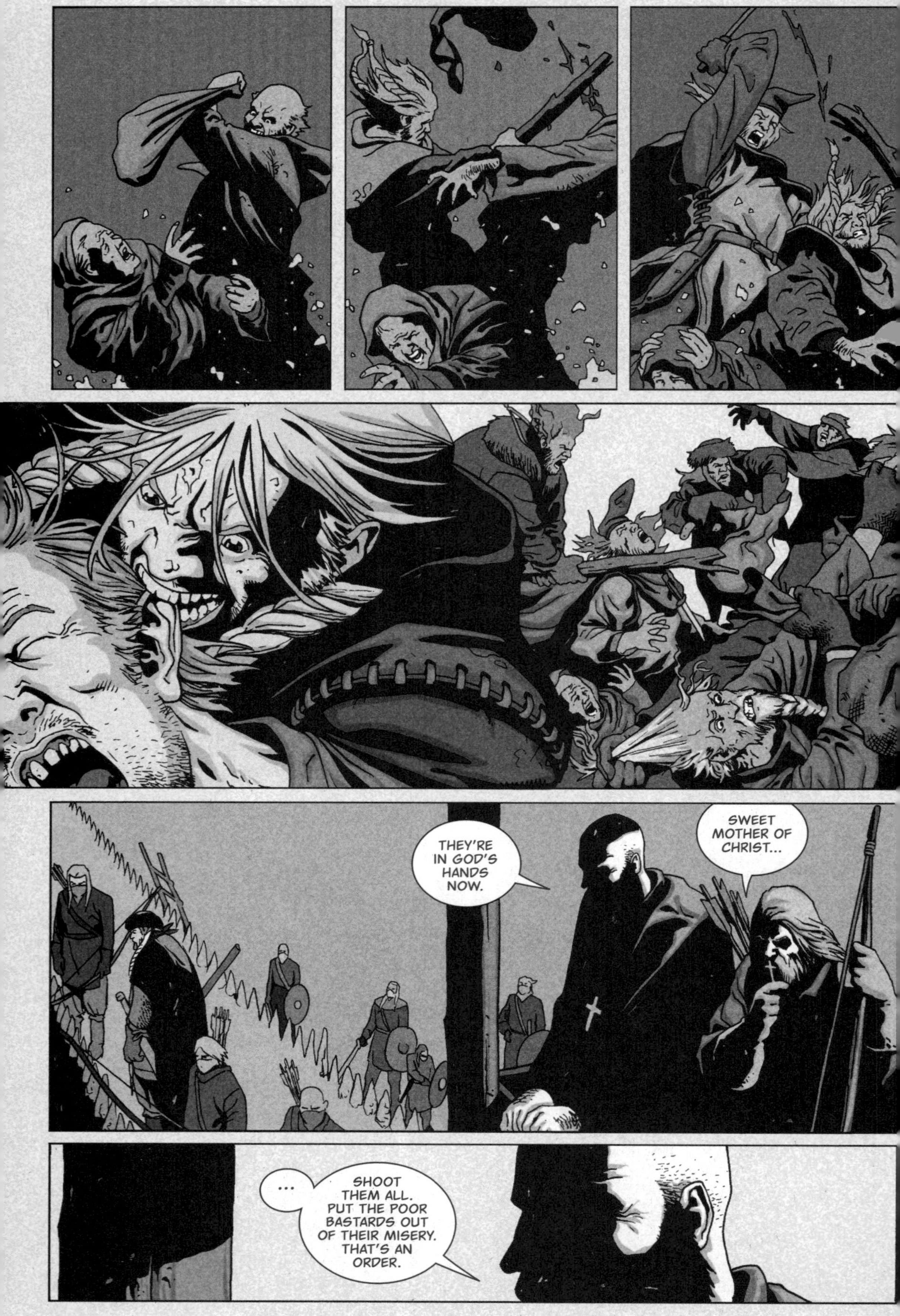
THEY'RE IN GOD'S HANDS NOW.
SWEET MOTHER OF CHRIST...
...
SHOOT THEM ALL. PUT THE POOR BASTARDS OUT OF THEIR MISERY. THAT'S AN ORDER.

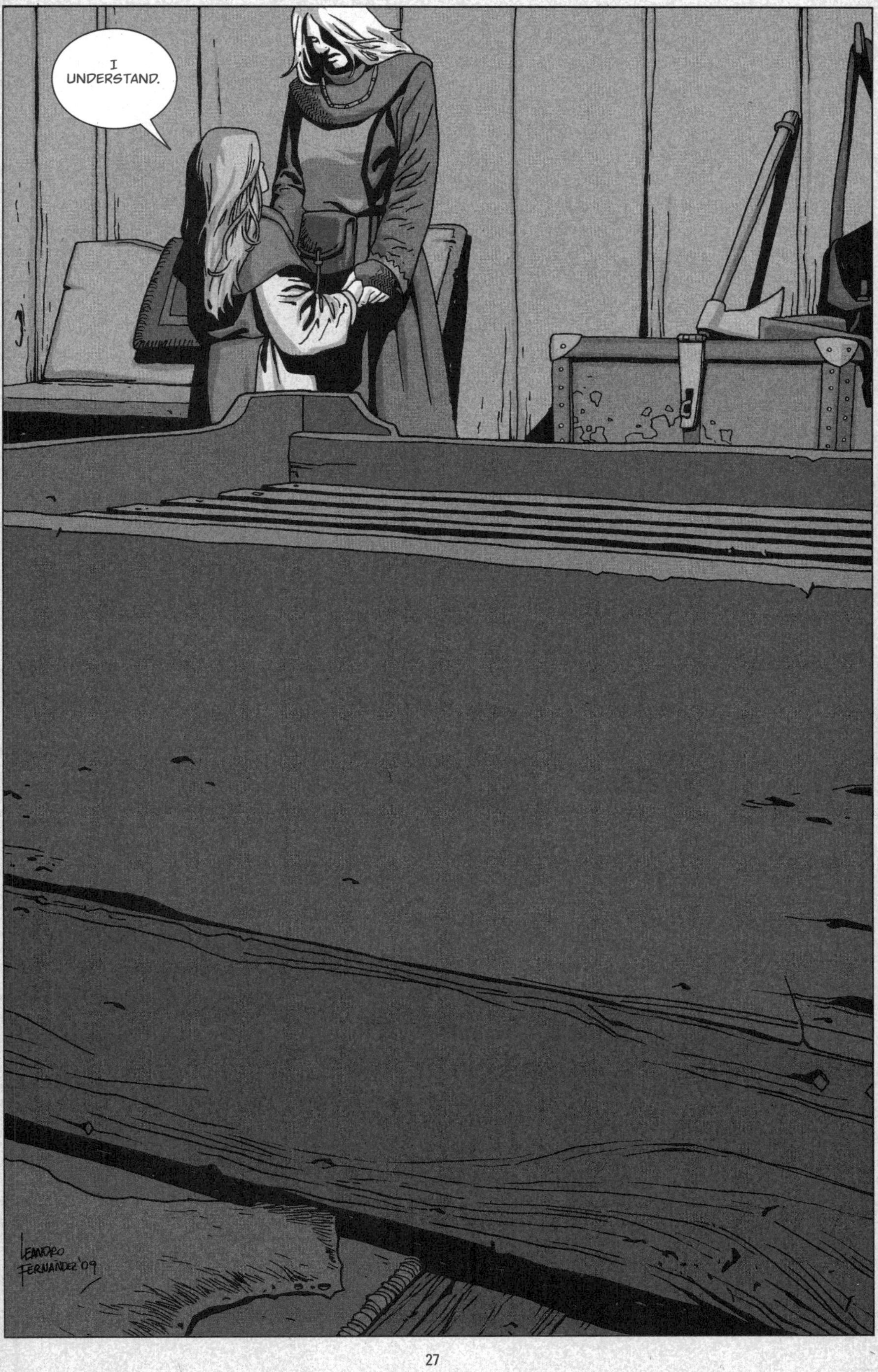
I UNDERSTAND.
LEANDRO FERNANDEZ '09

Part 2: Heads of Household

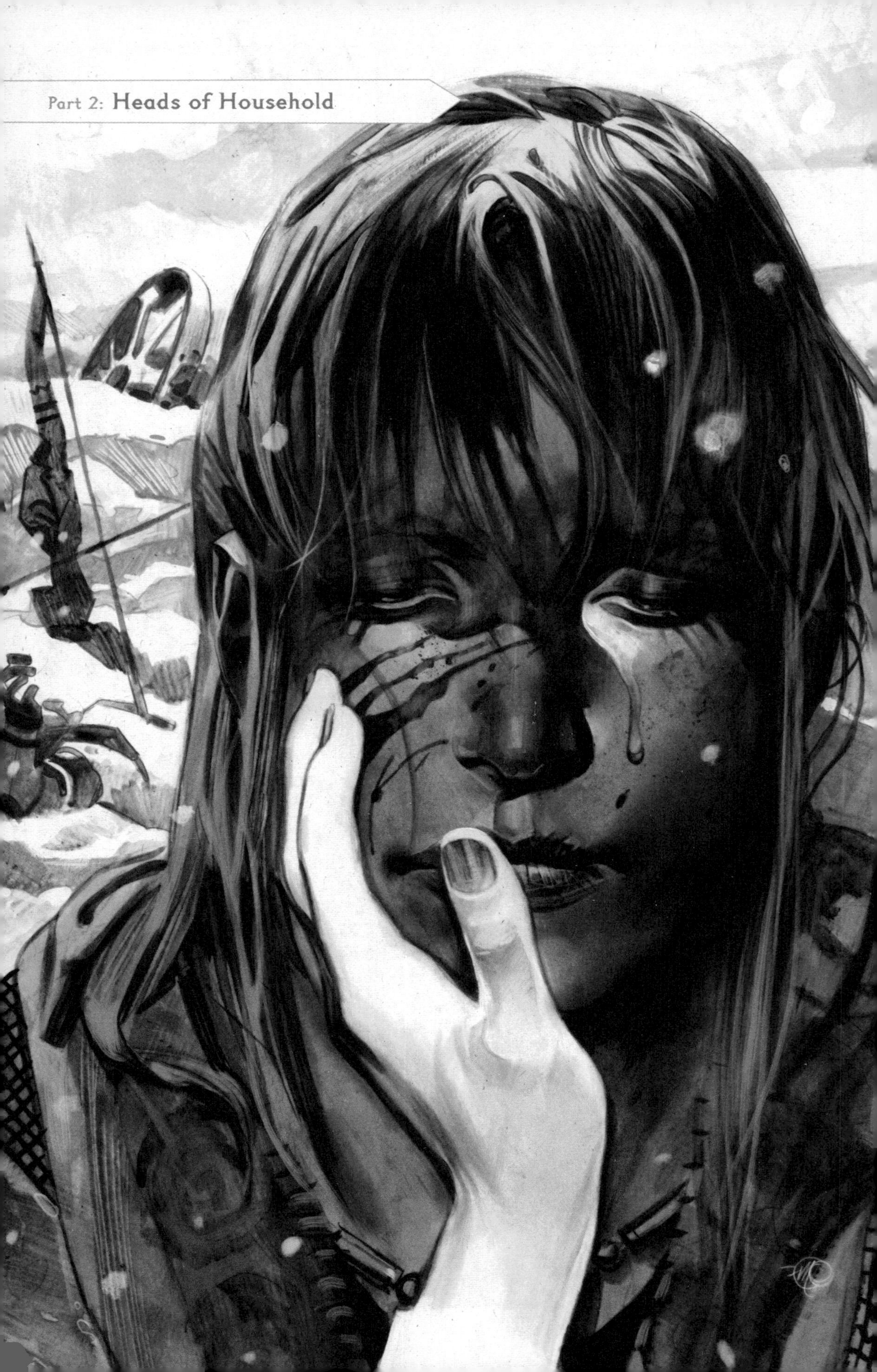

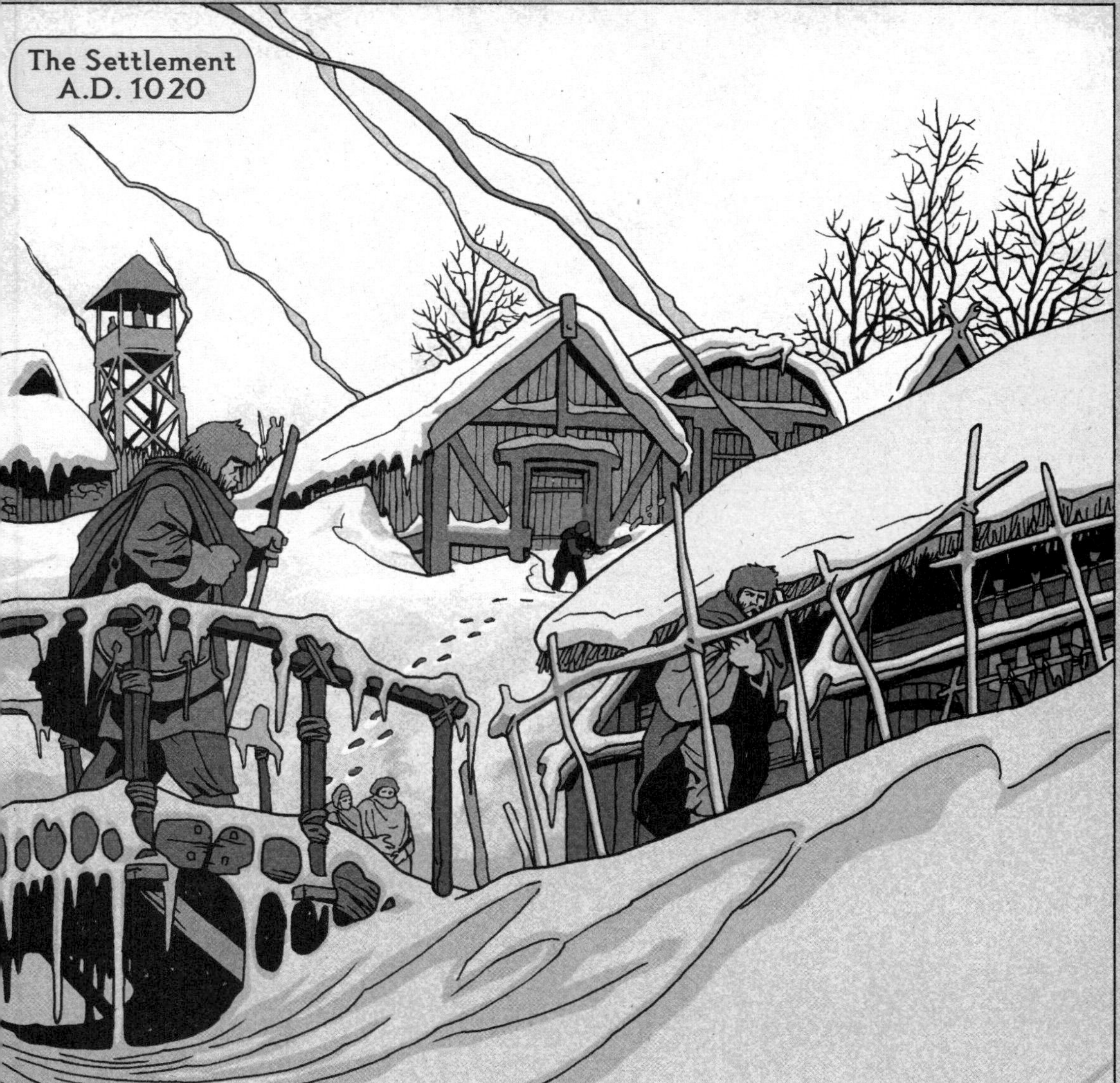
The Settlement
A.D. 1020

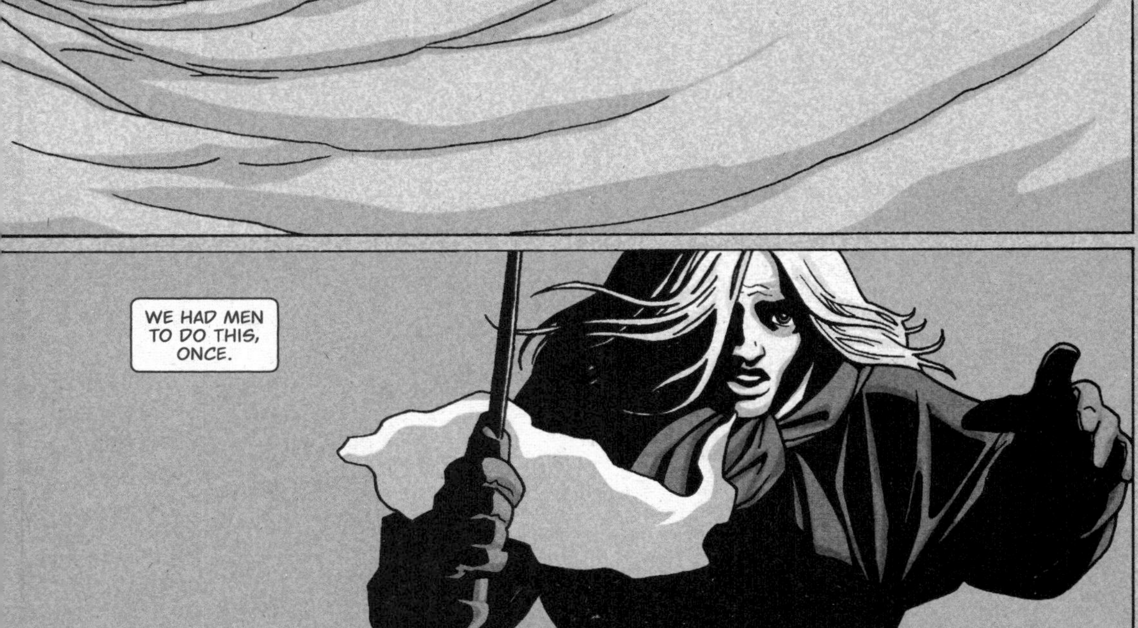
WE HAD MEN
TO DO THIS,
ONCE.

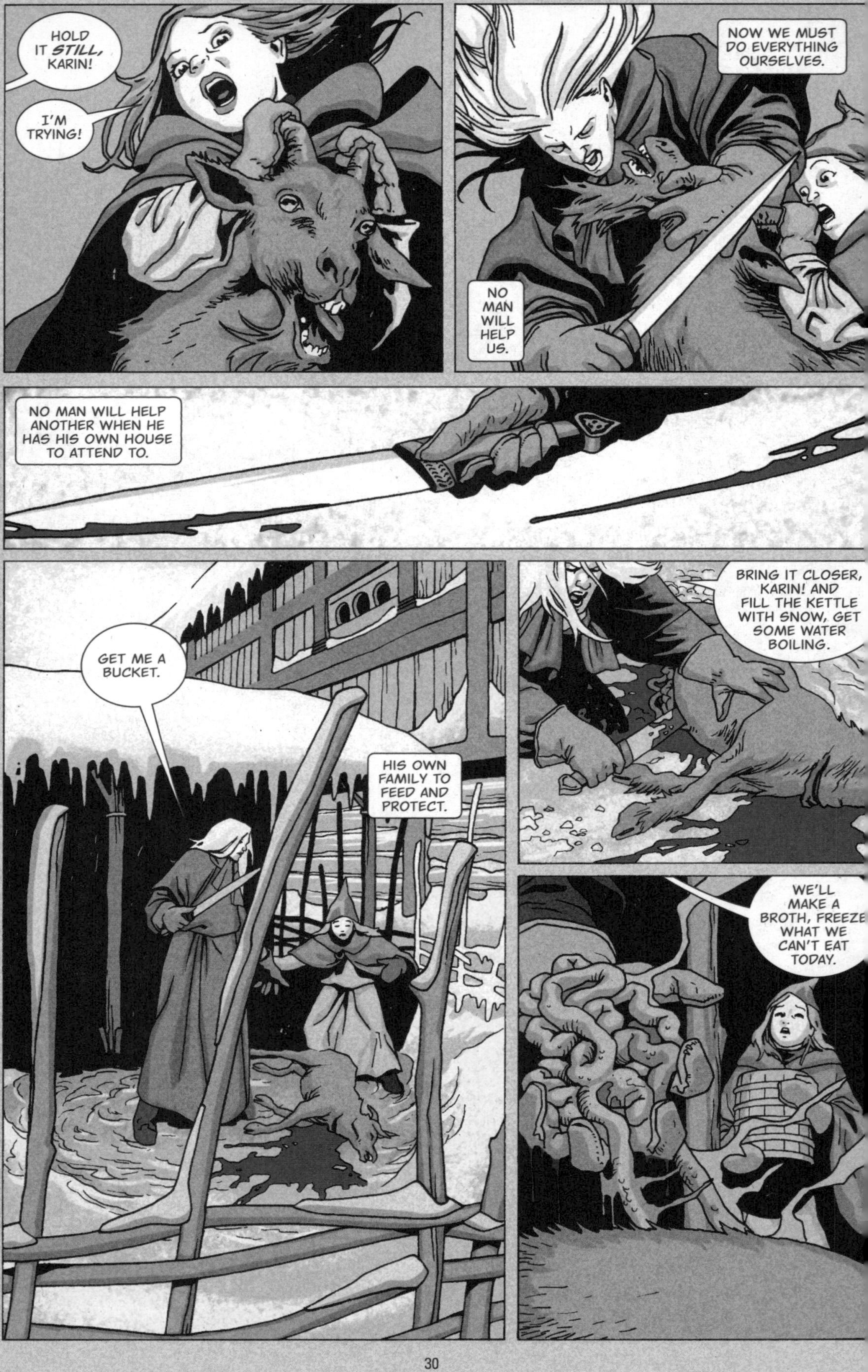
HOLD IT STILL, KARIN!
I'M TRYING!
NOW WE MUST DO EVERYTHING OURSELVES.
NO MAN WILL HELP US.
NO MAN WILL HELP ANOTHER WHEN HE HAS HIS OWN HOUSE TO ATTEND TO.
GET ME A BUCKET.
HIS OWN FAMILY TO FEED AND PROTECT.
BRING IT CLOSER, KARIN! AND FILL THE KETTLE WITH SNOW, GET SOME WATER BOILING.
WE'LL MAKE A BROTH, FREEZE WHAT WE CAN'T EAT TODAY.

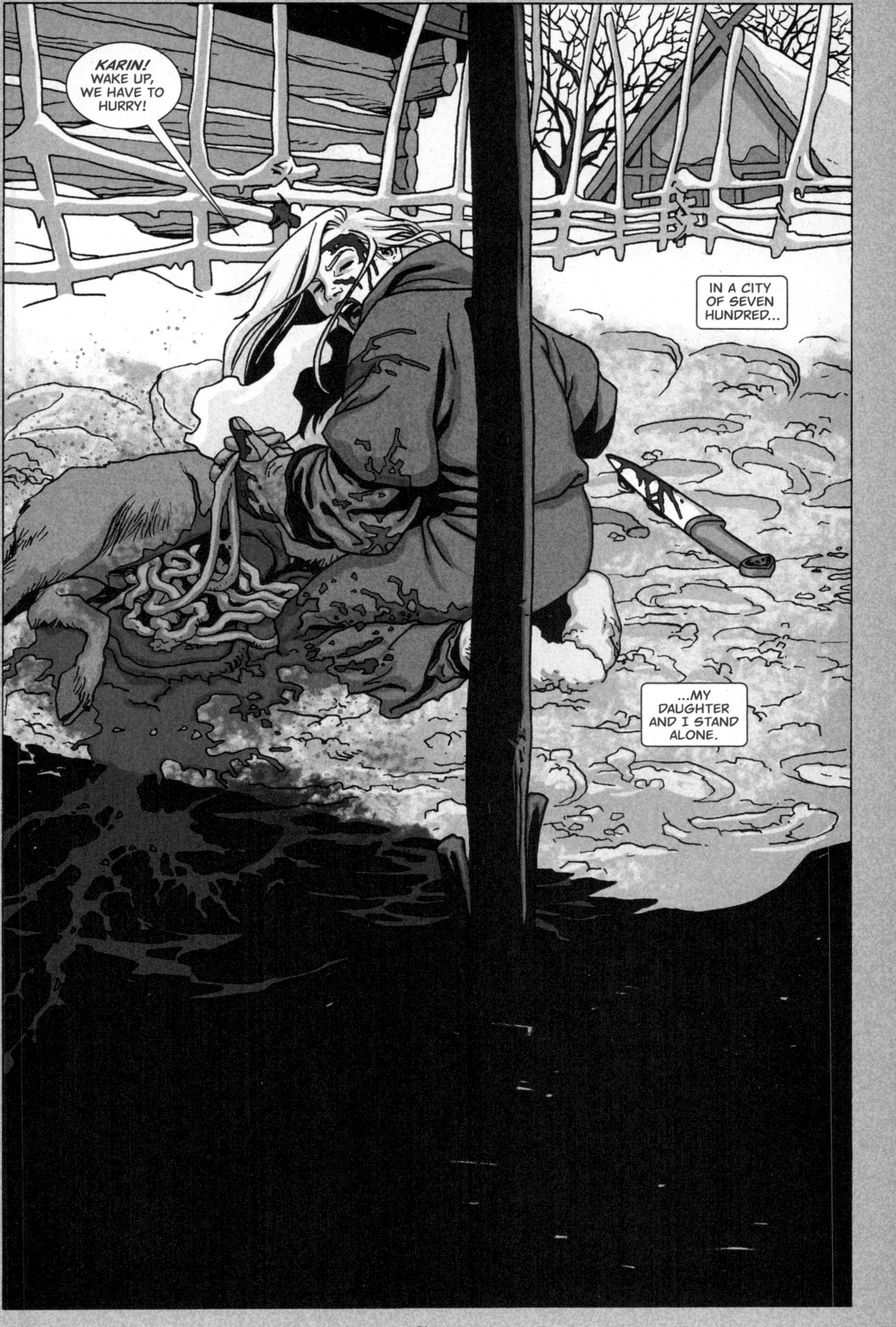
KARIN! WAKE UP, WE HAVE TO HURRY!
IN A CITY OF SEVEN HUNDRED...
...MY DAUGHTER AND I STAND ALONE.

KOFF
KOFF

I SAID AS MUCH TO BORIS AND HE LAUGHED UNTIL THE TEARS FROZE ON HIS CHEEKS.

THE TEMPERATURE DROPPED WITH THE SNOWFALL. WINTER WAS EVER A BRUTAL SEASON, AND THE WIND ROARED OFF THE RIVER AND WHISTLED THROUGH THE BIRCH TRUNKS...

THE MEN CLOSED THE GATES AND NAILED THEM SHUT. BORIS BLESSED THE ACT IN THREE LANGUAGES, THREE DIFFERENT FAITHS, AND SAID PRAYERS FOR THE DEAD THAT LAY OUTSIDE.

OVERNIGHT A DEEP SNOW FELL AND COVERED THE BODIES. PEOPLE CALLED IT A DIVINE ACT. IF SO, HE ONLY MET US HALFWAY, SINCE THE PAIN STILL MARKED OUR HEARTS AND SOULS, IF NOT THE EARTH.

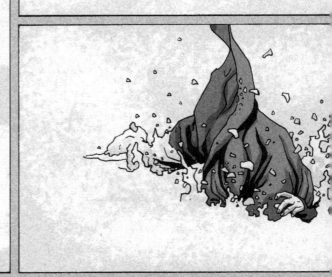

...AND TORE THE VOICES FROM OUR THROATS.

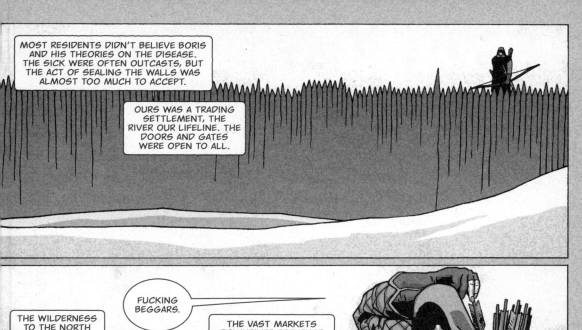

MOST RESIDENTS DIDN'T BELIEVE BORIS AND HIS THEORIES ON THE DISEASE. THE SICK WERE OFTEN OUTCASTS, BUT THE ACT OF SEALING THE WALLS WAS ALMOST TOO MUCH TO ACCEPT.

OURS WAS A TRADING SETTLEMENT, THE RIVER OUR LIFELINE. THE DOORS AND GATES WERE OPEN TO ALL.

THE WILDERNESS TO THE NORTH BORE PELTS AND IRON INGOTS, REINDEER ANTLERS AND SLAVES.

FUCKING BEGGARS.

THE VAST MARKETS DOWNRIVER RETURNED SILVER AND SWORD BLADES, FINE FABRICS DYED COLORS WE COULD SCARCELY DREAM OF.

MAY CHRIST HAVE MERCY ON THEIR WRETCHED SOULS.

THE FORESTS GAVE US WOOD AND MEAT, THE RIVERS AND STREAMS BEAR FISH, AND THE OUTLYING FARMS GROW APPLES AND WHEAT.

BUT THE FARMS ARE LOOTED AND BURNED, THE STREAMS FOULED BY DEAD BODIES.

FIREWOOD JUST OUT OF REACH, THE WATERS OF THE VOLGA OFF LIMITS.

WE ARE A CITY IN SELF-EXILE, THE DECISION MAKERS IN BITTER DISAGREEMENT.

AND OUR WINTERS LAST SEVEN MONTHS.

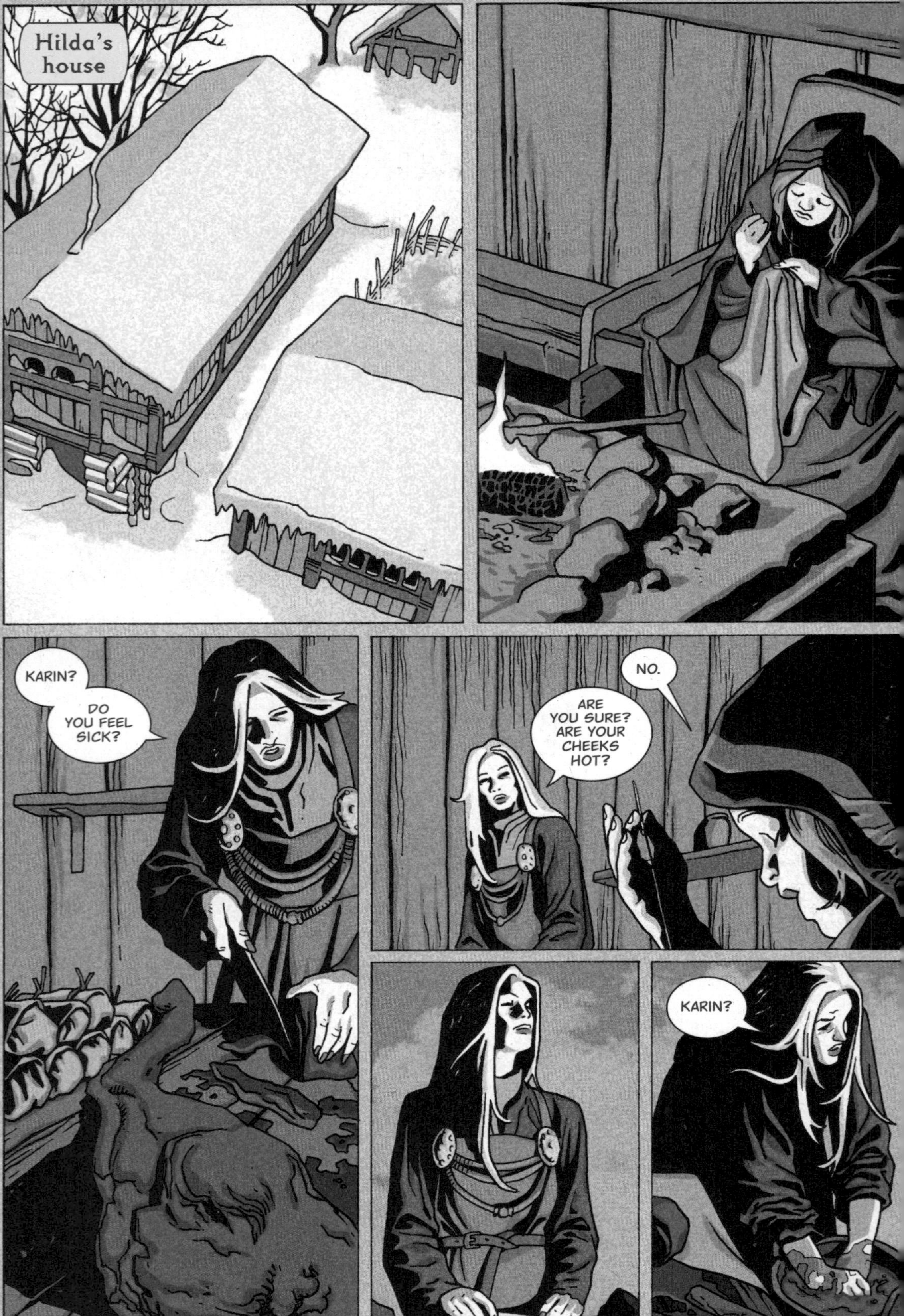
Hilda's house
KARIN?
DO YOU FEEL SICK?
NO.
ARE YOU SURE? ARE YOUR CHEEKS HOT?
KARIN?

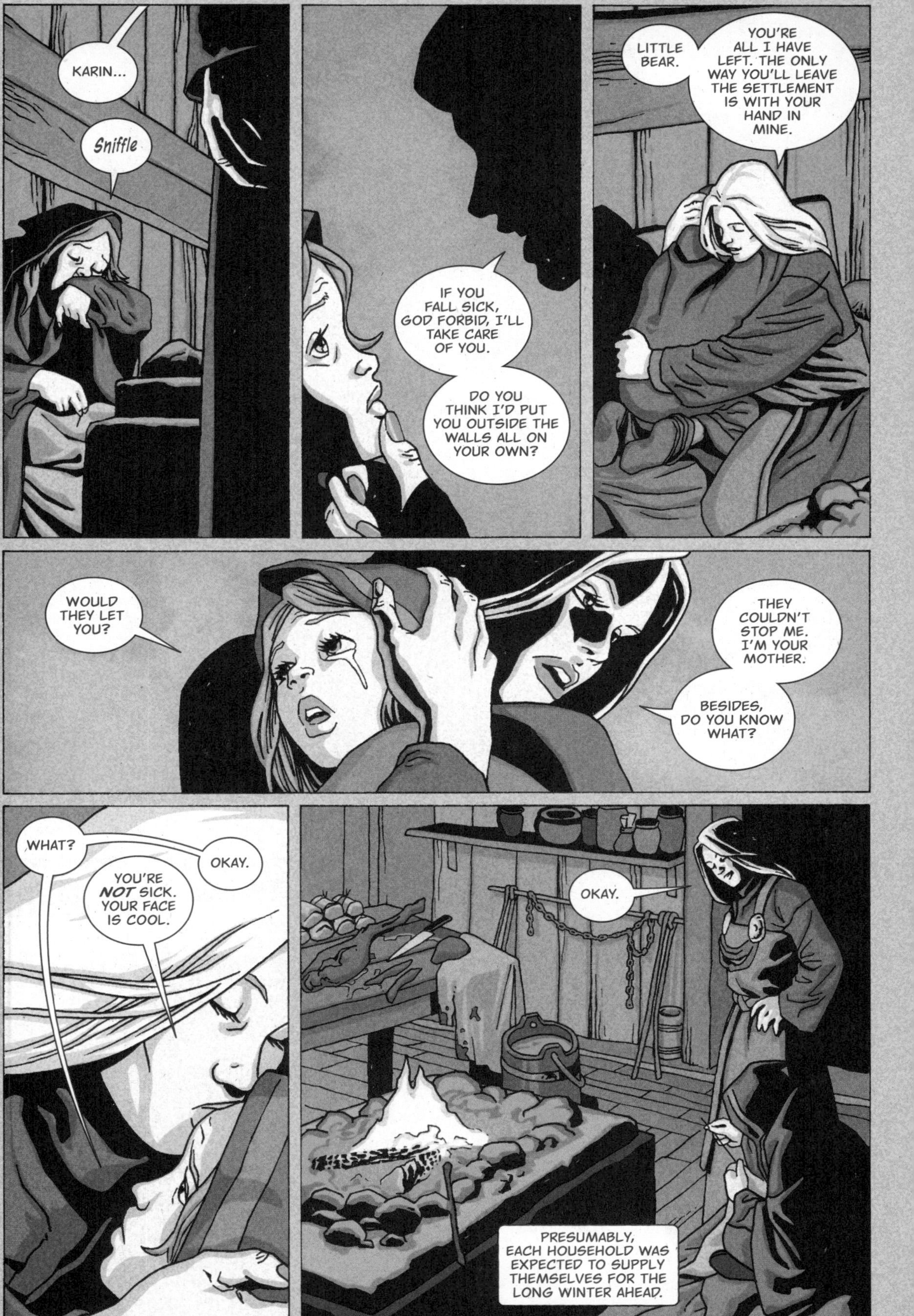
KARIN...
Sniffle
IF YOU FALL SICK, GOD FORBID, I'LL TAKE CARE OF YOU.
DO YOU THINK I'D PUT YOU OUTSIDE THE WALLS ALL ON YOUR OWN?
LITTLE BEAR.
YOU'RE ALL I HAVE LEFT. THE ONLY WAY YOU'LL LEAVE THE SETTLEMENT IS WITH YOUR HAND IN MINE.
WOULD THEY LET YOU?
THEY COULDN'T STOP ME. I'M YOUR MOTHER.
BESIDES, DO YOU KNOW WHAT?
WHAT?
YOU'RE ***NOT*** SICK. YOUR FACE IS COOL.
OKAY.
OKAY.
PRESUMABLY, EACH HOUSEHOLD WAS EXPECTED TO SUPPLY THEMSELVES FOR THE LONG WINTER AHEAD.

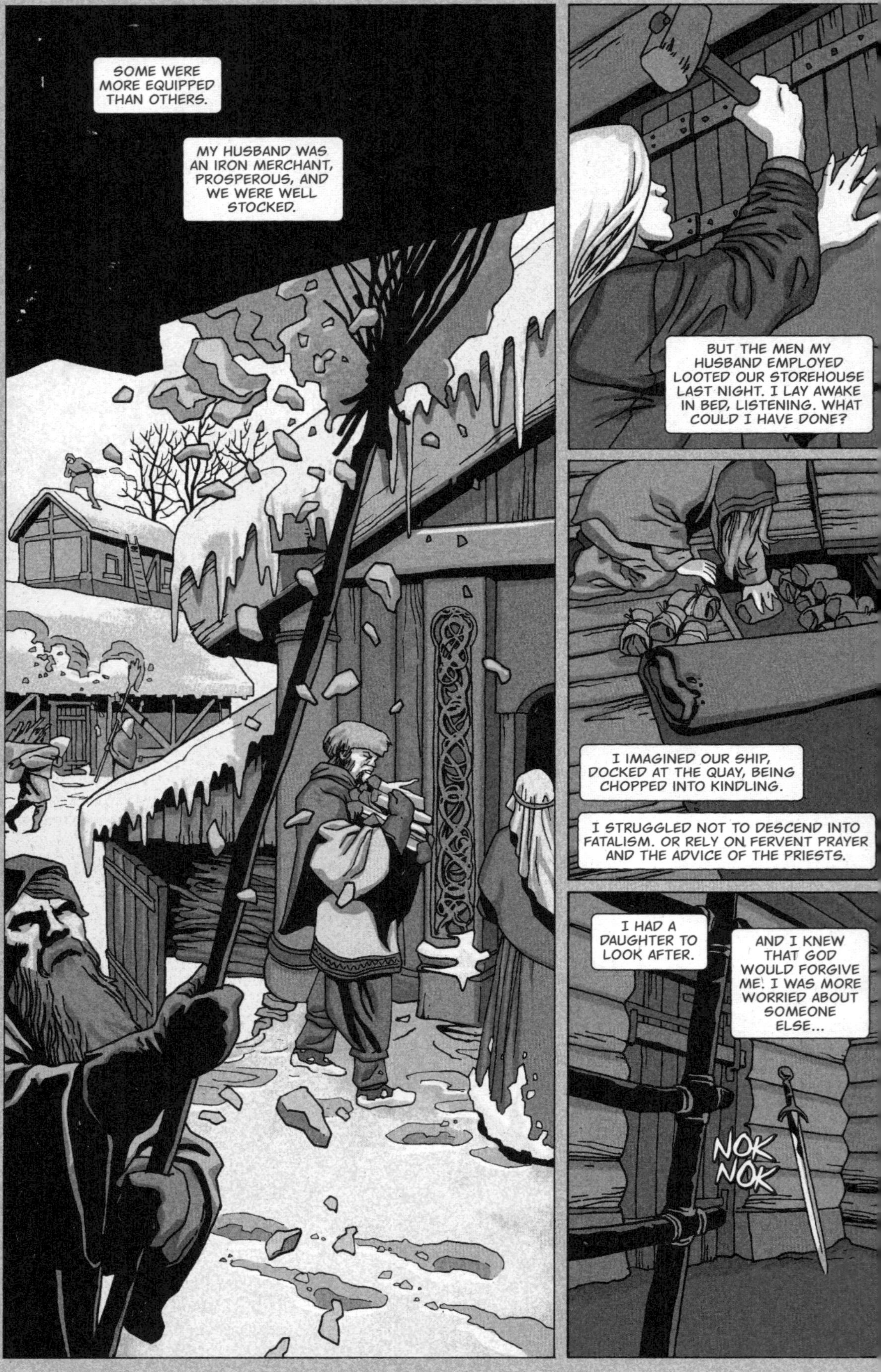
SOME WERE MORE EQUIPPED THAN OTHERS.
MY HUSBAND WAS AN IRON MERCHANT, PROSPEROUS, AND WE WERE WELL STOCKED.
BUT THE MEN MY HUSBAND EMPLOYED LOOTED OUR STOREHOUSE LAST NIGHT. I LAY AWAKE IN BED, LISTENING. WHAT COULD I HAVE DONE?
I IMAGINED OUR SHIP, DOCKED AT THE QUAY, BEING CHOPPED INTO KINDLING.
I STRUGGLED NOT TO DESCEND INTO FATALISM. OR RELY ON FERVENT PRAYER AND THE ADVICE OF THE PRIESTS.
I HAD A DAUGHTER TO LOOK AFTER.
AND I KNEW THAT GOD WOULD FORGIVE ME. I WAS MORE WORRIED ABOUT SOMEONE ELSE...
NOK NOK

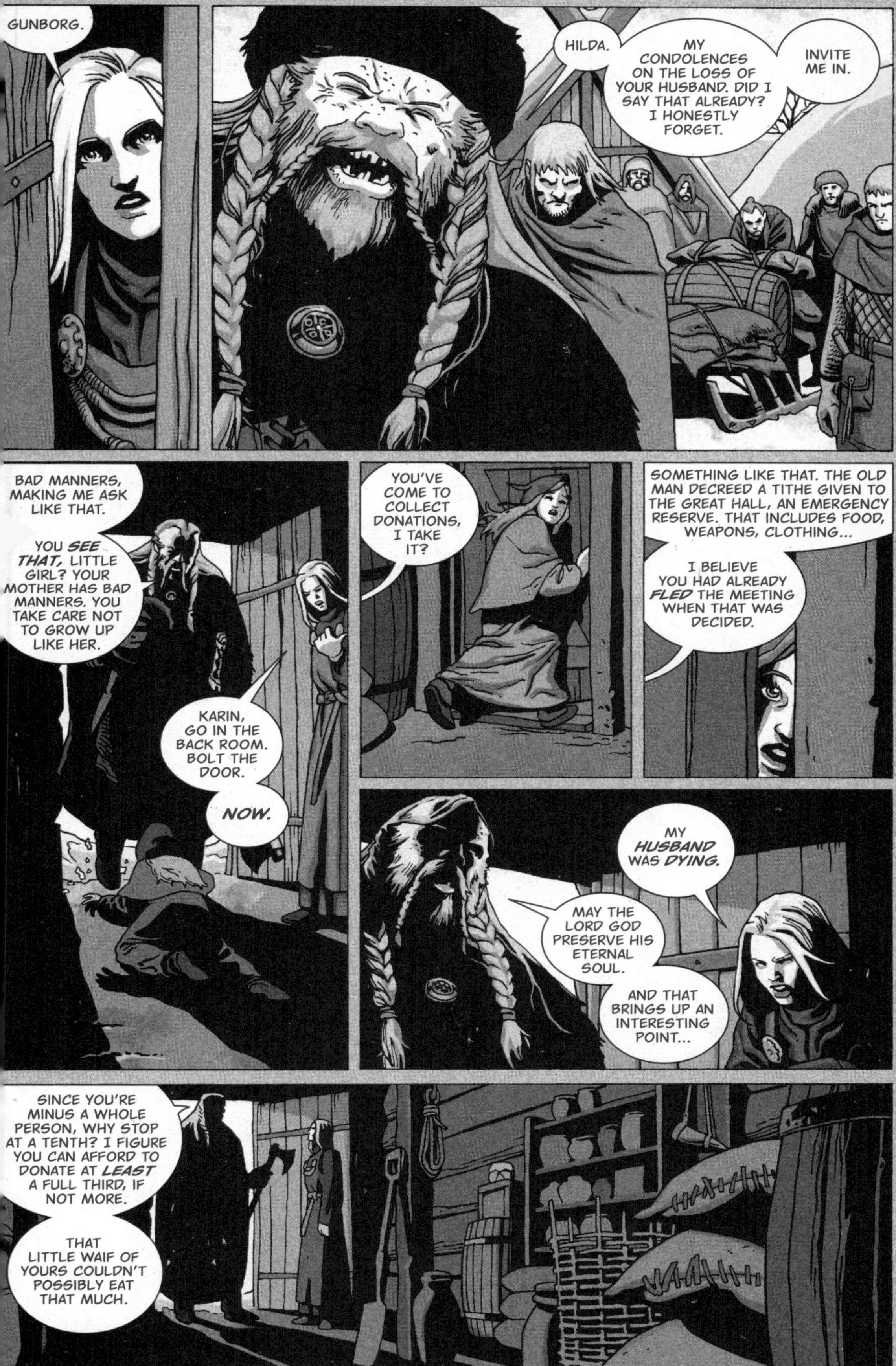
GUNBORG.
HILDA.
MY CONDOLENCES ON THE LOSS OF YOUR HUSBAND. DID I SAY THAT ALREADY? I HONESTLY FORGET.
INVITE ME IN.
BAD MANNERS, MAKING ME ASK LIKE THAT.
YOU SEE THAT, LITTLE GIRL? YOUR MOTHER HAS BAD MANNERS. YOU TAKE CARE NOT TO GROW UP LIKE HER.
KARIN, GO IN THE BACK ROOM. BOLT THE DOOR.
NOW.
YOU'VE COME TO COLLECT DONATIONS, I TAKE IT?
SOMETHING LIKE THAT. THE OLD MAN DECREED A TITHE GIVEN TO THE GREAT HALL, AN EMERGENCY RESERVE. THAT INCLUDES FOOD, WEAPONS, CLOTHING...
I BELIEVE YOU HAD ALREADY FLED THE MEETING WHEN THAT WAS DECIDED.
MY HUSBAND WAS DYING.
MAY THE LORD GOD PRESERVE HIS ETERNAL SOUL.
AND THAT BRINGS UP AN INTERESTING POINT...
SINCE YOU'RE MINUS A WHOLE PERSON, WHY STOP AT A TENTH? I FIGURE YOU CAN AFFORD TO DONATE AT LEAST A FULL THIRD, IF NOT MORE.
THAT LITTLE WAIF OF YOURS COULDN'T POSSIBLY EAT THAT MUCH.

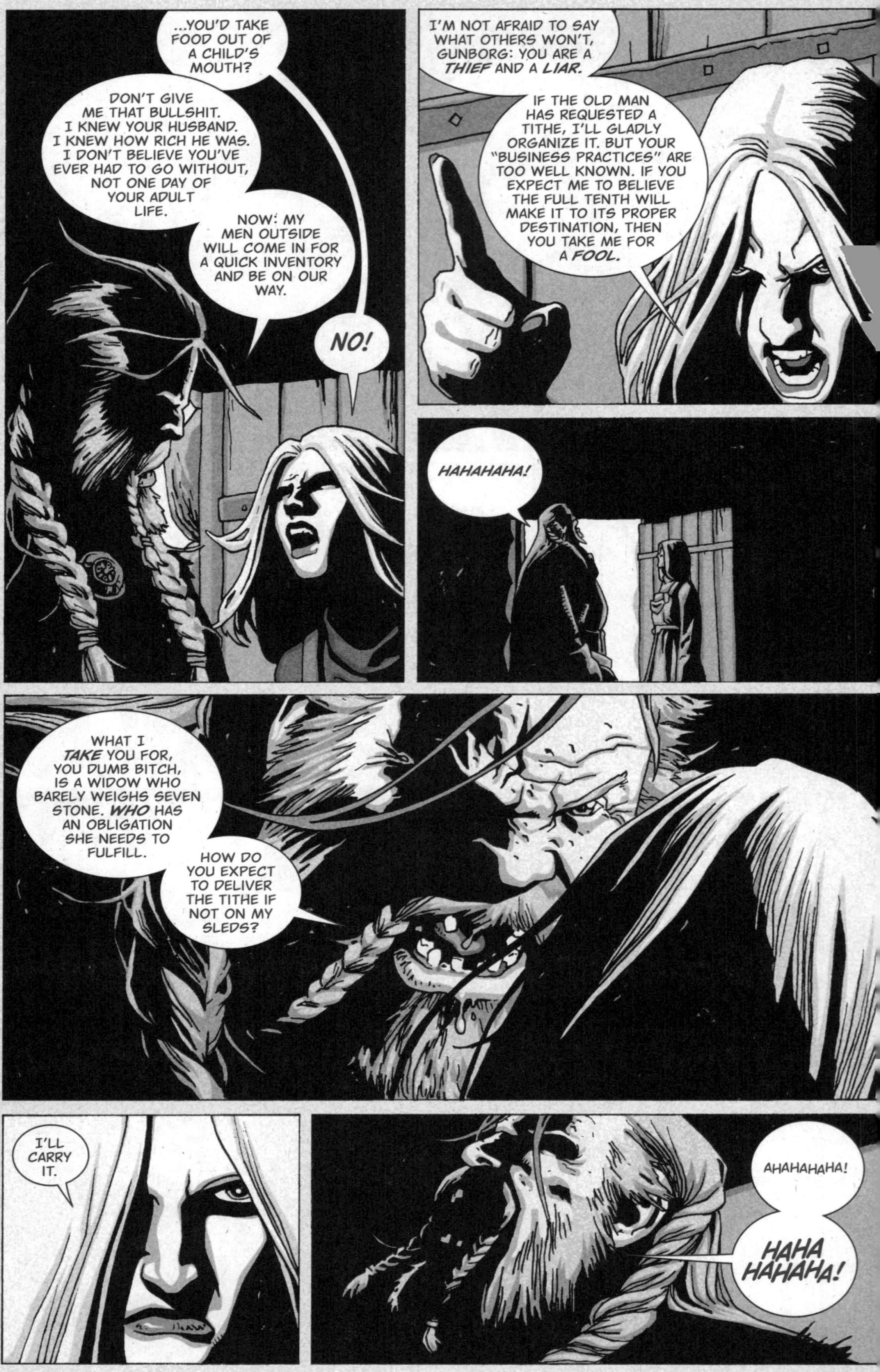
...YOU'D TAKE FOOD OUT OF A CHILD'S MOUTH?
DON'T GIVE ME THAT BULLSHIT. I KNEW YOUR HUSBAND. I KNEW HOW RICH HE WAS. I DON'T BELIEVE YOU'VE EVER HAD TO GO WITHOUT, NOT ONE DAY OF YOUR ADULT LIFE.
NOW: MY MEN OUTSIDE WILL COME IN FOR A QUICK INVENTORY AND BE ON OUR WAY.
NO!
I'M NOT AFRAID TO SAY WHAT OTHERS WON'T, GUNBORG: YOU ARE A THIEF AND A LIAR.
IF THE OLD MAN HAS REQUESTED A TITHE, I'LL GLADLY ORGANIZE IT. BUT YOUR "BUSINESS PRACTICES" ARE TOO WELL KNOWN. IF YOU EXPECT ME TO BELIEVE THE FULL TENTH WILL MAKE IT TO ITS PROPER DESTINATION, THEN YOU TAKE ME FOR A FOOL.
HAHAHAHA!
WHAT I TAKE YOU FOR, YOU DUMB BITCH, IS A WIDOW WHO BARELY WEIGHS SEVEN STONE. WHO HAS AN OBLIGATION SHE NEEDS TO FULFILL.
HOW DO YOU EXPECT TO DELIVER THE TITHE IF NOT ON MY SLEDS?
I'LL CARRY IT.
AHAHAHAHA!
HAHA HAHAHA!

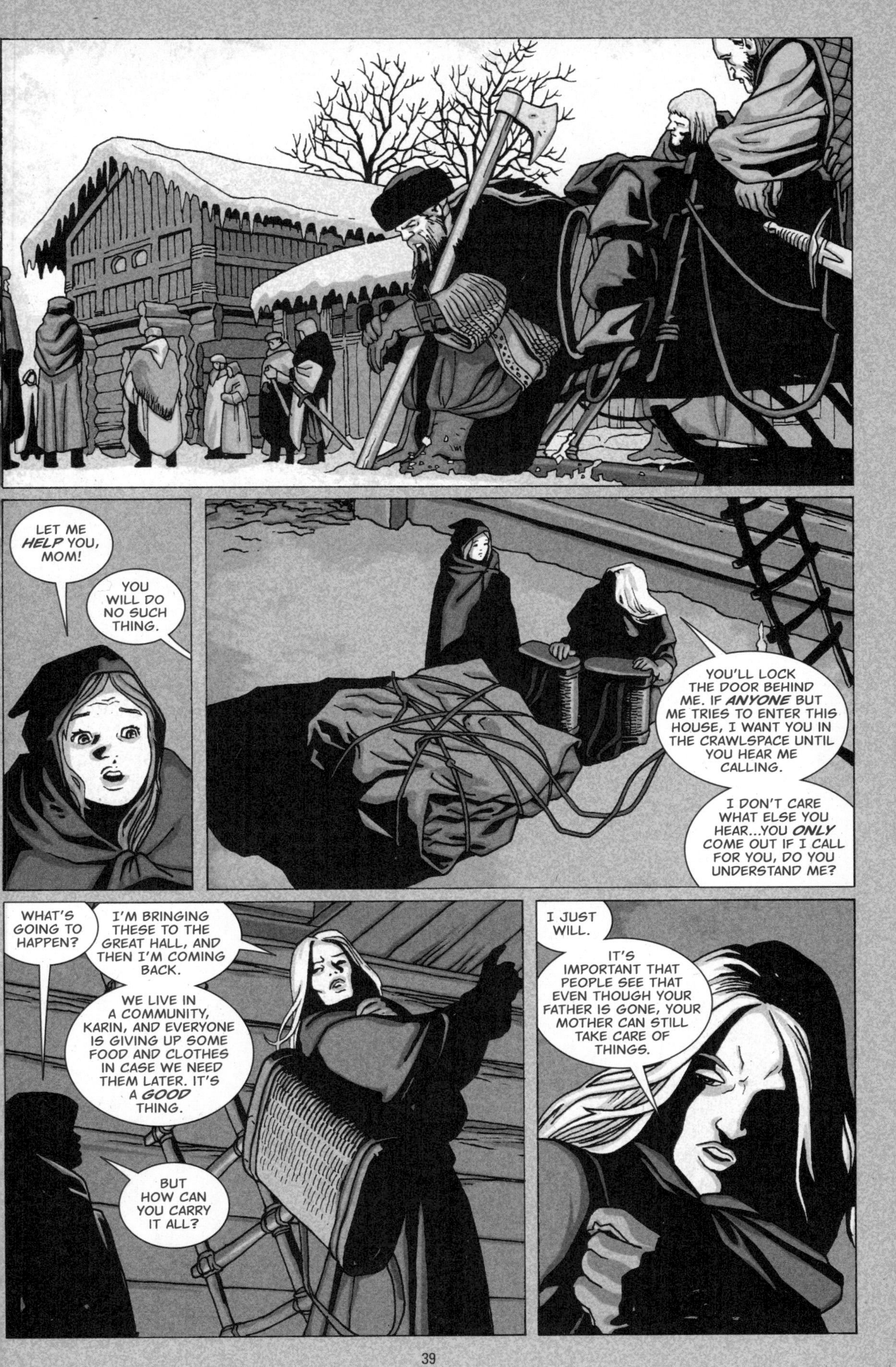
LET ME HELP YOU, MOM!
YOU WILL DO NO SUCH THING.
YOU'LL LOCK THE DOOR BEHIND ME. IF ANYONE BUT ME TRIES TO ENTER THIS HOUSE, I WANT YOU IN THE CRAWLSPACE UNTIL YOU HEAR ME CALLING.
I DON'T CARE WHAT ELSE YOU HEAR...YOU ONLY COME OUT IF I CALL FOR YOU, DO YOU UNDERSTAND ME?
WHAT'S GOING TO HAPPEN?
I'M BRINGING THESE TO THE GREAT HALL, AND THEN I'M COMING BACK.
WE LIVE IN A COMMUNITY, KARIN, AND EVERYONE IS GIVING UP SOME FOOD AND CLOTHES IN CASE WE NEED THEM LATER. IT'S A GOOD THING.
BUT HOW CAN YOU CARRY IT ALL?
I JUST WILL.
IT'S IMPORTANT THAT PEOPLE SEE THAT EVEN THOUGH YOUR FATHER IS GONE, YOUR MOTHER CAN STILL TAKE CARE OF THINGS.

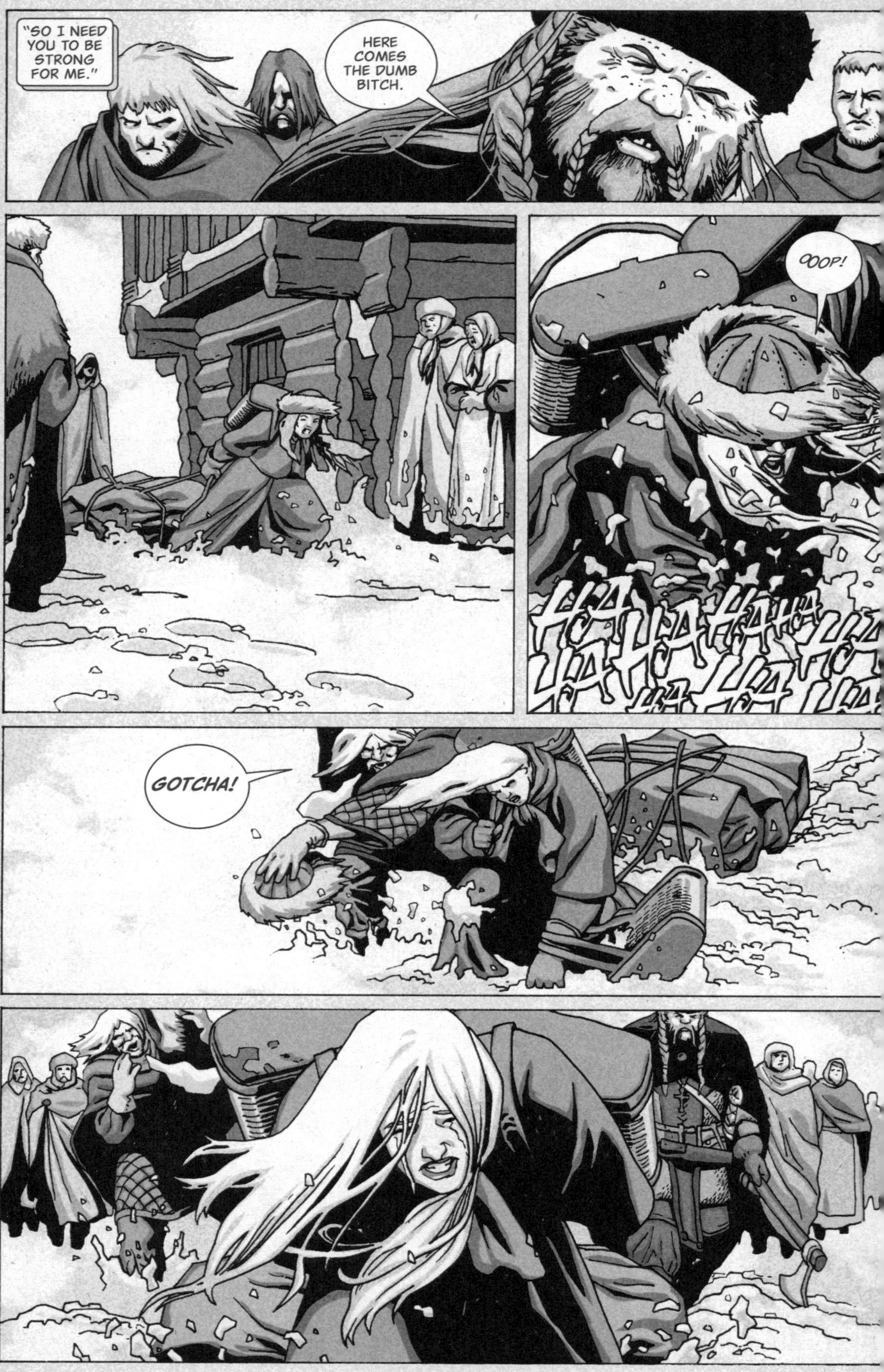
"SO I NEED YOU TO BE STRONG FOR ME."
HERE COMES THE DUMB BITCH.
OOOP!
HAHAHAHAHA
GOTCHA!

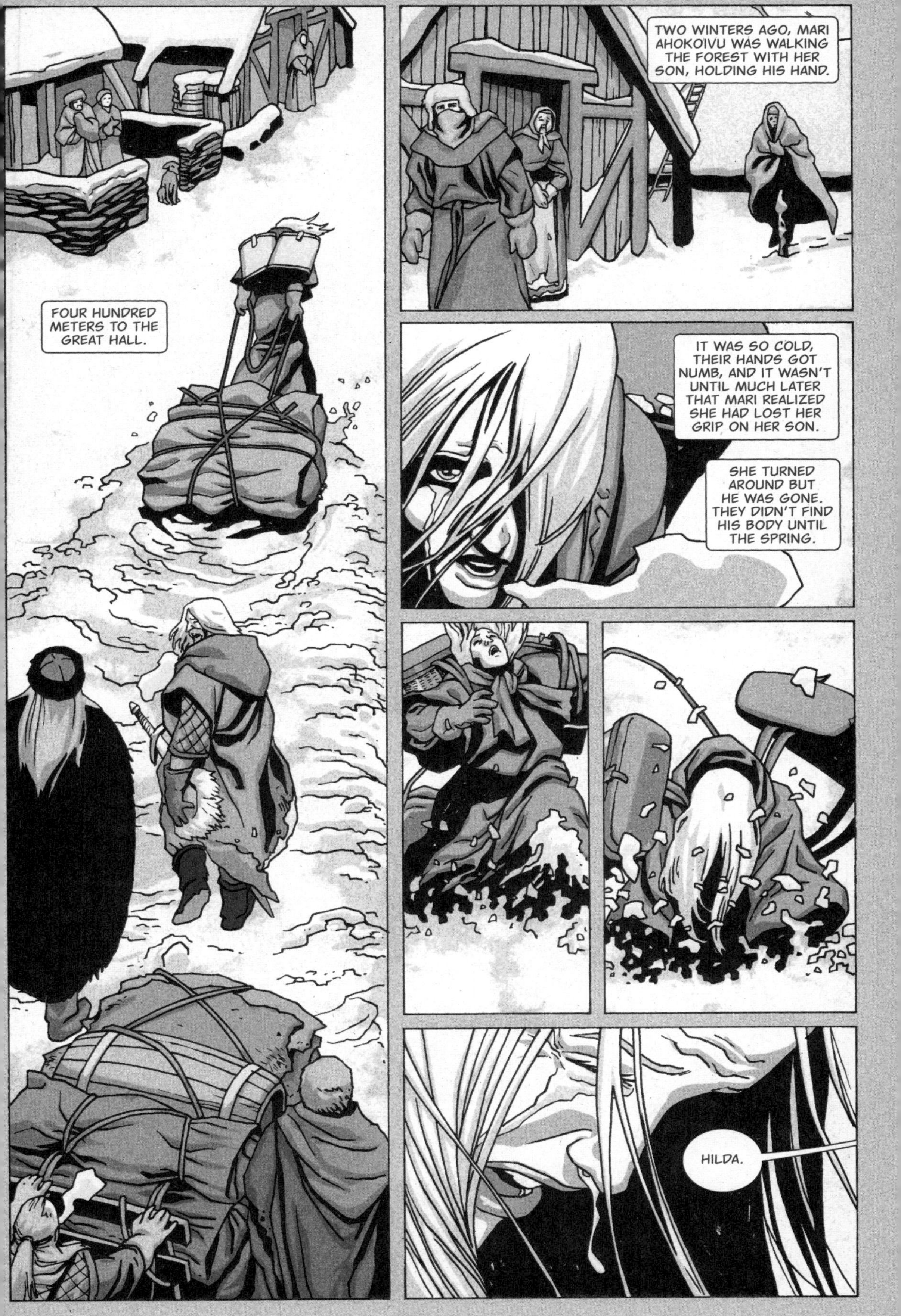
FOUR HUNDRED METERS TO THE GREAT HALL.
TWO WINTERS AGO, MARI AHOKOIVU WAS WALKING THE FOREST WITH HER SON, HOLDING HIS HAND.
IT WAS SO COLD, THEIR HANDS GOT NUMB, AND IT WASN'T UNTIL MUCH LATER THAT MARI REALIZED SHE HAD LOST HER GRIP ON HER SON.
SHE TURNED AROUND BUT HE WAS GONE. THEY DIDN'T FIND HIS BODY UNTIL THE SPRING.
HILDA.

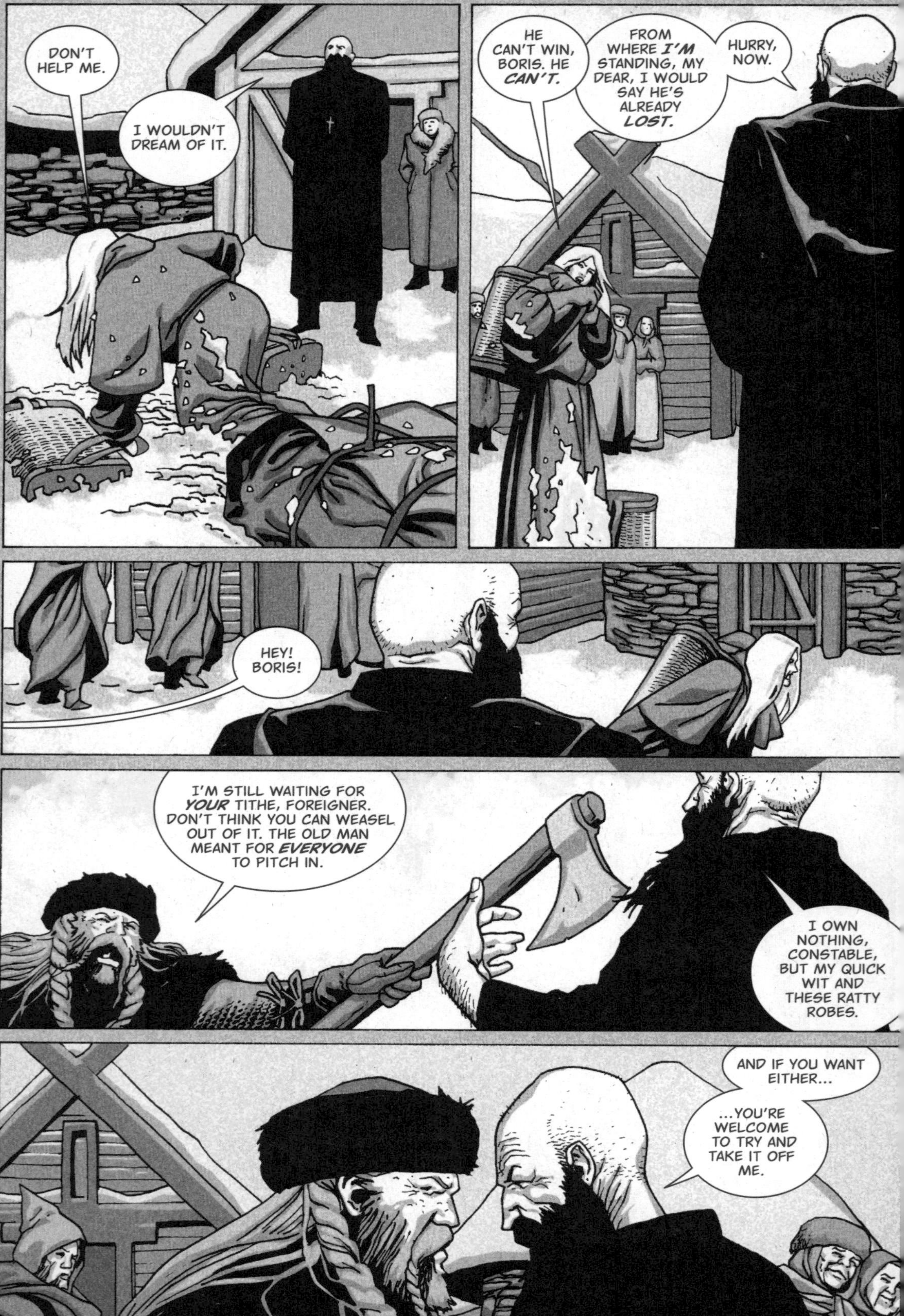
DON'T HELP ME.
I WOULDN'T DREAM OF IT.
HE CAN'T WIN, BORIS. HE *CAN'T.*
FROM WHERE *I'M* STANDING, MY DEAR, I WOULD SAY HE'S ALREADY *LOST.*
HURRY, NOW.
HEY! BORIS!
I'M STILL WAITING FOR *YOUR* TITHE, FOREIGNER. DON'T THINK YOU CAN WEASEL OUT OF IT. THE OLD MAN MEANT FOR *EVERYONE* TO PITCH IN.
I OWN NOTHING, CONSTABLE, BUT MY QUICK WIT AND THESE RATTY ROBES.
AND IF YOU WANT EITHER...
...YOU'RE WELCOME TO TRY AND TAKE IT OFF ME.

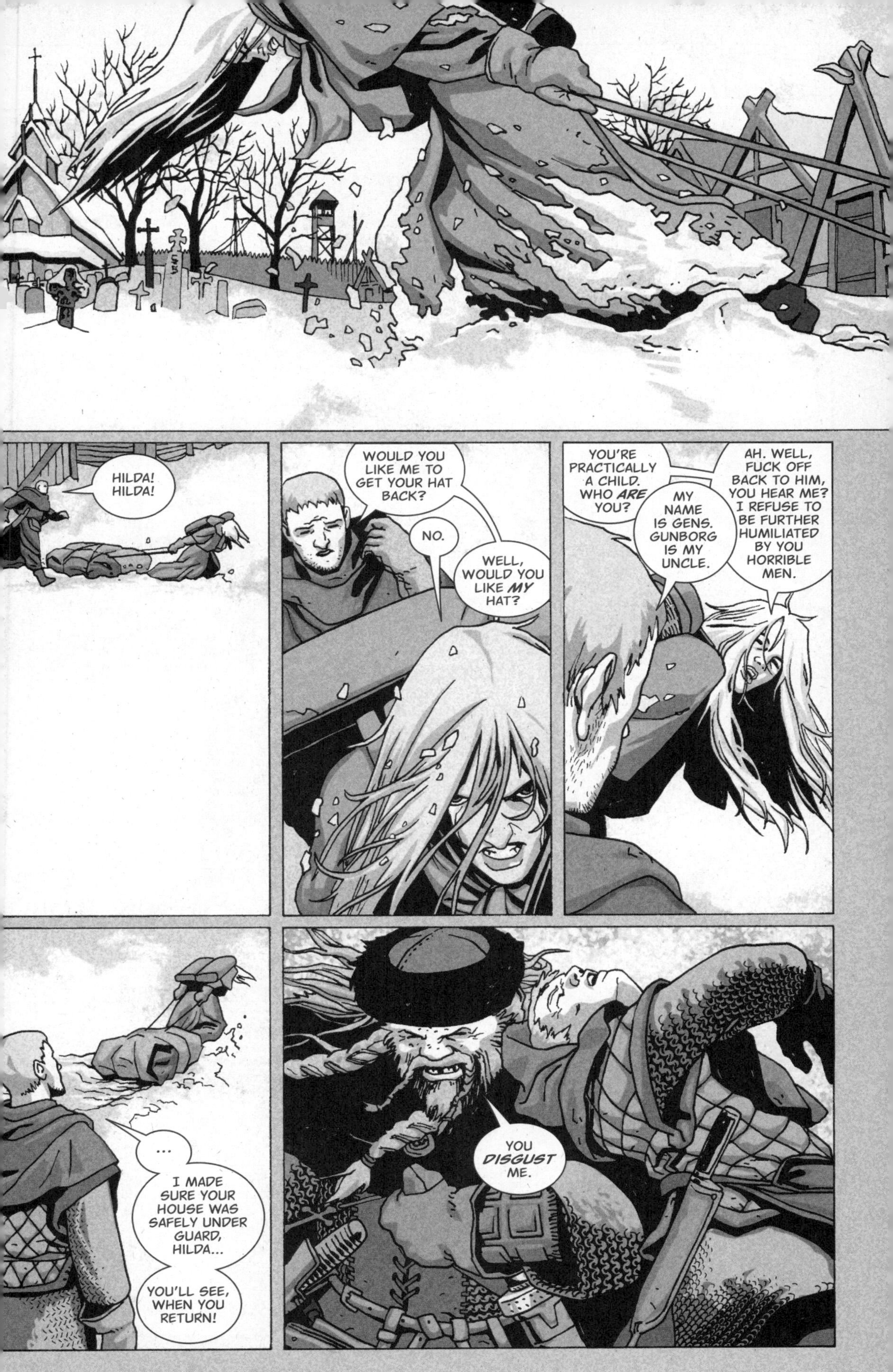
HILDA! HILDA!
WOULD YOU LIKE ME TO GET YOUR HAT BACK?
NO.
WELL, WOULD YOU LIKE MY HAT?
YOU'RE PRACTICALLY A CHILD. WHO ARE YOU?
MY NAME IS GENS. GUNBORG IS MY UNCLE.
AH. WELL, FUCK OFF BACK TO HIM, YOU HEAR ME? I REFUSE TO BE FURTHER HUMILIATED BY YOU HORRIBLE MEN.
...
I MADE SURE YOUR HOUSE WAS SAFELY UNDER GUARD, HILDA...
YOU'LL SEE, WHEN YOU RETURN!
YOU DISGUST ME.

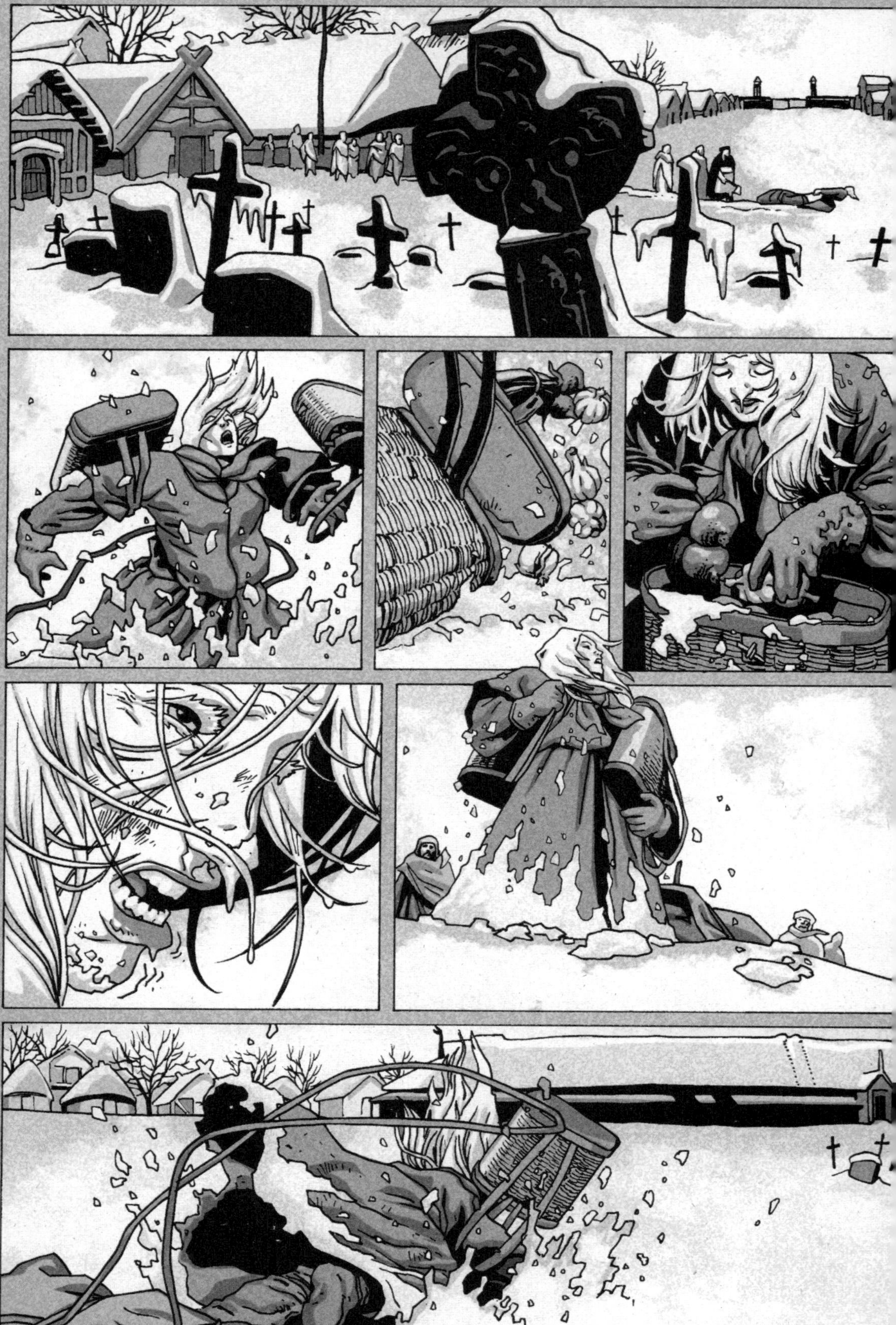

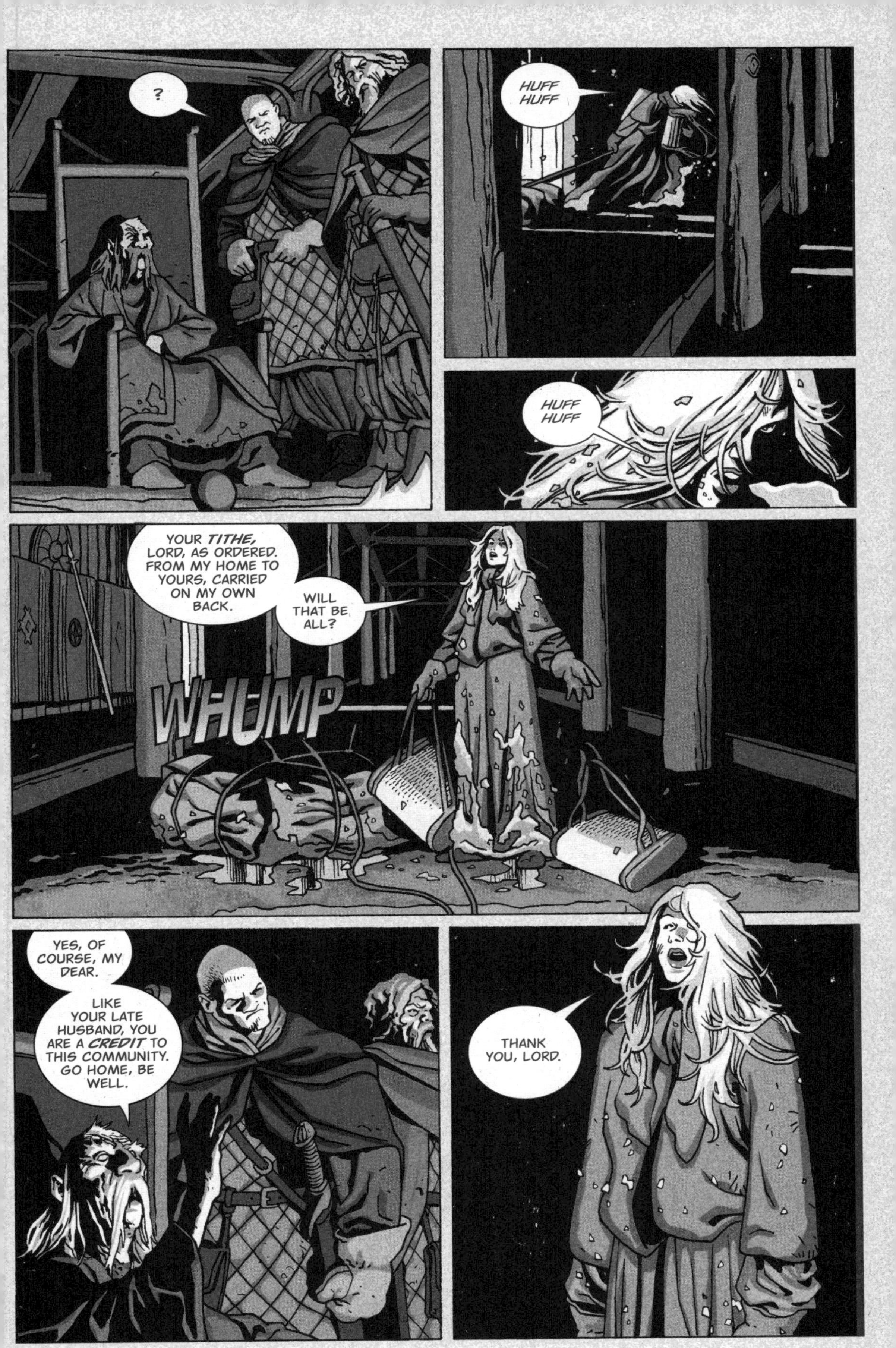
?
HUFF HUFF
HUFF HUFF
YOUR TITHE, LORD, AS ORDERED. FROM MY HOME TO YOURS, CARRIED ON MY OWN BACK.
WILL THAT BE ALL?
WHUMP
YES, OF COURSE, MY DEAR.
LIKE YOUR LATE HUSBAND, YOU ARE A CREDIT TO THIS COMMUNITY. GO HOME, BE WELL.
THANK YOU, LORD.

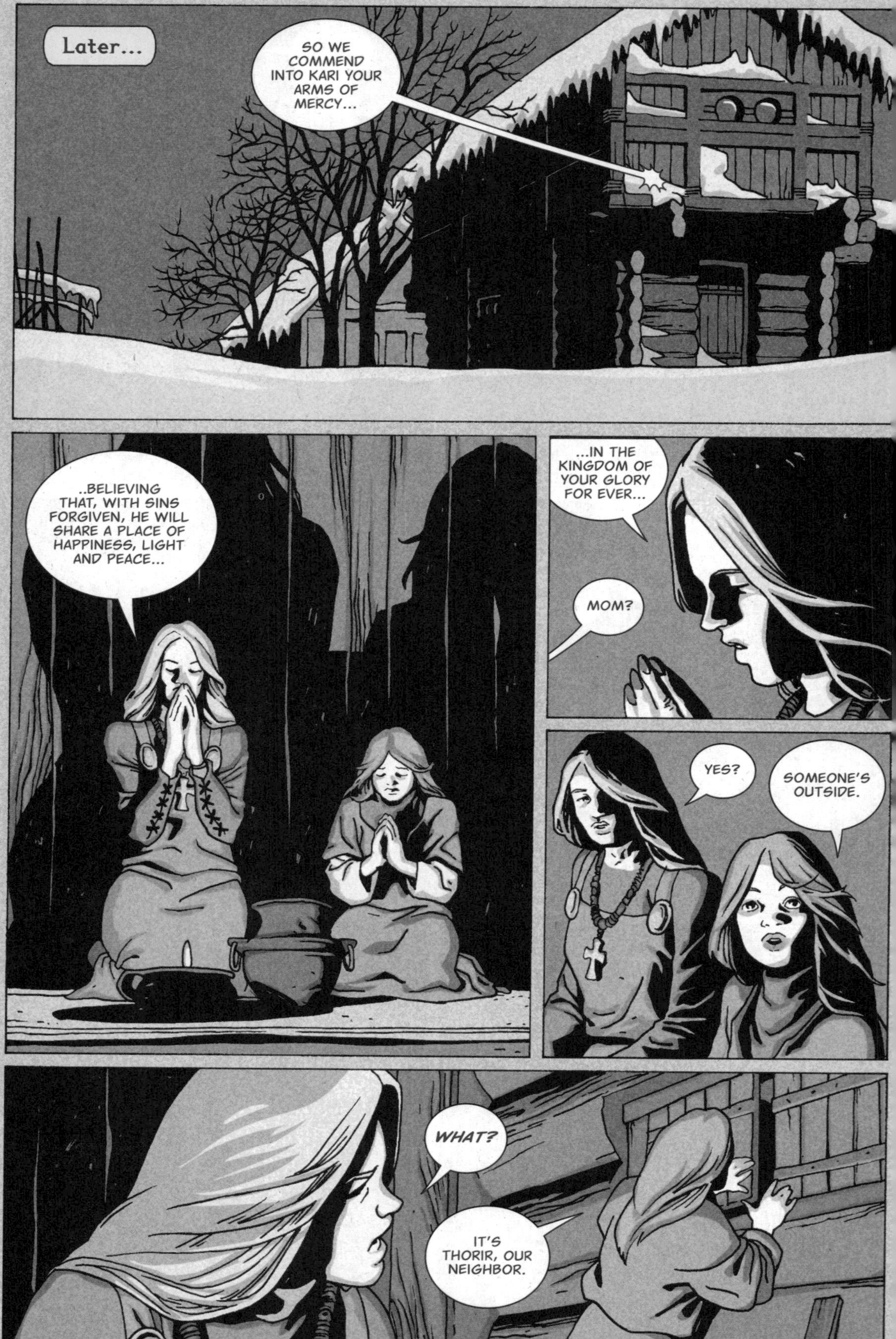
Later...
SO WE COMMEND INTO KARI YOUR ARMS OF MERCY...
..BELIEVING THAT, WITH SINS FORGIVEN, HE WILL SHARE A PLACE OF HAPPINESS, LIGHT AND PEACE...
...IN THE KINGDOM OF YOUR GLORY FOR EVER...
MOM?
YES?
SOMEONE'S OUTSIDE.
WHAT?
IT'S THORIR, OUR NEIGHBOR.

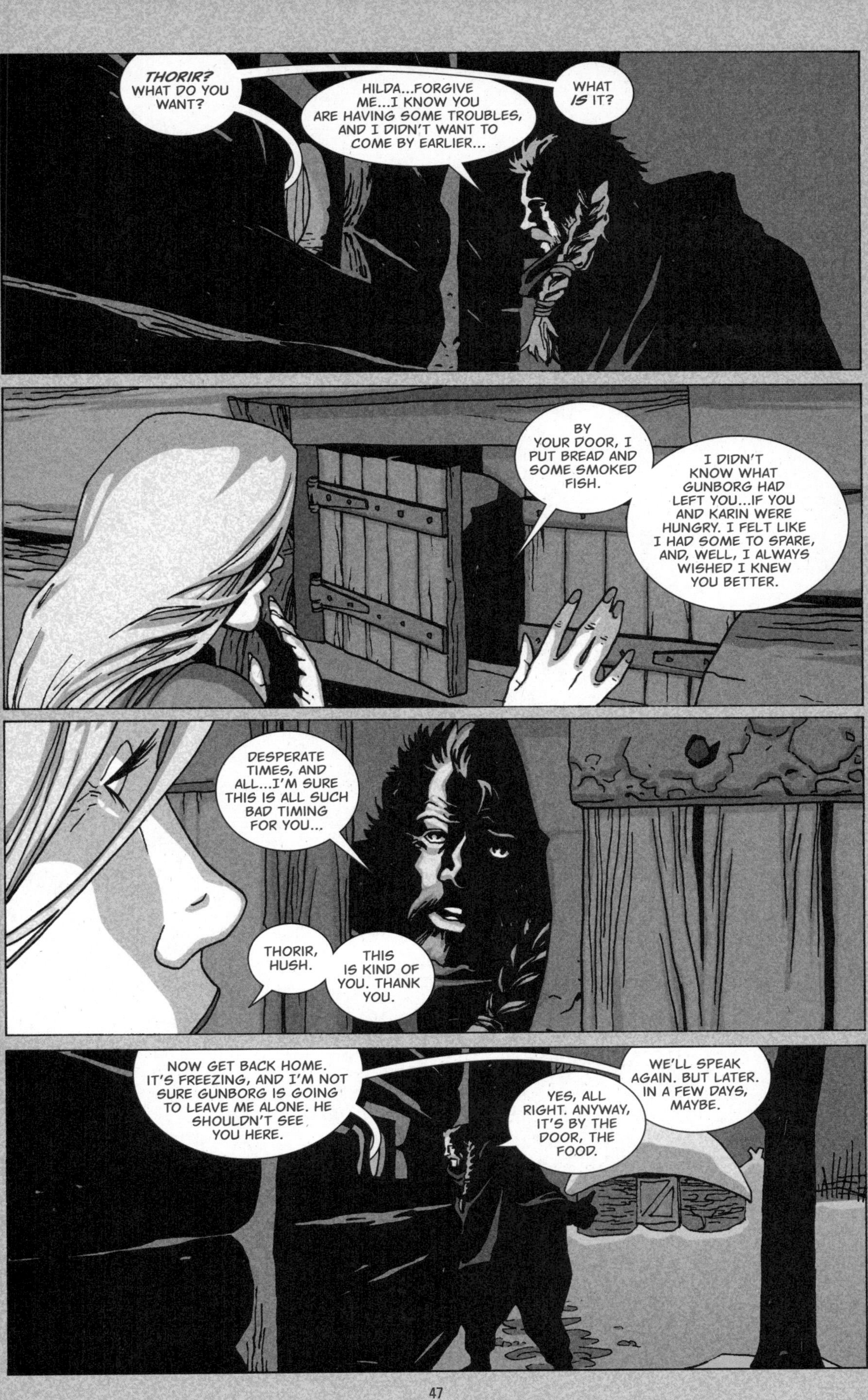
THORIR? WHAT DO YOU WANT?
HILDA...FORGIVE ME...I KNOW YOU ARE HAVING SOME TROUBLES, AND I DIDN'T WANT TO COME BY EARLIER...
WHAT IS IT?
BY YOUR DOOR, I PUT BREAD AND SOME SMOKED FISH.
I DIDN'T KNOW WHAT GUNBORG HAD LEFT YOU...IF YOU AND KARIN WERE HUNGRY. I FELT LIKE I HAD SOME TO SPARE, AND, WELL, I ALWAYS WISHED I KNEW YOU BETTER.
DESPERATE TIMES, AND ALL...I'M SURE THIS IS ALL SUCH BAD TIMING FOR YOU...
THORIR, HUSH.
THIS IS KIND OF YOU. THANK YOU.
NOW GET BACK HOME. IT'S FREEZING, AND I'M NOT SURE GUNBORG IS GOING TO LEAVE ME ALONE. HE SHOULDN'T SEE YOU HERE.
WE'LL SPEAK AGAIN. BUT LATER. IN A FEW DAYS, MAYBE.
YES, ALL RIGHT. ANYWAY, IT'S BY THE DOOR, THE FOOD.

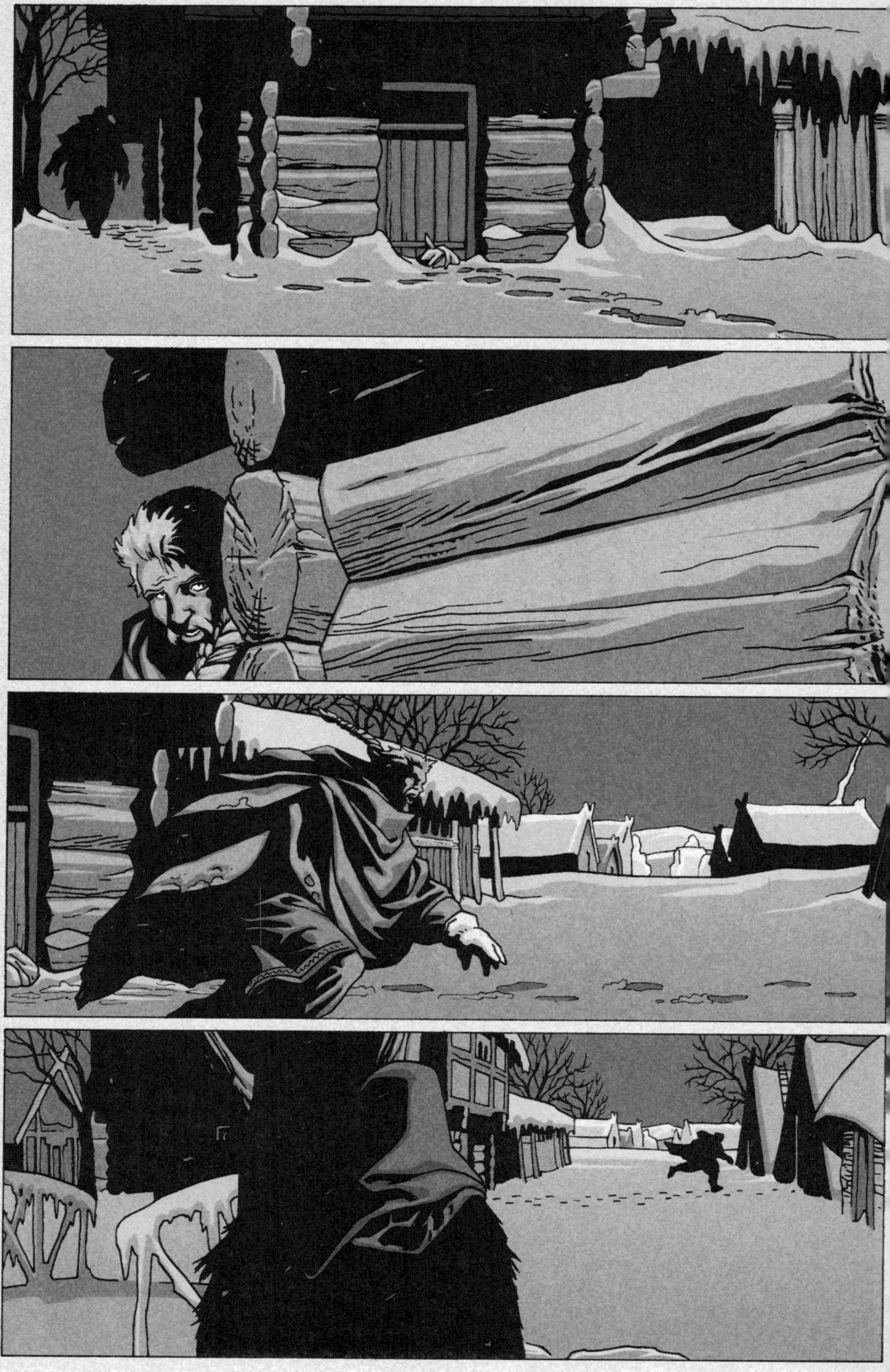

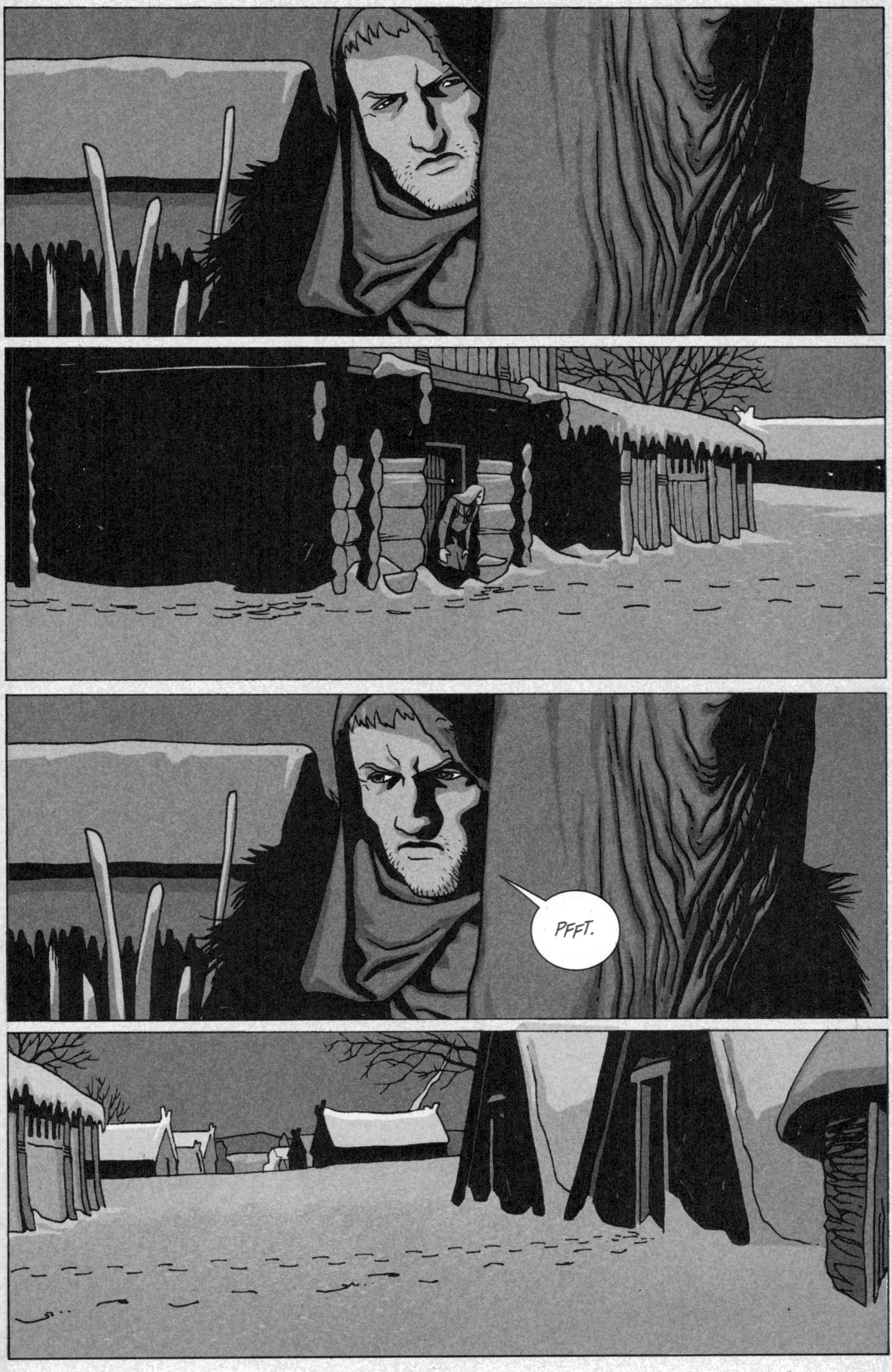
PFFT.

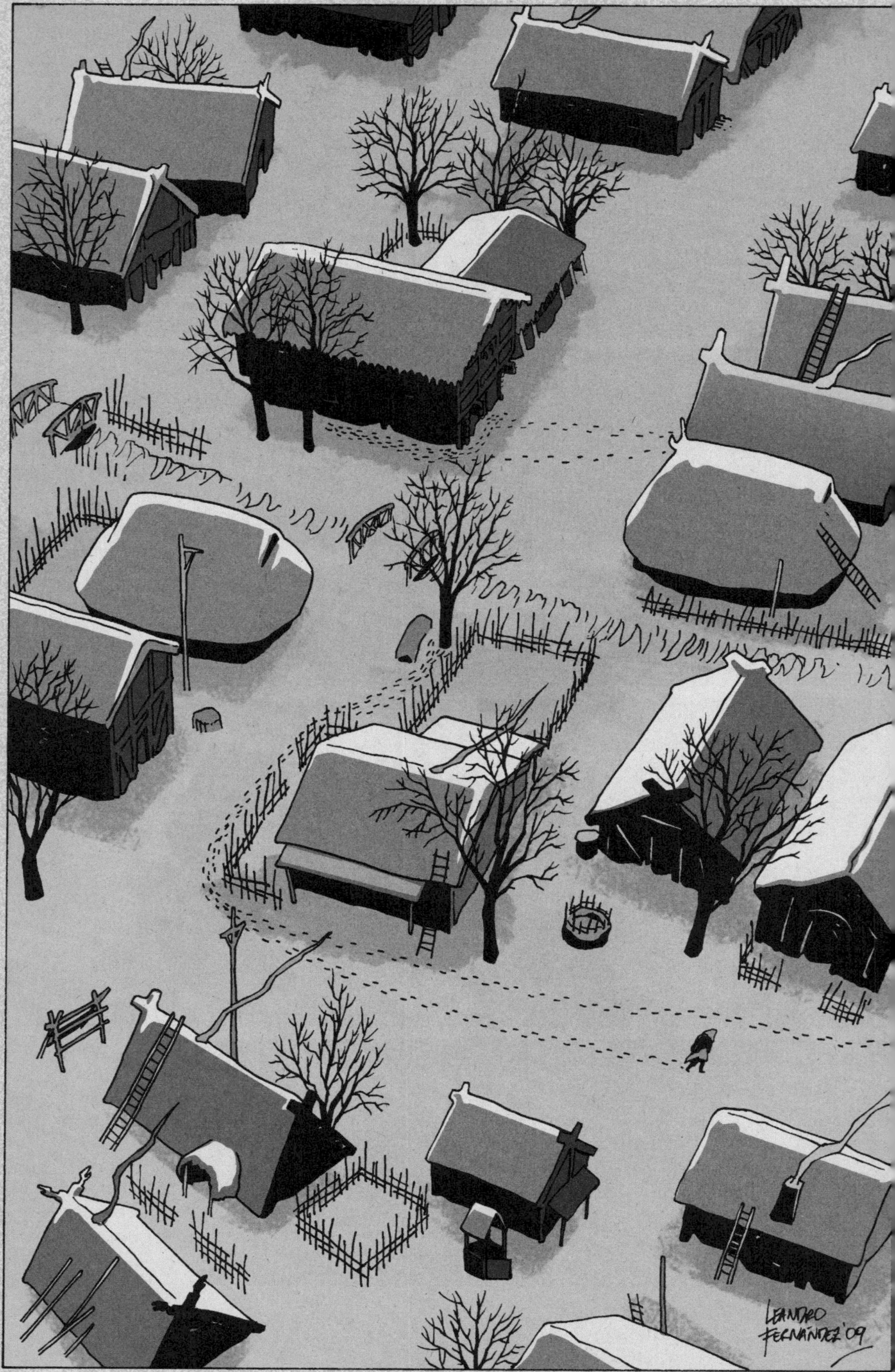
LEANDRO FERNÁNDEZ '09

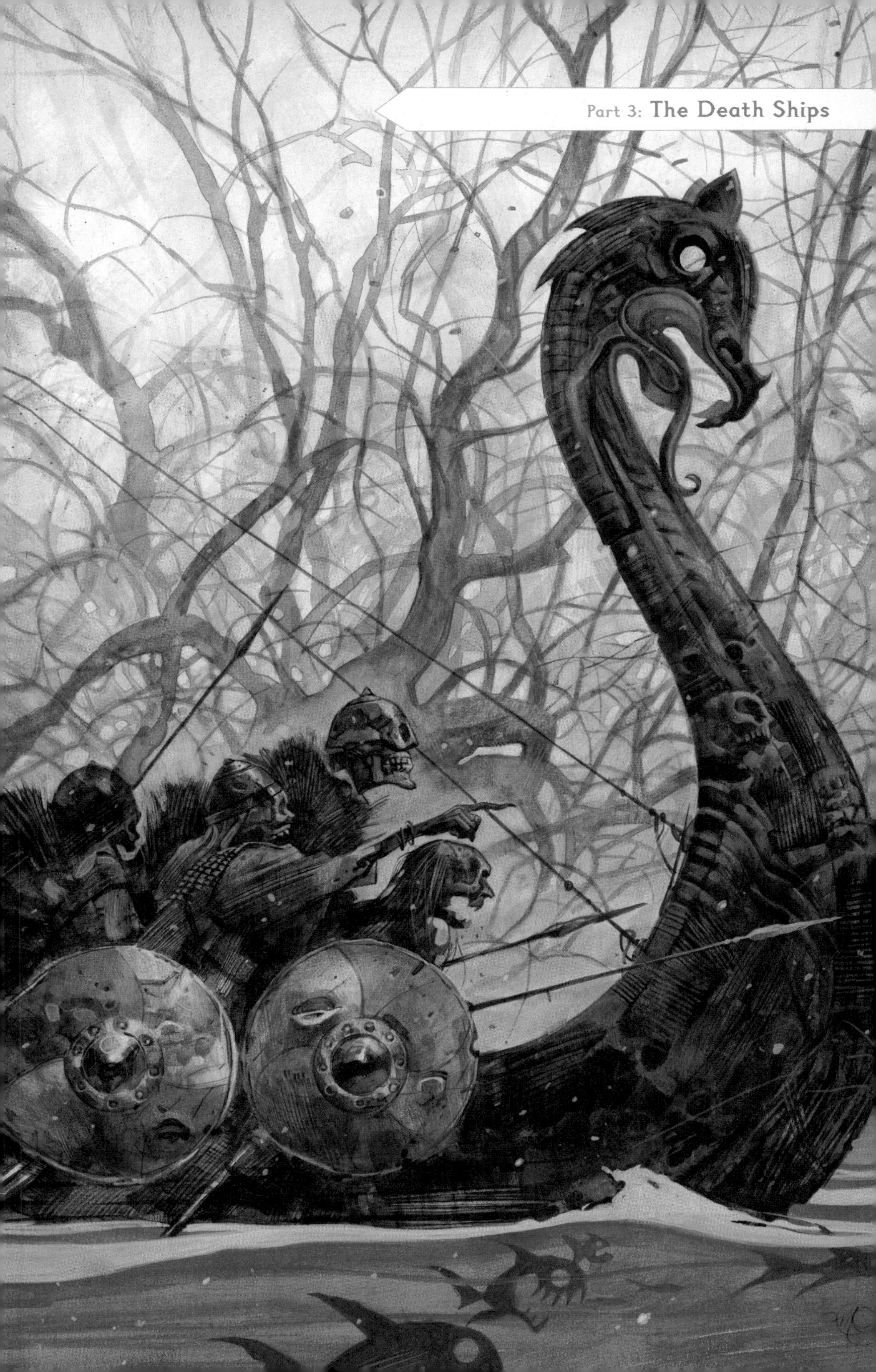

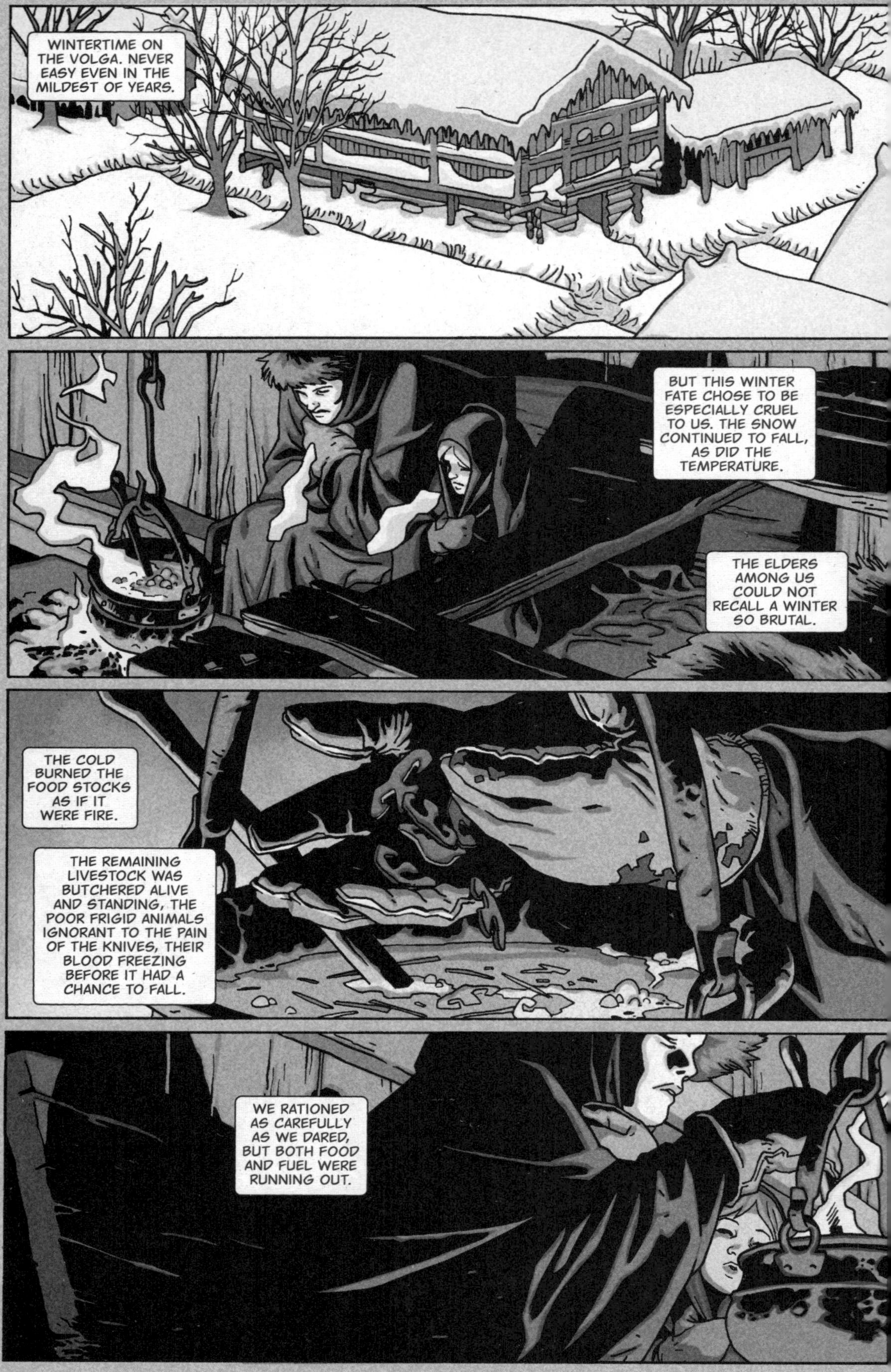
WINTERTIME ON THE VOLGA. NEVER EASY EVEN IN THE MILDEST OF YEARS.
BUT THIS WINTER FATE CHOSE TO BE ESPECIALLY CRUEL TO US. THE SNOW CONTINUED TO FALL, AS DID THE TEMPERATURE.
THE ELDERS AMONG US COULD NOT RECALL A WINTER SO BRUTAL.
THE COLD BURNED THE FOOD STOCKS AS IF IT WERE FIRE.
THE REMAINING LIVESTOCK WAS BUTCHERED ALIVE AND STANDING, THE POOR FRIGID ANIMALS IGNORANT TO THE PAIN OF THE KNIVES, THEIR BLOOD FREEZING BEFORE IT HAD A CHANCE TO FALL.
WE RATIONED AS CAREFULLY AS WE DARED, BUT BOTH FOOD AND FUEL WERE RUNNING OUT.

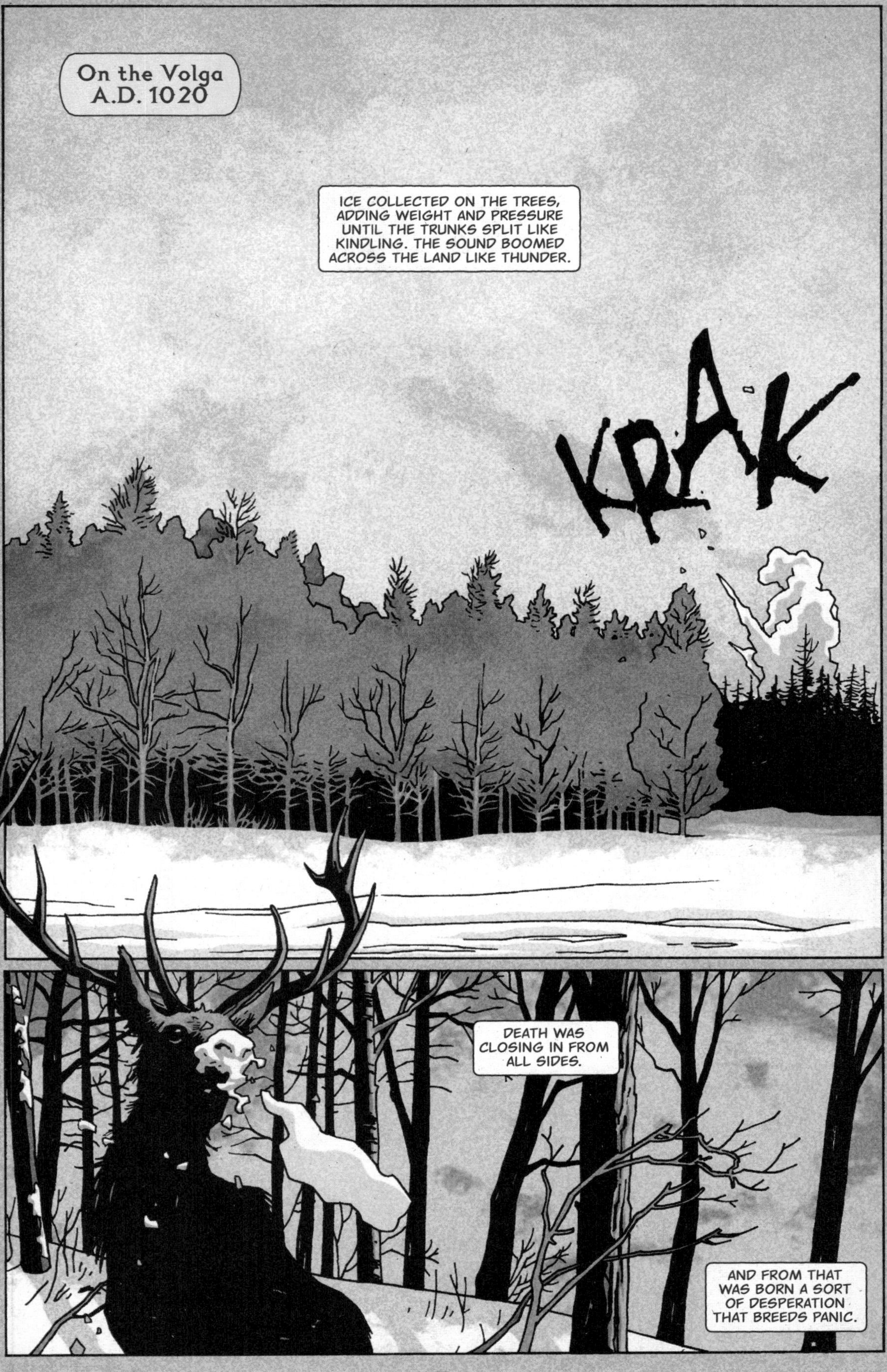
On the Volga
A.D. 1020
ICE COLLECTED ON THE TREES, ADDING WEIGHT AND PRESSURE UNTIL THE TRUNKS SPLIT LIKE KINDLING. THE SOUND BOOMED ACROSS THE LAND LIKE THUNDER.
KRAK
DEATH WAS CLOSING IN FROM ALL SIDES.
AND FROM THAT WAS BORN A SORT OF DESPERATION THAT BREEDS PANIC.

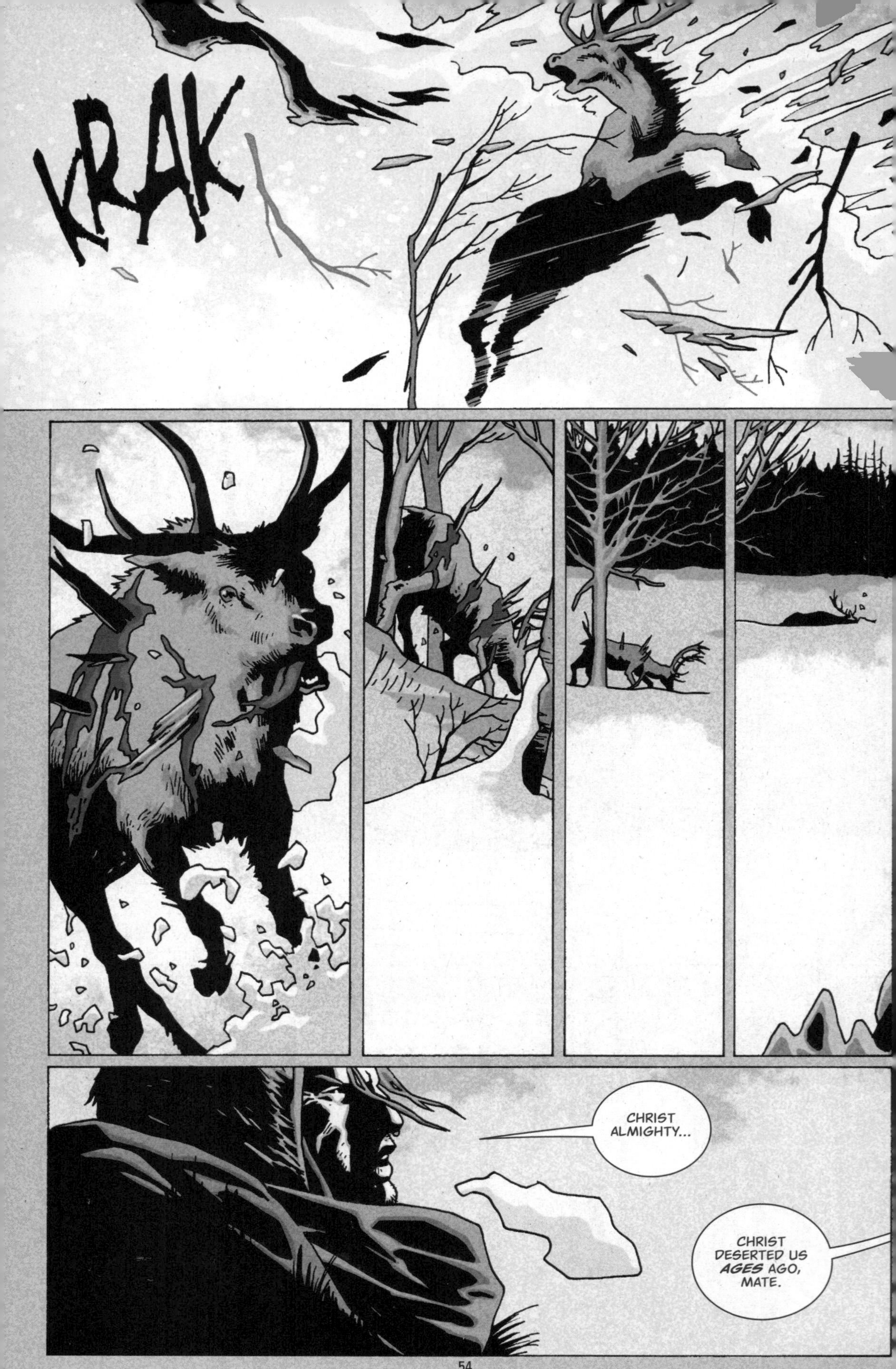
KRAK
CHRIST ALMIGHTY...
CHRIST DESERTED US *AGES* AGO, MATE.

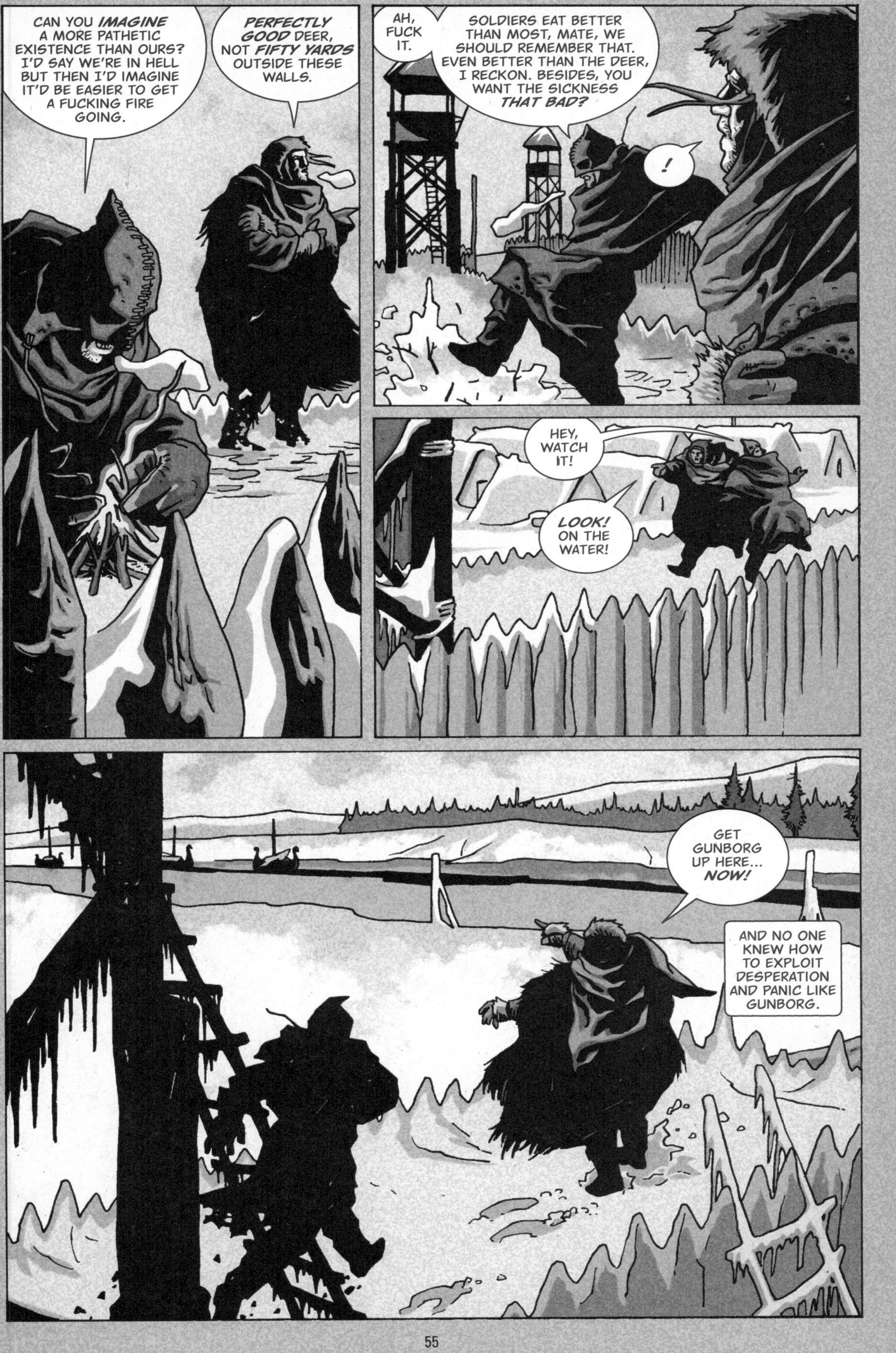
CAN YOU IMAGINE A MORE PATHETIC EXISTENCE THAN OURS? I'D SAY WE'RE IN HELL BUT THEN I'D IMAGINE IT'D BE EASIER TO GET A FUCKING FIRE GOING.
PERFECTLY GOOD DEER, NOT FIFTY YARDS OUTSIDE THESE WALLS.
AH, FUCK IT.
SOLDIERS EAT BETTER THAN MOST, MATE, WE SHOULD REMEMBER THAT. EVEN BETTER THAN THE DEER, I RECKON. BESIDES, YOU WANT THE SICKNESS THAT BAD?
!
HEY, WATCH IT!
LOOK! ON THE WATER!
GET GUNBORG UP HERE... NOW!
AND NO ONE KNEW HOW TO EXPLOIT DESPERATION AND PANIC LIKE GUNBORG.

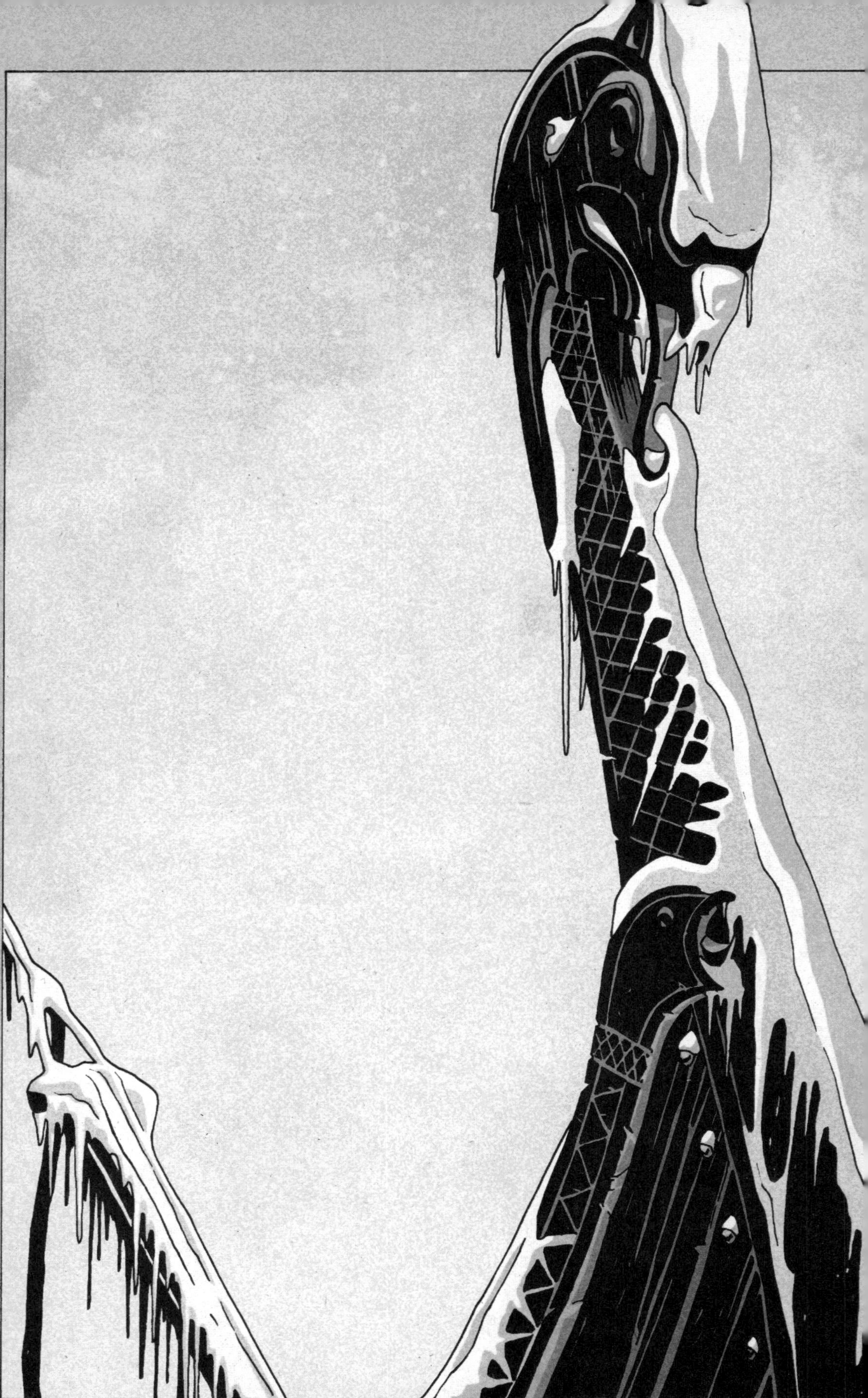

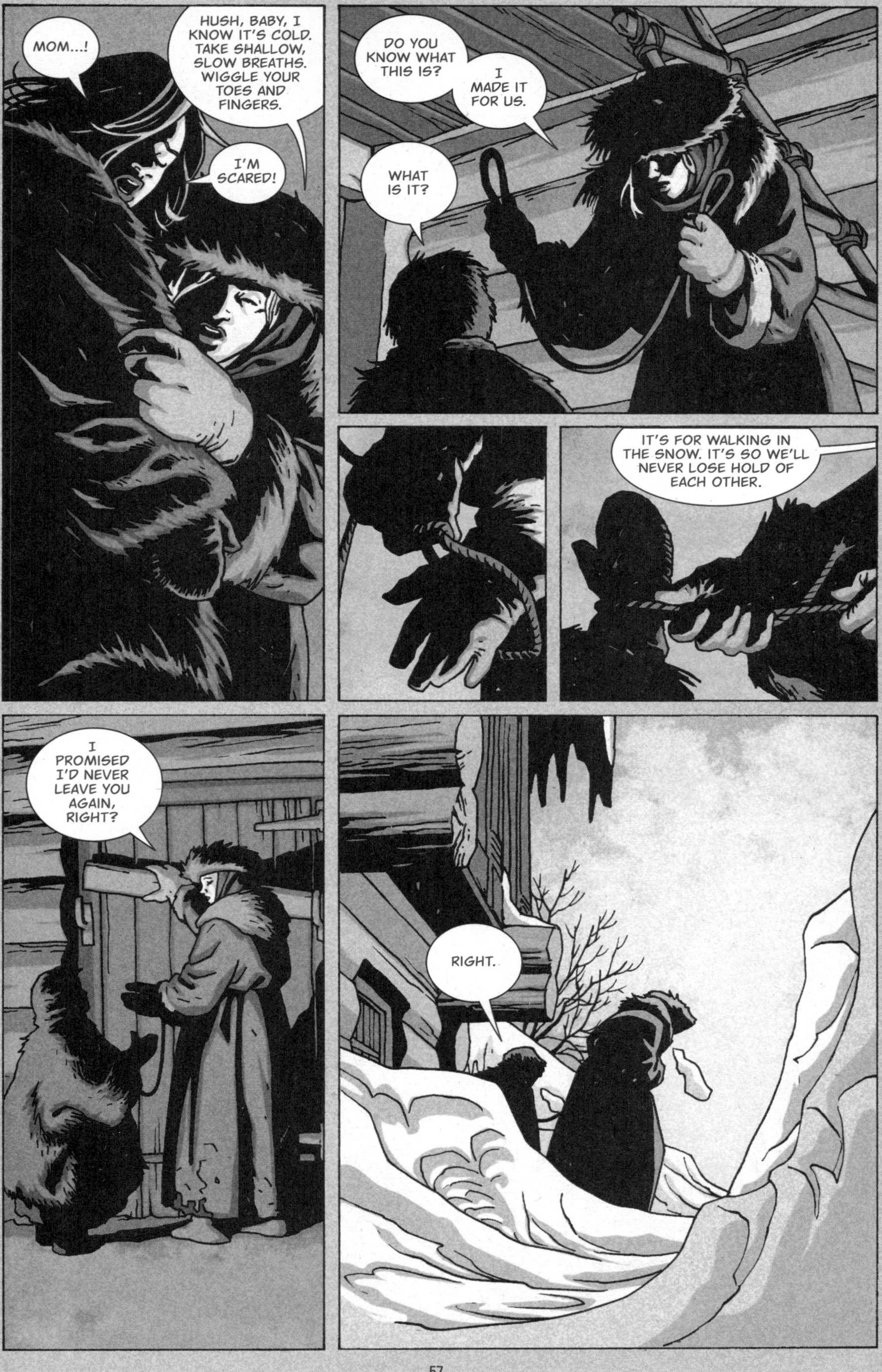
MOM...!
HUSH, BABY, I KNOW IT'S COLD. TAKE SHALLOW, SLOW BREATHS. WIGGLE YOUR TOES AND FINGERS.
I'M SCARED!
DO YOU KNOW WHAT THIS IS?
I MADE IT FOR US.
WHAT IS IT?
IT'S FOR WALKING IN THE SNOW. IT'S SO WE'LL NEVER LOSE HOLD OF EACH OTHER.
I PROMISED I'D NEVER LEAVE YOU AGAIN, RIGHT?
RIGHT.

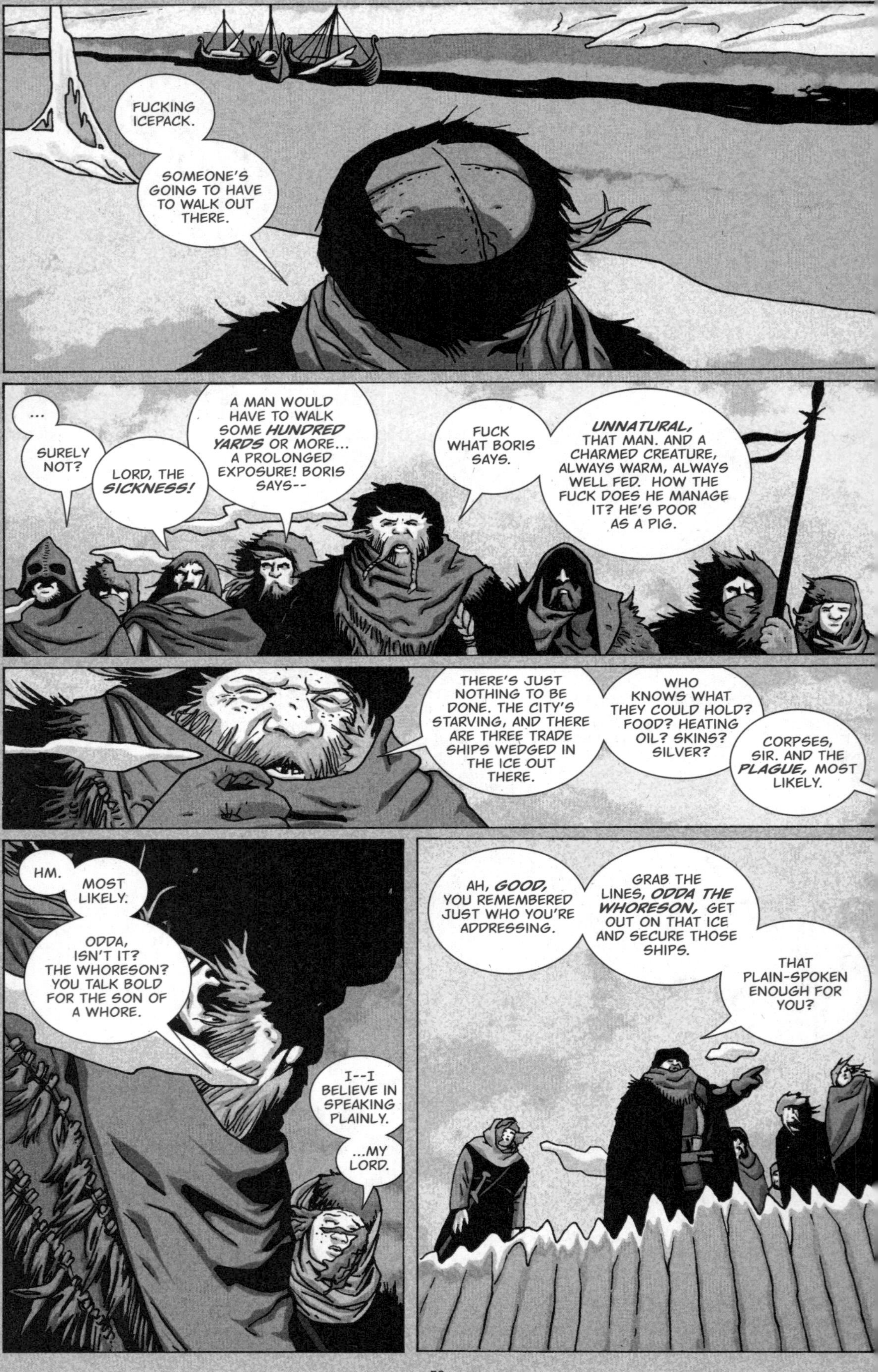

FUCKING ICEPACK.
SOMEONE'S GOING TO HAVE TO WALK OUT THERE.
...
SURELY NOT?
LORD, THE SICKNESS!
A MAN WOULD HAVE TO WALK SOME HUNDRED YARDS OR MORE... A PROLONGED EXPOSURE! BORIS SAYS--
FUCK WHAT BORIS SAYS.
UNNATURAL, THAT MAN. AND A CHARMED CREATURE, ALWAYS WARM, ALWAYS WELL FED. HOW THE FUCK DOES HE MANAGE IT? HE'S POOR AS A PIG.
THERE'S JUST NOTHING TO BE DONE. THE CITY'S STARVING, AND THERE ARE THREE TRADE SHIPS WEDGED IN THE ICE OUT THERE.
WHO KNOWS WHAT THEY COULD HOLD? FOOD? HEATING OIL? SKINS? SILVER?
CORPSES, SIR. AND THE PLAGUE, MOST LIKELY.
HM.
MOST LIKELY.
ODDA, ISN'T IT? THE WHORESON? YOU TALK BOLD FOR THE SON OF A WHORE.
I--I BELIEVE IN SPEAKING PLAINLY.
...MY LORD.
AH, GOOD, YOU REMEMBERED JUST WHO YOU'RE ADDRESSING.
GRAB THE LINES, ODDA THE WHORESON, GET OUT ON THAT ICE AND SECURE THOSE SHIPS.
THAT PLAIN-SPOKEN ENOUGH FOR YOU?

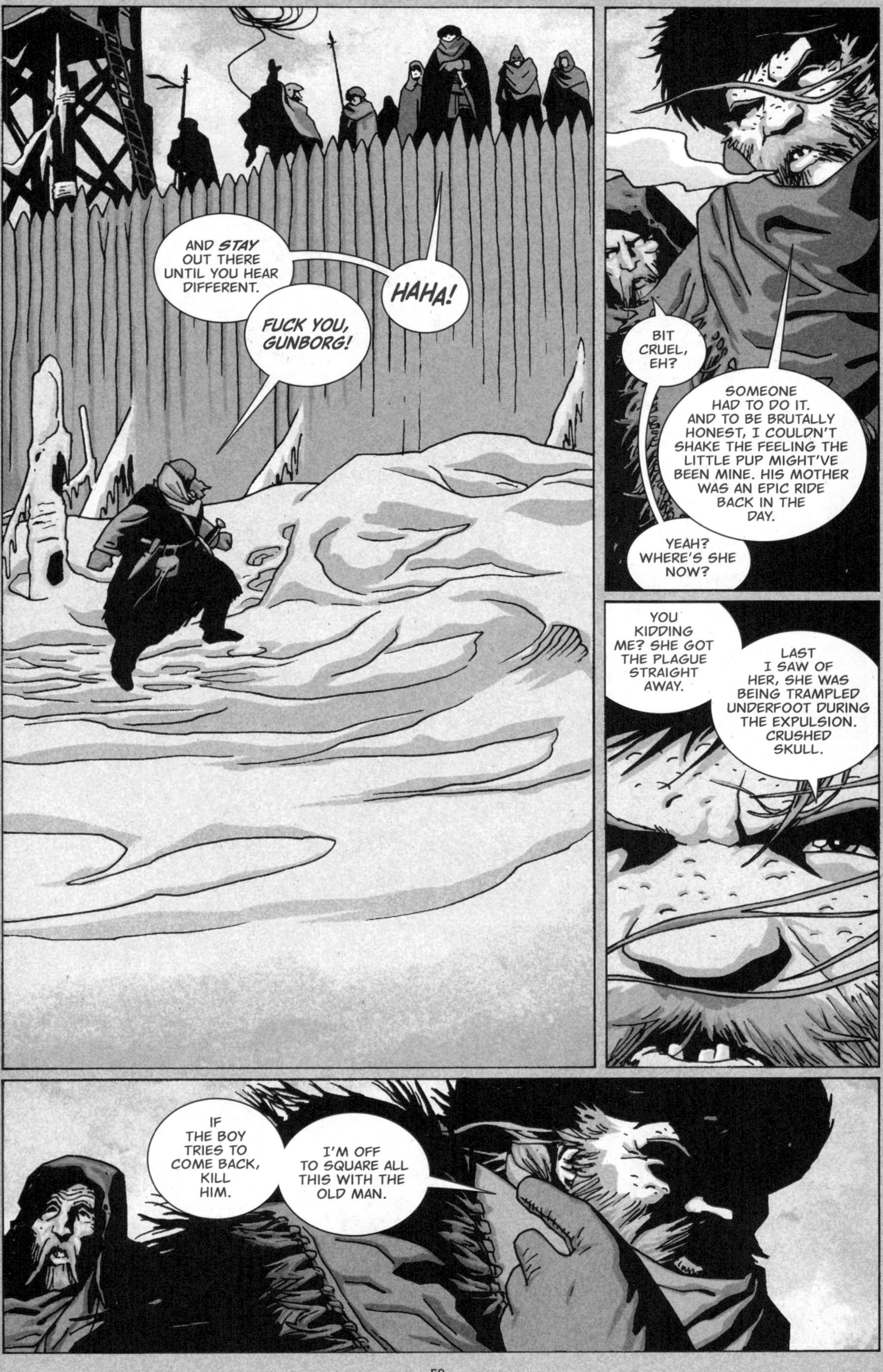
AND STAY OUT THERE UNTIL YOU HEAR DIFFERENT.
HAHA!
FUCK YOU, GUNBORG!
BIT CRUEL, EH?
SOMEONE HAD TO DO IT. AND TO BE BRUTALLY HONEST, I COULDN'T SHAKE THE FEELING THE LITTLE PUP MIGHT'VE BEEN MINE. HIS MOTHER WAS AN EPIC RIDE BACK IN THE DAY.
YEAH? WHERE'S SHE NOW?
YOU KIDDING ME? SHE GOT THE PLAGUE STRAIGHT AWAY.
LAST I SAW OF HER, SHE WAS BEING TRAMPLED UNDERFOOT DURING THE EXPULSION. CRUSHED SKULL.
IF THE BOY TRIES TO COME BACK, KILL HIM.
I'M OFF TO SQUARE ALL THIS WITH THE OLD MAN.

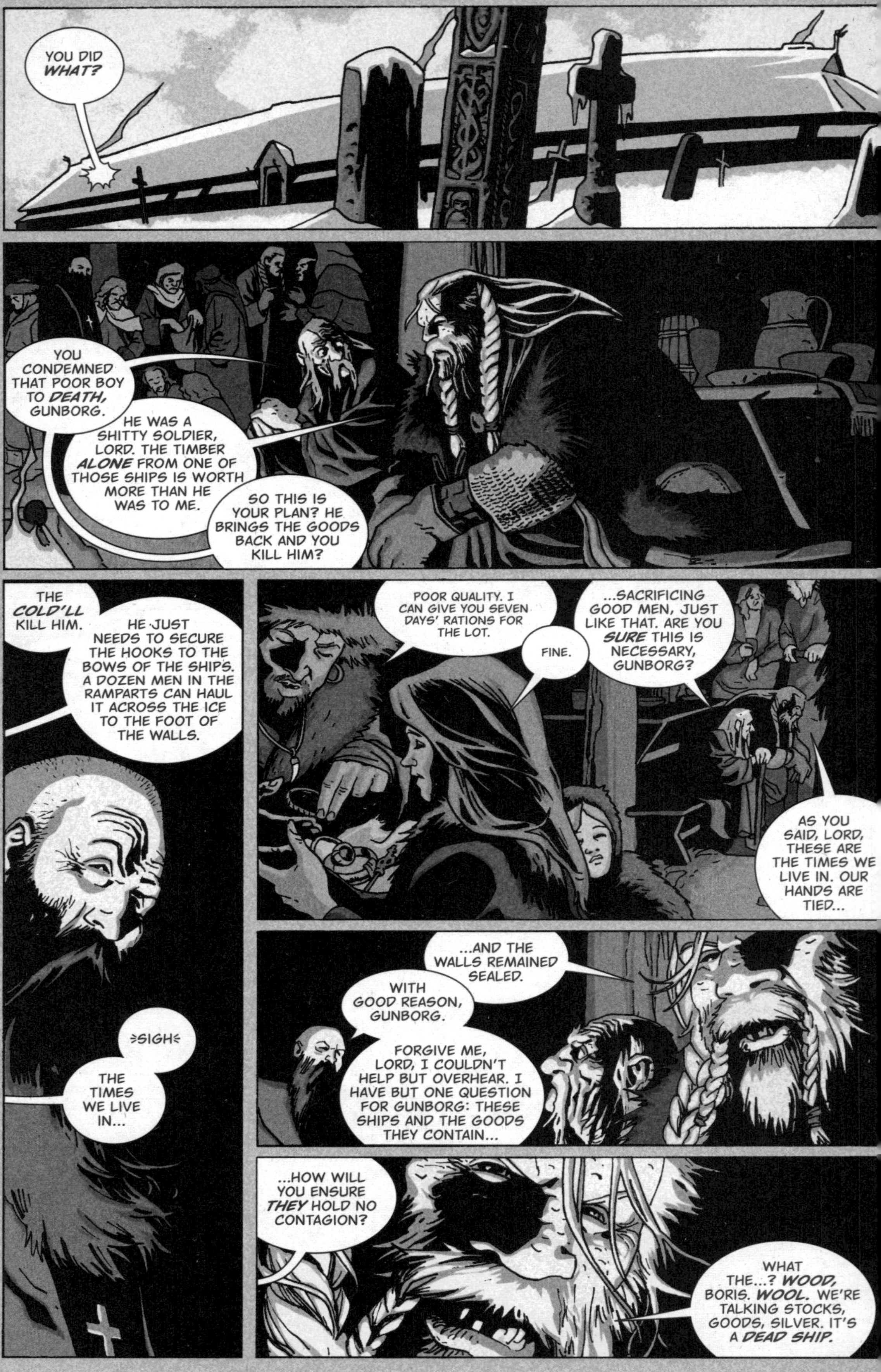
YOU DID WHAT?
YOU CONDEMNED THAT POOR BOY TO DEATH, GUNBORG.
HE WAS A SHITTY SOLDIER, LORD. THE TIMBER ALONE FROM ONE OF THOSE SHIPS IS WORTH MORE THAN HE WAS TO ME.
SO THIS IS YOUR PLAN? HE BRINGS THE GOODS BACK AND YOU KILL HIM?
THE COLD'LL KILL HIM.
HE JUST NEEDS TO SECURE THE HOOKS TO THE BOWS OF THE SHIPS. A DOZEN MEN IN THE RAMPARTS CAN HAUL IT ACROSS THE ICE TO THE FOOT OF THE WALLS.
SIGH
THE TIMES WE LIVE IN...
POOR QUALITY. I CAN GIVE YOU SEVEN DAYS' RATIONS FOR THE LOT.
FINE.
...SACRIFICING GOOD MEN, JUST LIKE THAT. ARE YOU SURE THIS IS NECESSARY, GUNBORG?
AS YOU SAID, LORD, THESE ARE THE TIMES WE LIVE IN. OUR HANDS ARE TIED...
...AND THE WALLS REMAINED SEALED.
WITH GOOD REASON, GUNBORG.
FORGIVE ME, LORD, I COULDN'T HELP BUT OVERHEAR. I HAVE BUT ONE QUESTION FOR GUNBORG: THESE SHIPS AND THE GOODS THEY CONTAIN...
...HOW WILL YOU ENSURE THEY HOLD NO CONTAGION?
WHAT THE...? WOOD, BORIS. WOOL. WE'RE TALKING STOCKS, GOODS, SILVER. IT'S A DEAD SHIP.

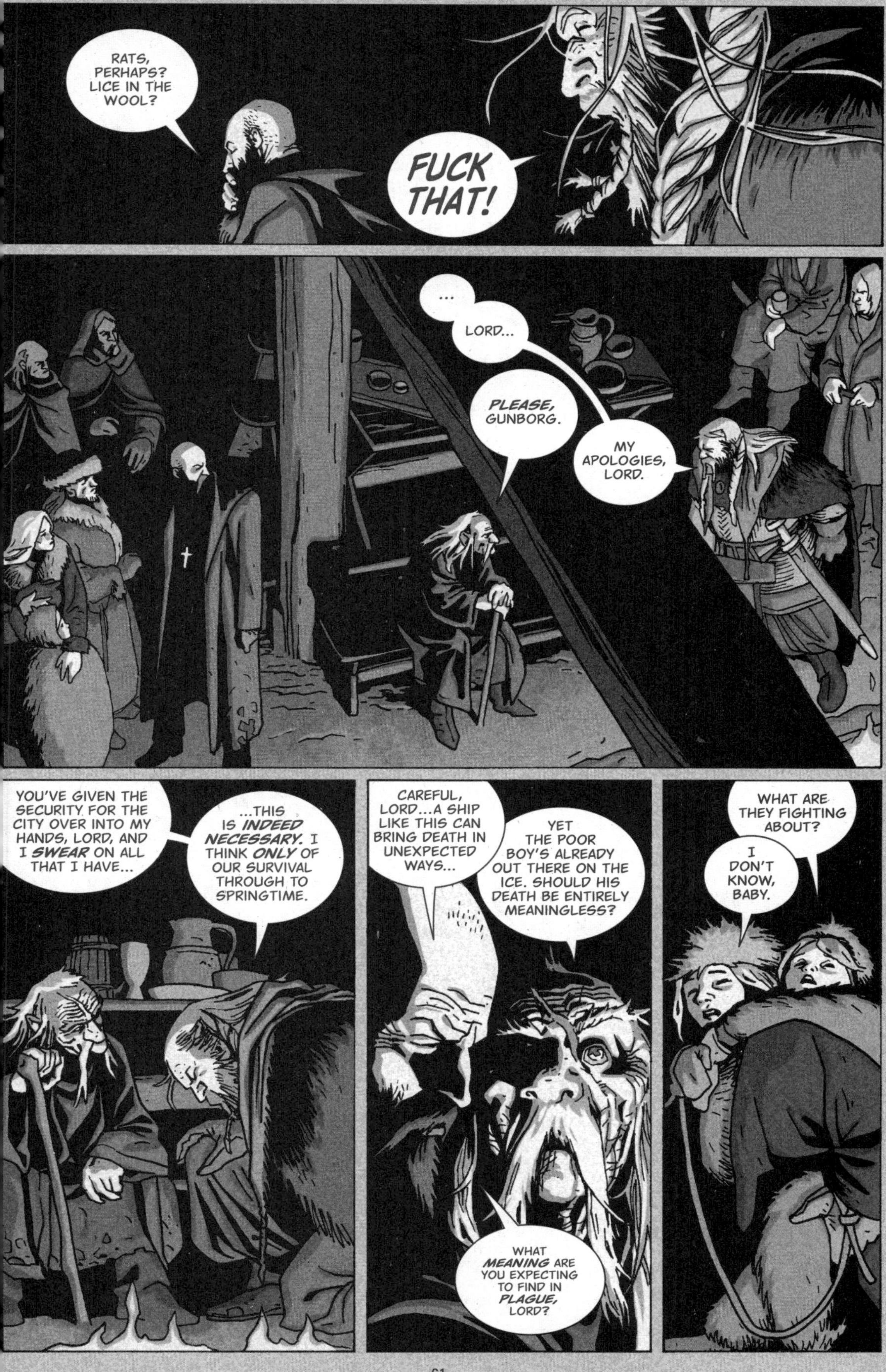

RATS, PERHAPS? LICE IN THE WOOL?
FUCK THAT!
...
LORD...
PLEASE, GUNBORG.
MY APOLOGIES, LORD.
YOU'VE GIVEN THE SECURITY FOR THE CITY OVER INTO MY HANDS, LORD, AND I SWEAR ON ALL THAT I HAVE...
...THIS IS INDEED NECESSARY. I THINK ONLY OF OUR SURVIVAL THROUGH TO SPRINGTIME.
CAREFUL, LORD...A SHIP LIKE THIS CAN BRING DEATH IN UNEXPECTED WAYS...
YET THE POOR BOY'S ALREADY OUT THERE ON THE ICE. SHOULD HIS DEATH BE ENTIRELY MEANINGLESS?
WHAT MEANING ARE YOU EXPECTING TO FIND IN PLAGUE, LORD?
WHAT ARE THEY FIGHTING ABOUT?
I DON'T KNOW, BABY.

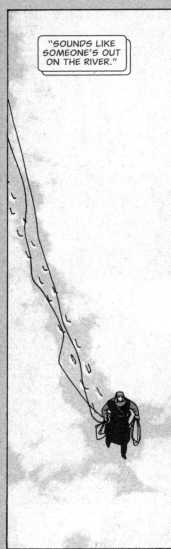

"SOUNDS LIKE SOMEONE'S OUT ON THE RIVER."

SNIF

PRICKS.

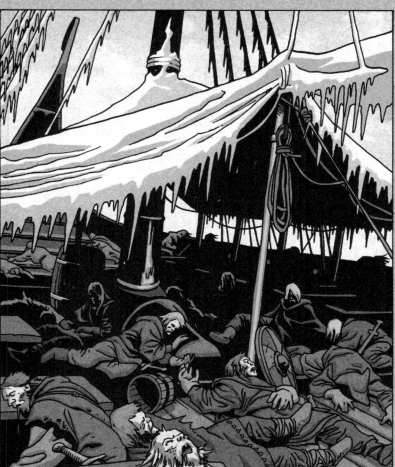

WHUFF.

THERE'S THE SIGNAL. GET THE MEN ONTO THE LINES.

HOLD ON, WHAT'S THAT?

...

GARRRR!

THUNK

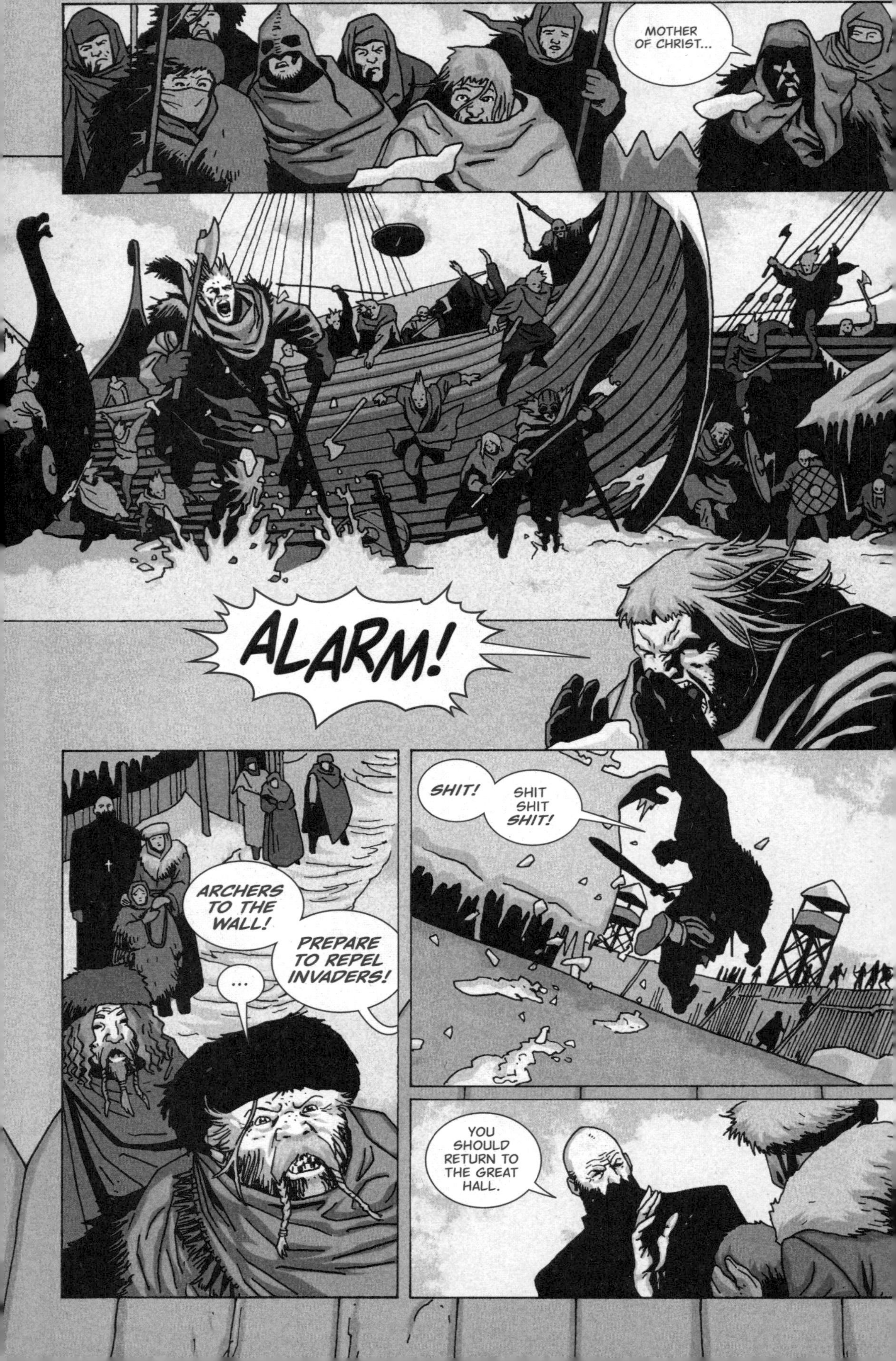
MOTHER OF CHRIST...
ALARM!
ARCHERS TO THE WALL!
PREPARE TO REPEL INVADERS!
...
SHIT!
SHIT SHIT SHIT!
YOU SHOULD RETURN TO THE GREAT HALL.

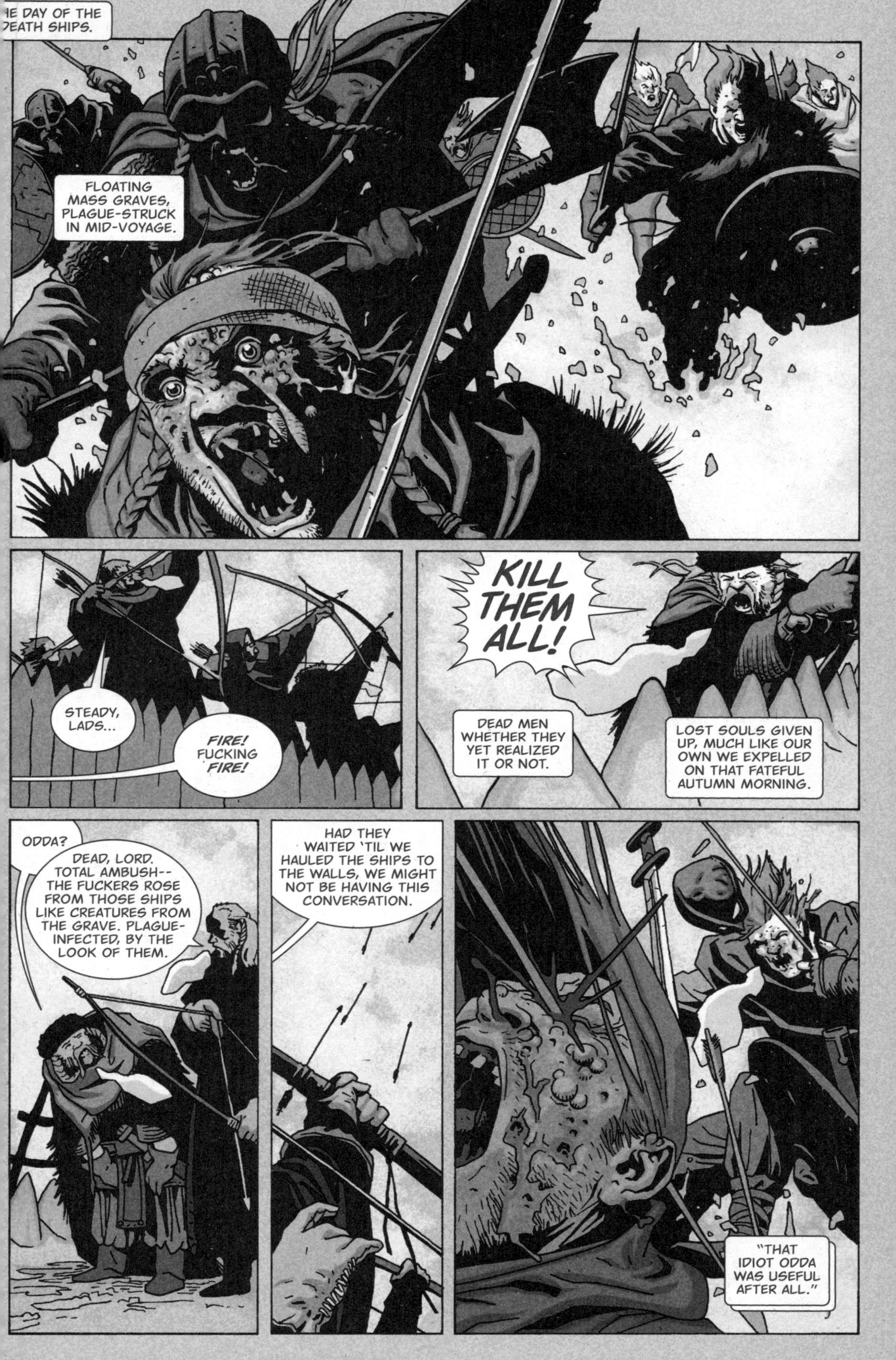
HE DAY OF THE
DEATH SHIPS.
FLOATING MASS GRAVES, PLAGUE-STRUCK IN MID-VOYAGE.
STEADY, LADS...
FIRE! FUCKING *FIRE!*
KILL THEM ALL!
DEAD MEN WHETHER THEY YET REALIZED IT OR NOT.
LOST SOULS GIVEN UP, MUCH LIKE OUR OWN WE EXPELLED ON THAT FATEFUL AUTUMN MORNING.
ODDA?
DEAD, LORD. TOTAL AMBUSH-- THE FUCKERS ROSE FROM THOSE SHIPS LIKE CREATURES FROM THE GRAVE. PLAGUE-INFECTED, BY THE LOOK OF THEM.
HAD THEY WAITED 'TIL WE HAULED THE SHIPS TO THE WALLS, WE MIGHT NOT BE HAVING THIS CONVERSATION.
"THAT IDIOT ODDA WAS USEFUL AFTER ALL."

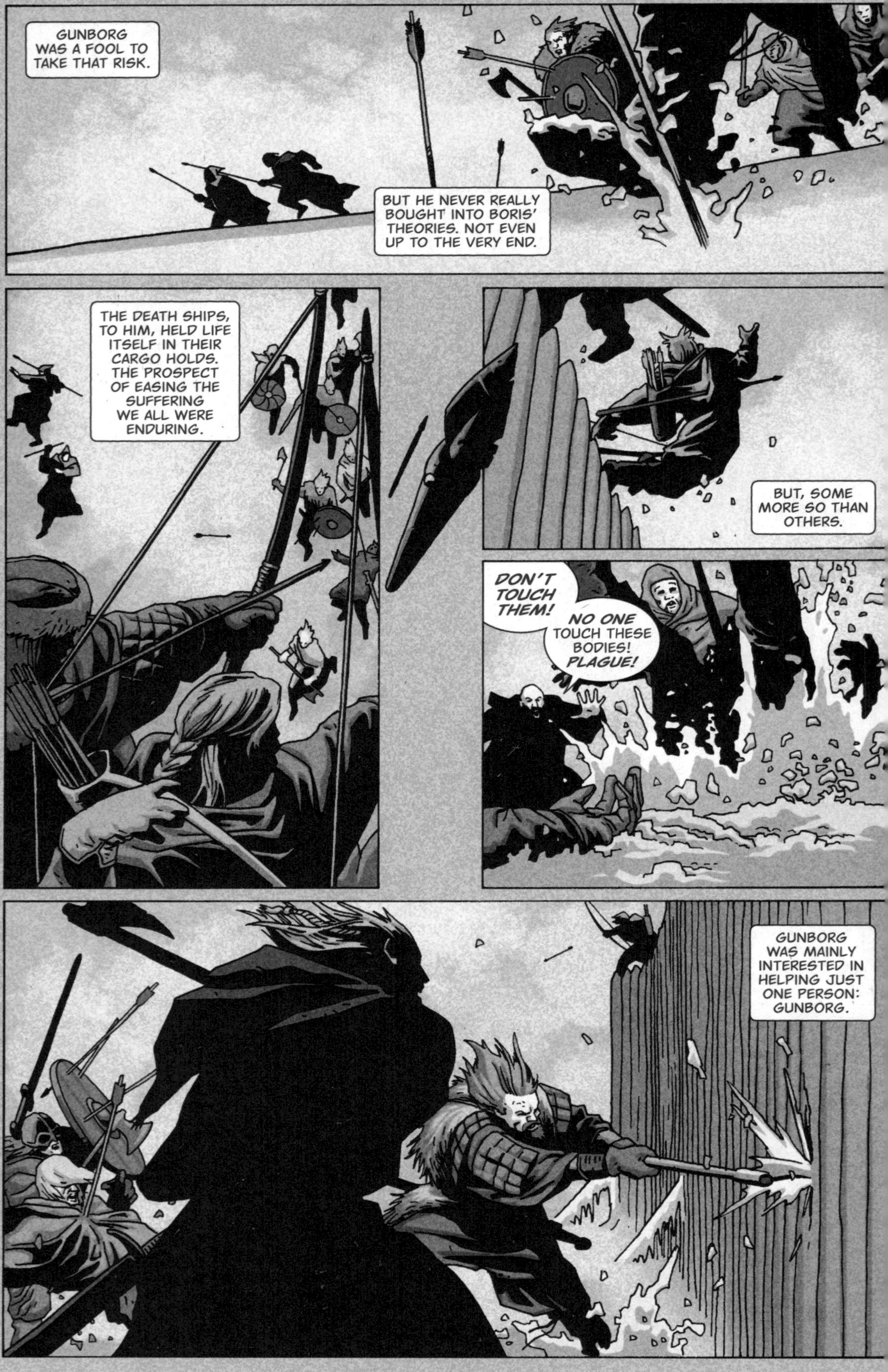
GUNBORG WAS A FOOL TO TAKE THAT RISK.
BUT HE NEVER REALLY BOUGHT INTO BORIS' THEORIES. NOT EVEN UP TO THE VERY END.
THE DEATH SHIPS, TO HIM, HELD LIFE ITSELF IN THEIR CARGO HOLDS. THE PROSPECT OF EASING THE SUFFERING WE ALL WERE ENDURING.
BUT, SOME MORE SO THAN OTHERS.
DON'T TOUCH THEM!
NO ONE TOUCH THESE BODIES! PLAGUE!
GUNBORG WAS MAINLY INTERESTED IN HELPING JUST ONE PERSON: GUNBORG.

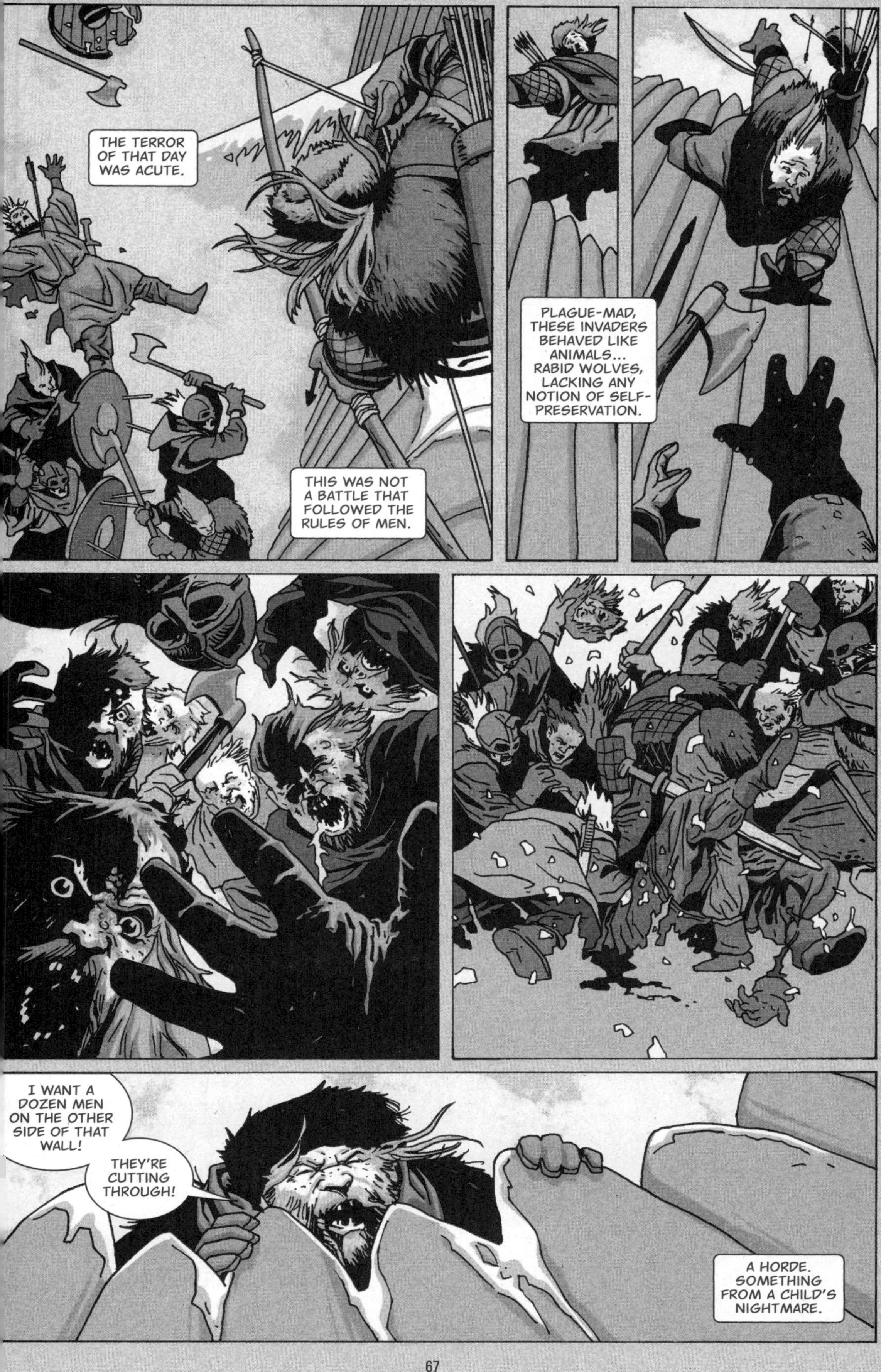
THE TERROR OF THAT DAY WAS ACUTE.
THIS WAS NOT A BATTLE THAT FOLLOWED THE RULES OF MEN.
PLAGUE-MAD, THESE INVADERS BEHAVED LIKE ANIMALS... RABID WOLVES, LACKING ANY NOTION OF SELF-PRESERVATION.
I WANT A DOZEN MEN ON THE OTHER SIDE OF THAT WALL!
THEY'RE CUTTING THROUGH!
A HORDE. SOMETHING FROM A CHILD'S NIGHTMARE.

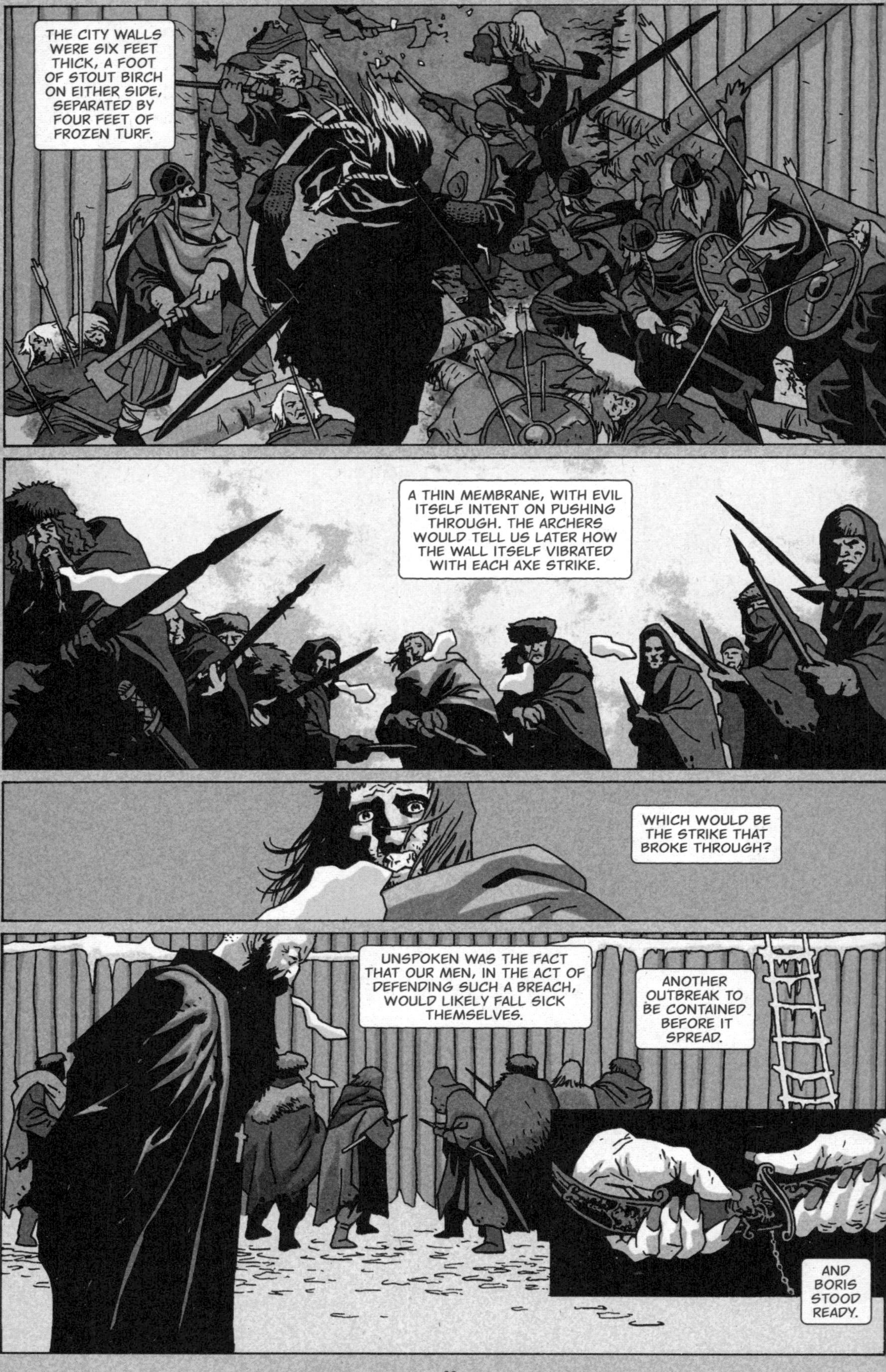
THE CITY WALLS WERE SIX FEET THICK, A FOOT OF STOUT BIRCH ON EITHER SIDE, SEPARATED BY FOUR FEET OF FROZEN TURF.
A THIN MEMBRANE, WITH EVIL ITSELF INTENT ON PUSHING THROUGH. THE ARCHERS WOULD TELL US LATER HOW THE WALL ITSELF VIBRATED WITH EACH AXE STRIKE.
WHICH WOULD BE THE STRIKE THAT BROKE THROUGH?
UNSPOKEN WAS THE FACT THAT OUR MEN, IN THE ACT OF DEFENDING SUCH A BREACH, WOULD LIKELY FALL SICK THEMSELVES.
ANOTHER OUTBREAK TO BE CONTAINED BEFORE IT SPREAD.
AND BORIS STOOD READY.

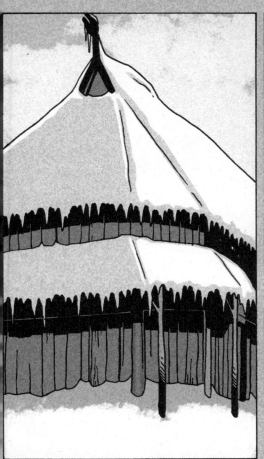

I LOVE YOU.

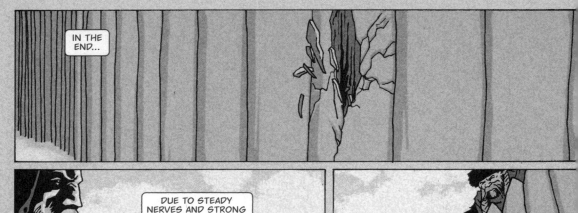

IN THE END...

DUE TO STEADY NERVES AND STRONG DEFENSES...

THE DAY WAS WON.

BUT IT WAS A LESSON LEARNED TERRIBLY, AS WELL AS A STARK REMINDER THAT WE ARE WELL AND TRULY ALONE.

OUTSIDE THESE WALLS, THE REFUGE WE'VE BUILT FOR OURSELVES, IS A LAND GODFORSAKEN, A VIOLENT AND SICK PLACE.

BUT TODAY, AT LEAST, WE SURVIVE.

GOD BE PRAISED.

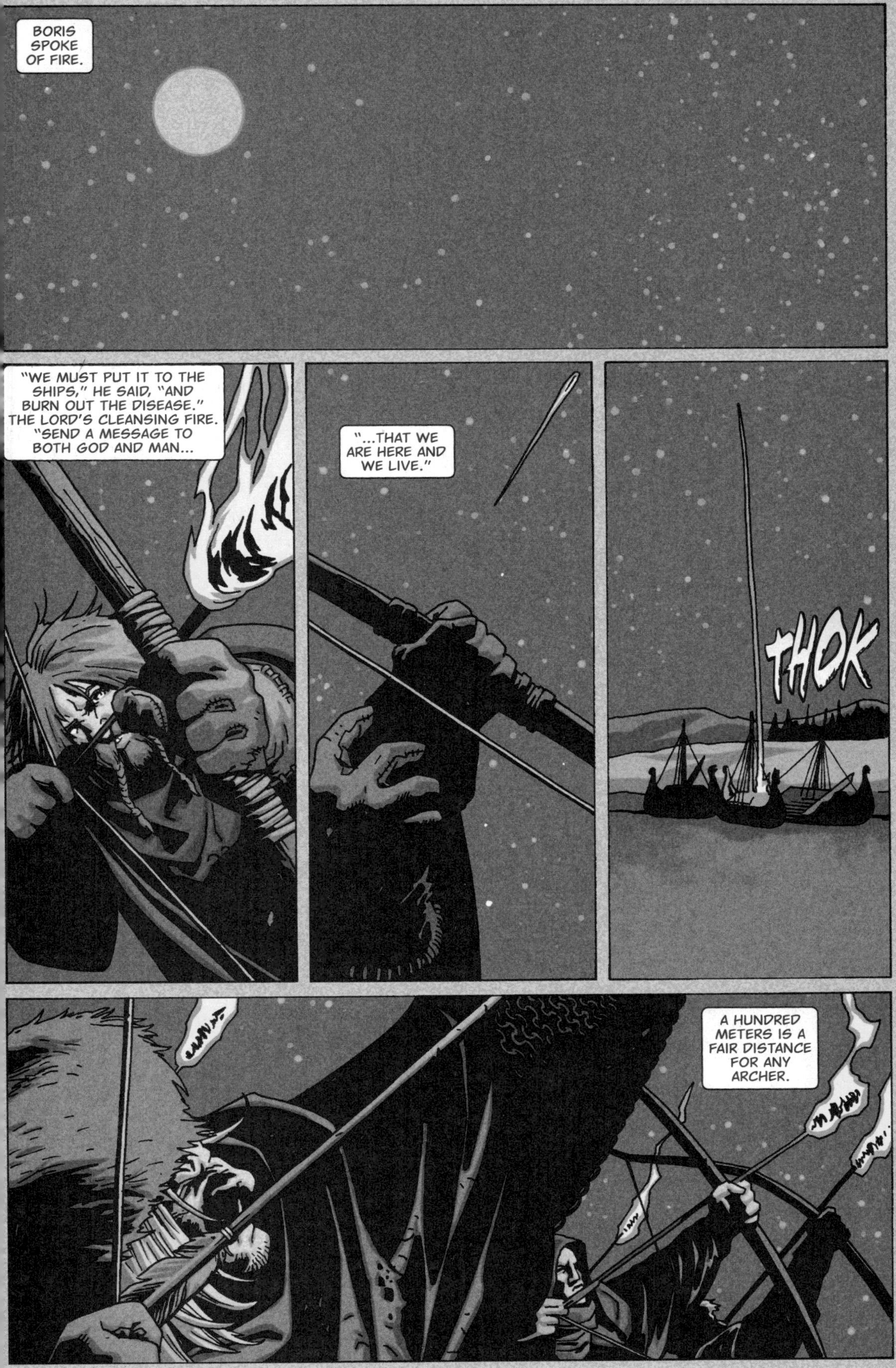
BORIS SPOKE OF FIRE.
"WE MUST PUT IT TO THE SHIPS," HE SAID, "AND BURN OUT THE DISEASE." THE LORD'S CLEANSING FIRE. "SEND A MESSAGE TO BOTH GOD AND MAN...
"...THAT WE ARE HERE AND WE LIVE."
THOK
A HUNDRED METERS IS A FAIR DISTANCE FOR ANY ARCHER.

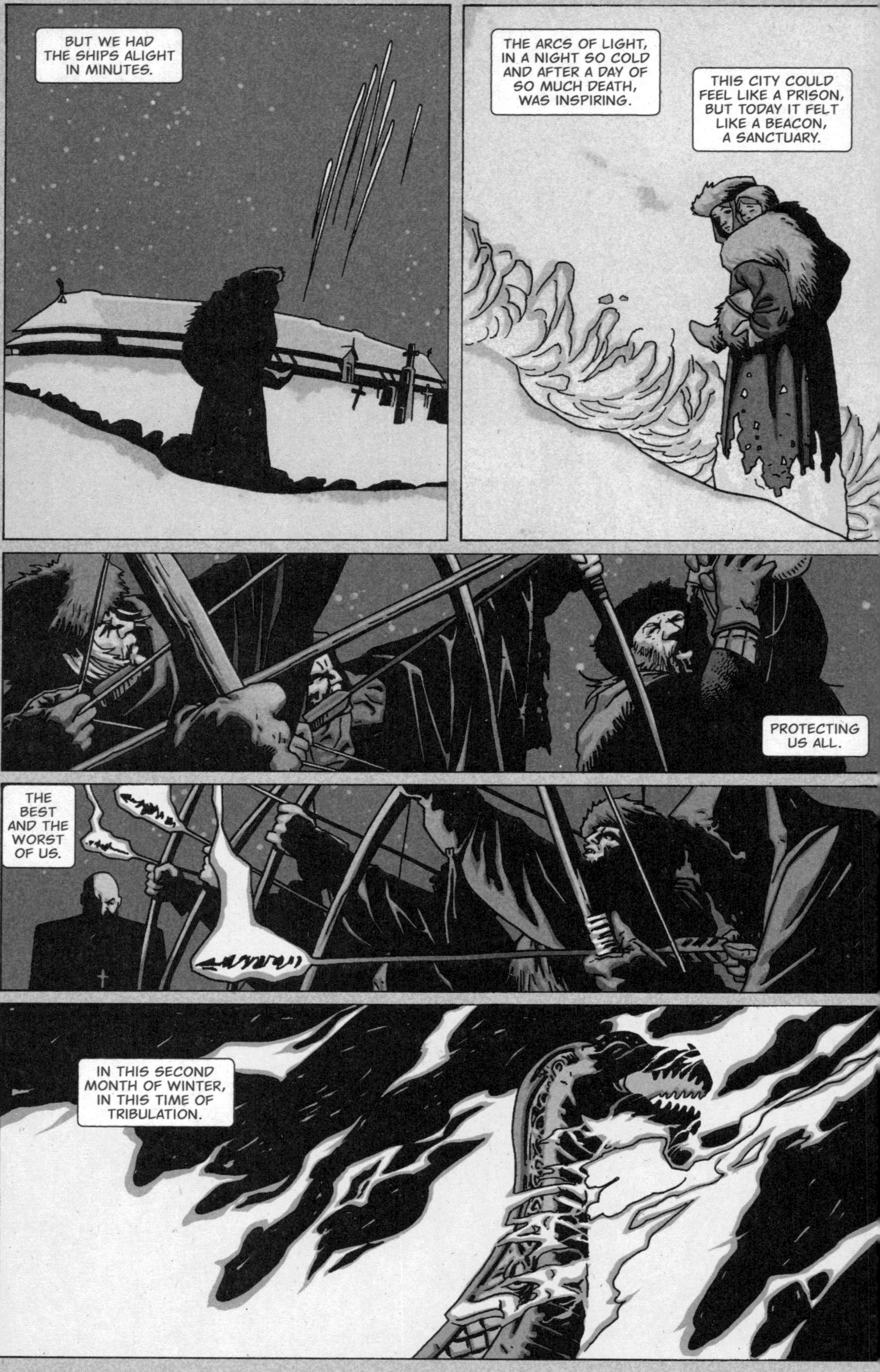
BUT WE HAD THE SHIPS ALIGHT IN MINUTES.
THE ARCS OF LIGHT, IN A NIGHT SO COLD AND AFTER A DAY OF SO MUCH DEATH, WAS INSPIRING.
THIS CITY COULD FEEL LIKE A PRISON, BUT TODAY IT FELT LIKE A BEACON, A SANCTUARY.
PROTECTING US ALL.
THE BEST AND THE WORST OF US.
IN THIS SECOND MONTH OF WINTER, IN THIS TIME OF TRIBULATION.

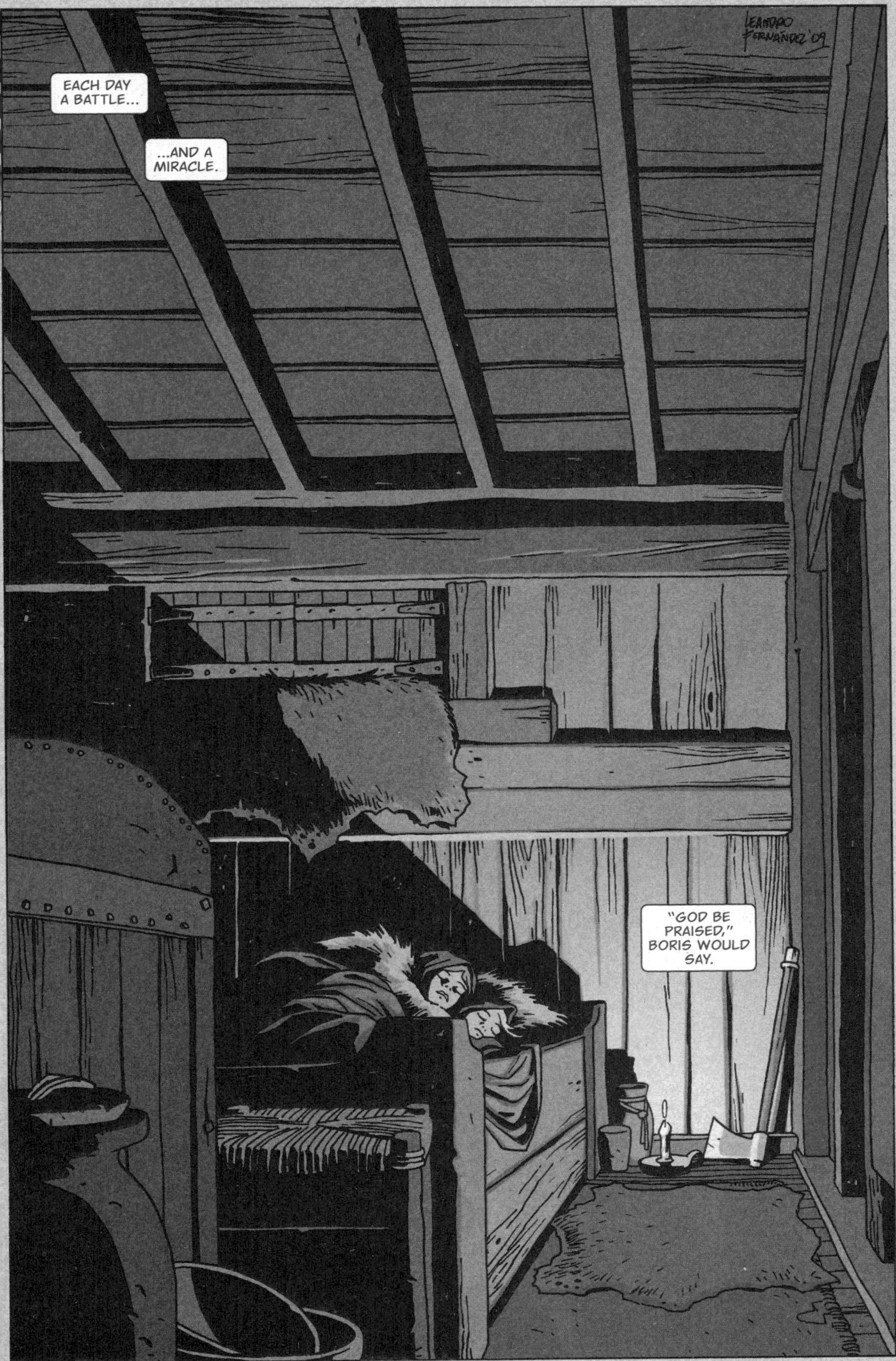
EACH DAY A BATTLE...
...AND A MIRACLE.
"GOD BE PRAISED," BORIS WOULD SAY.
LEANDRO FERNÁNDEZ '09

Part 4: Exposure

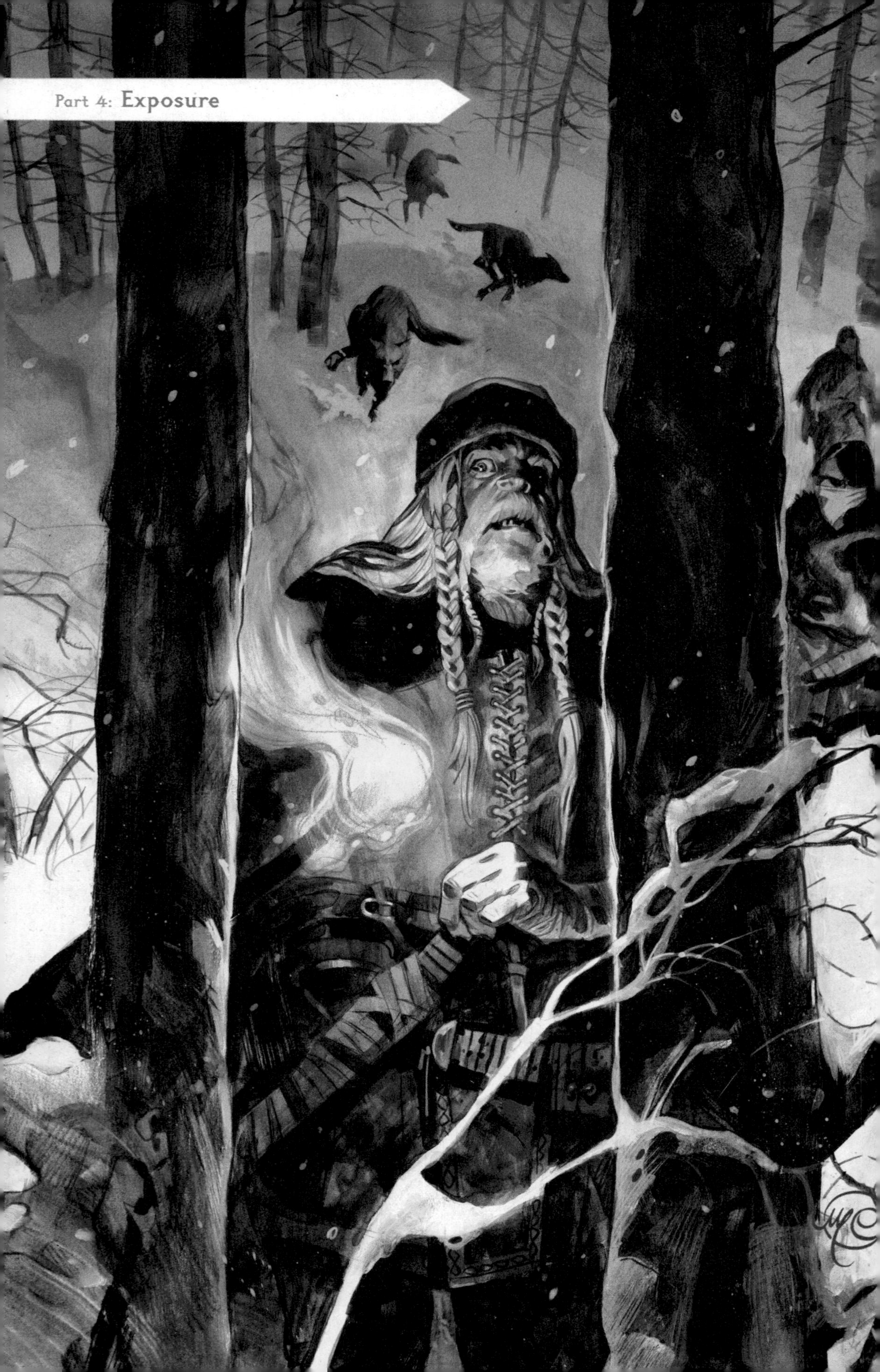

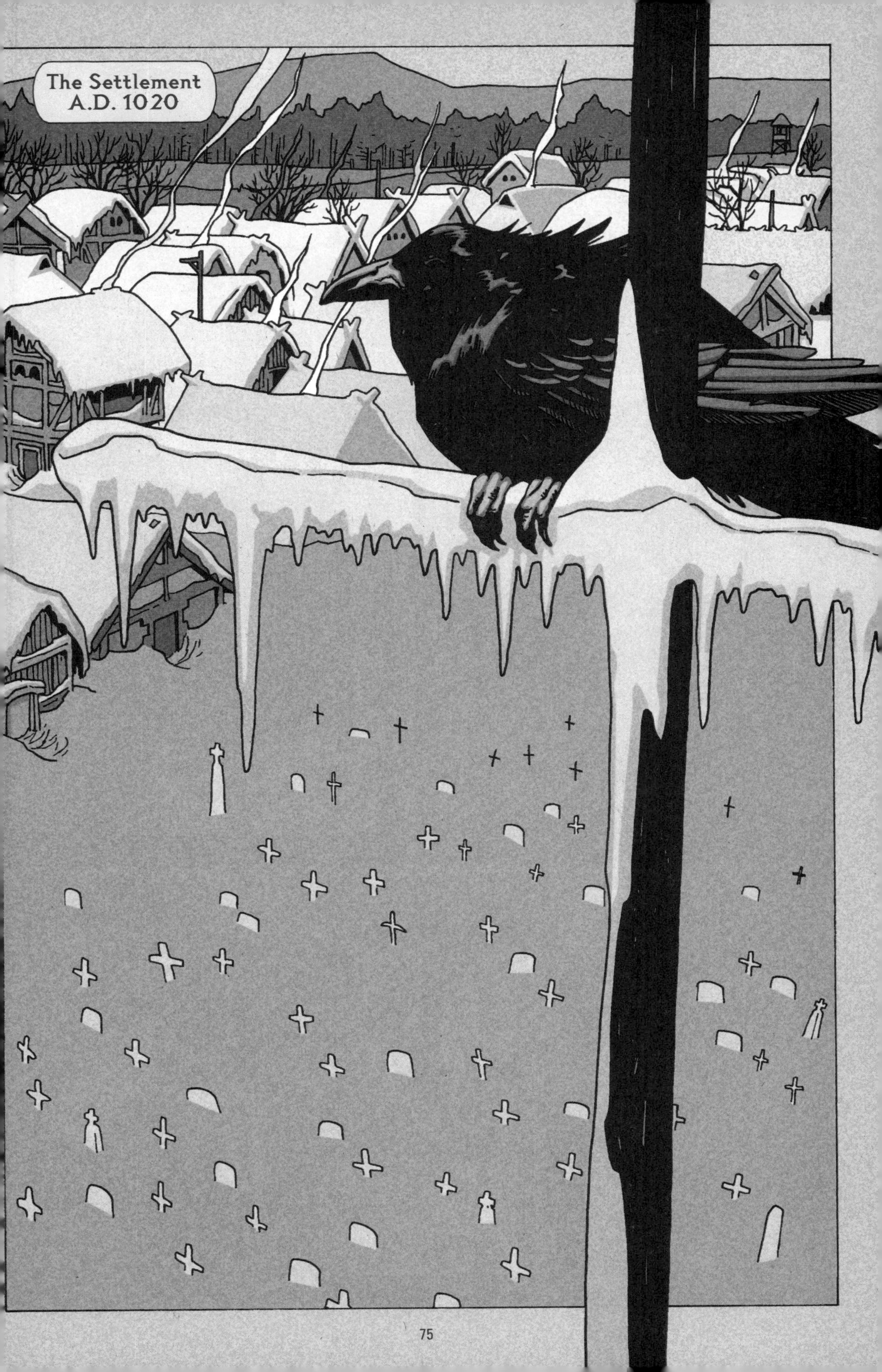
The Settlement
A.D. 1020

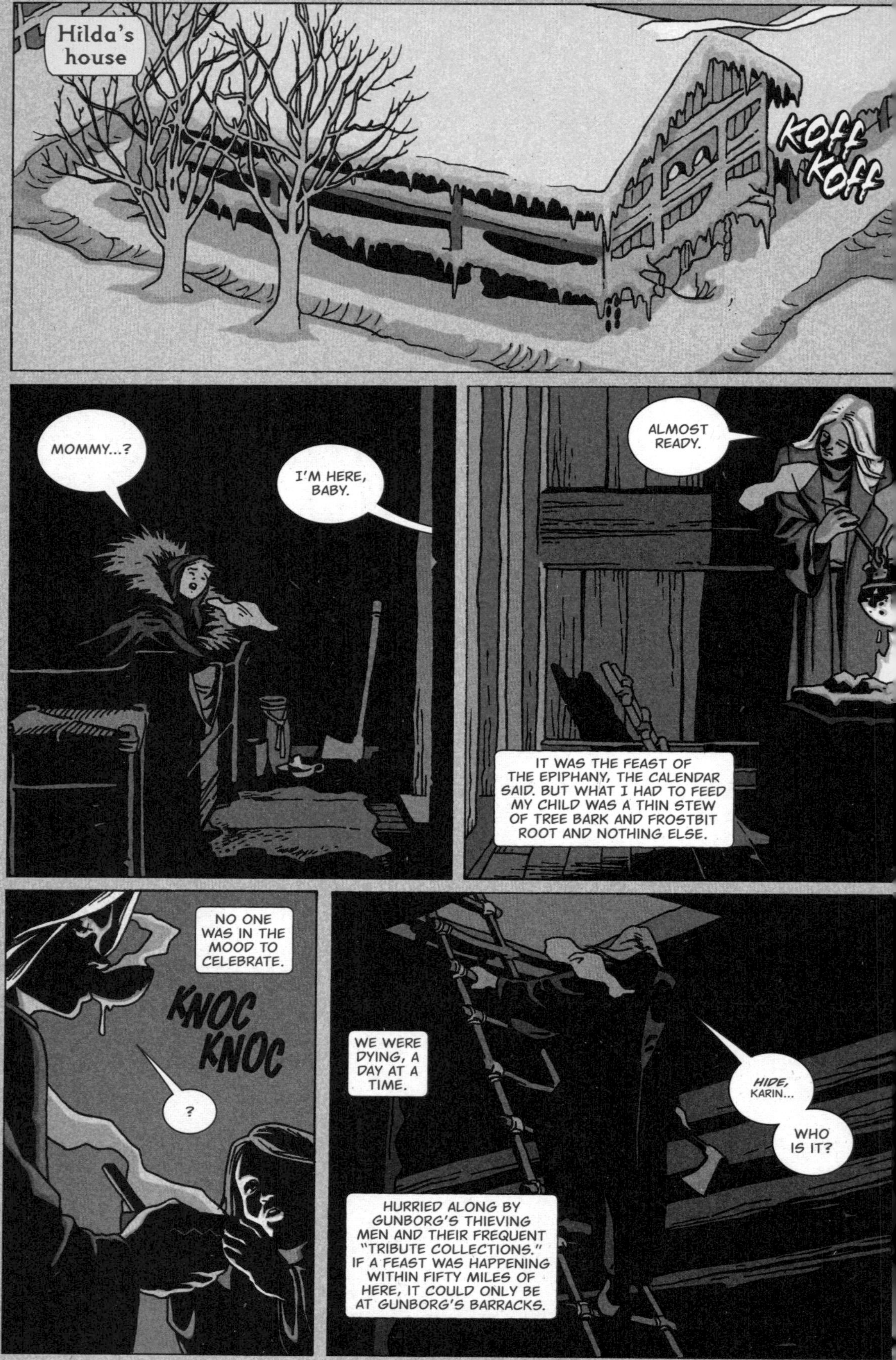
Hilda's house
KOFF KOFF
MOMMY...?
I'M HERE, BABY.
ALMOST READY.
IT WAS THE FEAST OF THE EPIPHANY, THE CALENDAR SAID. BUT WHAT I HAD TO FEED MY CHILD WAS A THIN STEW OF TREE BARK AND FROSTBIT ROOT AND NOTHING ELSE.
NO ONE WAS IN THE MOOD TO CELEBRATE.
KNOC KNOC
?
WE WERE DYING, A DAY AT A TIME.
HURRIED ALONG BY GUNBORG'S THIEVING MEN AND THEIR FREQUENT "TRIBUTE COLLECTIONS." IF A FEAST WAS HAPPENING WITHIN FIFTY MILES OF HERE, IT COULD ONLY BE AT GUNBORG'S BARRACKS.
HIDE, KARIN...
WHO IS IT?

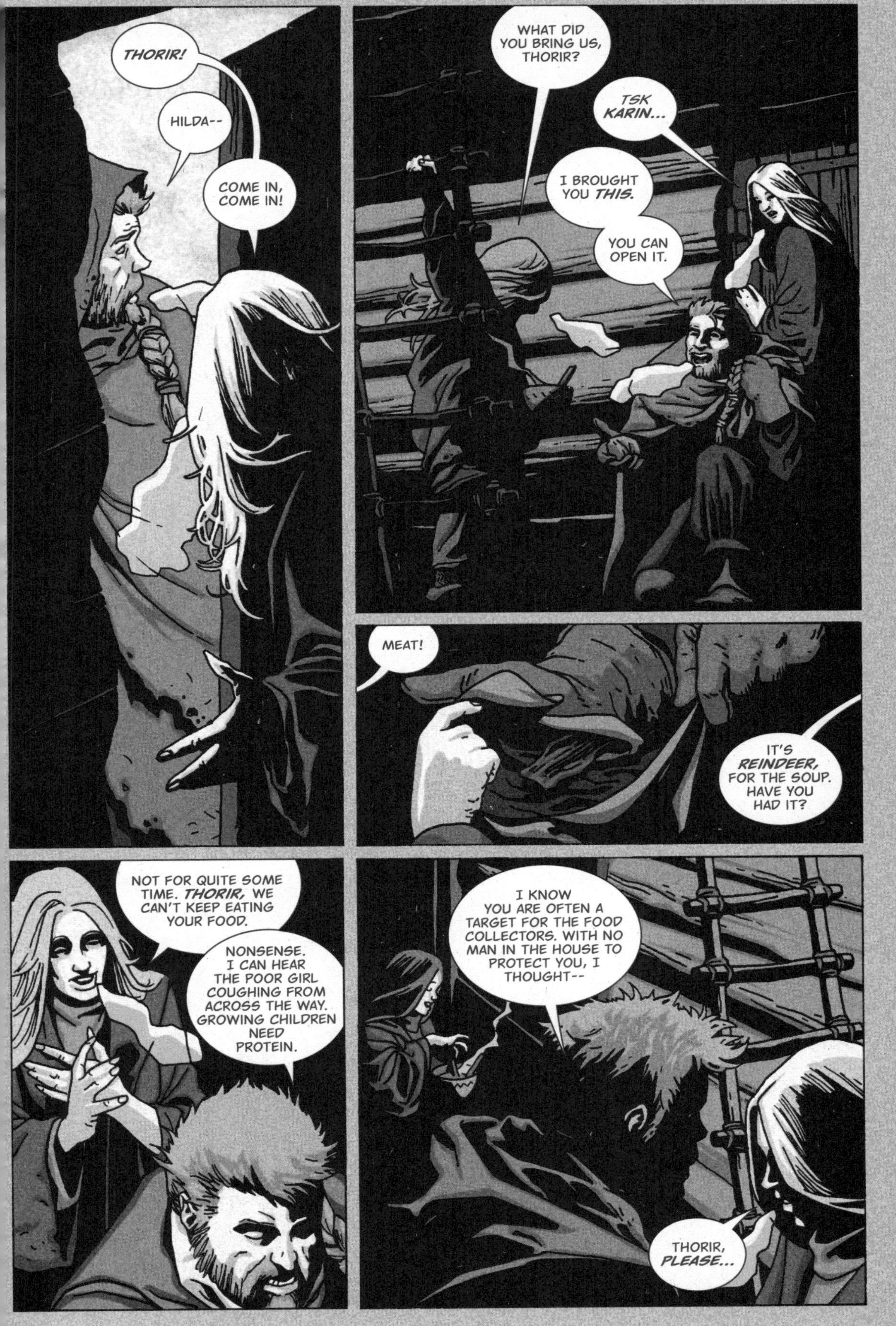
THORIR!
HILDA--
COME IN, COME IN!
WHAT DID YOU BRING US, THORIR?
TSK KARIN...
I BROUGHT YOU THIS.
YOU CAN OPEN IT.
MEAT!
IT'S REINDEER, FOR THE SOUP. HAVE YOU HAD IT?
NOT FOR QUITE SOME TIME. THORIR, WE CAN'T KEEP EATING YOUR FOOD.
NONSENSE. I CAN HEAR THE POOR GIRL COUGHING FROM ACROSS THE WAY. GROWING CHILDREN NEED PROTEIN.
I KNOW YOU ARE OFTEN A TARGET FOR THE FOOD COLLECTORS. WITH NO MAN IN THE HOUSE TO PROTECT YOU, I THOUGHT--
THORIR, PLEASE...

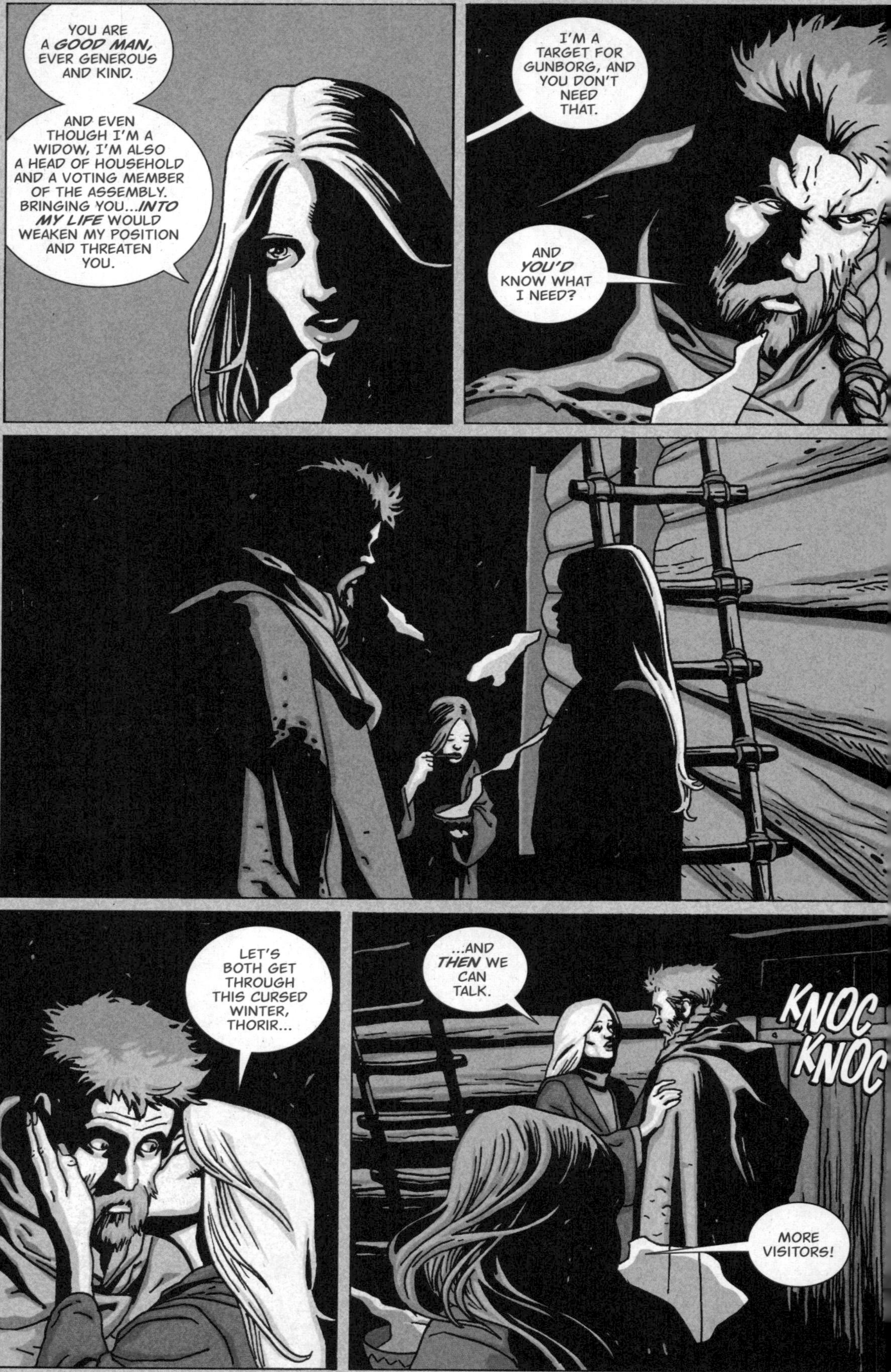
YOU ARE A GOOD MAN, EVER GENEROUS AND KIND.
AND EVEN THOUGH I'M A WIDOW, I'M ALSO A HEAD OF HOUSEHOLD AND A VOTING MEMBER OF THE ASSEMBLY. BRINGING YOU...INTO MY LIFE WOULD WEAKEN MY POSITION AND THREATEN YOU.
I'M A TARGET FOR GUNBORG, AND YOU DON'T NEED THAT.
AND YOU'D KNOW WHAT I NEED?
LET'S BOTH GET THROUGH THIS CURSED WINTER, THORIR...
...AND THEN WE CAN TALK.
KNOC KNOC
MORE VISITORS!

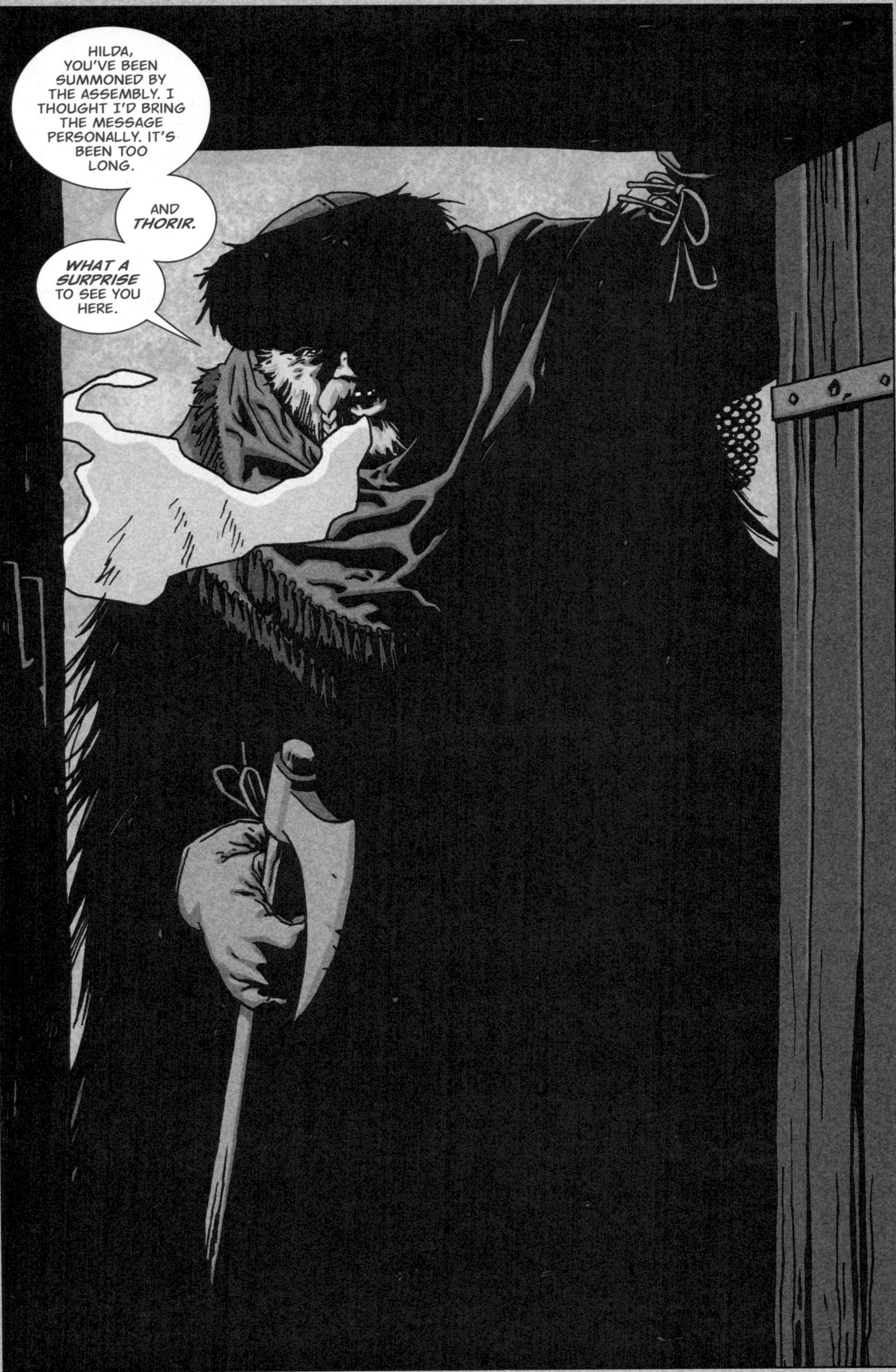
HILDA, YOU'VE BEEN SUMMONED BY THE ASSEMBLY. I THOUGHT I'D BRING THE MESSAGE PERSONALLY. IT'S BEEN TOO LONG.
AND *THORIR.*
WHAT A SURPRISE TO SEE YOU HERE.

The Great Hall

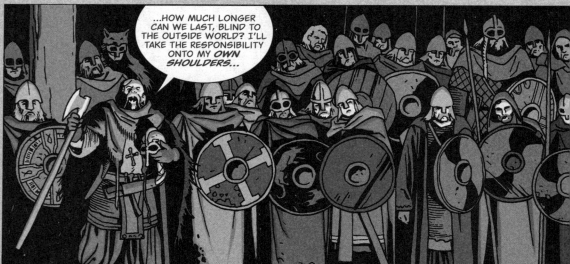

...HOW MUCH LONGER CAN WE LAST, BLIND TO THE OUTSIDE WORLD? I'LL TAKE THE RESPONSIBILITY ONTO MY *OWN* SHOULDERS...

...FOR THE *GOOD* OF US *ALL*.

YOU'LL BE *EXPOSED*, GUNBORG. *ALL OF YOU* WILL BE EXPOSED.

YOU DON'T KNOW THAT!

THE FUCKING COLD DAMN NEAR KILLS EVERYTHING IT TOUCHES, WHY NOT THIS DISEASE AS WELL? WE COULD BE STARVING OURSELVES FOR *NOTHING!*

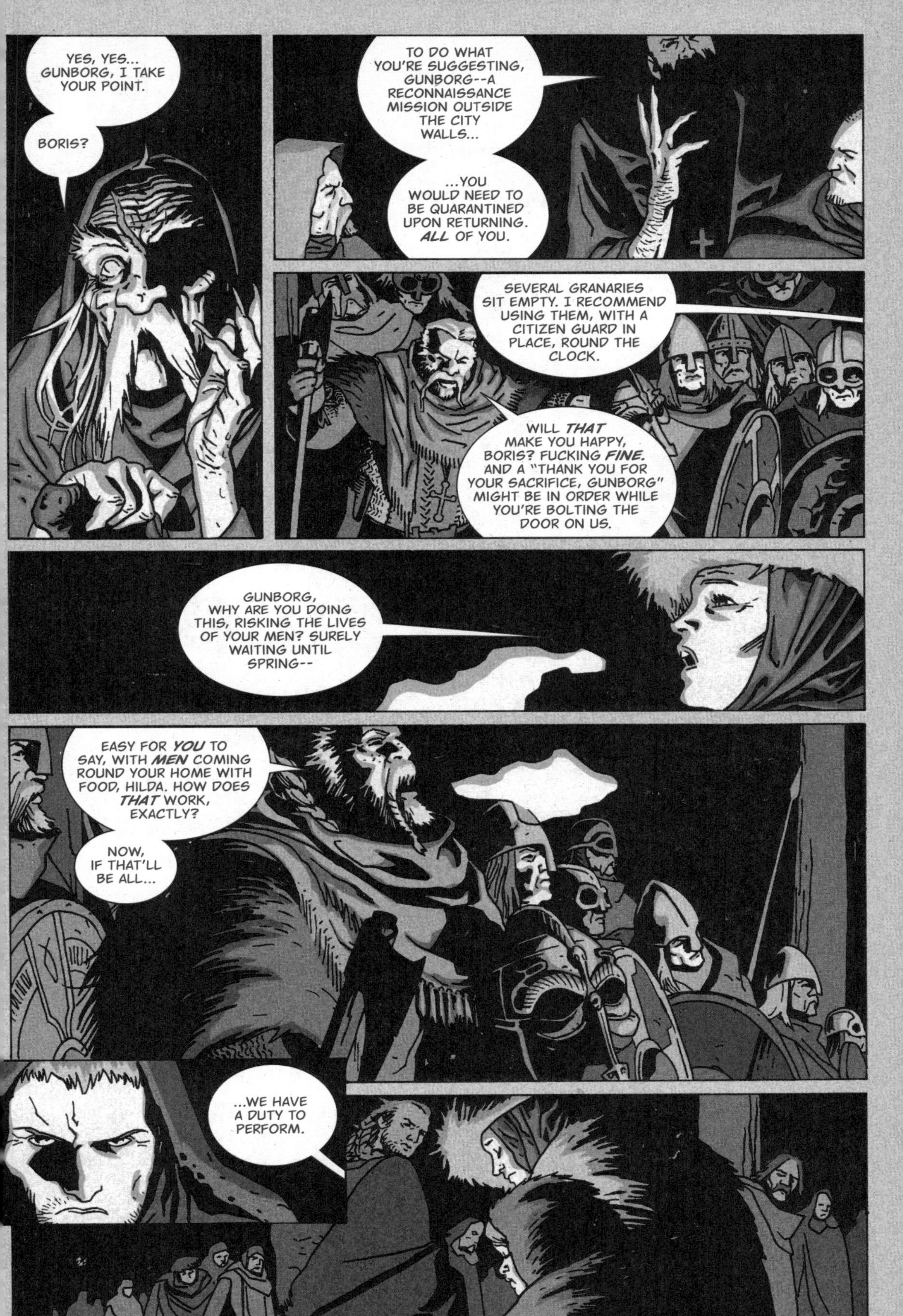
YES, YES... GUNBORG, I TAKE YOUR POINT.
BORIS?
TO DO WHAT YOU'RE SUGGESTING, GUNBORG--A RECONNAISSANCE MISSION OUTSIDE THE CITY WALLS...
...YOU WOULD NEED TO BE QUARANTINED UPON RETURNING. ALL OF YOU.
SEVERAL GRANARIES SIT EMPTY. I RECOMMEND USING THEM, WITH A CITIZEN GUARD IN PLACE, ROUND THE CLOCK.
WILL THAT MAKE YOU HAPPY, BORIS? FUCKING FINE. AND A "THANK YOU FOR YOUR SACRIFICE, GUNBORG" MIGHT BE IN ORDER WHILE YOU'RE BOLTING THE DOOR ON US.
GUNBORG, WHY ARE YOU DOING THIS, RISKING THE LIVES OF YOUR MEN? SURELY WAITING UNTIL SPRING--
EASY FOR YOU TO SAY, WITH MEN COMING ROUND YOUR HOME WITH FOOD, HILDA. HOW DOES THAT WORK, EXACTLY?
NOW, IF THAT'LL BE ALL...
...WE HAVE A DUTY TO PERFORM.

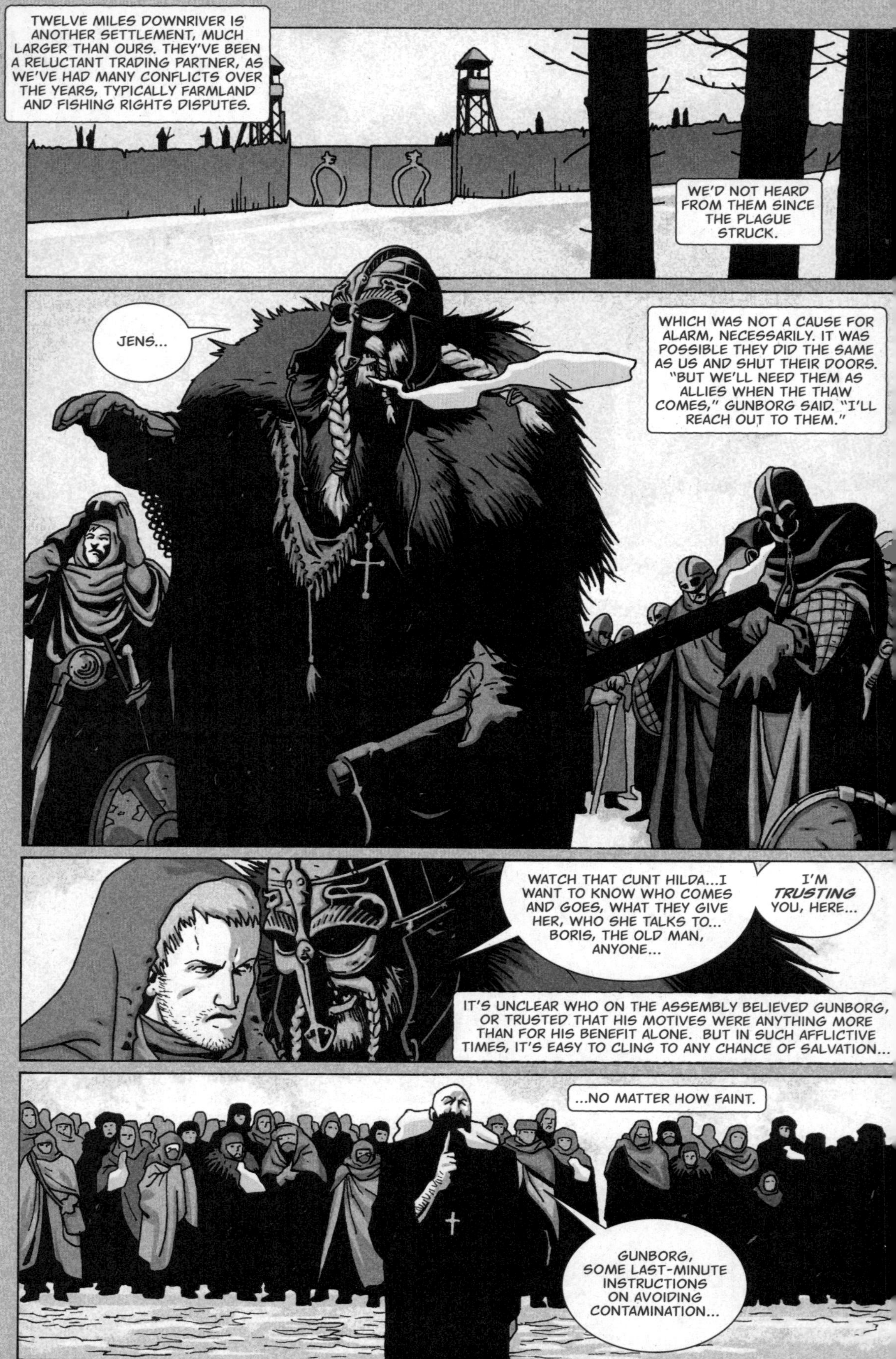
TWELVE MILES DOWNRIVER IS ANOTHER SETTLEMENT, MUCH LARGER THAN OURS. THEY'VE BEEN A RELUCTANT TRADING PARTNER, AS WE'VE HAD MANY CONFLICTS OVER THE YEARS, TYPICALLY FARMLAND AND FISHING RIGHTS DISPUTES.
WE'D NOT HEARD FROM THEM SINCE THE PLAGUE STRUCK.
JENS...
WHICH WAS NOT A CAUSE FOR ALARM, NECESSARILY. IT WAS POSSIBLE THEY DID THE SAME AS US AND SHUT THEIR DOORS. "BUT WE'LL NEED THEM AS ALLIES WHEN THE THAW COMES," GUNBORG SAID. "I'LL REACH OUT TO THEM."
WATCH THAT CUNT HILDA...I WANT TO KNOW WHO COMES AND GOES, WHAT THEY GIVE HER, WHO SHE TALKS TO... BORIS, THE OLD MAN, ANYONE...
I'M *TRUSTING* YOU, HERE...
IT'S UNCLEAR WHO ON THE ASSEMBLY BELIEVED GUNBORG, OR TRUSTED THAT HIS MOTIVES WERE ANYTHING MORE THAN FOR HIS BENEFIT ALONE. BUT IN SUCH AFFLICTIVE TIMES, IT'S EASY TO CLING TO ANY CHANCE OF SALVATION...
...NO MATTER HOW FAINT.
GUNBORG, SOME LAST-MINUTE INSTRUCTIONS ON AVOIDING CONTAMINATION...

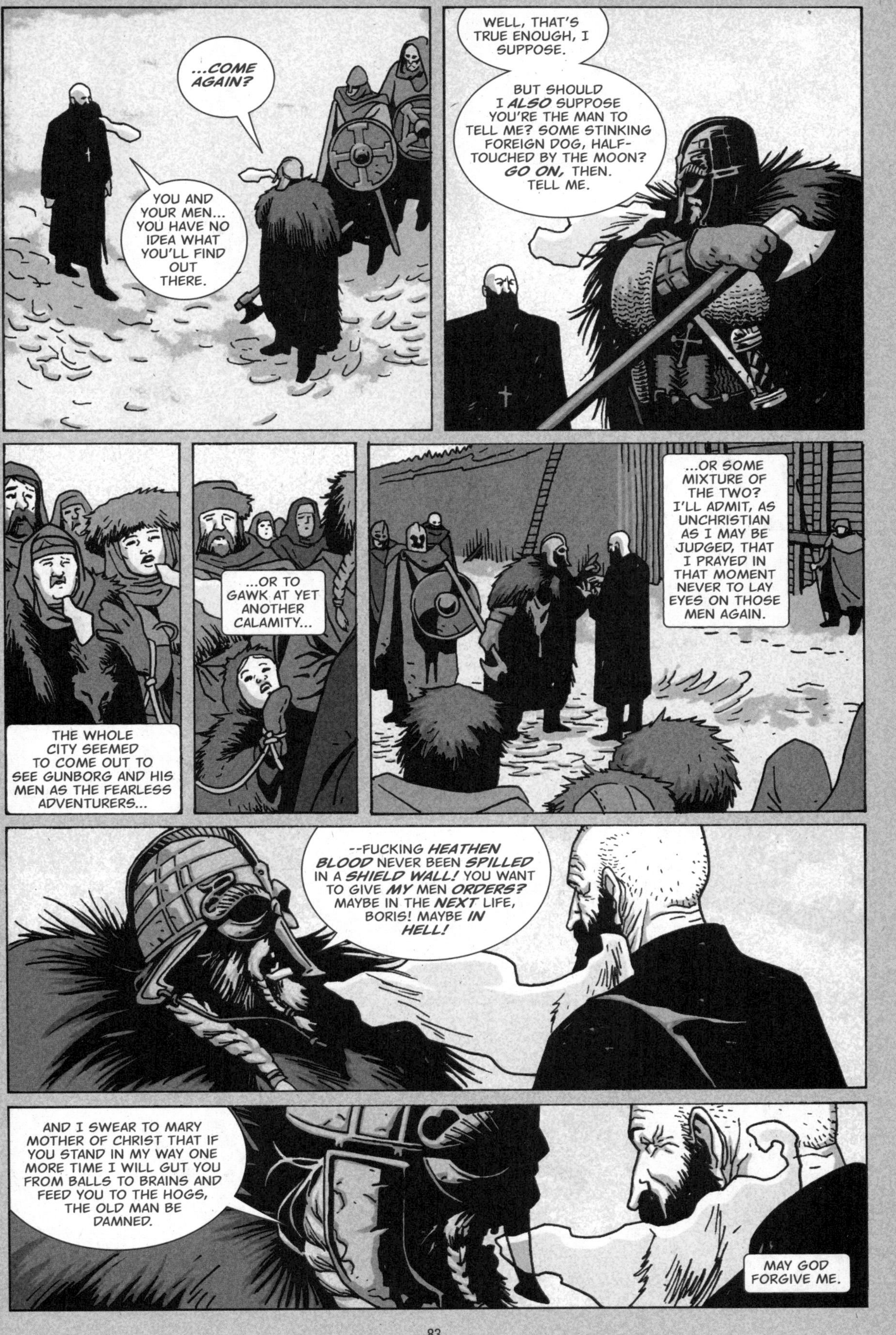
...COME AGAIN?
YOU AND YOUR MEN... YOU HAVE NO IDEA WHAT YOU'LL FIND OUT THERE.
WELL, THAT'S TRUE ENOUGH, I SUPPOSE.
BUT SHOULD I ALSO SUPPOSE YOU'RE THE MAN TO TELL ME? SOME STINKING FOREIGN DOG, HALF-TOUCHED BY THE MOON? GO ON, THEN. TELL ME.
THE WHOLE CITY SEEMED TO COME OUT TO SEE GUNBORG AND HIS MEN AS THE FEARLESS ADVENTURERS...
...OR TO GAWK AT YET ANOTHER CALAMITY...
...OR SOME MIXTURE OF THE TWO? I'LL ADMIT, AS UNCHRISTIAN AS I MAY BE JUDGED, THAT I PRAYED IN THAT MOMENT NEVER TO LAY EYES ON THOSE MEN AGAIN.
--FUCKING HEATHEN BLOOD NEVER BEEN SPILLED IN A SHIELD WALL! YOU WANT TO GIVE MY MEN ORDERS? MAYBE IN THE NEXT LIFE, BORIS! MAYBE IN HELL!
AND I SWEAR TO MARY MOTHER OF CHRIST THAT IF YOU STAND IN MY WAY ONE MORE TIME I WILL GUT YOU FROM BALLS TO BRAINS AND FEED YOU TO THE HOGS, THE OLD MAN BE DAMNED.
MAY GOD FORGIVE ME.

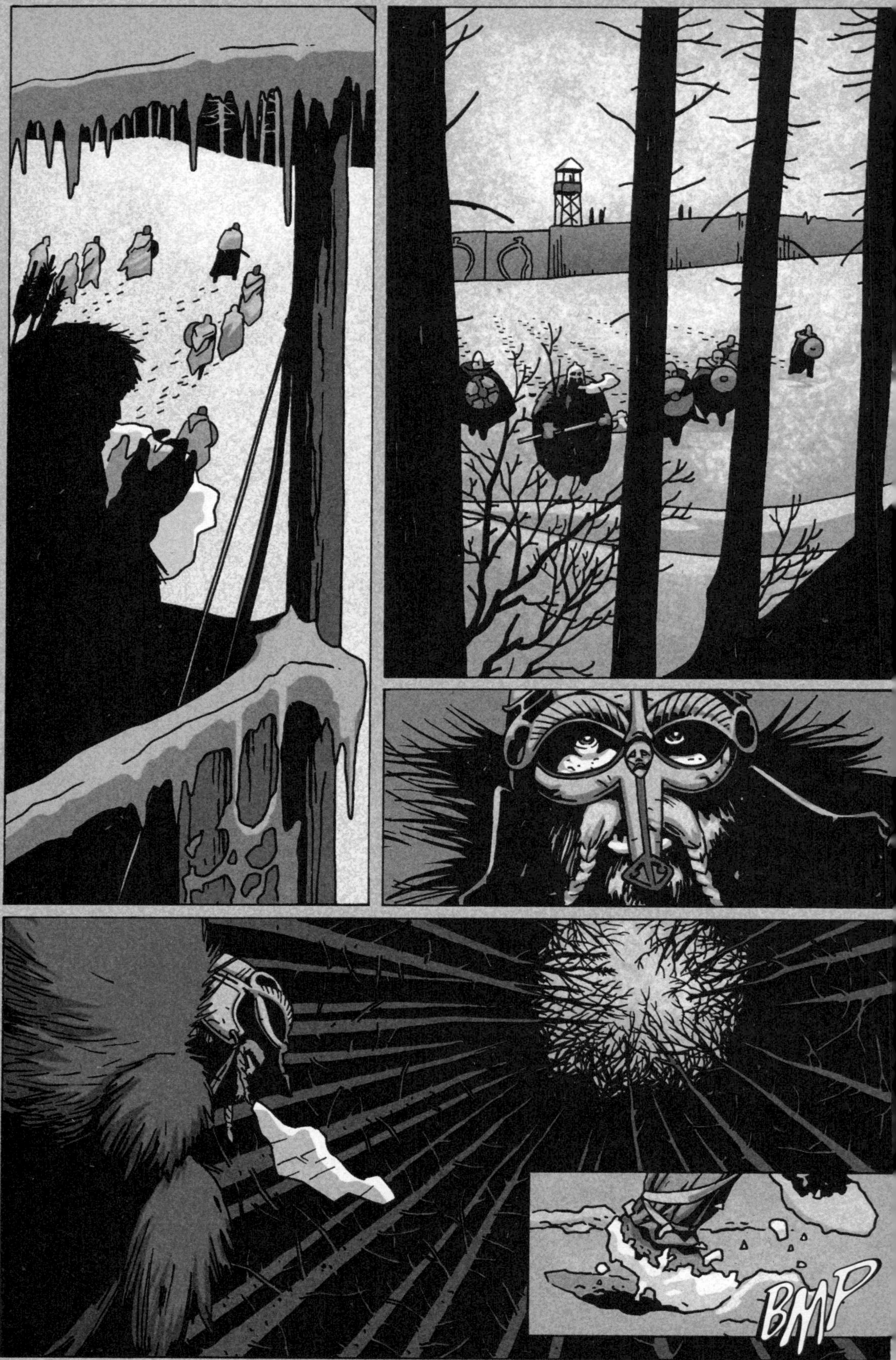
BMP

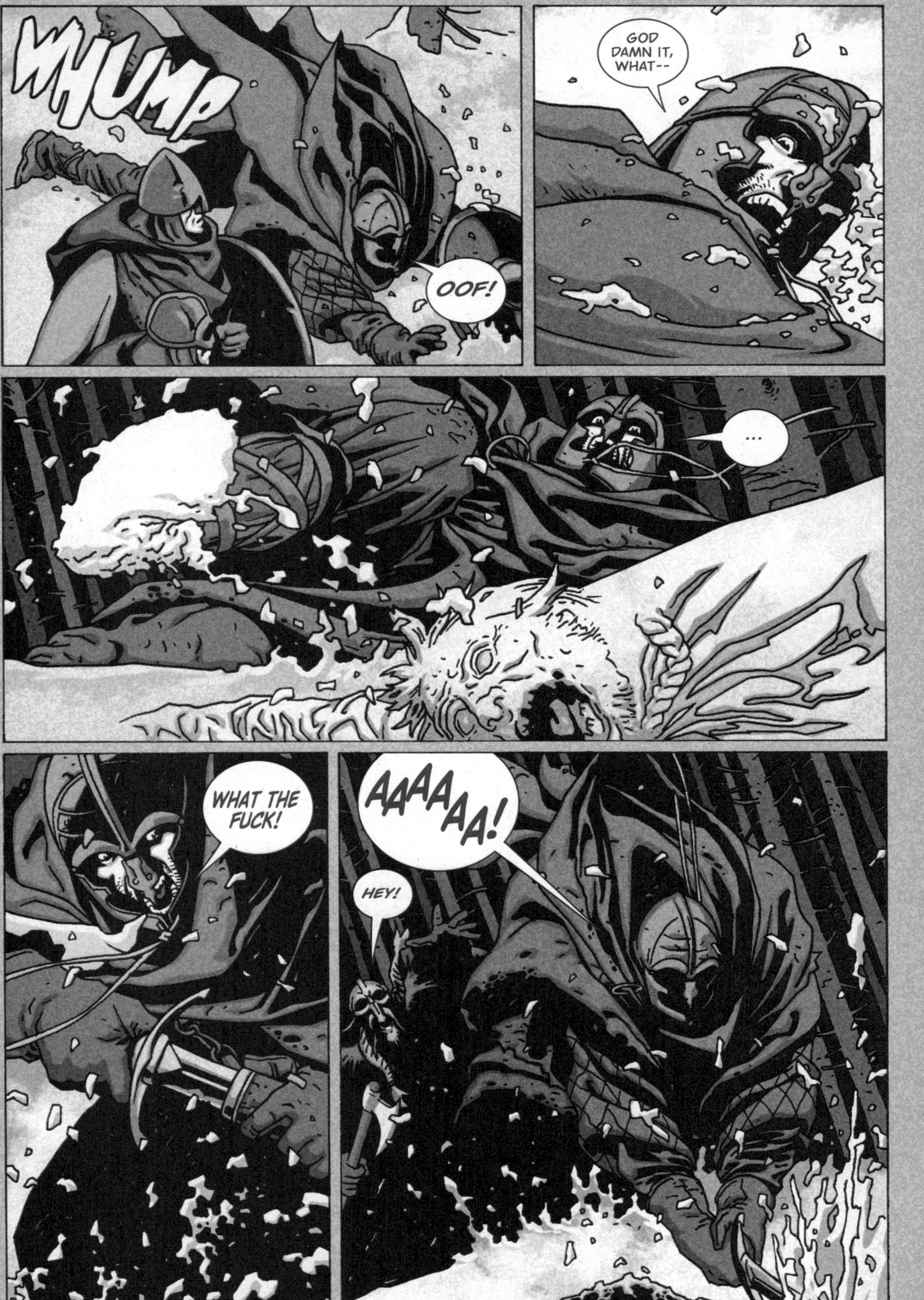
WHUMP
OOF!
GOD DAMN IT, WHAT--
...
WHAT THE FUCK!
AAAAAAA!
HEY!

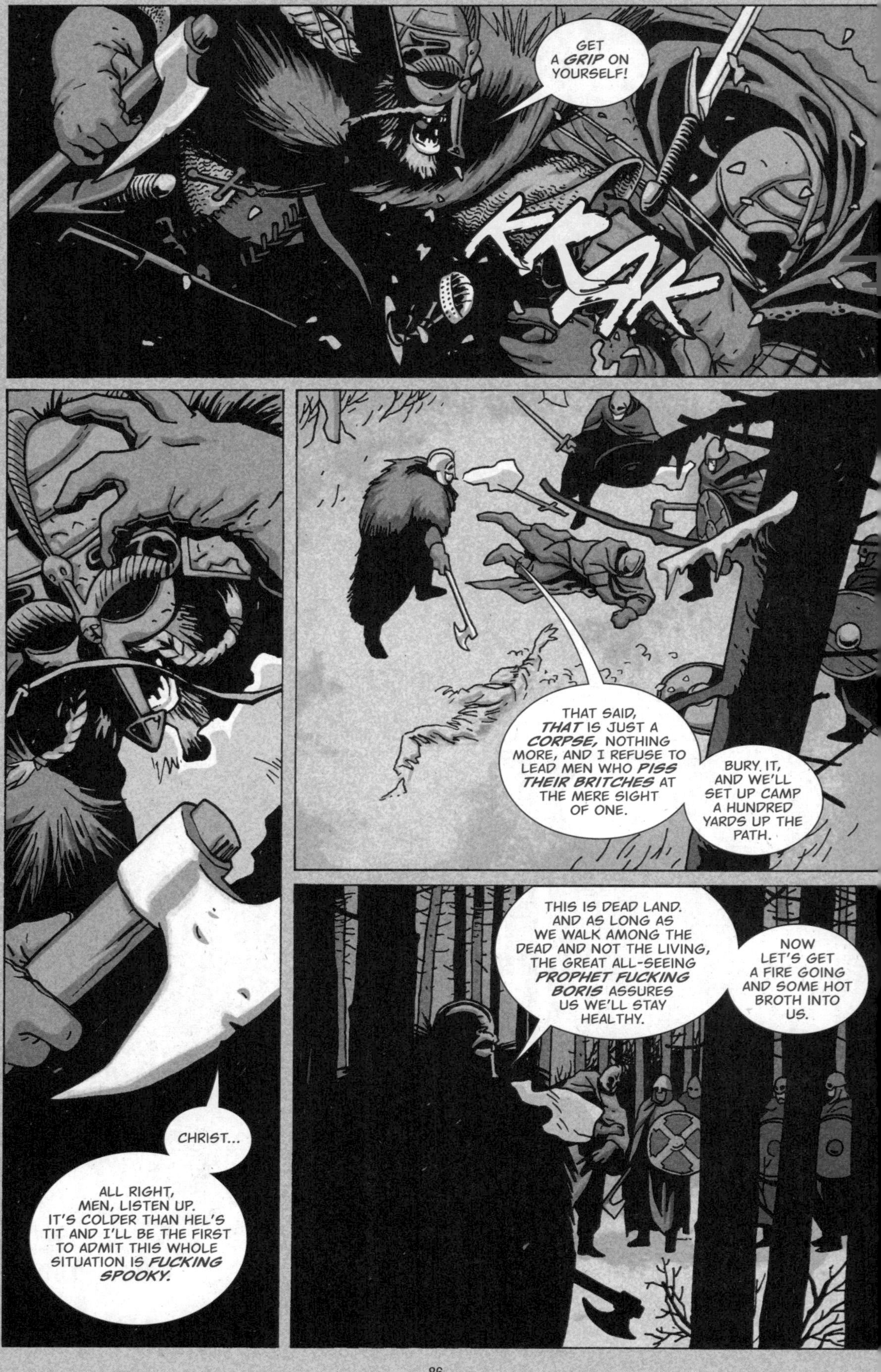
GET A *GRIP* ON YOURSELF!
KRAK
CHRIST...
ALL RIGHT, MEN, LISTEN UP. IT'S COLDER THAN HEL'S TIT AND I'LL BE THE FIRST TO ADMIT THIS WHOLE SITUATION IS *FUCKING SPOOKY.*
THAT SAID, *THAT* IS JUST A *CORPSE,* NOTHING MORE, AND I REFUSE TO LEAD MEN WHO *PISS THEIR BRITCHES* AT THE MERE SIGHT OF ONE.
BURY IT, AND WE'LL SET UP CAMP A HUNDRED YARDS UP THE PATH.
THIS IS DEAD LAND. AND AS LONG AS WE WALK AMONG THE DEAD AND NOT THE LIVING, THE GREAT ALL-SEEING *PROPHET FUCKING BORIS* ASSURES US WE'LL STAY HEALTHY.
NOW LET'S GET A FIRE GOING AND SOME HOT BROTH INTO US.

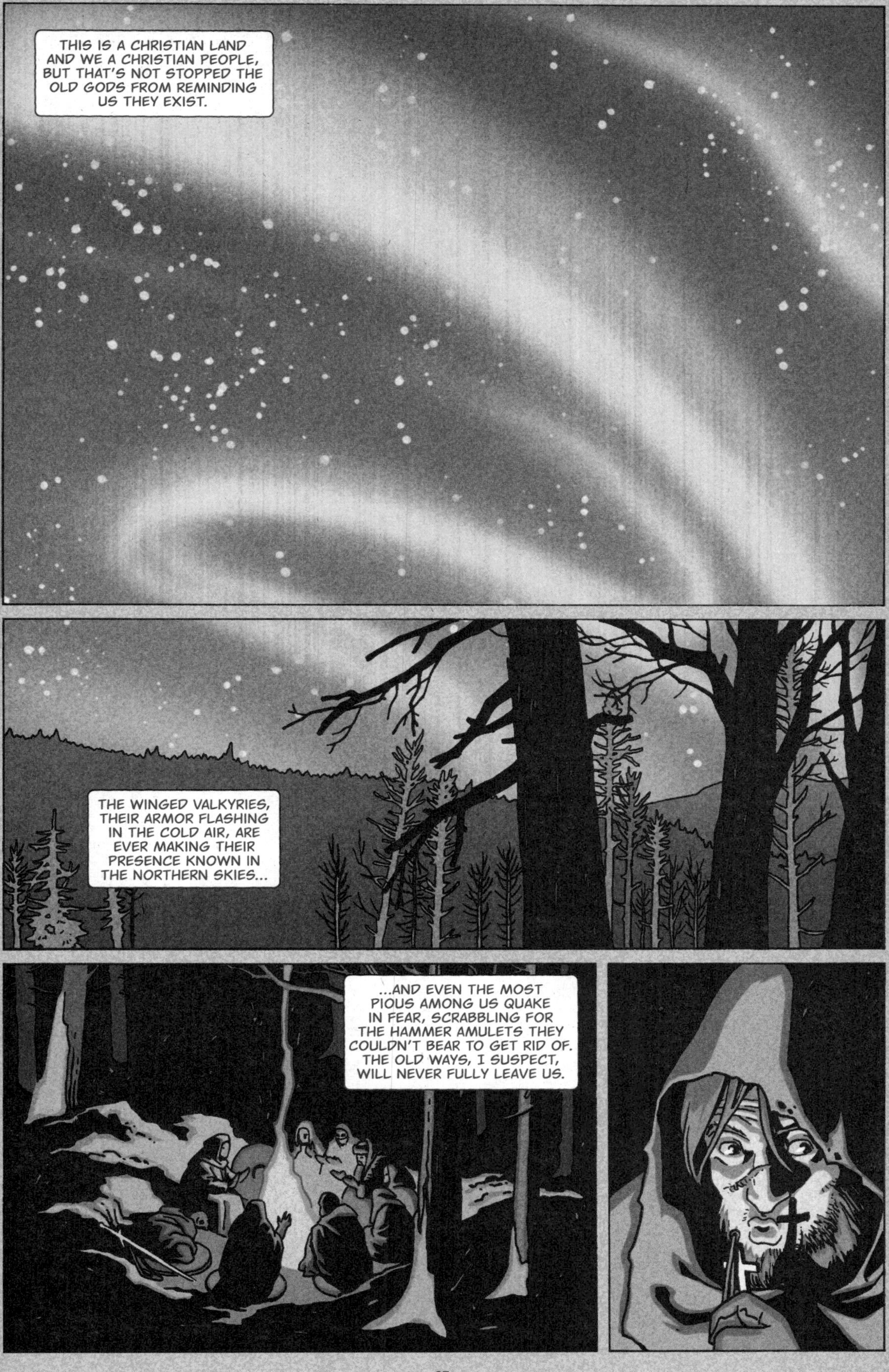
THIS IS A CHRISTIAN LAND AND WE A CHRISTIAN PEOPLE, BUT THAT'S NOT STOPPED THE OLD GODS FROM REMINDING US THEY EXIST.
THE WINGED VALKYRIES, THEIR ARMOR FLASHING IN THE COLD AIR, ARE EVER MAKING THEIR PRESENCE KNOWN IN THE NORTHERN SKIES...
...AND EVEN THE MOST PIOUS AMONG US QUAKE IN FEAR, SCRABBLING FOR THE HAMMER AMULETS THEY COULDN'T BEAR TO GET RID OF. THE OLD WAYS, I SUSPECT, WILL NEVER FULLY LEAVE US.

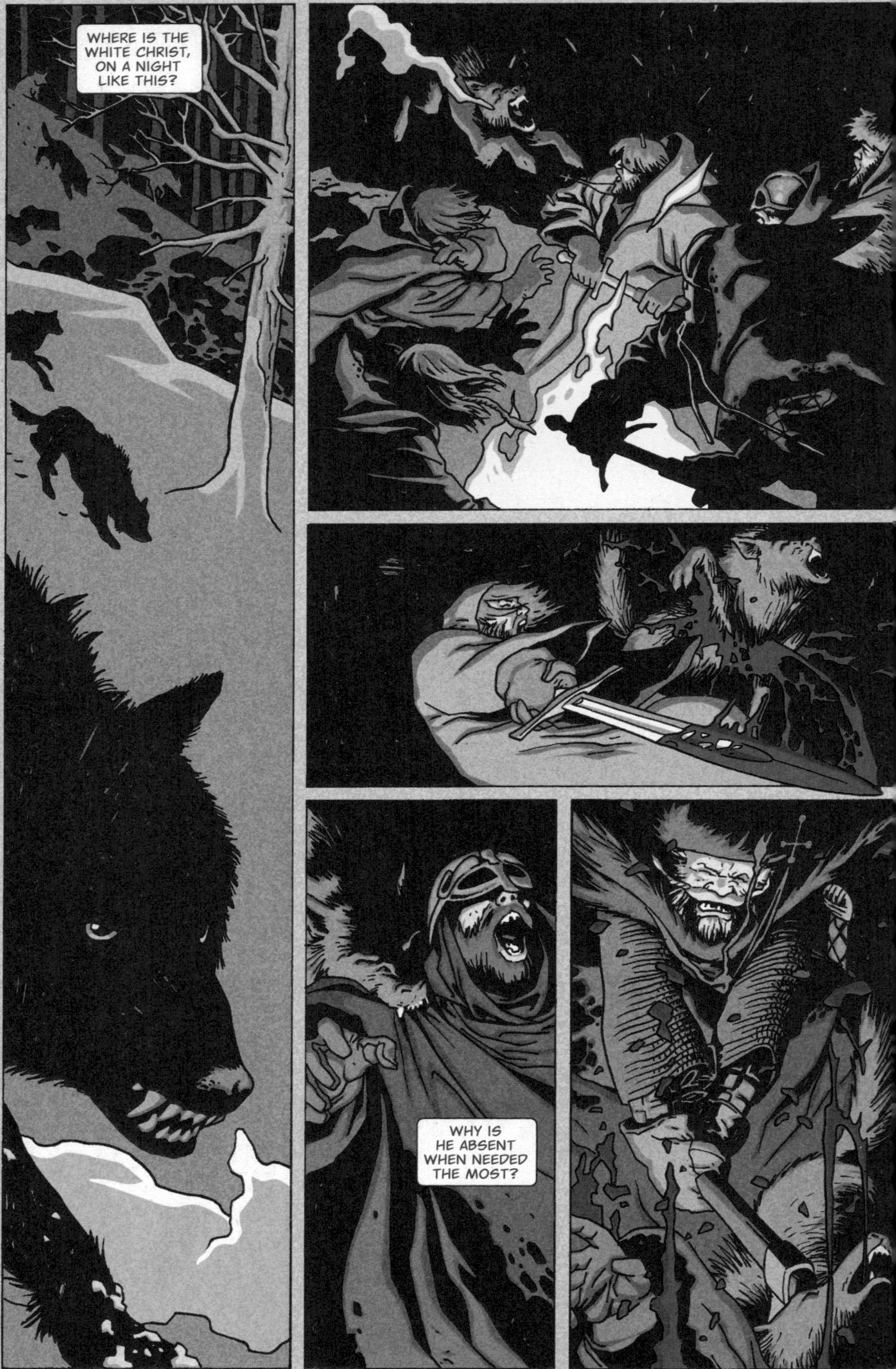
WHERE IS THE WHITE CHRIST, ON A NIGHT LIKE THIS?
WHY IS HE ABSENT WHEN NEEDED THE MOST?

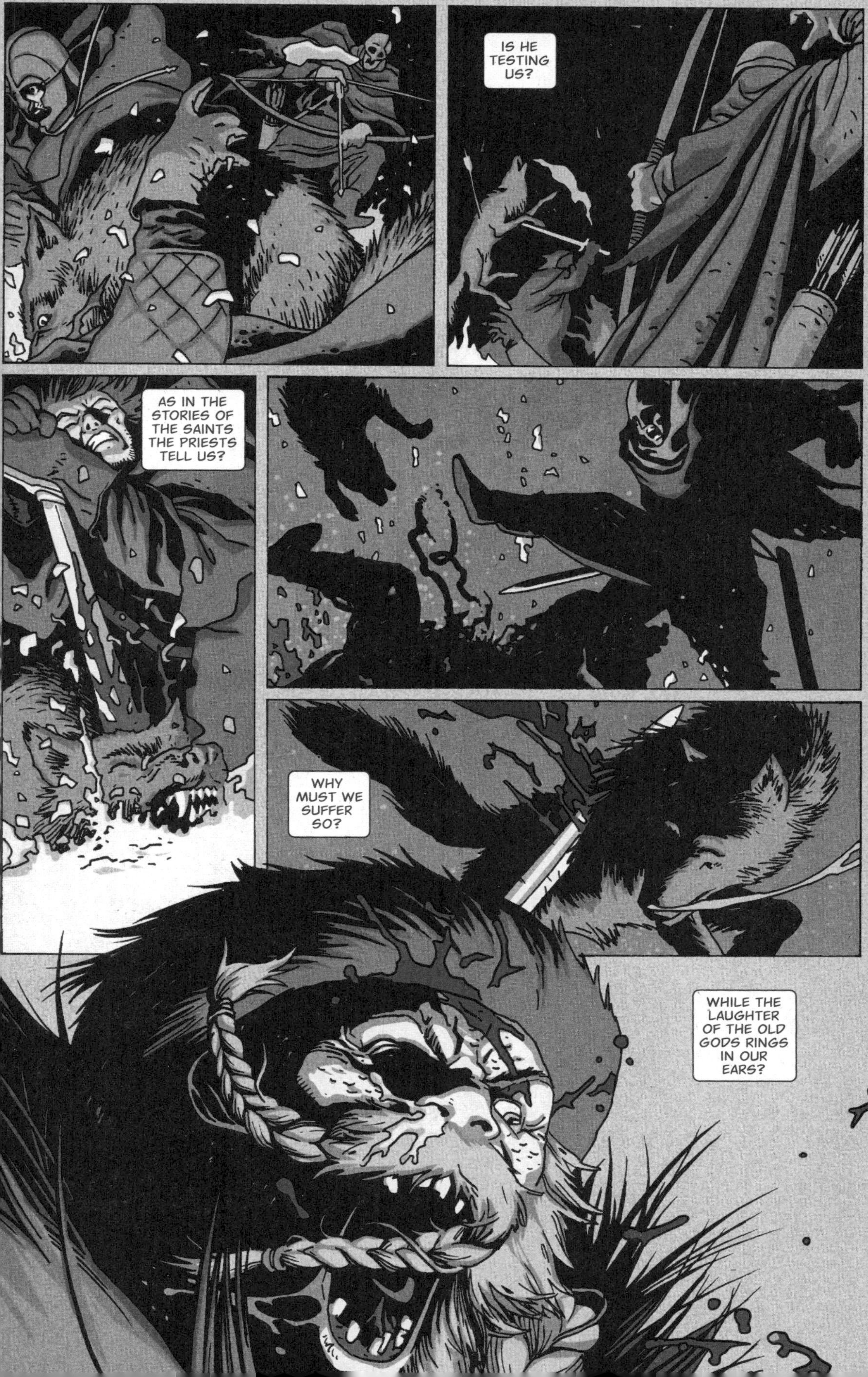
IS HE TESTING US?
AS IN THE STORIES OF THE SAINTS THE PRIESTS TELL US?
WHY MUST WE SUFFER SO?
WHILE THE LAUGHTER OF THE OLD GODS RINGS IN OUR EARS?

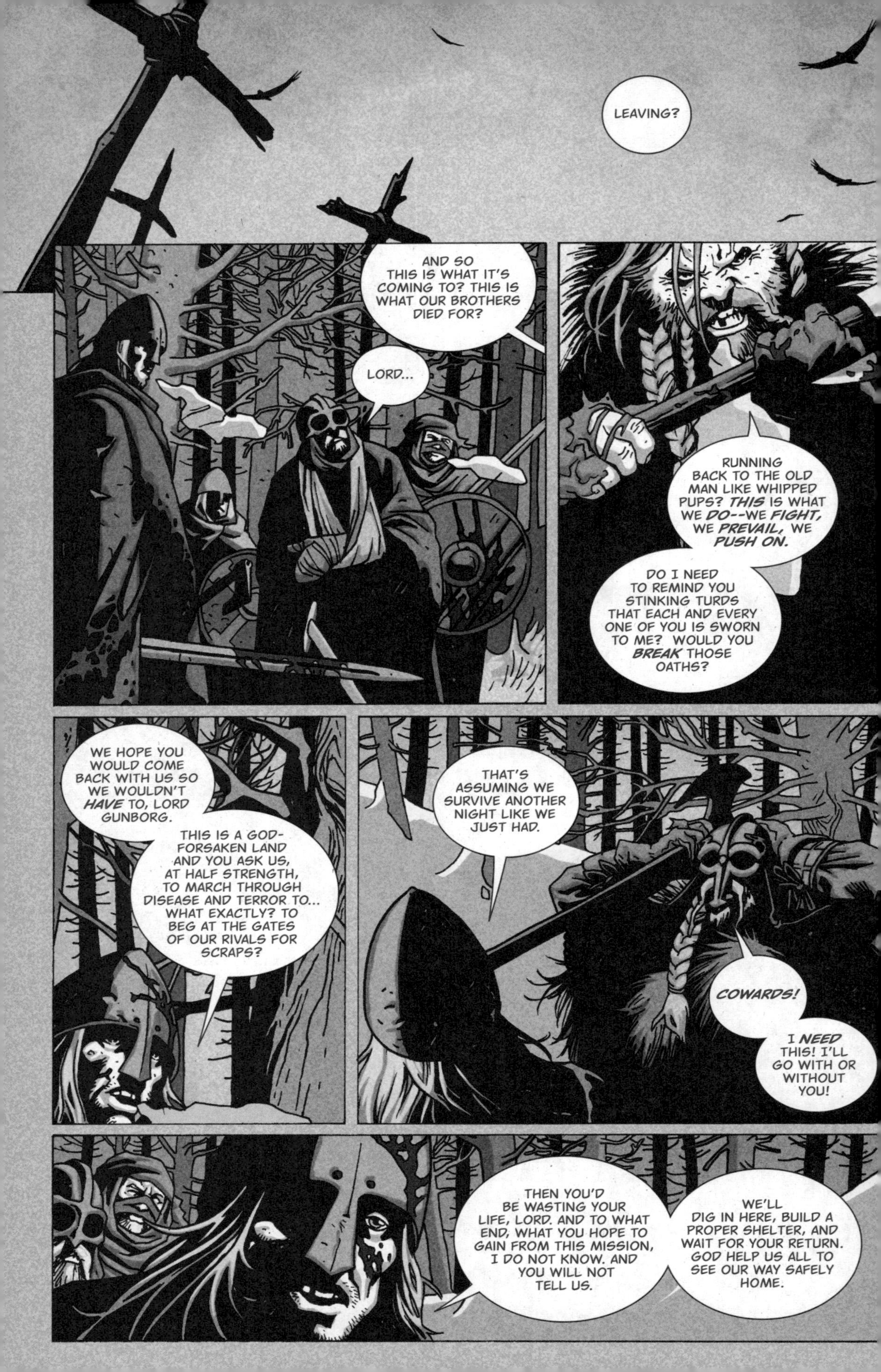
LEAVING?
AND SO THIS IS WHAT IT'S COMING TO? THIS IS WHAT OUR BROTHERS DIED FOR?
LORD...
RUNNING BACK TO THE OLD MAN LIKE WHIPPED PUPS? THIS IS WHAT WE DO--WE FIGHT, WE PREVAIL, WE PUSH ON.
DO I NEED TO REMIND YOU STINKING TURDS THAT EACH AND EVERY ONE OF YOU IS SWORN TO ME? WOULD YOU BREAK THOSE OATHS?
WE HOPE YOU WOULD COME BACK WITH US SO WE WOULDN'T HAVE TO, LORD GUNBORG.
THIS IS A GOD-FORSAKEN LAND AND YOU ASK US, AT HALF STRENGTH, TO MARCH THROUGH DISEASE AND TERROR TO... WHAT EXACTLY? TO BEG AT THE GATES OF OUR RIVALS FOR SCRAPS?
THAT'S ASSUMING WE SURVIVE ANOTHER NIGHT LIKE WE JUST HAD.
COWARDS!
I NEED THIS! I'LL GO WITH OR WITHOUT YOU!
THEN YOU'D BE WASTING YOUR LIFE, LORD. AND TO WHAT END, WHAT YOU HOPE TO GAIN FROM THIS MISSION, I DO NOT KNOW. AND YOU WILL NOT TELL US.
WE'LL DIG IN HERE, BUILD A PROPER SHELTER, AND WAIT FOR YOUR RETURN. GOD HELP US ALL TO SEE OUR WAY SAFELY HOME.

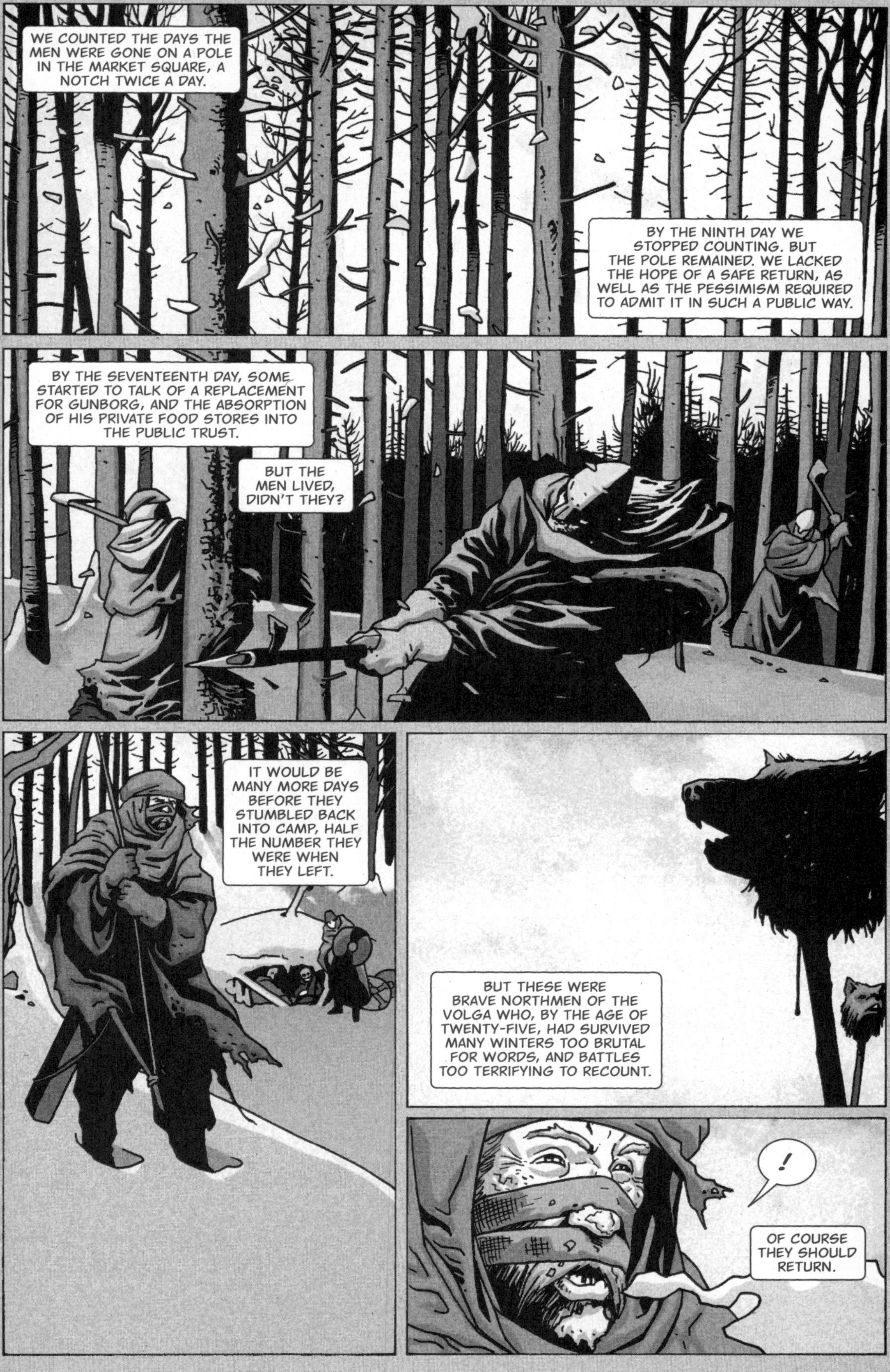
WE COUNTED THE DAYS THE MEN WERE GONE ON A POLE IN THE MARKET SQUARE, A NOTCH TWICE A DAY.
BY THE NINTH DAY WE STOPPED COUNTING. BUT THE POLE REMAINED. WE LACKED THE HOPE OF A SAFE RETURN, AS WELL AS THE PESSIMISM REQUIRED TO ADMIT IT IN SUCH A PUBLIC WAY.
BY THE SEVENTEENTH DAY, SOME STARTED TO TALK OF A REPLACEMENT FOR GUNBORG, AND THE ABSORPTION OF HIS PRIVATE FOOD STORES INTO THE PUBLIC TRUST.
BUT THE MEN LIVED, DIDN'T THEY?
IT WOULD BE MANY MORE DAYS BEFORE THEY STUMBLED BACK INTO CAMP, HALF THE NUMBER THEY WERE WHEN THEY LEFT.
BUT THESE WERE BRAVE NORTHMEN OF THE VOLGA WHO, BY THE AGE OF TWENTY-FIVE, HAD SURVIVED MANY WINTERS TOO BRUTAL FOR WORDS, AND BATTLES TOO TERRIFYING TO RECOUNT.
!
OF COURSE THEY SHOULD RETURN.

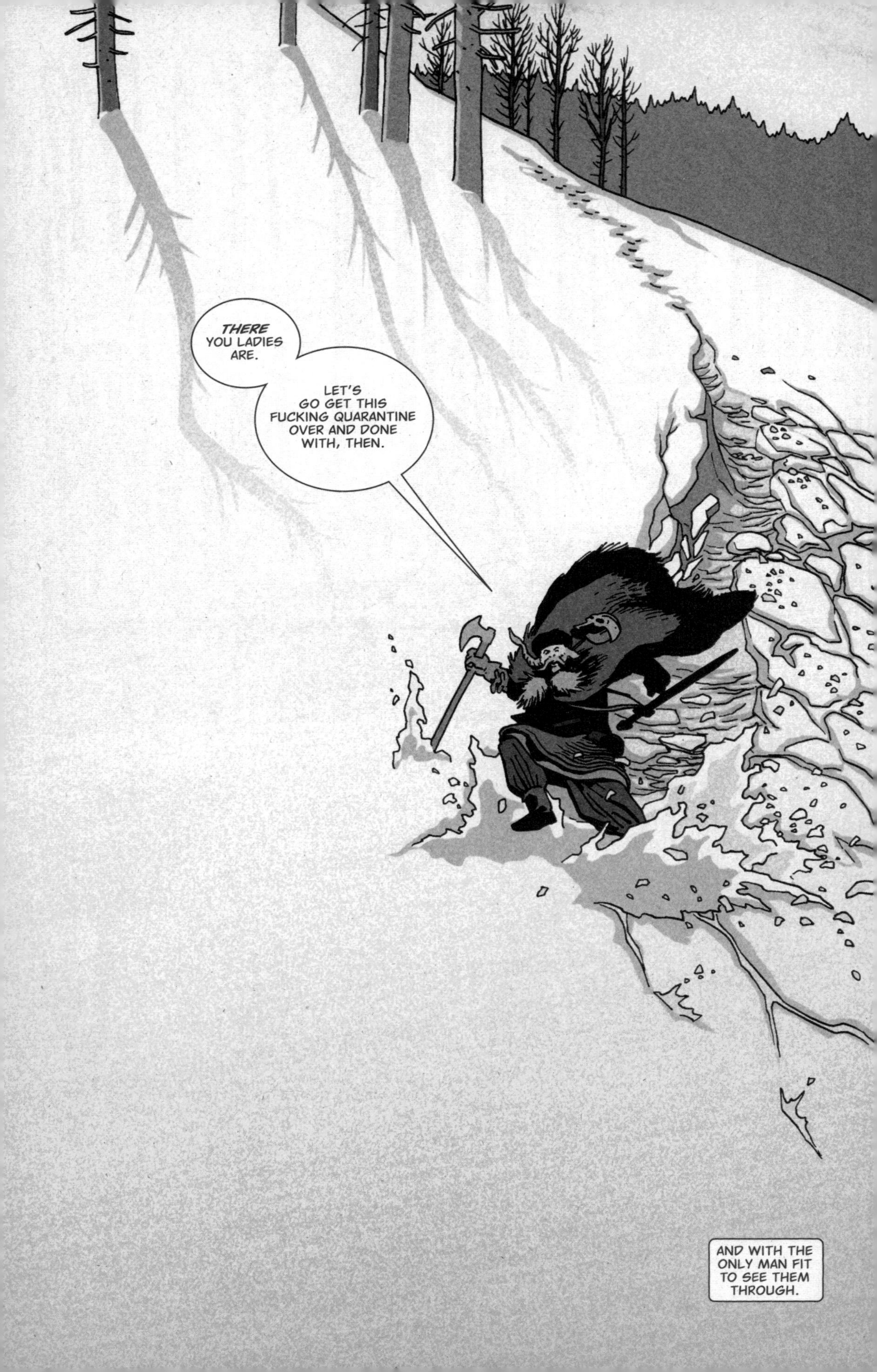
THERE YOU LADIES ARE.
LET'S GO GET THIS FUCKING QUARANTINE OVER AND DONE WITH, THEN.
AND WITH THE ONLY MAN FIT TO SEE THEM THROUGH.

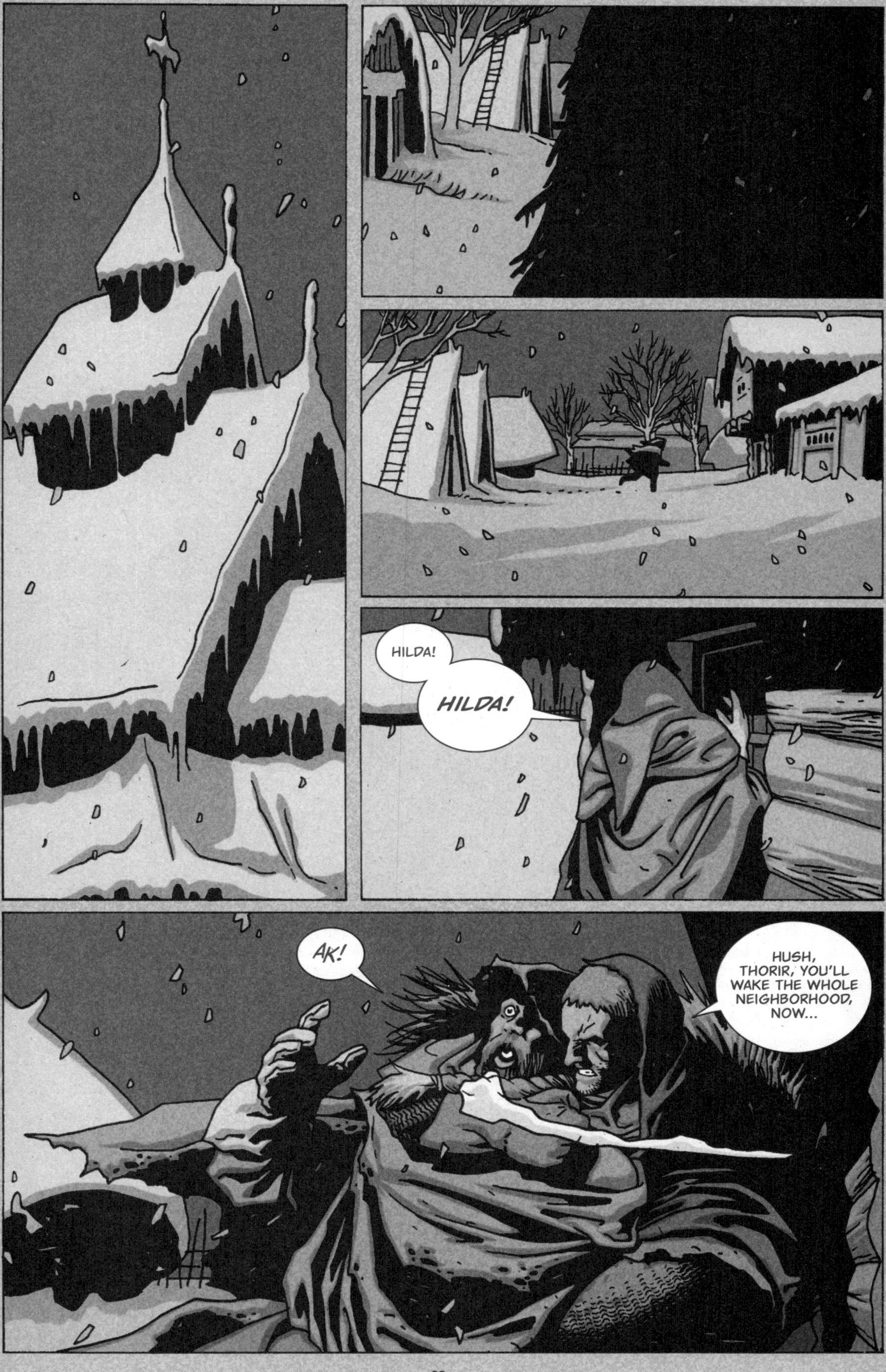
HILDA!
HILDA!
AK!
HUSH, THORIR, YOU'LL WAKE THE WHOLE NEIGHBORHOOD, NOW...

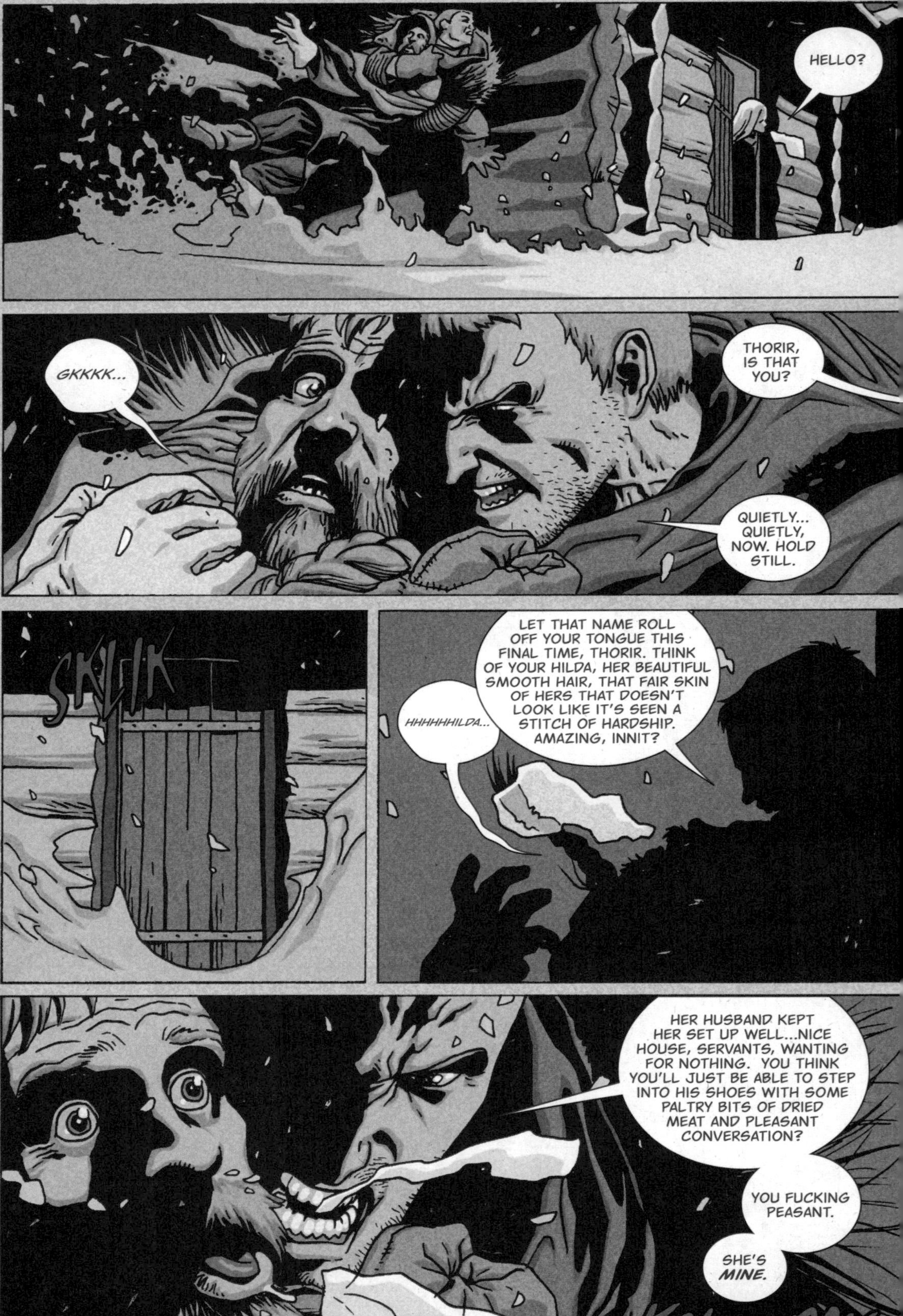
HELLO?
GKKKK...
THORIR, IS THAT YOU?
QUIETLY... QUIETLY, NOW. HOLD STILL.
SKLIK
LET THAT NAME ROLL OFF YOUR TONGUE THIS FINAL TIME, THORIR. THINK OF YOUR HILDA, HER BEAUTIFUL SMOOTH HAIR, THAT FAIR SKIN OF HERS THAT DOESN'T LOOK LIKE IT'S SEEN A STITCH OF HARDSHIP. AMAZING, INNIT?
HHHHHHILDA...
HER HUSBAND KEPT HER SET UP WELL...NICE HOUSE, SERVANTS, WANTING FOR NOTHING. YOU THINK YOU'LL JUST BE ABLE TO STEP INTO HIS SHOES WITH SOME PALTRY BITS OF DRIED MEAT AND PLEASANT CONVERSATION?
YOU FUCKING PEASANT.
SHE'S *MINE.*
KRIK KRAK

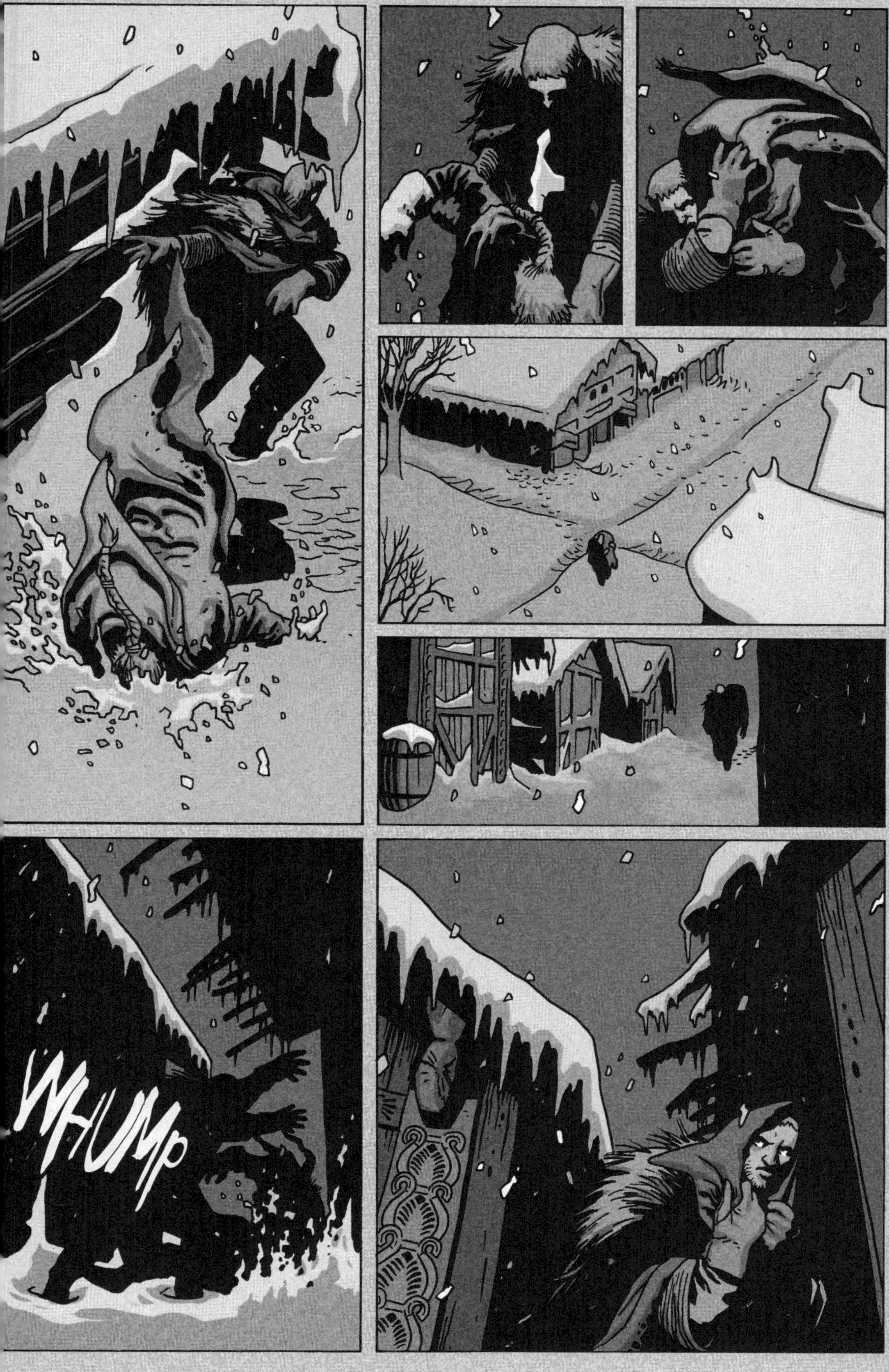
WHUMp

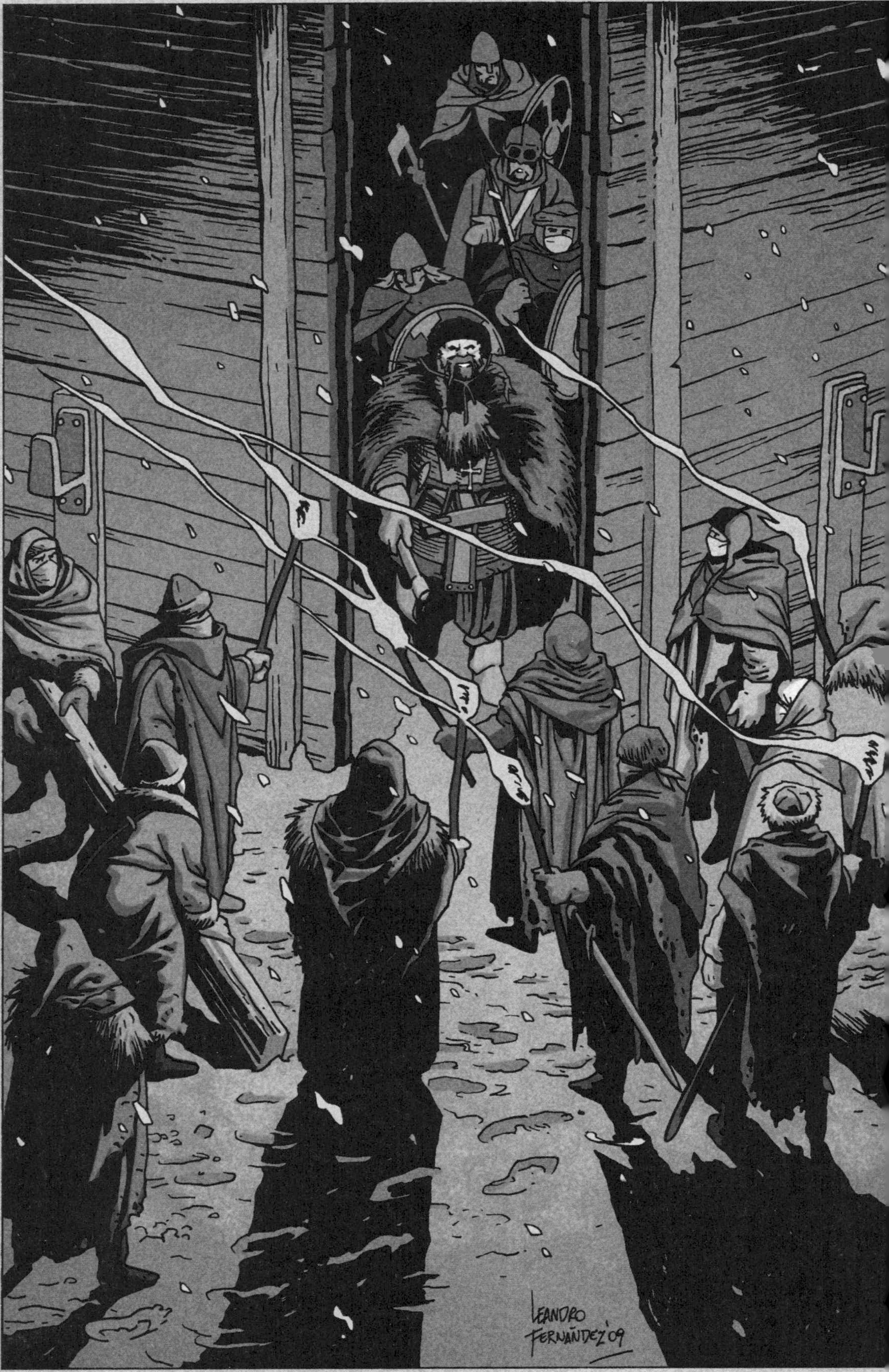
LEANDRO
FERNÁNDEZ '09

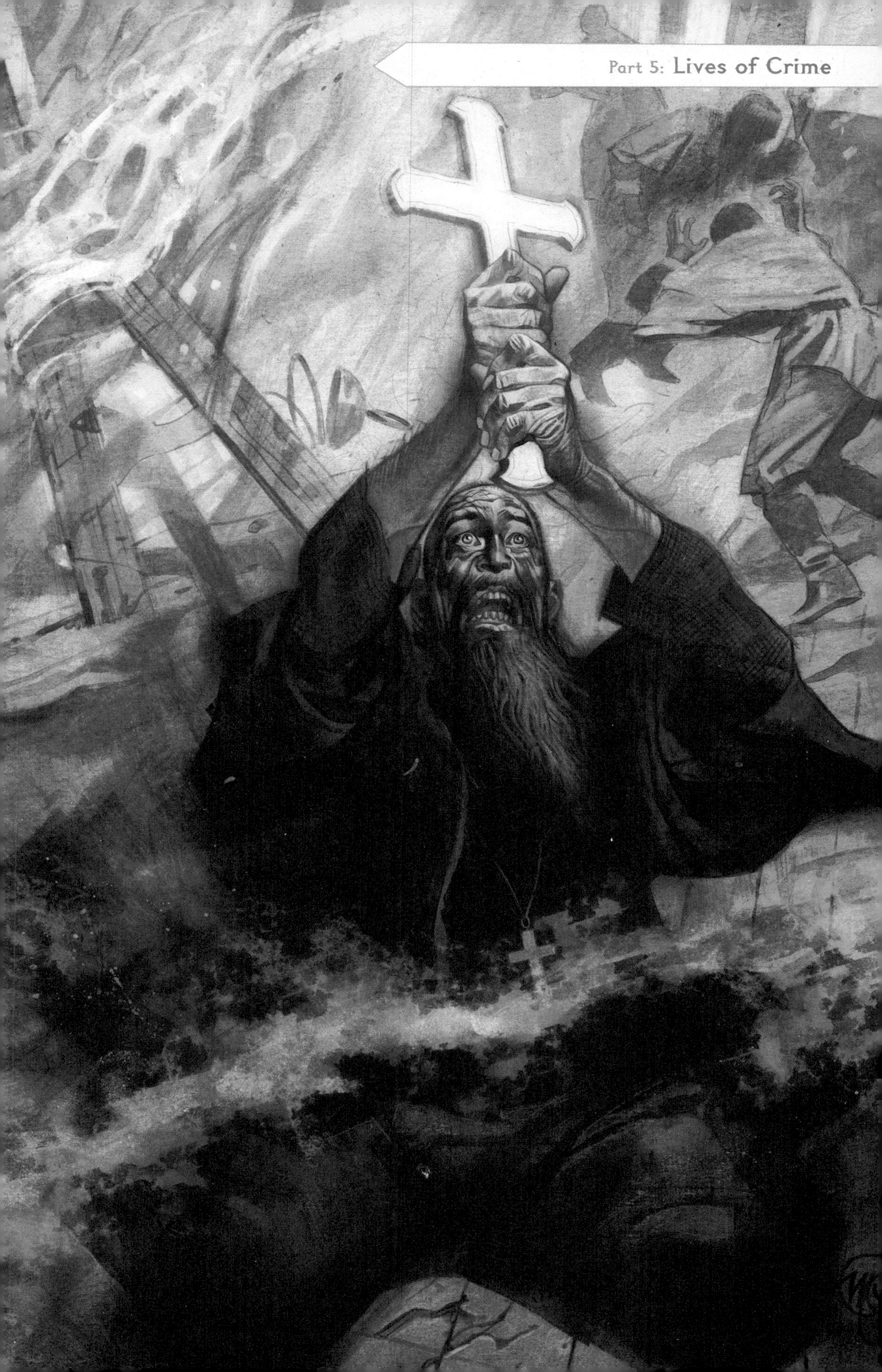

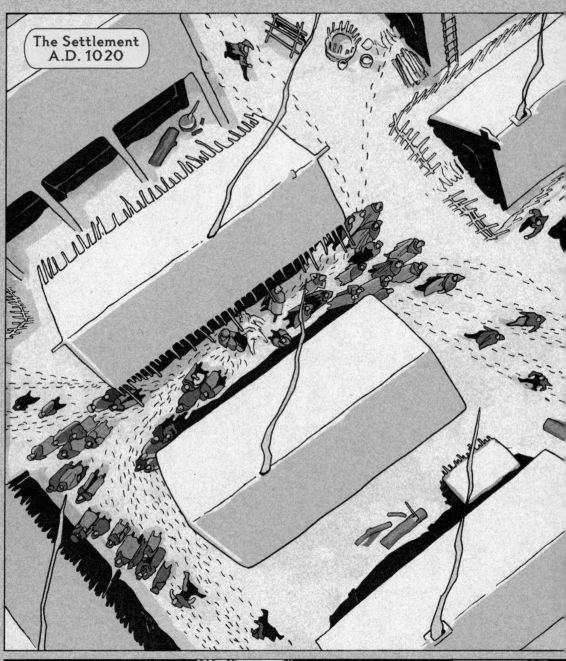

The Settlement
A.D. 1020

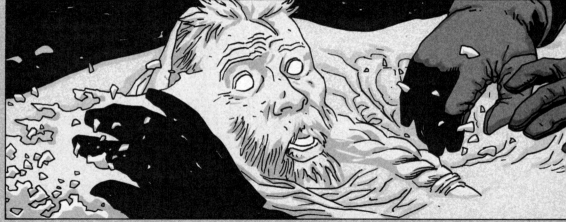

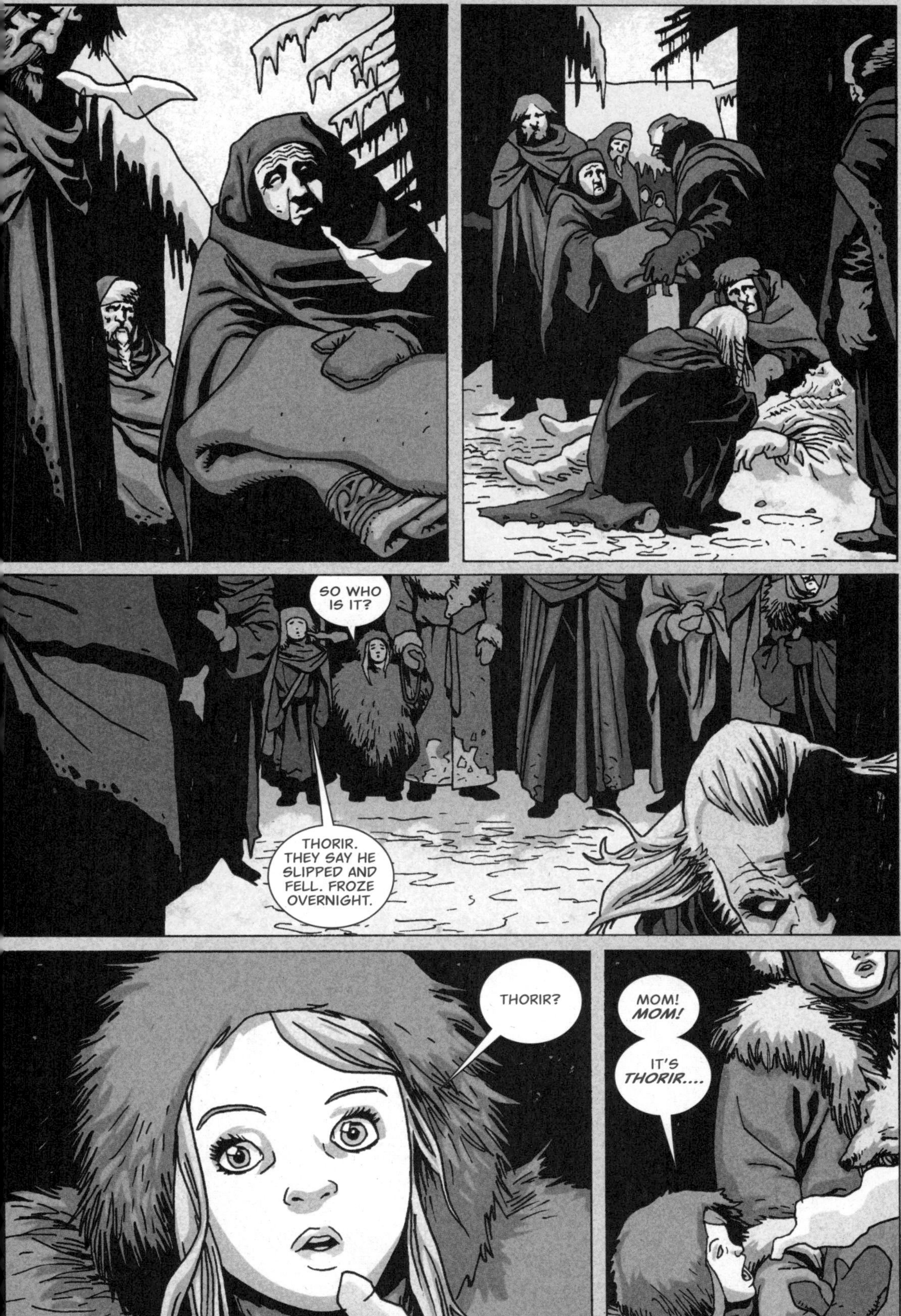
SO WHO IS IT?
THORIR. THEY SAY HE SLIPPED AND FELL. FROZE OVERNIGHT.
THORIR?
MOM! MOM!
IT'S THORIR....

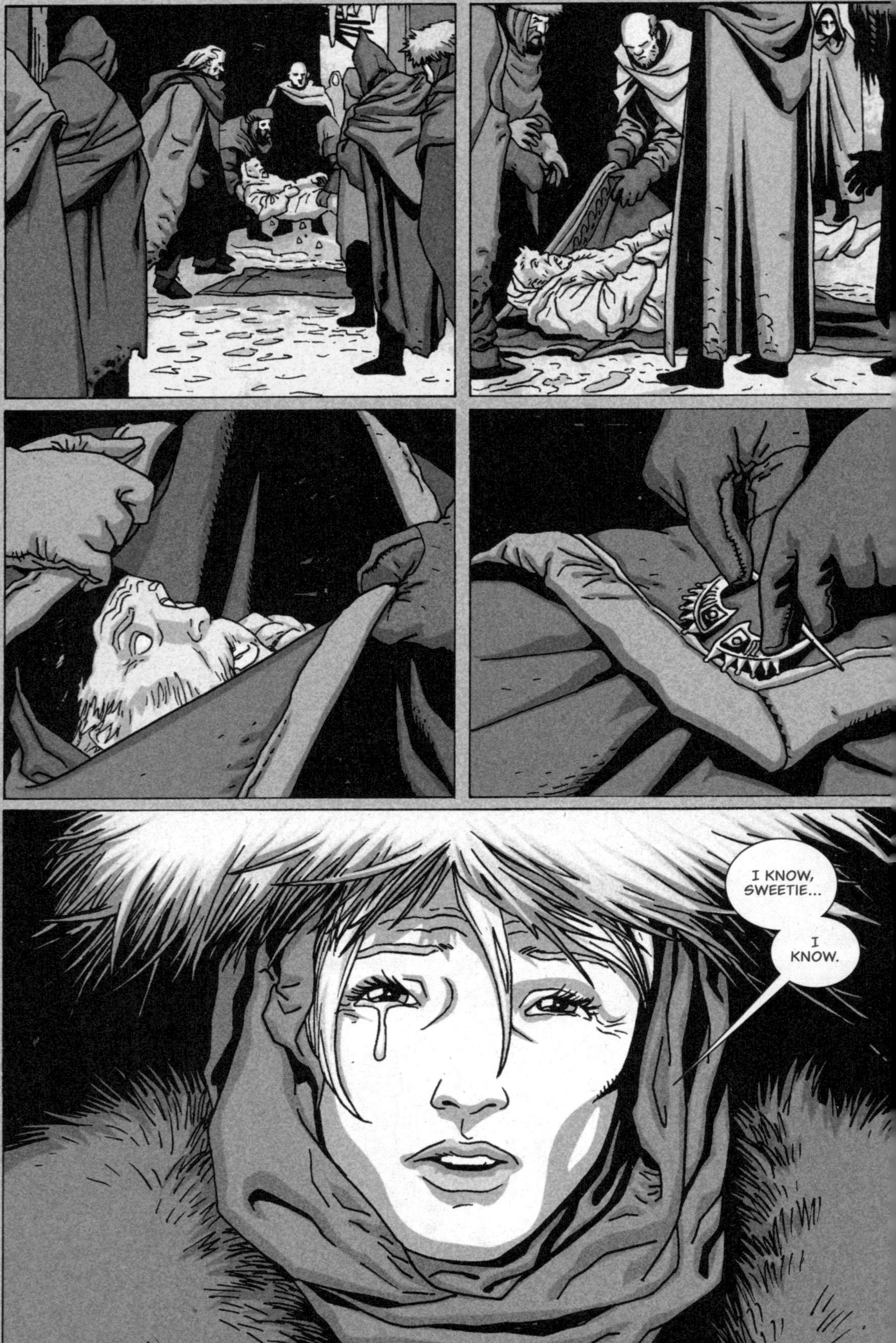
I KNOW, SWEETIE...
I KNOW.

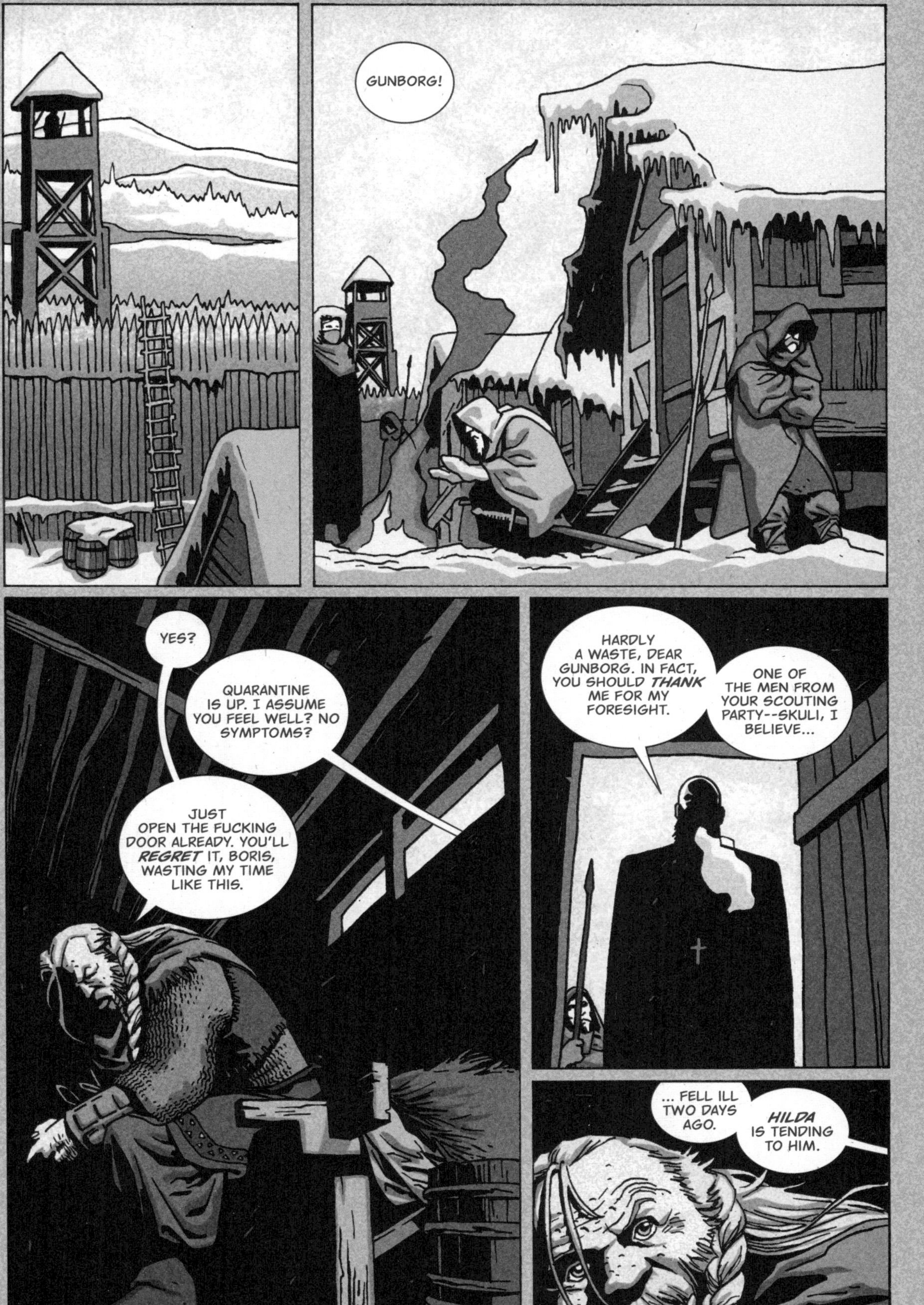
GUNBORG!
YES?
QUARANTINE IS UP. I ASSUME YOU FEEL WELL? NO SYMPTOMS?
JUST OPEN THE FUCKING DOOR ALREADY. YOU'LL REGRET IT, BORIS, WASTING MY TIME LIKE THIS.
HARDLY A WASTE, DEAR GUNBORG. IN FACT, YOU SHOULD THANK ME FOR MY FORESIGHT.
ONE OF THE MEN FROM YOUR SCOUTING PARTY--SKULI, I BELIEVE...
... FELL ILL TWO DAYS AGO.
HILDA IS TENDING TO HIM.

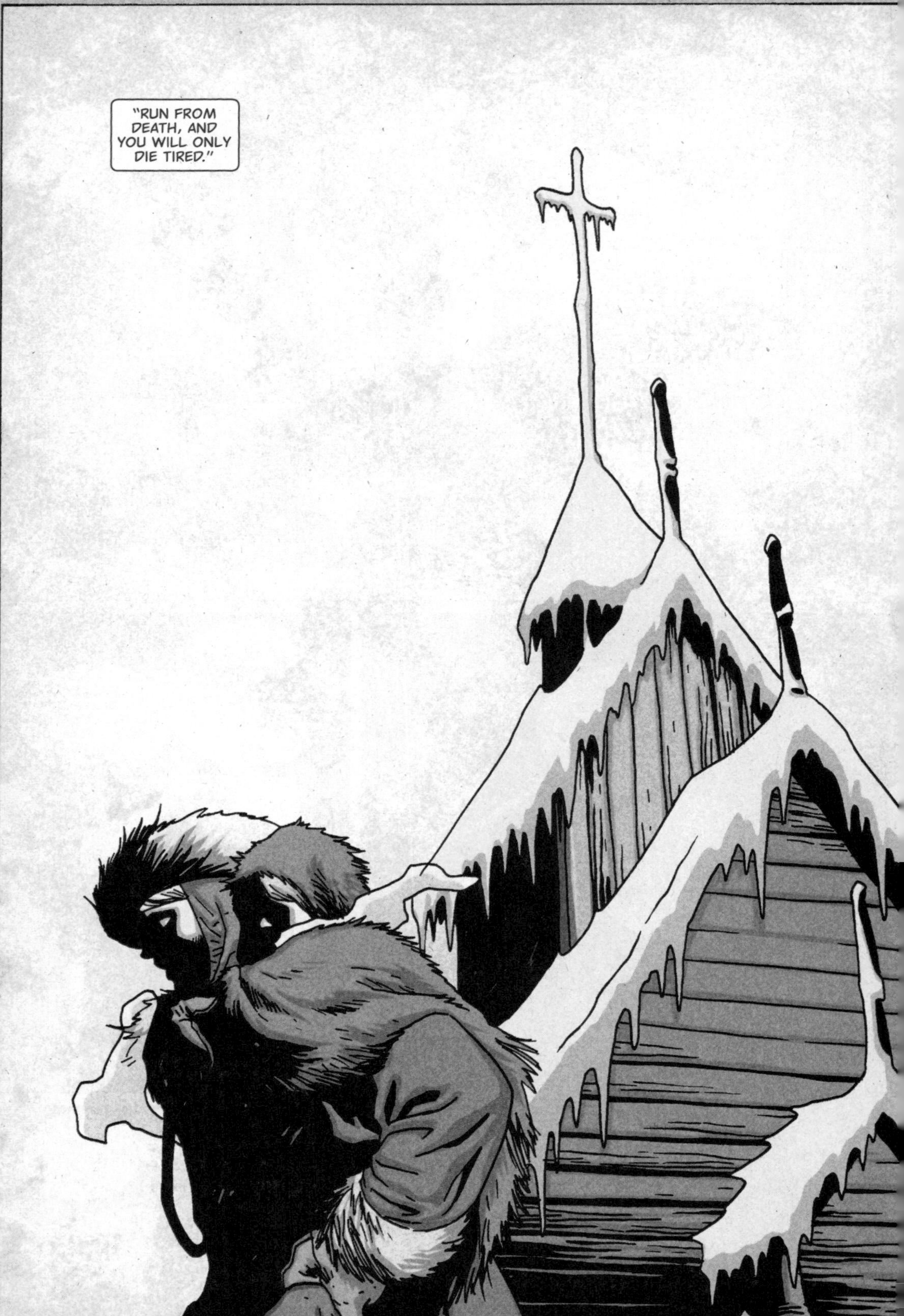
"RUN FROM DEATH, AND YOU WILL ONLY DIE TIRED."

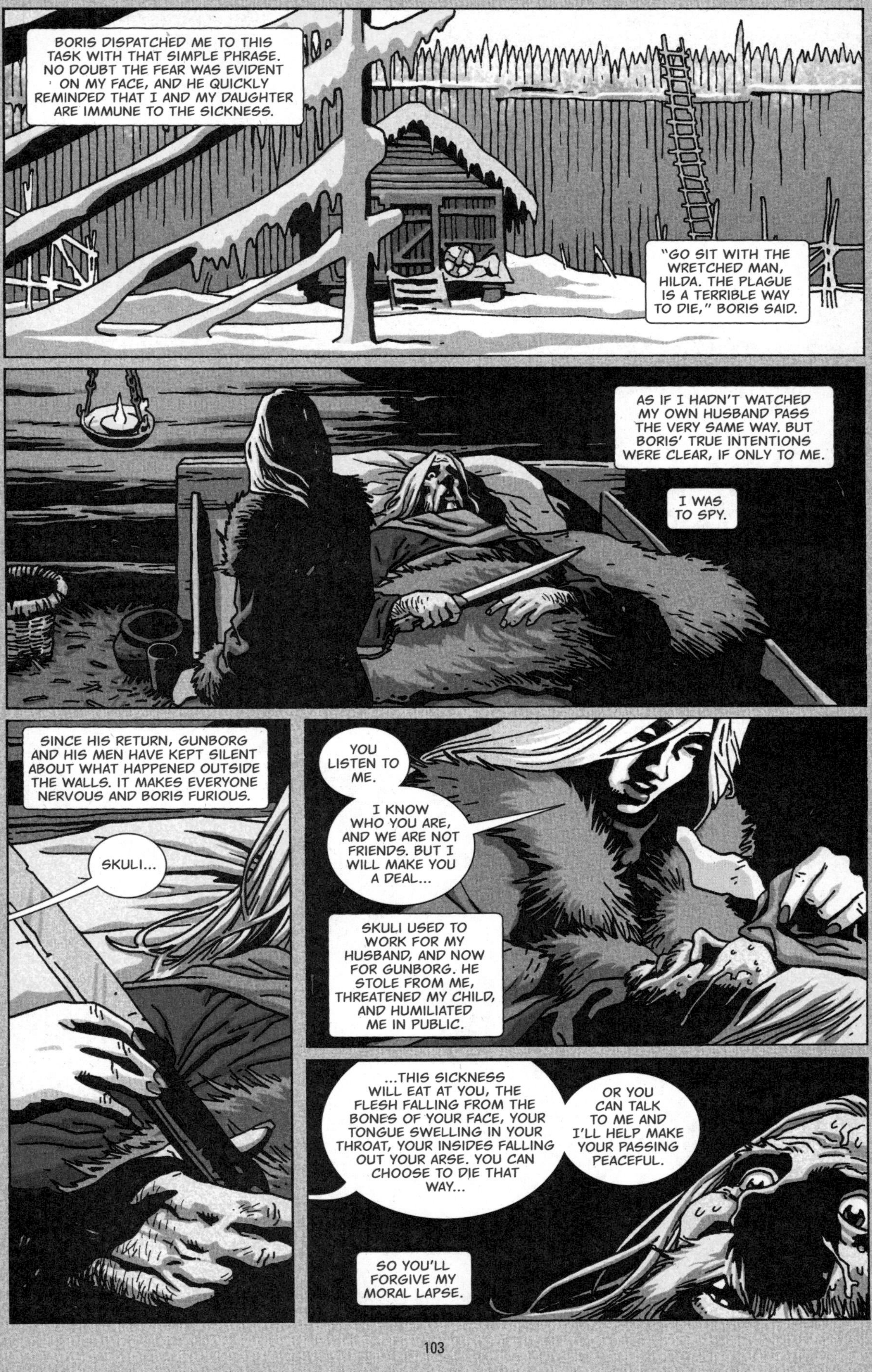
BORIS DISPATCHED ME TO THIS TASK WITH THAT SIMPLE PHRASE. NO DOUBT THE FEAR WAS EVIDENT ON MY FACE, AND HE QUICKLY REMINDED THAT I AND MY DAUGHTER ARE IMMUNE TO THE SICKNESS.
"GO SIT WITH THE WRETCHED MAN, HILDA. THE PLAGUE IS A TERRIBLE WAY TO DIE," BORIS SAID.
AS IF I HADN'T WATCHED MY OWN HUSBAND PASS THE VERY SAME WAY. BUT BORIS' TRUE INTENTIONS WERE CLEAR, IF ONLY TO ME.
I WAS TO SPY.
SINCE HIS RETURN, GUNBORG AND HIS MEN HAVE KEPT SILENT ABOUT WHAT HAPPENED OUTSIDE THE WALLS. IT MAKES EVERYONE NERVOUS AND BORIS FURIOUS.
SKULI...
YOU LISTEN TO ME.
I KNOW WHO YOU ARE, AND WE ARE NOT FRIENDS. BUT I WILL MAKE YOU A DEAL...
SKULI USED TO WORK FOR MY HUSBAND, AND NOW FOR GUNBORG. HE STOLE FROM ME, THREATENED MY CHILD, AND HUMILIATED ME IN PUBLIC.
...THIS SICKNESS WILL EAT AT YOU, THE FLESH FALLING FROM THE BONES OF YOUR FACE, YOUR TONGUE SWELLING IN YOUR THROAT, YOUR INSIDES FALLING OUT YOUR ARSE. YOU CAN CHOOSE TO DIE THAT WAY...
OR YOU CAN TALK TO ME AND I'LL HELP MAKE YOUR PASSING PEACEFUL.
SO YOU'LL FORGIVE MY MORAL LAPSE.

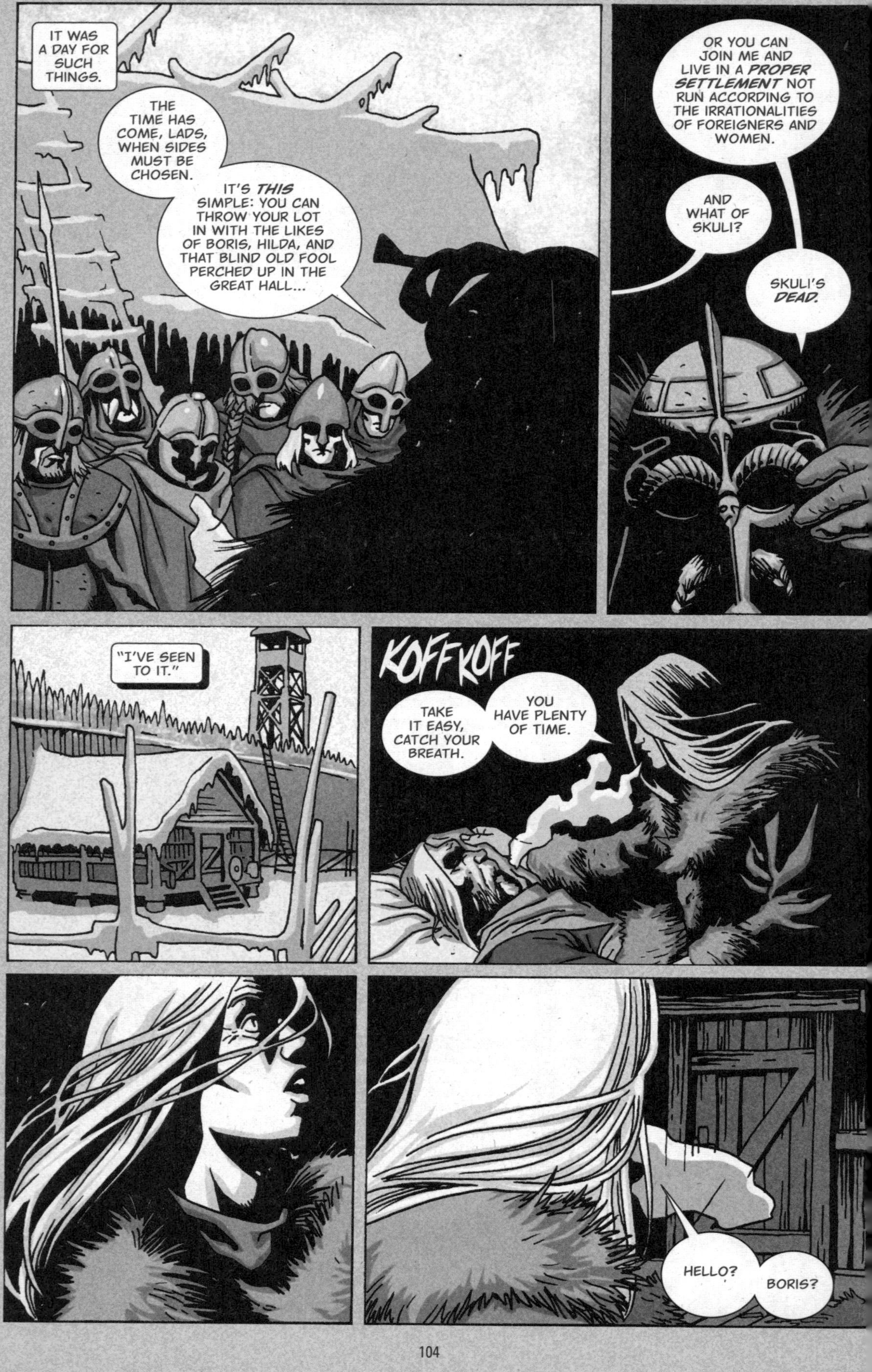

IT WAS A DAY FOR SUCH THINGS.
THE TIME HAS COME, LADS, WHEN SIDES MUST BE CHOSEN.
IT'S THIS SIMPLE: YOU CAN THROW YOUR LOT IN WITH THE LIKES OF BORIS, HILDA, AND THAT BLIND OLD FOOL PERCHED UP IN THE GREAT HALL...
OR YOU CAN JOIN ME AND LIVE IN A PROPER SETTLEMENT NOT RUN ACCORDING TO THE IRRATIONALITIES OF FOREIGNERS AND WOMEN.
AND WHAT OF SKULI?
SKULI'S DEAD.
"I'VE SEEN TO IT."
KOFF KOFF
TAKE IT EASY, CATCH YOUR BREATH.
YOU HAVE PLENTY OF TIME.
HELLO?
BORIS?

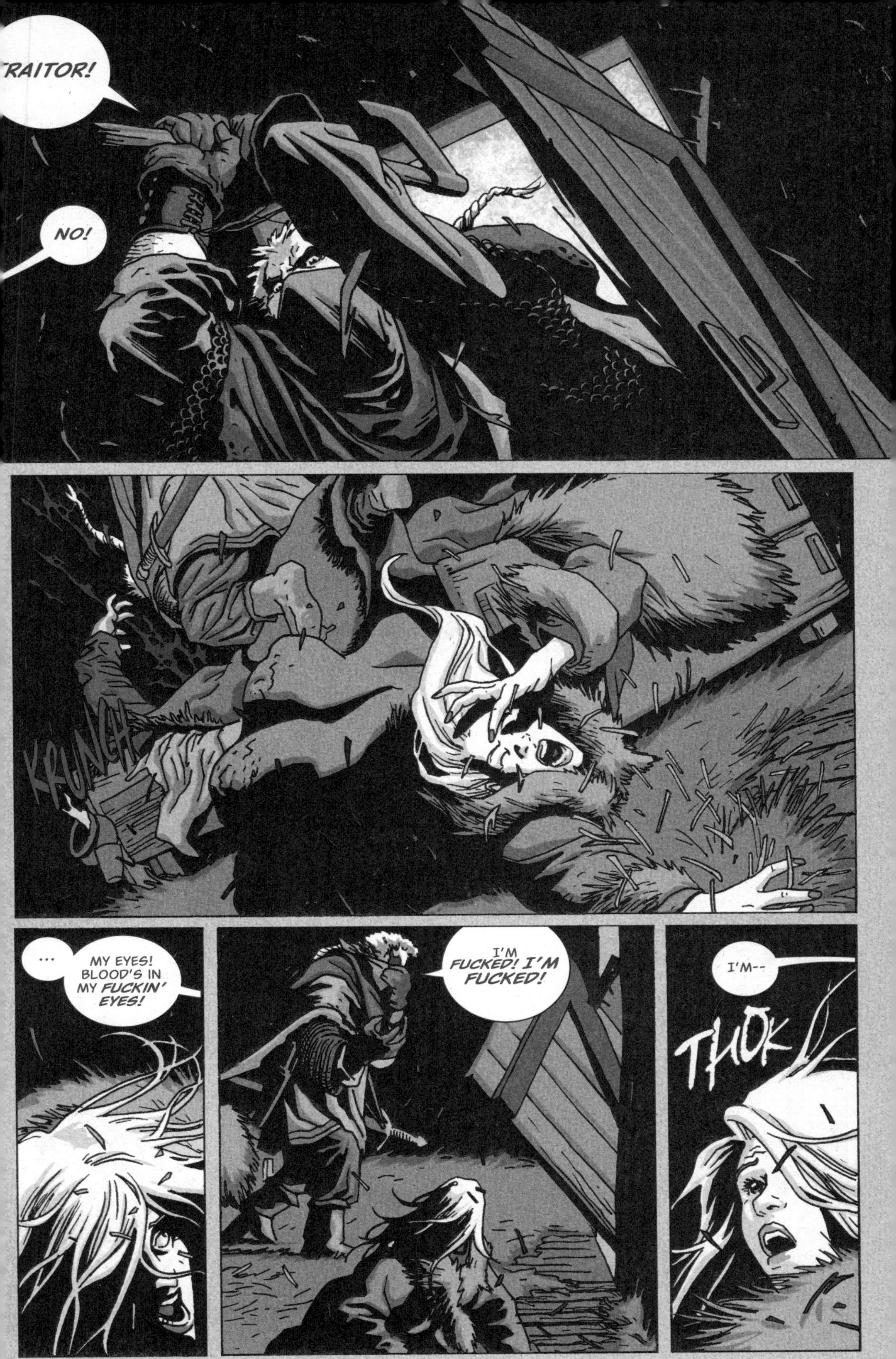

TRAITOR!
NO!
KRUNCH
...
MY EYES! BLOOD'S IN MY FUCKIN' EYES!
I'M FUCKED! I'M FUCKED!
I'M--
THOK

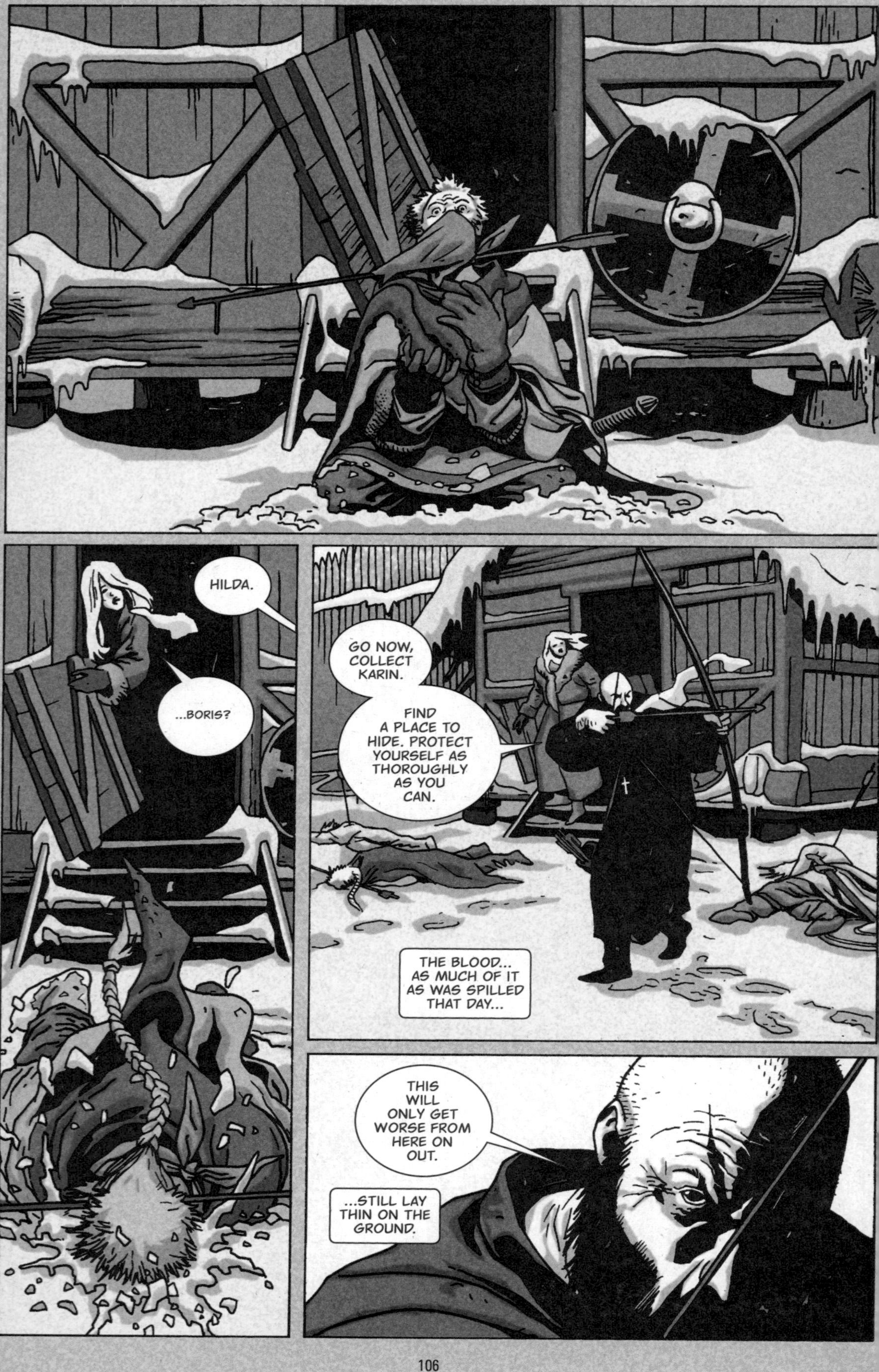
HILDA.
...BORIS?
GO NOW, COLLECT KARIN.
FIND A PLACE TO HIDE. PROTECT YOURSELF AS THOROUGHLY AS YOU CAN.
THE BLOOD... AS MUCH OF IT AS WAS SPILLED THAT DAY...
THIS WILL ONLY GET WORSE FROM HERE ON OUT.
...STILL LAY THIN ON THE GROUND.

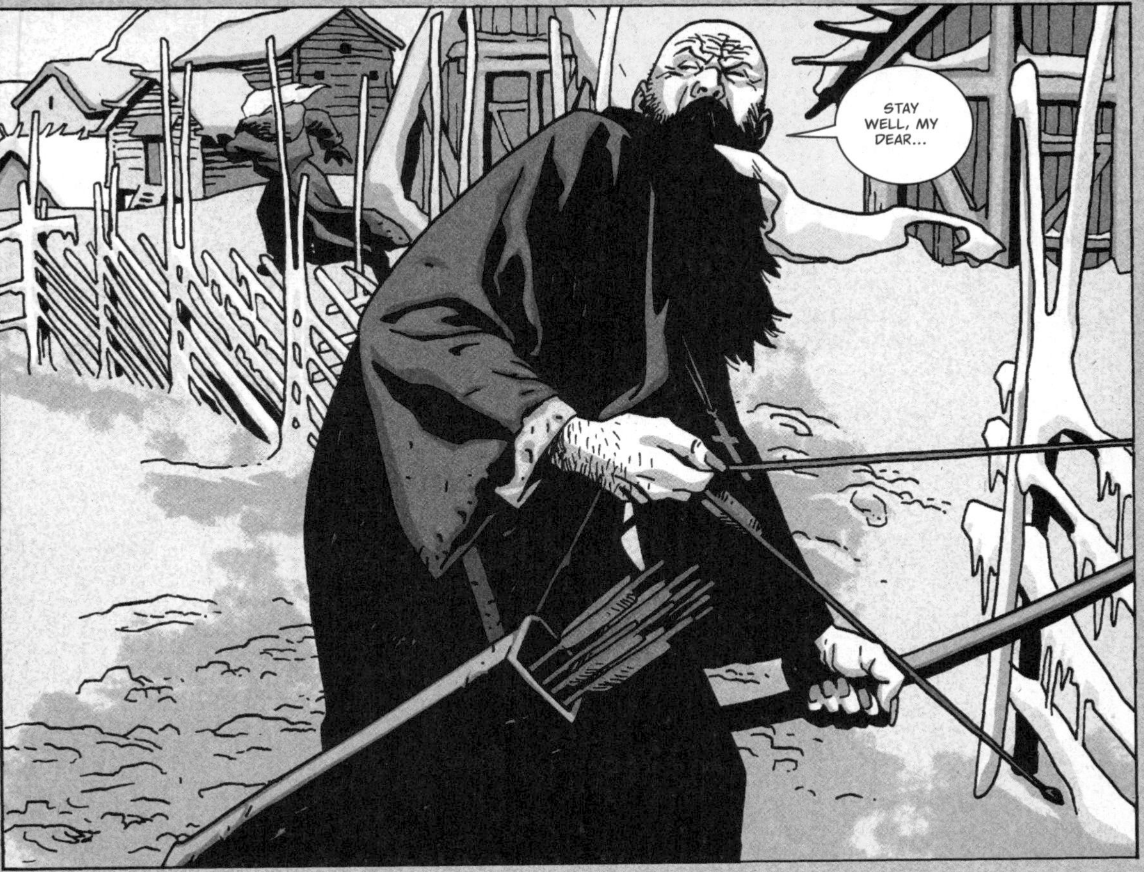
STAY WELL, MY DEAR...

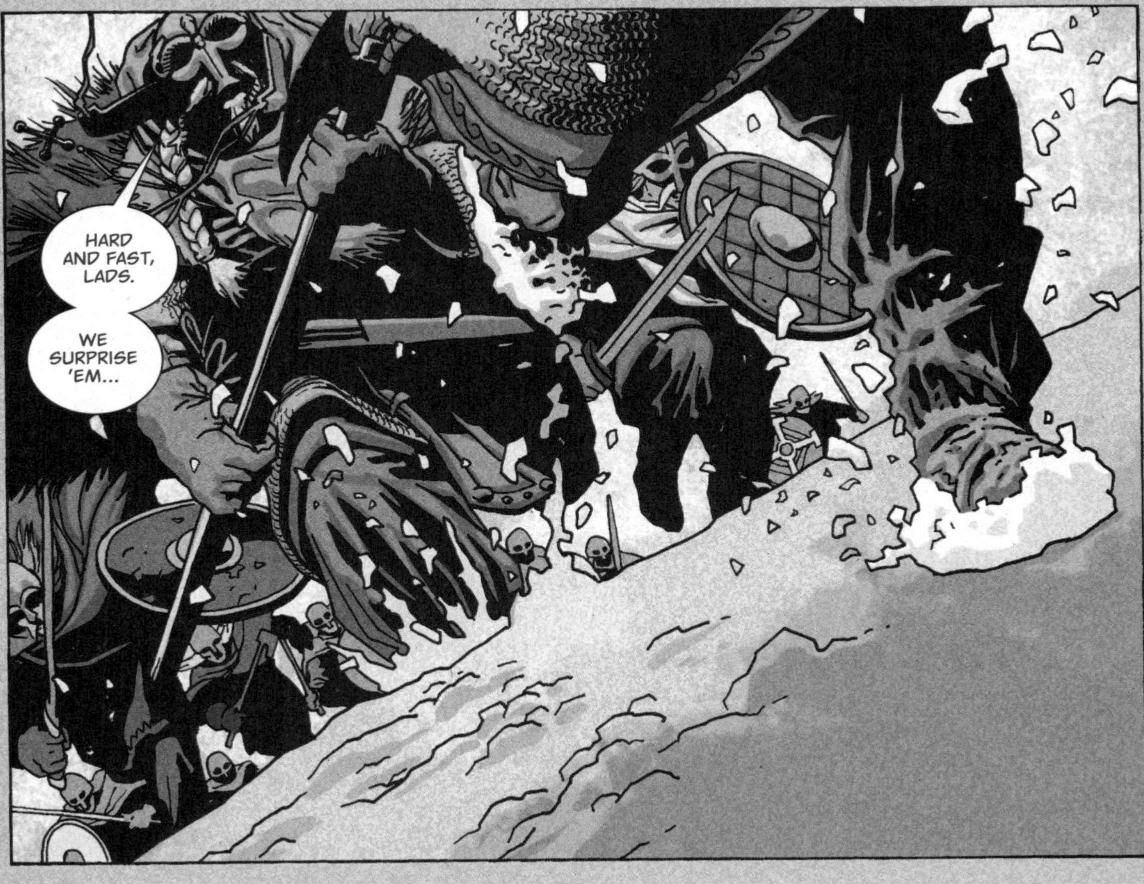
HARD AND FAST, LADS.
WE SURPRISE 'EM...

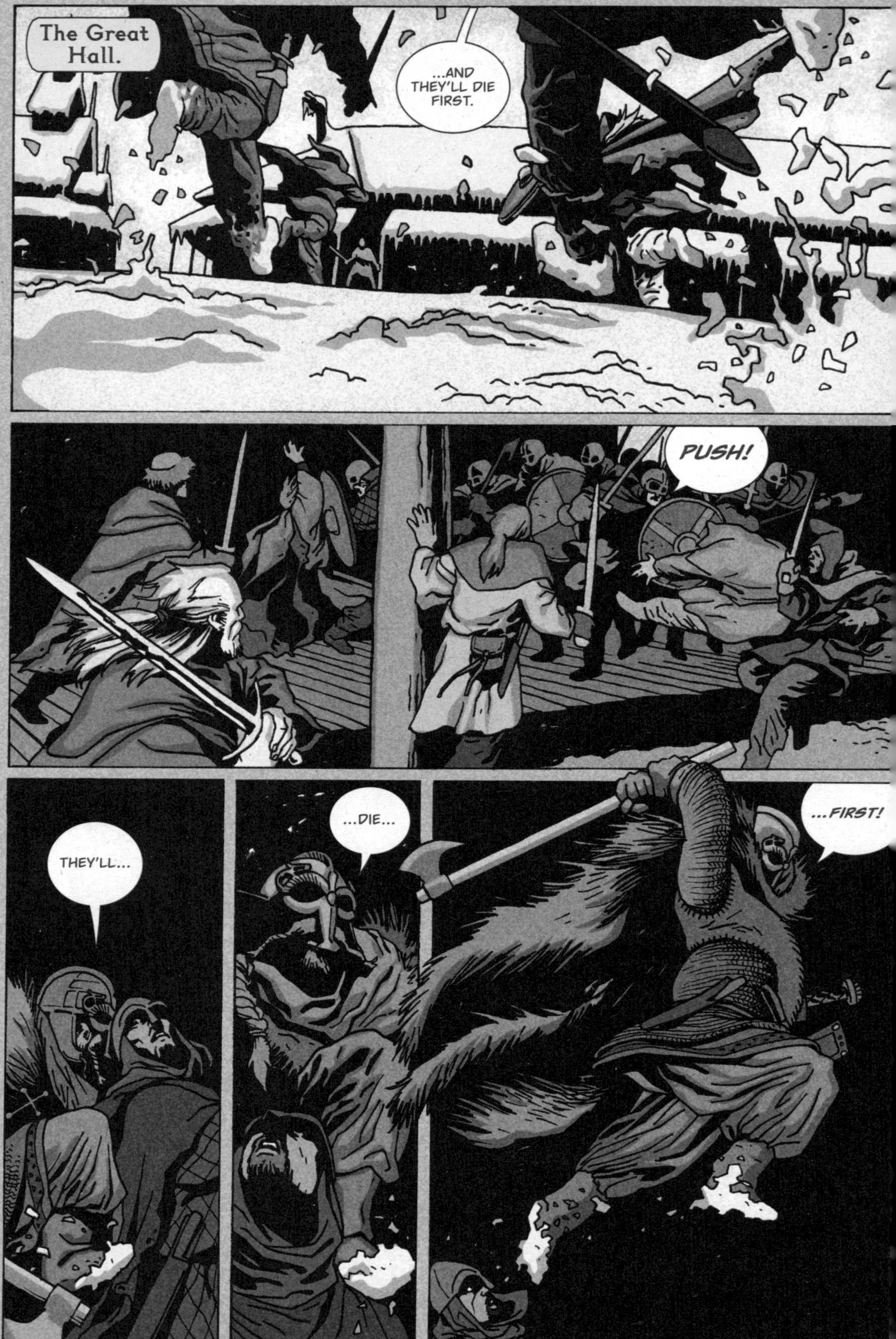
The Great Hall.
...AND THEY'LL DIE FIRST.
PUSH!
THEY'LL...
...DIE...
...FIRST!

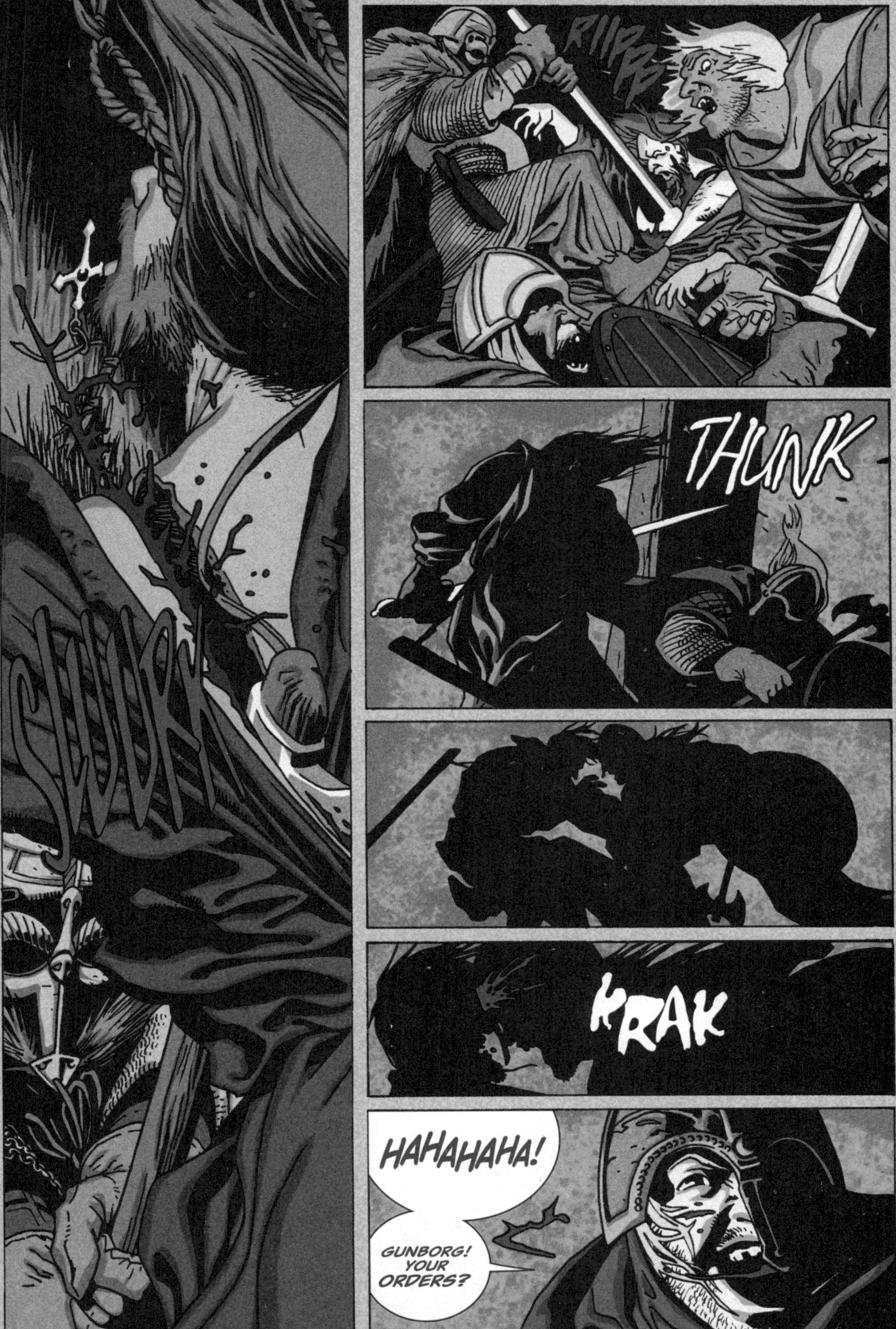
RIIPP
THUNK
KRAK
HAHAHAHA!
GUNBORG! YOUR ORDERS?

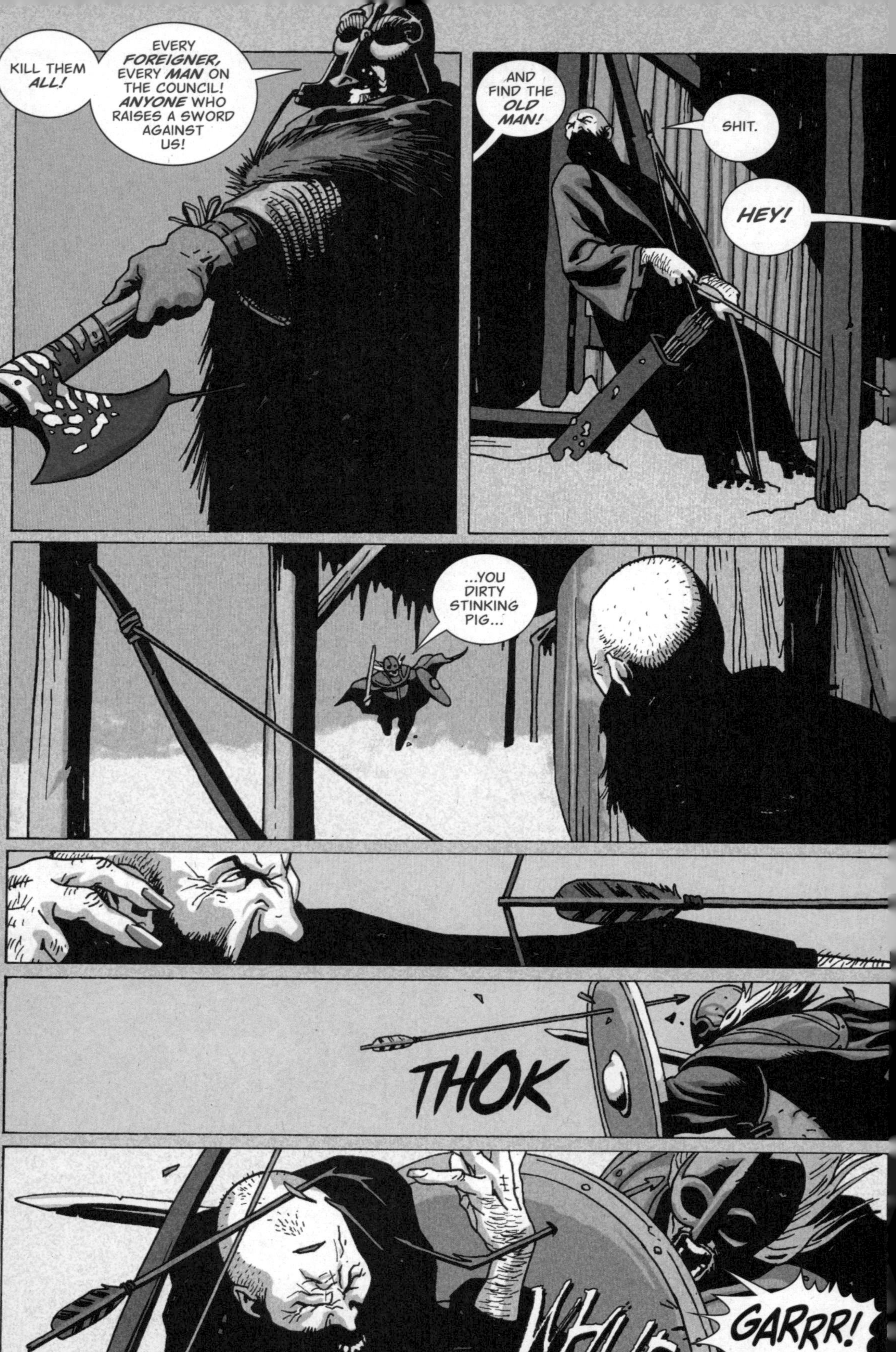
KILL THEM ALL!
EVERY FOREIGNER, EVERY MAN ON THE COUNCIL! ANYONE WHO RAISES A SWORD AGAINST US!
AND FIND THE OLD MAN!
SHIT.
HEY!
...YOU DIRTY STINKING PIG...
THOK
WHUF
GARRR!

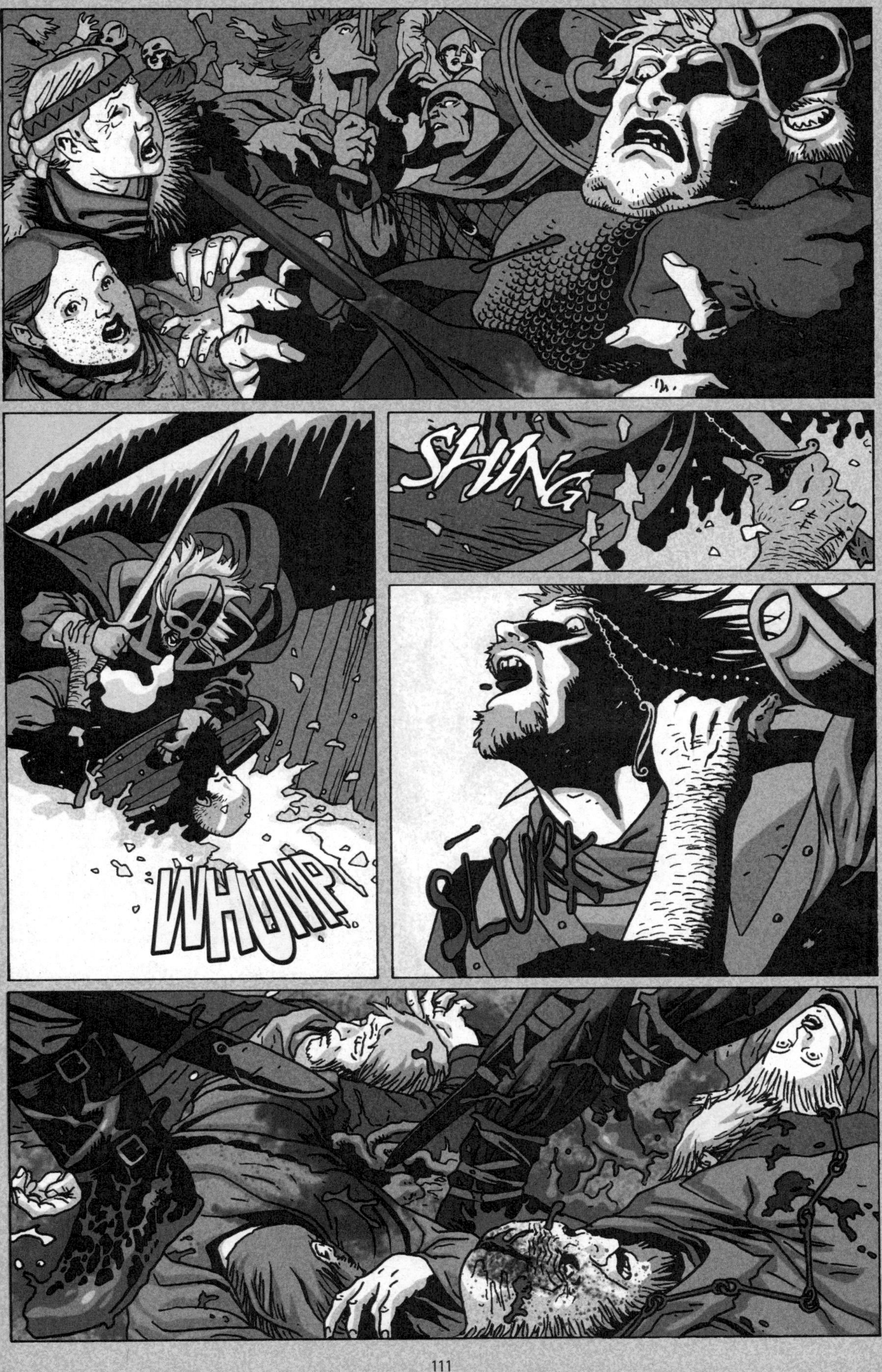
WHUMP
SHING
SLURK

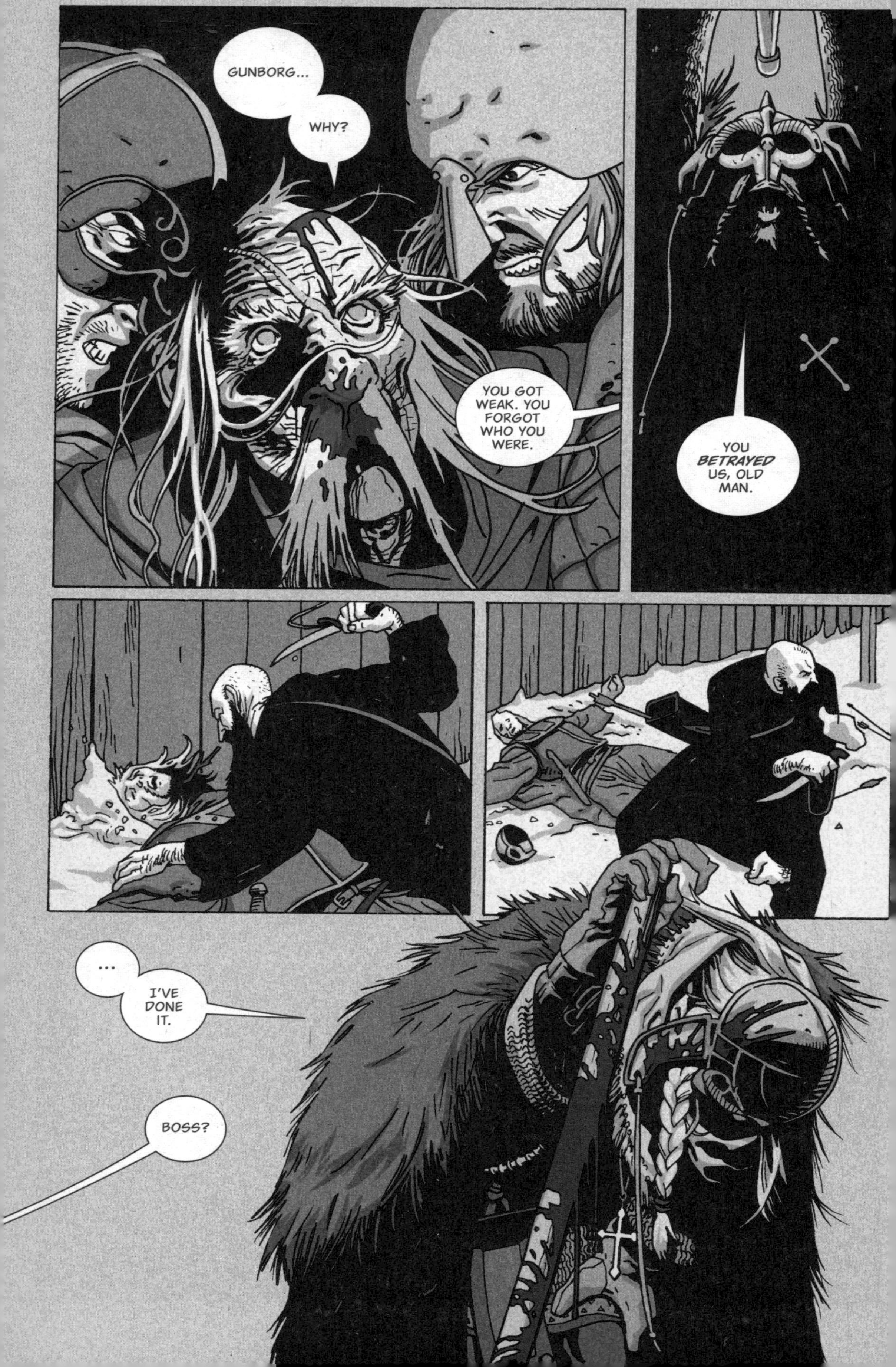
GUNBORG...
WHY?
YOU GOT WEAK. YOU FORGOT WHO YOU WERE.
YOU *BETRAYED* US, OLD MAN.
... I'VE DONE IT.
BOSS?

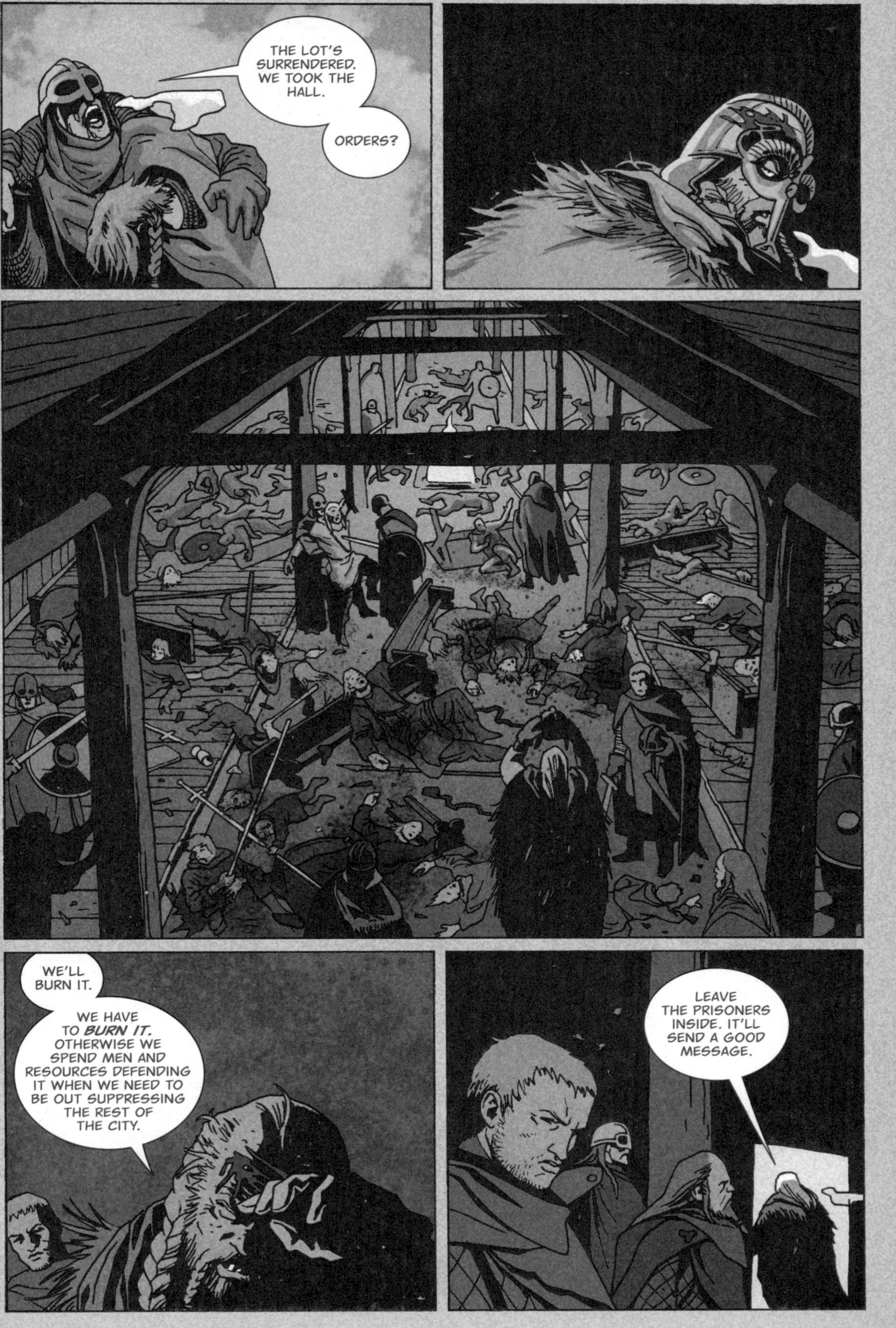
THE LOT'S SURRENDERED. WE TOOK THE HALL.
ORDERS?
WE'LL BURN IT.
WE HAVE TO *BURN IT.* OTHERWISE WE SPEND MEN AND RESOURCES DEFENDING IT WHEN WE NEED TO BE OUT SUPPRESSING THE REST OF THE CITY.
LEAVE THE PRISONERS INSIDE. IT'LL SEND A GOOD MESSAGE.

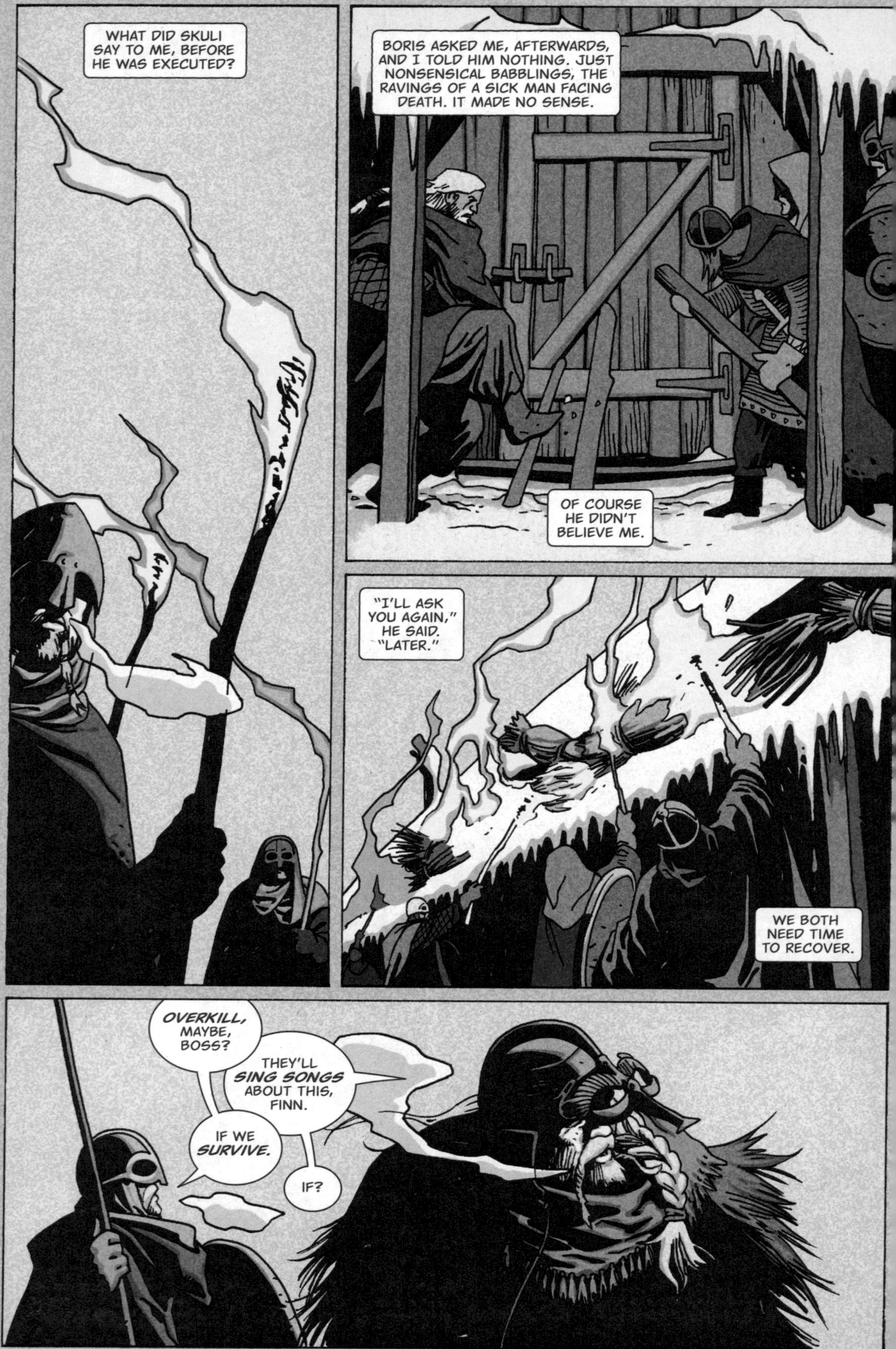
WHAT DID SKULI SAY TO ME, BEFORE HE WAS EXECUTED?
BORIS ASKED ME, AFTERWARDS, AND I TOLD HIM NOTHING. JUST NONSENSICAL BABBLINGS, THE RAVINGS OF A SICK MAN FACING DEATH. IT MADE NO SENSE.
OF COURSE HE DIDN'T BELIEVE ME.
"I'LL ASK YOU AGAIN," HE SAID. "LATER."
WE BOTH NEED TIME TO RECOVER.
OVERKILL, MAYBE, BOSS?
THEY'LL SING SONGS ABOUT THIS, FINN.
IF WE SURVIVE.
IF?

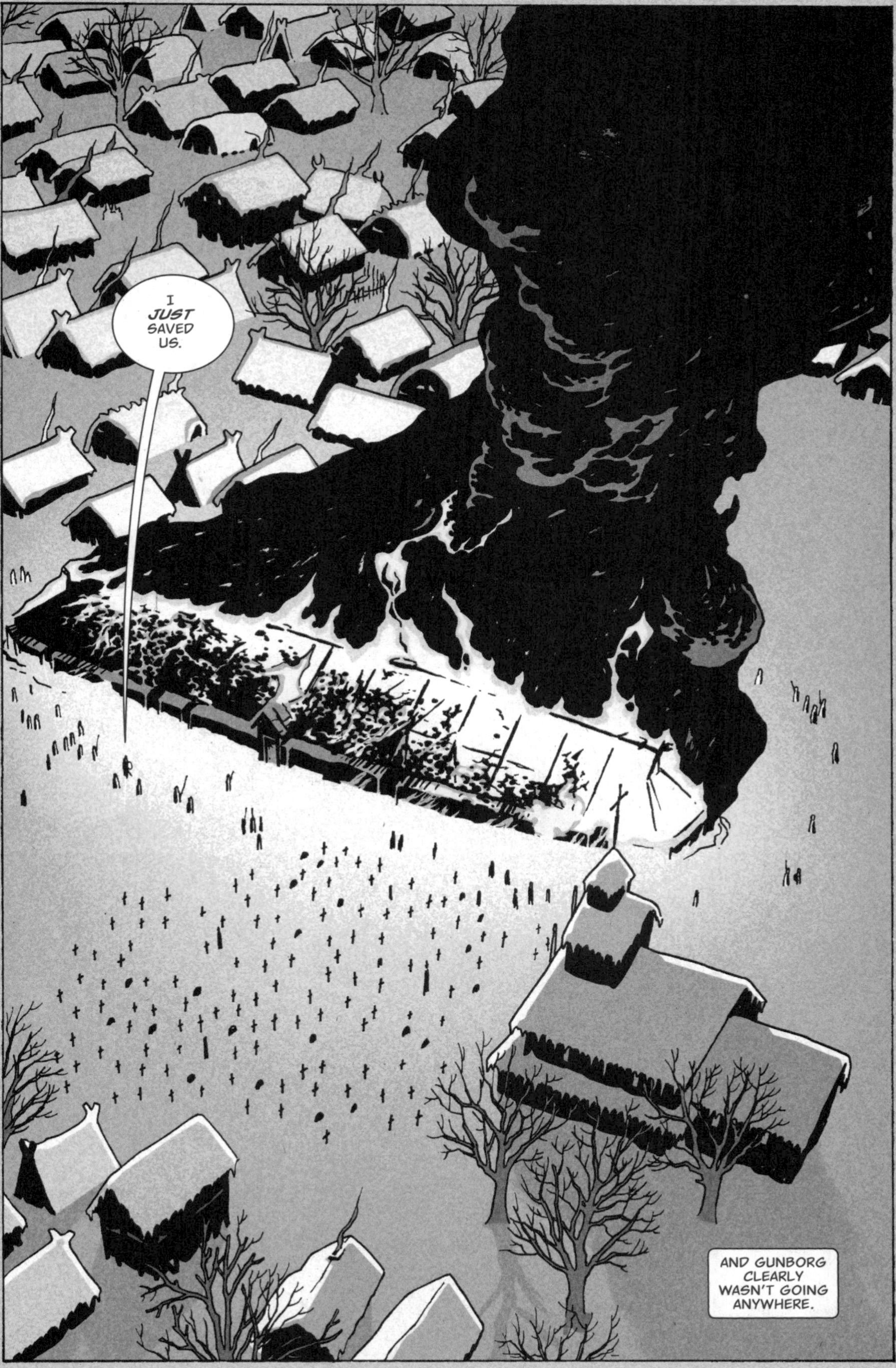
I JUST SAVED US.
AND GUNBORG CLEARLY WASN'T GOING ANYWHERE.

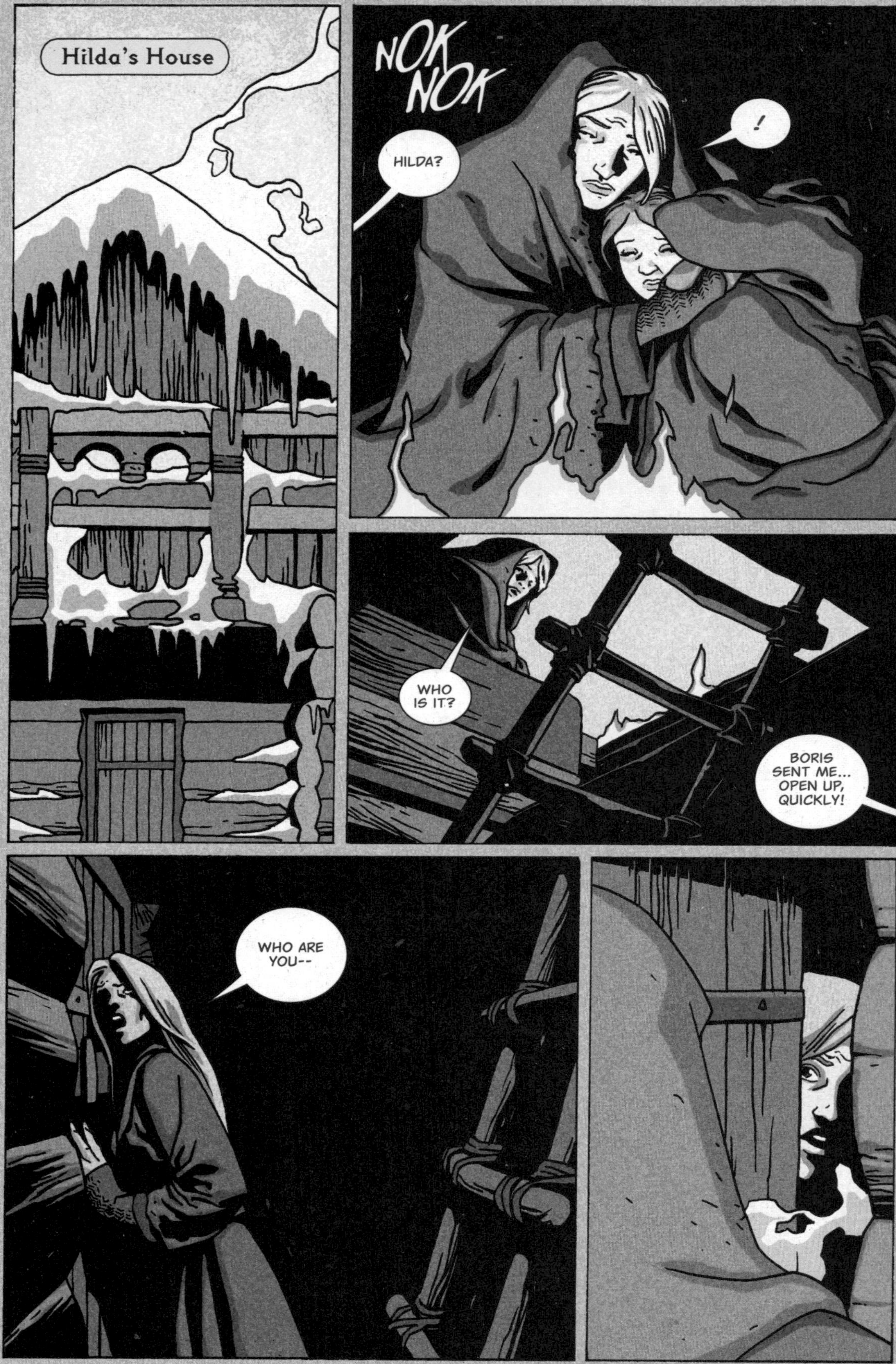
Hilda's House
NOK NOK
HILDA?
!
WHO IS IT?
BORIS SENT ME... OPEN UP, QUICKLY!
WHO ARE YOU--

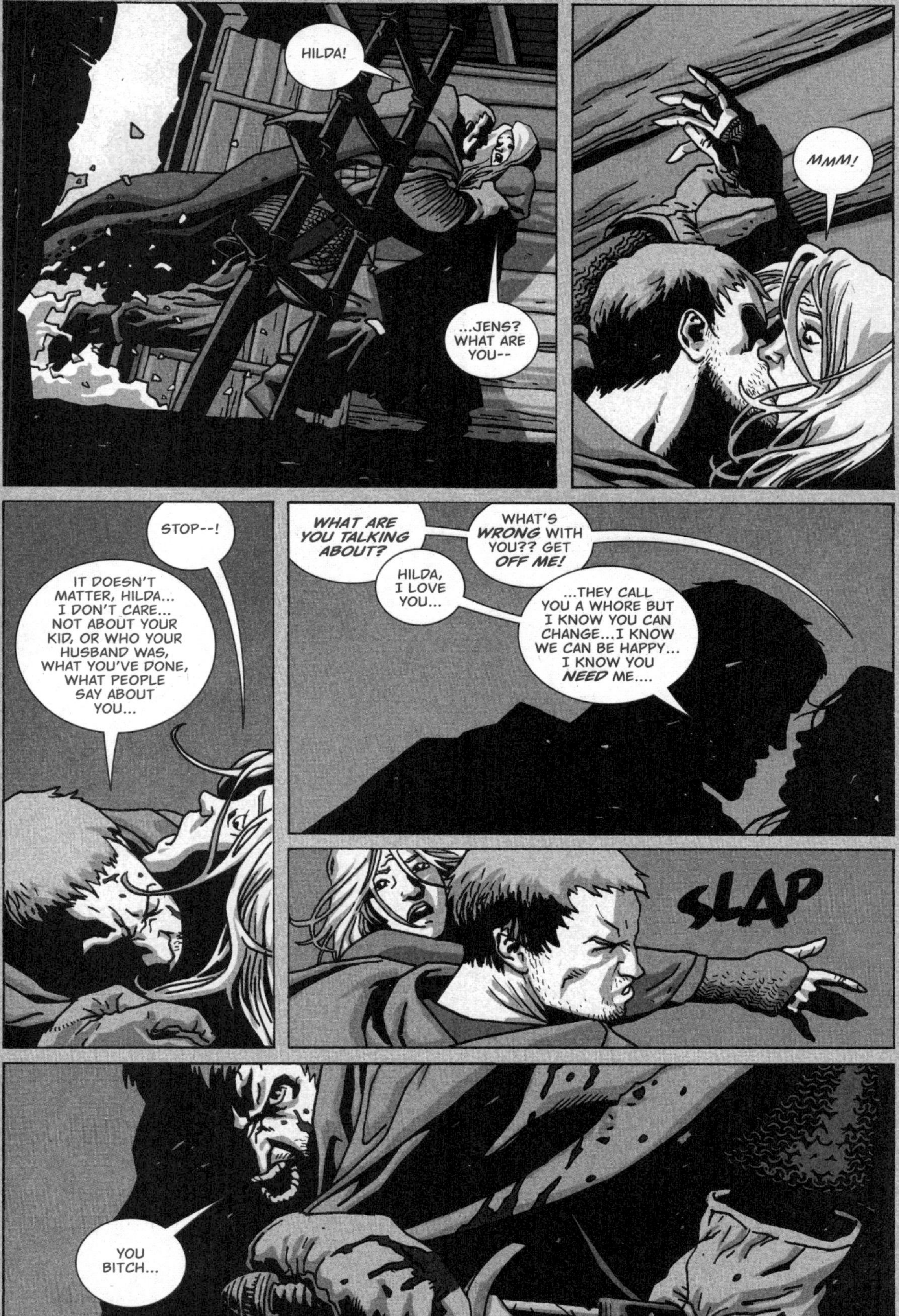
HILDA!
...JENS? WHAT ARE YOU--
MMM!
STOP--!
IT DOESN'T MATTER, HILDA... I DON'T CARE... NOT ABOUT YOUR KID, OR WHO YOUR HUSBAND WAS, WHAT YOU'VE DONE, WHAT PEOPLE SAY ABOUT YOU...
WHAT ARE YOU TALKING ABOUT?
WHAT'S WRONG WITH YOU?? GET OFF ME!
HILDA, I LOVE YOU...
...THEY CALL YOU A WHORE BUT I KNOW YOU CAN CHANGE...I KNOW WE CAN BE HAPPY... I KNOW YOU NEED ME....
SLAP
YOU BITCH...

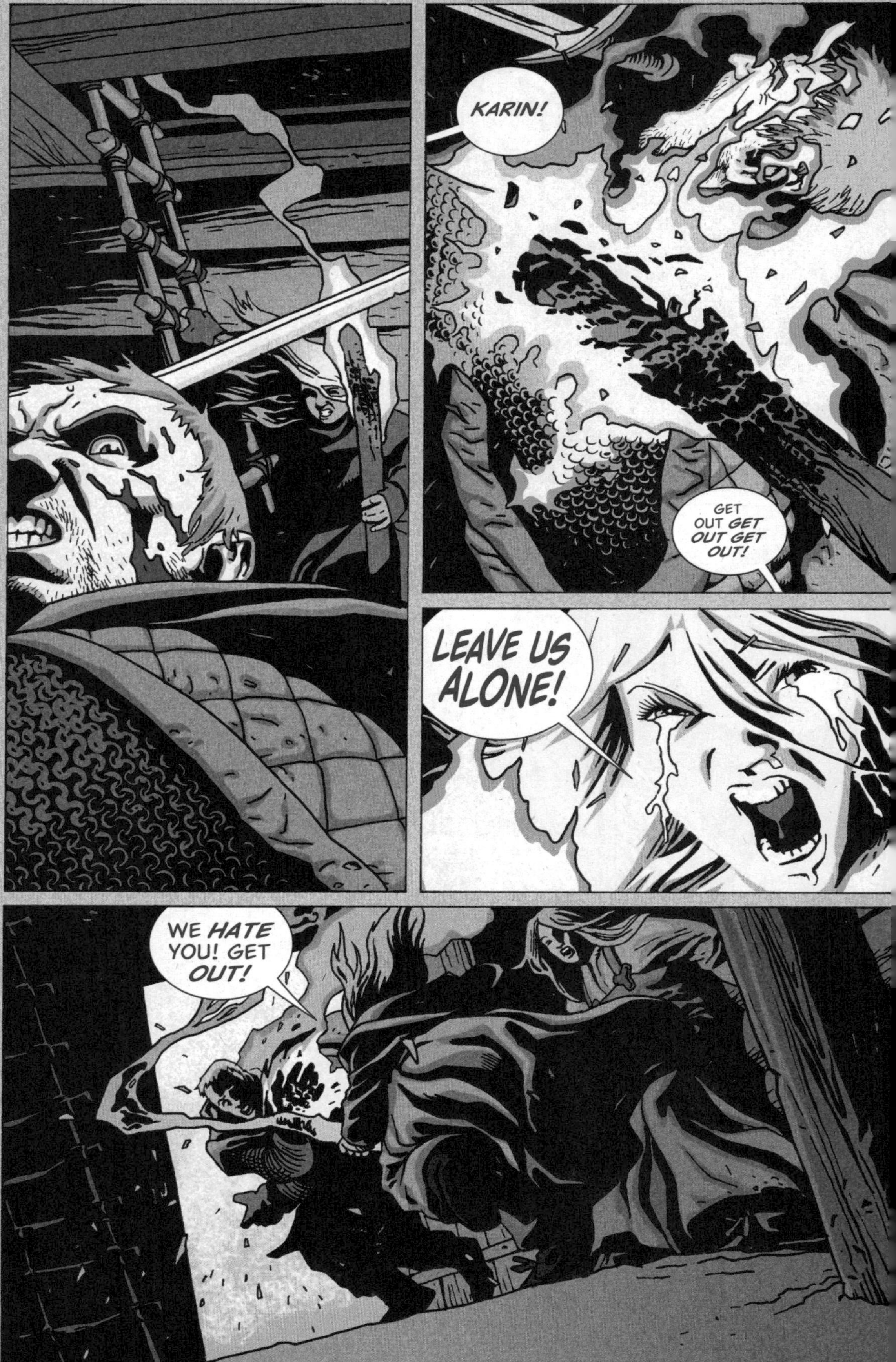
KARIN!
GET OUT GET OUT GET OUT!
LEAVE US ALONE!
WE HATE YOU! GET OUT!

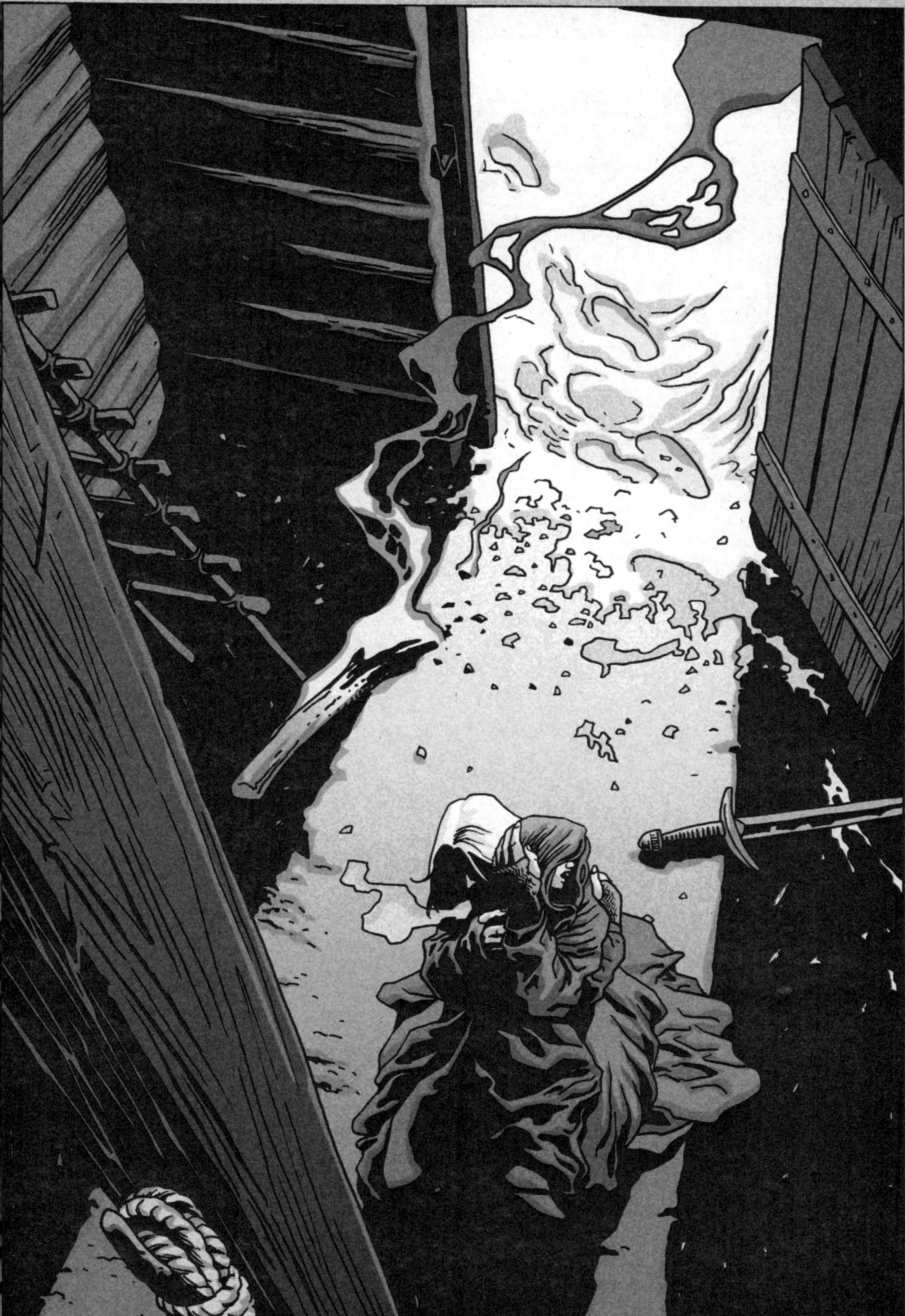
LEANDRO
FERNANDEZ '10

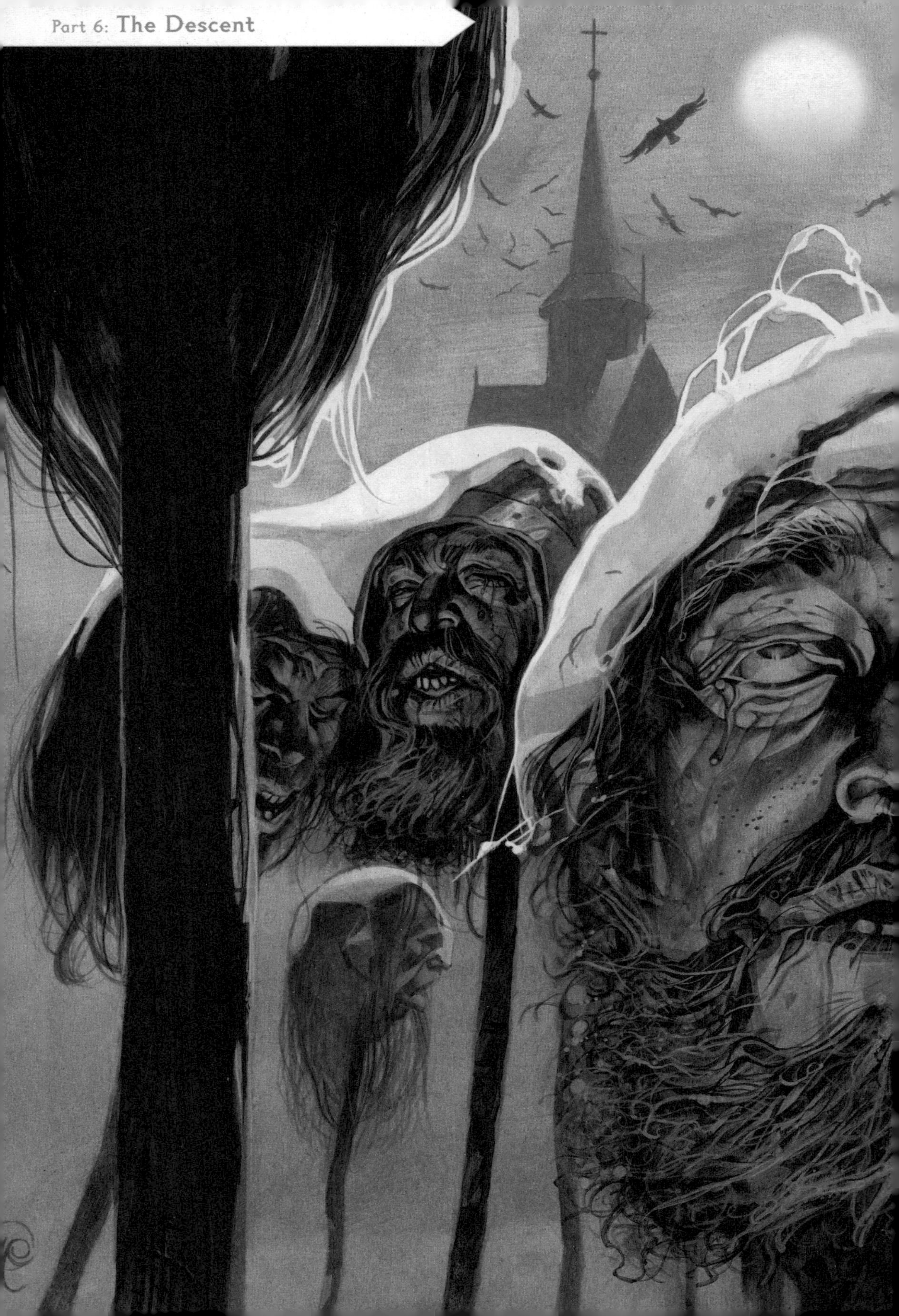

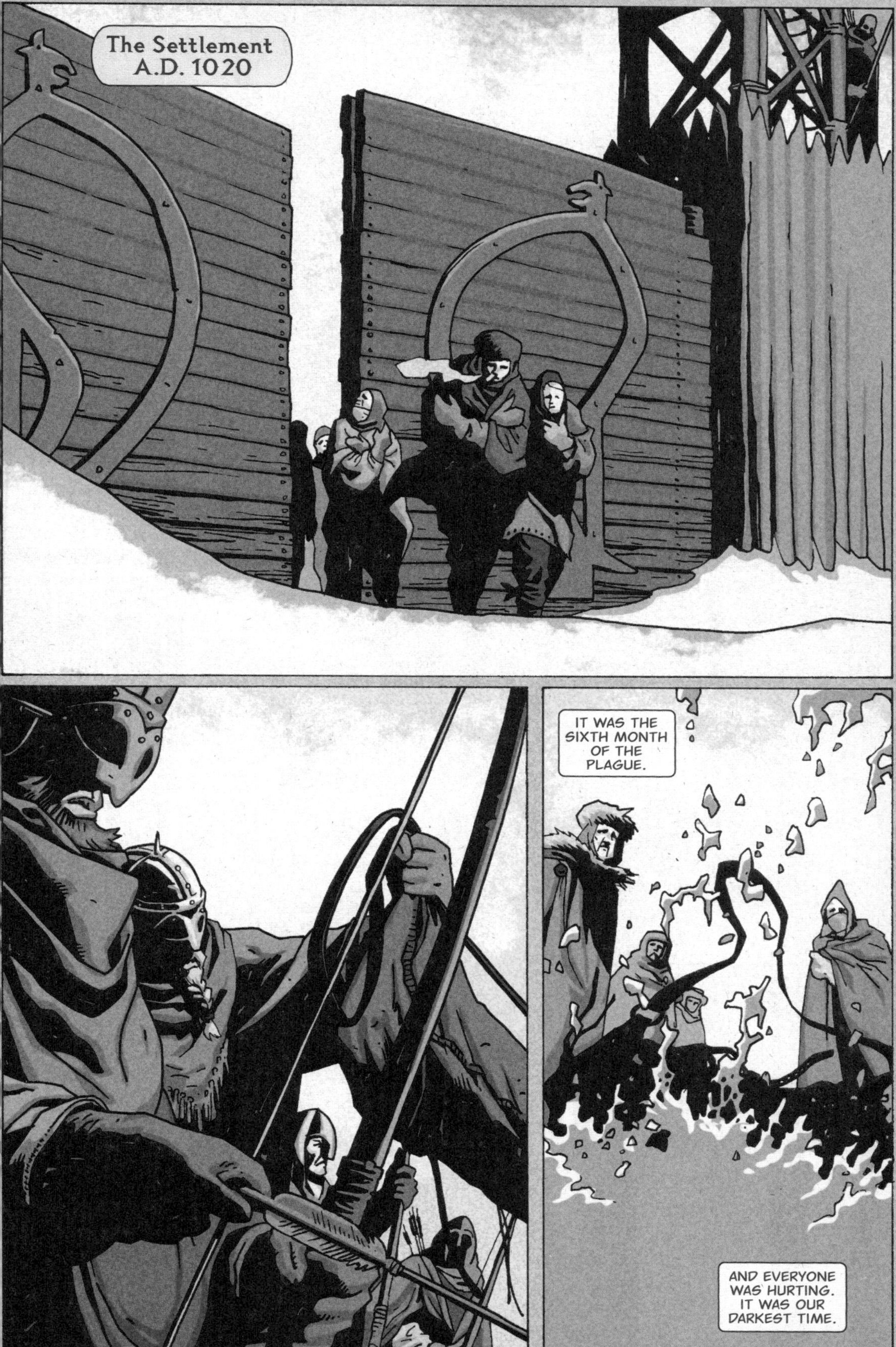
The Settlement
A.D. 1020
IT WAS THE SIXTH MONTH OF THE PLAGUE.
AND EVERYONE WAS HURTING. IT WAS OUR DARKEST TIME.

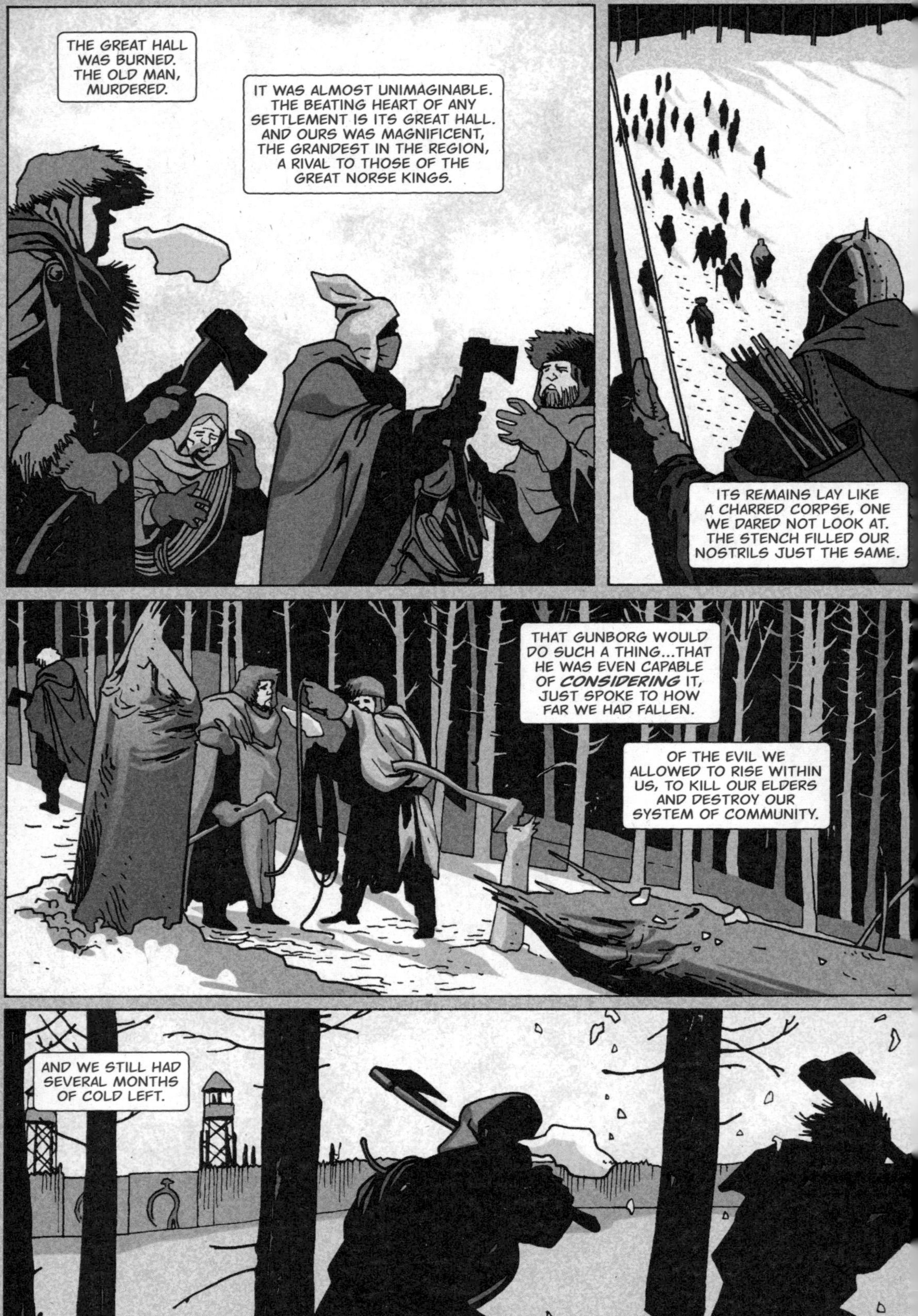
THE GREAT HALL WAS BURNED. THE OLD MAN, MURDERED.
IT WAS ALMOST UNIMAGINABLE. THE BEATING HEART OF ANY SETTLEMENT IS ITS GREAT HALL. AND OURS WAS MAGNIFICENT, THE GRANDEST IN THE REGION, A RIVAL TO THOSE OF THE GREAT NORSE KINGS.
ITS REMAINS LAY LIKE A CHARRED CORPSE, ONE WE DARED NOT LOOK AT. THE STENCH FILLED OUR NOSTRILS JUST THE SAME.
THAT GUNBORG WOULD DO SUCH A THING...THAT HE WAS EVEN CAPABLE OF *CONSIDERING* IT, JUST SPOKE TO HOW FAR WE HAD FALLEN.
OF THE EVIL WE ALLOWED TO RISE WITHIN US, TO KILL OUR ELDERS AND DESTROY OUR SYSTEM OF COMMUNITY.
AND WE STILL HAD SEVERAL MONTHS OF COLD LEFT.

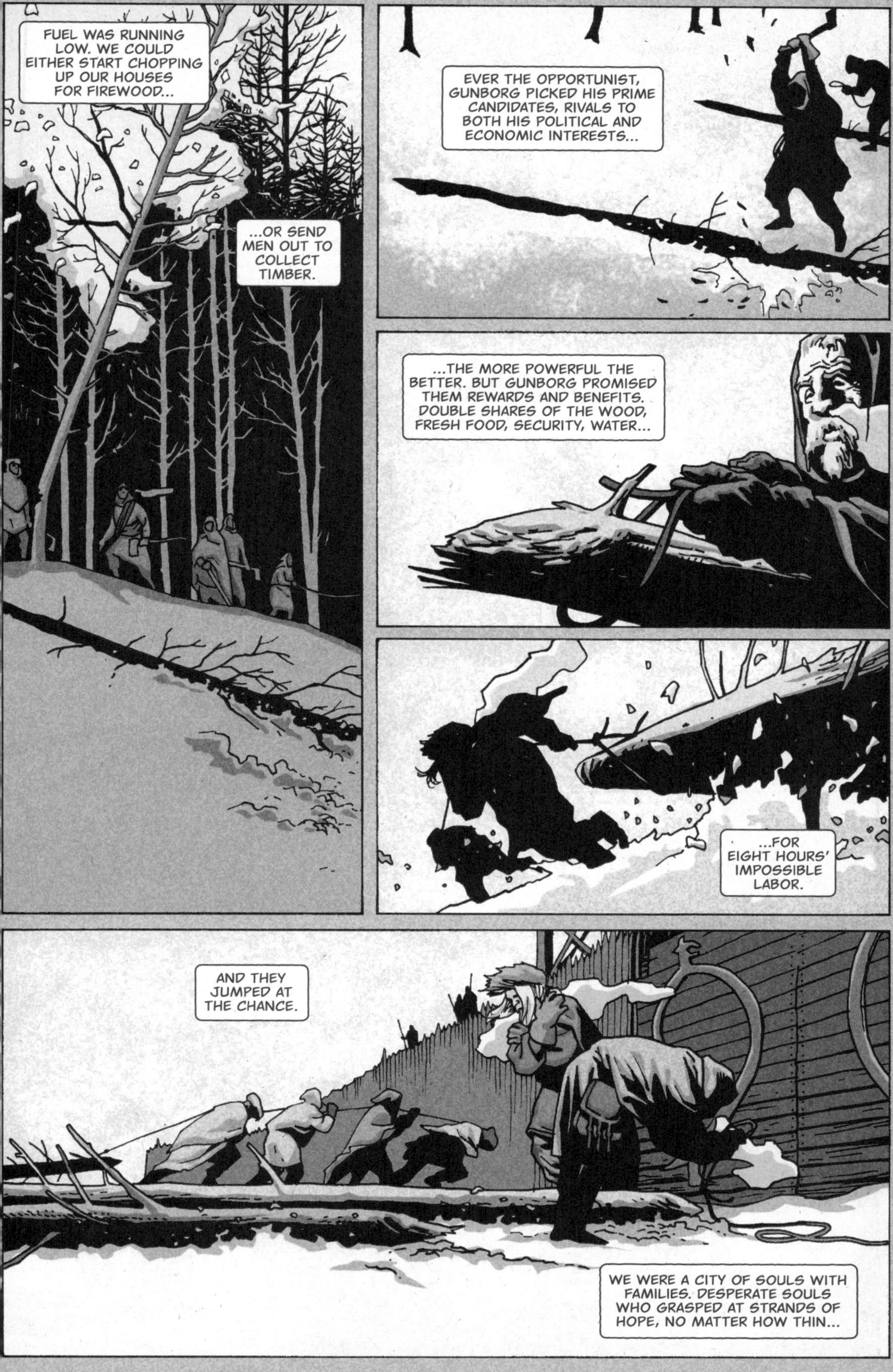
FUEL WAS RUNNING LOW. WE COULD EITHER START CHOPPING UP OUR HOUSES FOR FIREWOOD...
...OR SEND MEN OUT TO COLLECT TIMBER.
EVER THE OPPORTUNIST, GUNBORG PICKED HIS PRIME CANDIDATES, RIVALS TO BOTH HIS POLITICAL AND ECONOMIC INTERESTS...
...THE MORE POWERFUL THE BETTER. BUT GUNBORG PROMISED THEM REWARDS AND BENEFITS. DOUBLE SHARES OF THE WOOD, FRESH FOOD, SECURITY, WATER...
...FOR EIGHT HOURS' IMPOSSIBLE LABOR.
AND THEY JUMPED AT THE CHANCE.
WE WERE A CITY OF SOULS WITH FAMILIES. DESPERATE SOULS WHO GRASPED AT STRANDS OF HOPE, NO MATTER HOW THIN...

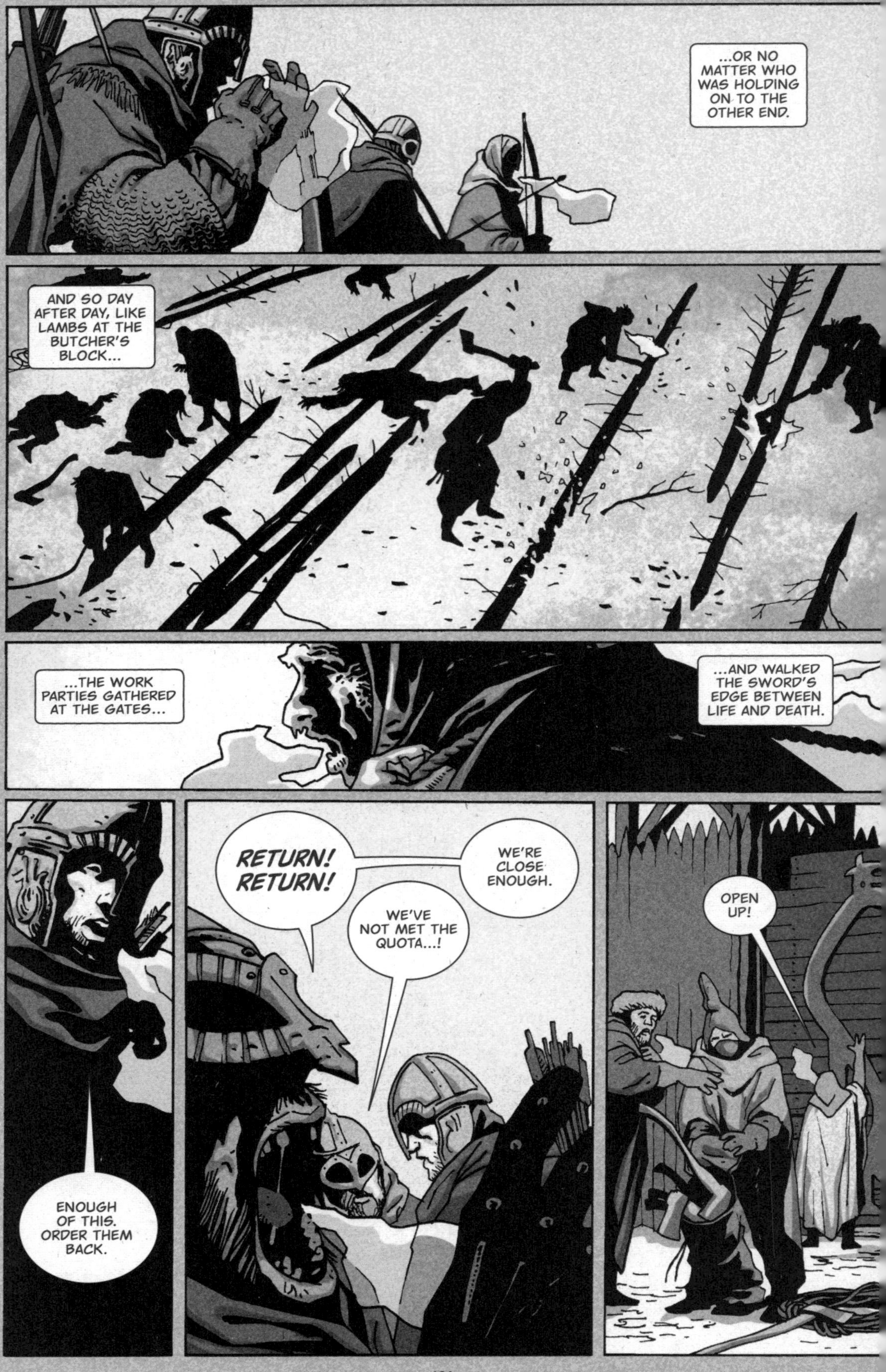
...OR NO MATTER WHO WAS HOLDING ON TO THE OTHER END.
AND SO DAY AFTER DAY, LIKE LAMBS AT THE BUTCHER'S BLOCK...
...THE WORK PARTIES GATHERED AT THE GATES...
...AND WALKED THE SWORD'S EDGE BETWEEN LIFE AND DEATH.
ENOUGH OF THIS. ORDER THEM BACK.
RETURN! RETURN!
WE'RE CLOSE ENOUGH.
WE'VE NOT MET THE QUOTA...!
OPEN UP!

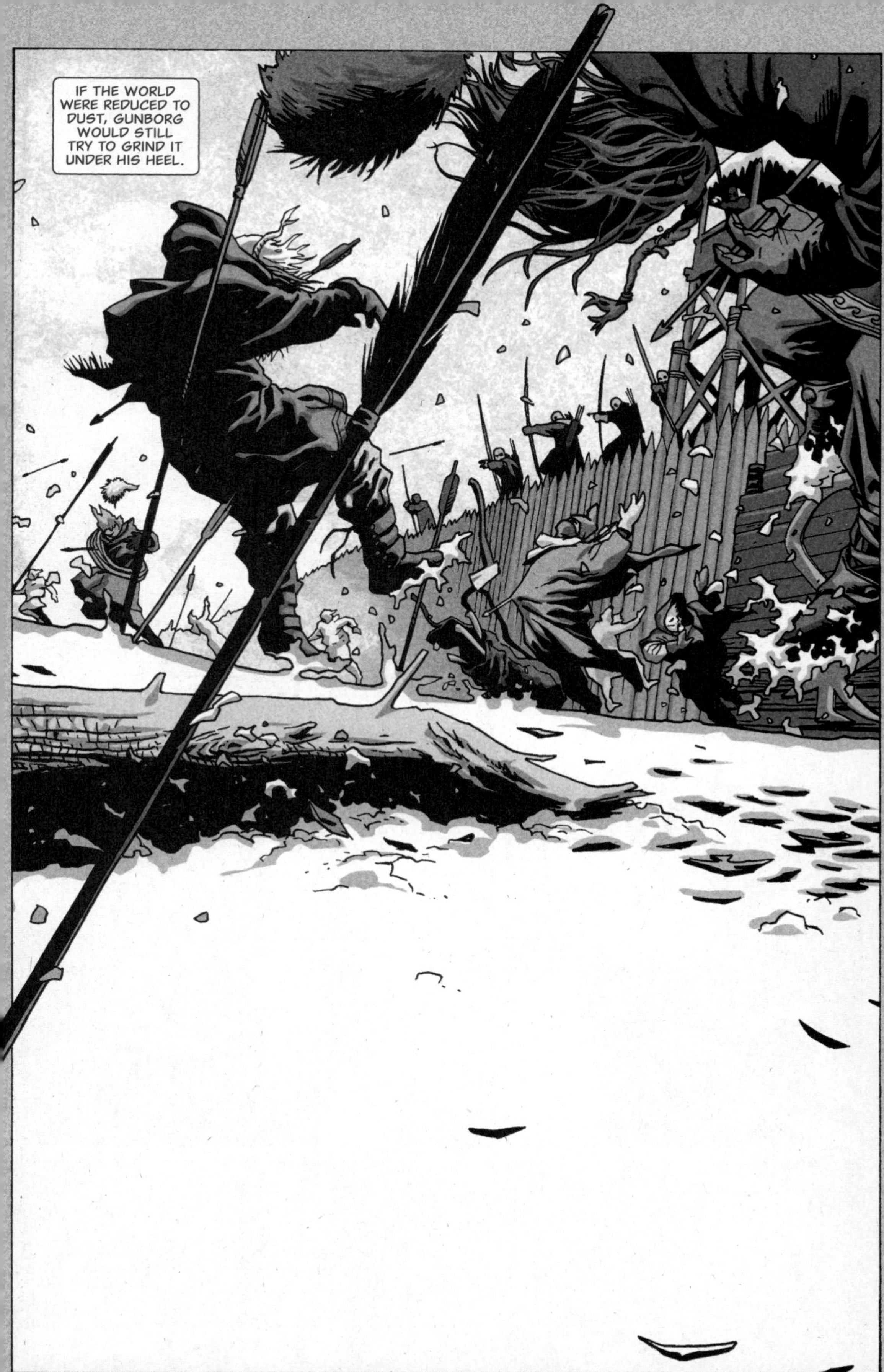
IF THE WORLD WERE REDUCED TO DUST, GUNBORG WOULD STILL TRY TO GRIND IT UNDER HIS HEEL.

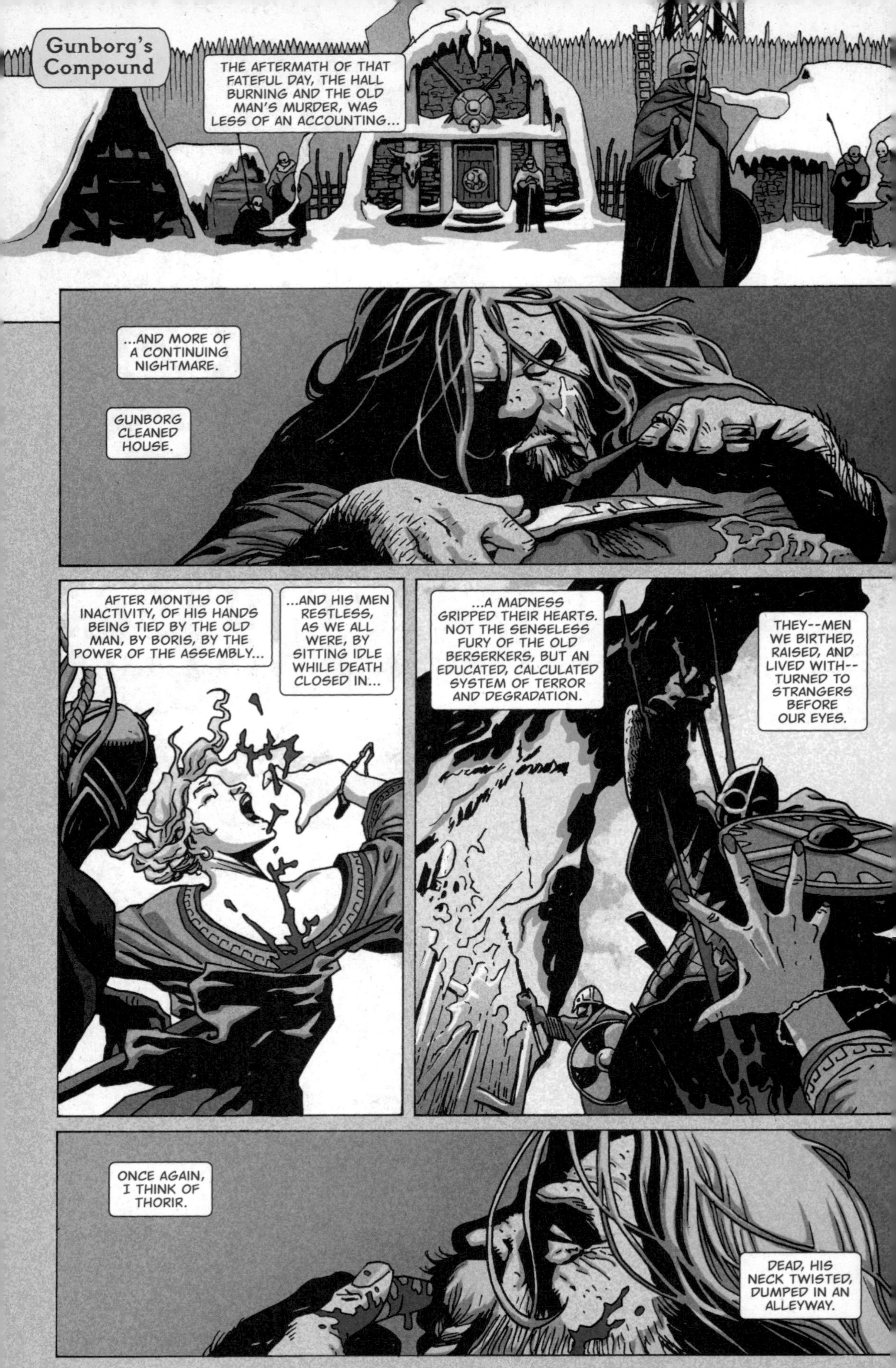
Gunborg's Compound
THE AFTERMATH OF THAT FATEFUL DAY, THE HALL BURNING AND THE OLD MAN'S MURDER, WAS LESS OF AN ACCOUNTING...
...AND MORE OF A CONTINUING NIGHTMARE.
GUNBORG CLEANED HOUSE.
AFTER MONTHS OF INACTIVITY, OF HIS HANDS BEING TIED BY THE OLD MAN, BY BORIS, BY THE POWER OF THE ASSEMBLY...
...AND HIS MEN RESTLESS, AS WE ALL WERE, BY SITTING IDLE WHILE DEATH CLOSED IN...
...A MADNESS GRIPPED THEIR HEARTS. NOT THE SENSELESS FURY OF THE OLD BERSERKERS, BUT AN EDUCATED, CALCULATED SYSTEM OF TERROR AND DEGRADATION.
THEY--MEN WE BIRTHED, RAISED, AND LIVED WITH--TURNED TO STRANGERS BEFORE OUR EYES.
ONCE AGAIN, I THINK OF THORIR.
DEAD, HIS NECK TWISTED, DUMPED IN AN ALLEYWAY.

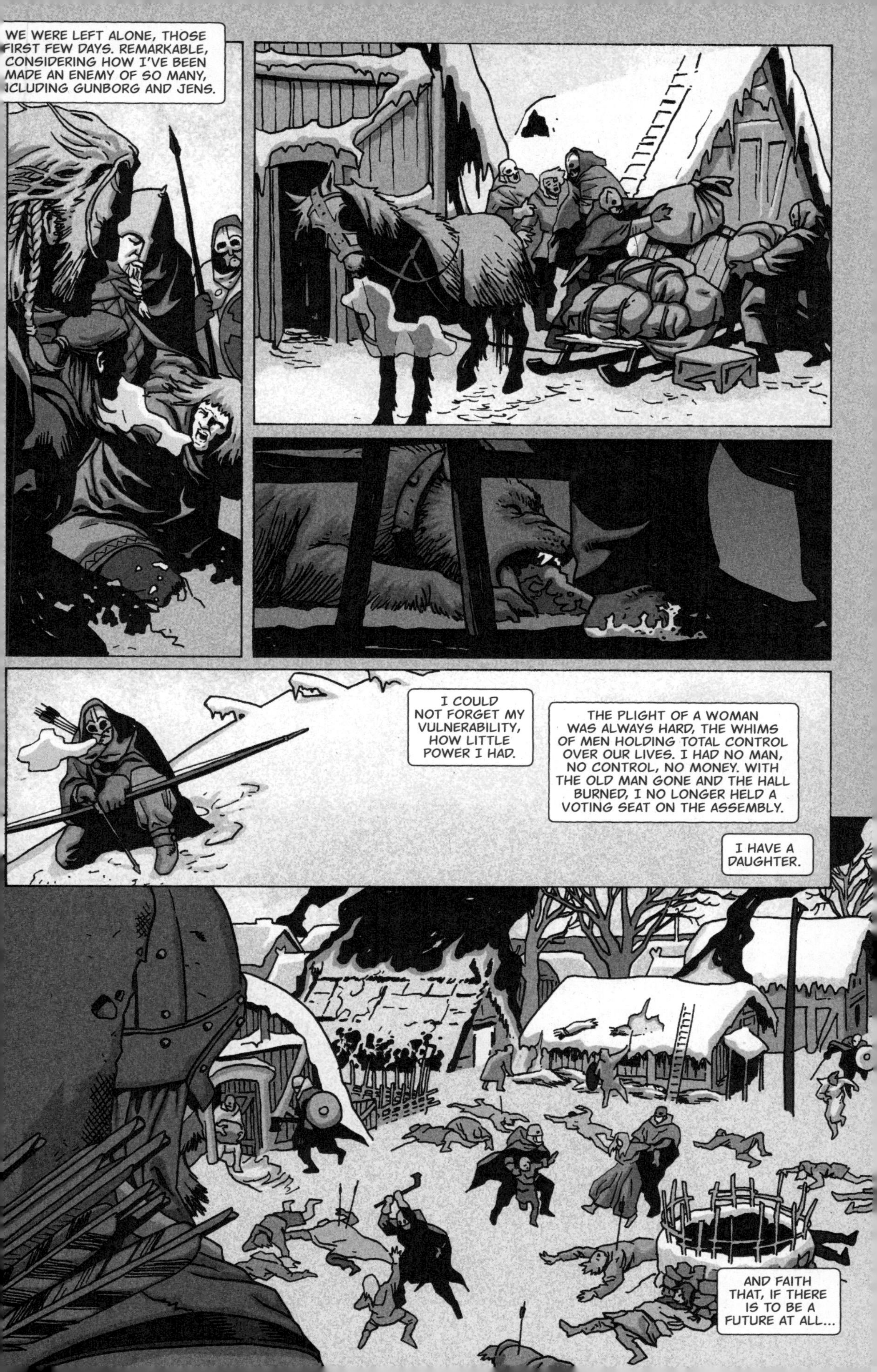
WE WERE LEFT ALONE, THOSE FIRST FEW DAYS. REMARKABLE, CONSIDERING HOW I'VE BEEN MADE AN ENEMY OF SO MANY, INCLUDING GUNBORG AND JENS.
I COULD NOT FORGET MY VULNERABILITY, HOW LITTLE POWER I HAD.
THE PLIGHT OF A WOMAN WAS ALWAYS HARD, THE WHIMS OF MEN HOLDING TOTAL CONTROL OVER OUR LIVES. I HAD NO MAN, NO CONTROL, NO MONEY. WITH THE OLD MAN GONE AND THE HALL BURNED, I NO LONGER HELD A VOTING SEAT ON THE ASSEMBLY.
I HAVE A DAUGHTER.
AND FAITH THAT, IF THERE IS TO BE A FUTURE AT ALL...

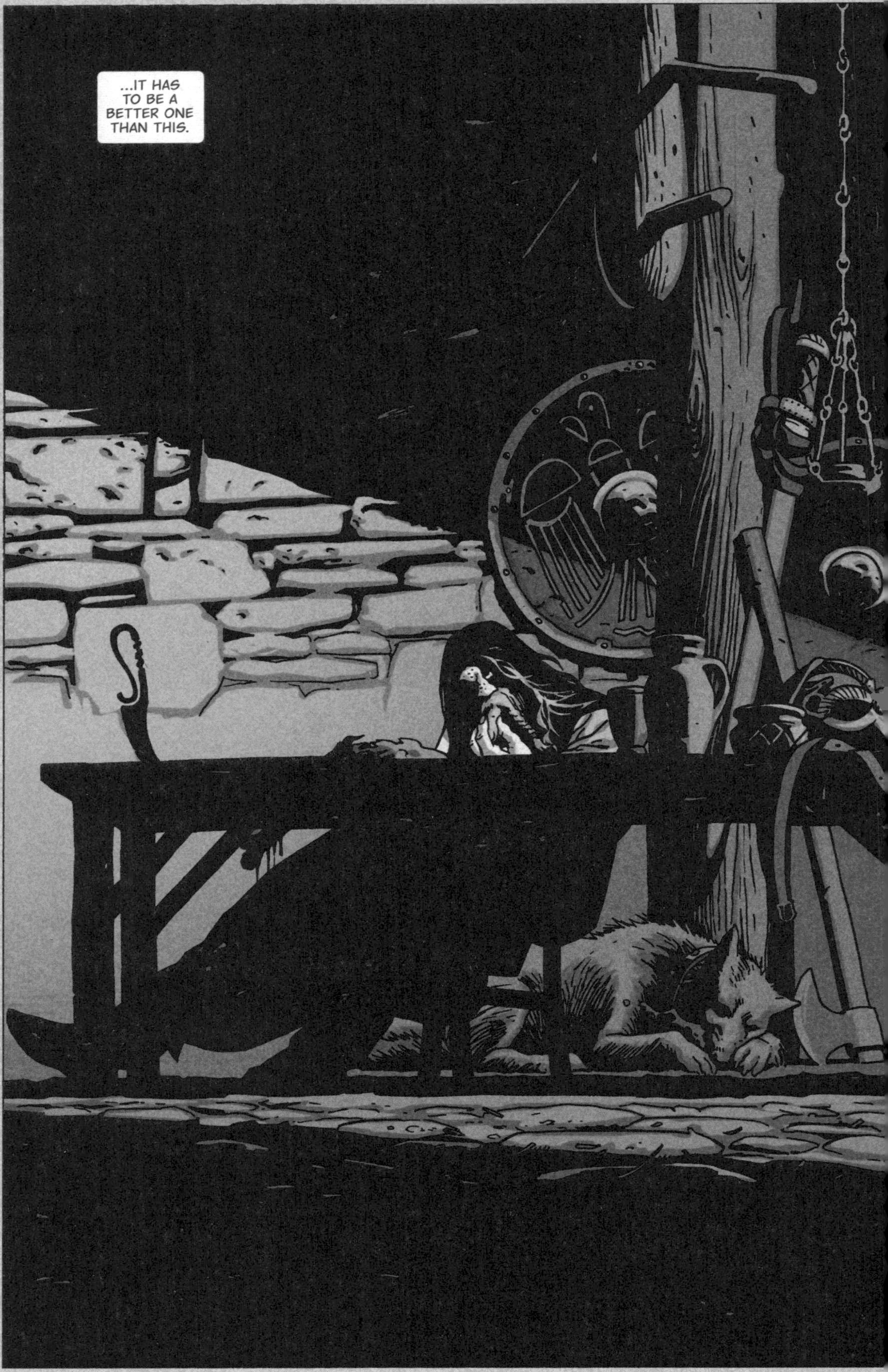
...IT HAS TO BE A BETTER ONE THAN THIS.

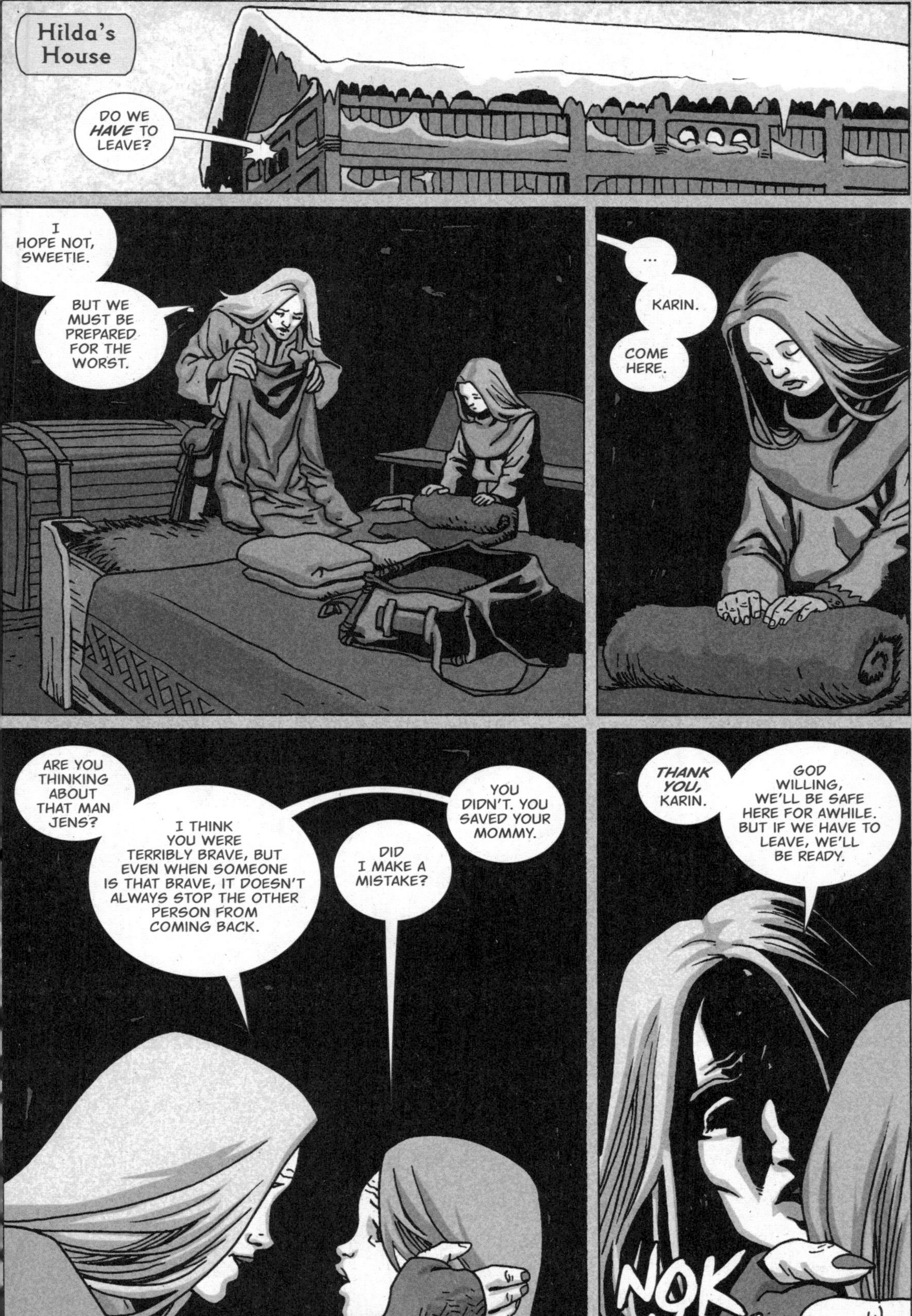

Hilda's House
DO WE *HAVE* TO LEAVE?
I HOPE NOT, SWEETIE.
BUT WE MUST BE PREPARED FOR THE WORST.
...
KARIN.
COME HERE.
ARE YOU THINKING ABOUT THAT MAN JENS?
I THINK YOU WERE TERRIBLY BRAVE, BUT EVEN WHEN SOMEONE IS THAT BRAVE, IT DOESN'T ALWAYS STOP THE OTHER PERSON FROM COMING BACK.
DID I MAKE A MISTAKE?
YOU DIDN'T. YOU SAVED YOUR MOMMY.
THANK YOU, KARIN.
GOD WILLING, WE'LL BE SAFE HERE FOR AWHILE. BUT IF WE HAVE TO LEAVE, WE'LL BE READY.
NOK NOK

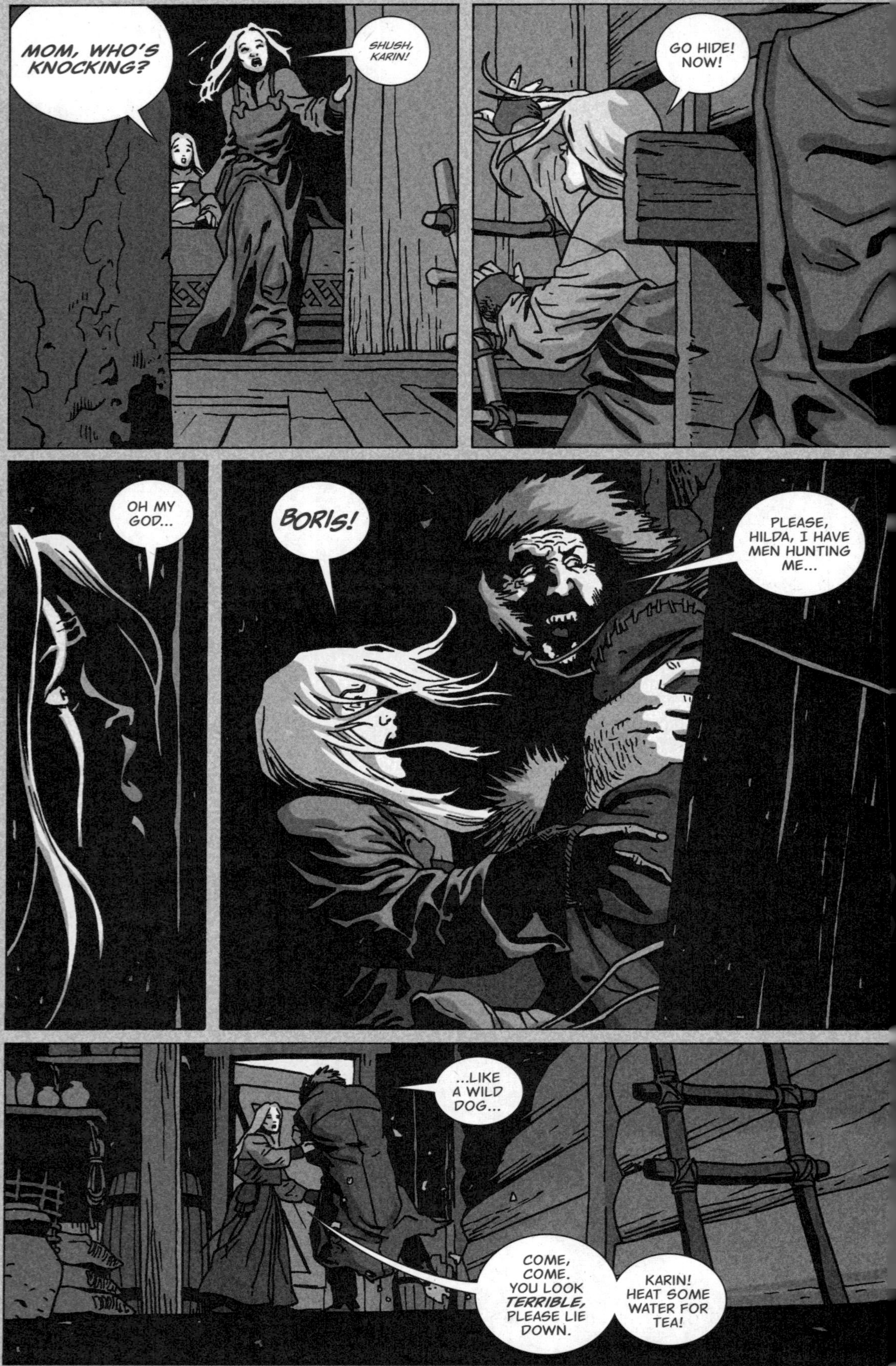
MOM, WHO'S KNOCKING?
SHUSH, KARIN!
GO HIDE! NOW!
OH MY GOD...
BORIS!
PLEASE, HILDA, I HAVE MEN HUNTING ME...
...LIKE A WILD DOG...
COME, COME. YOU LOOK *TERRIBLE*, PLEASE LIE DOWN.
KARIN! HEAT SOME WATER FOR TEA!

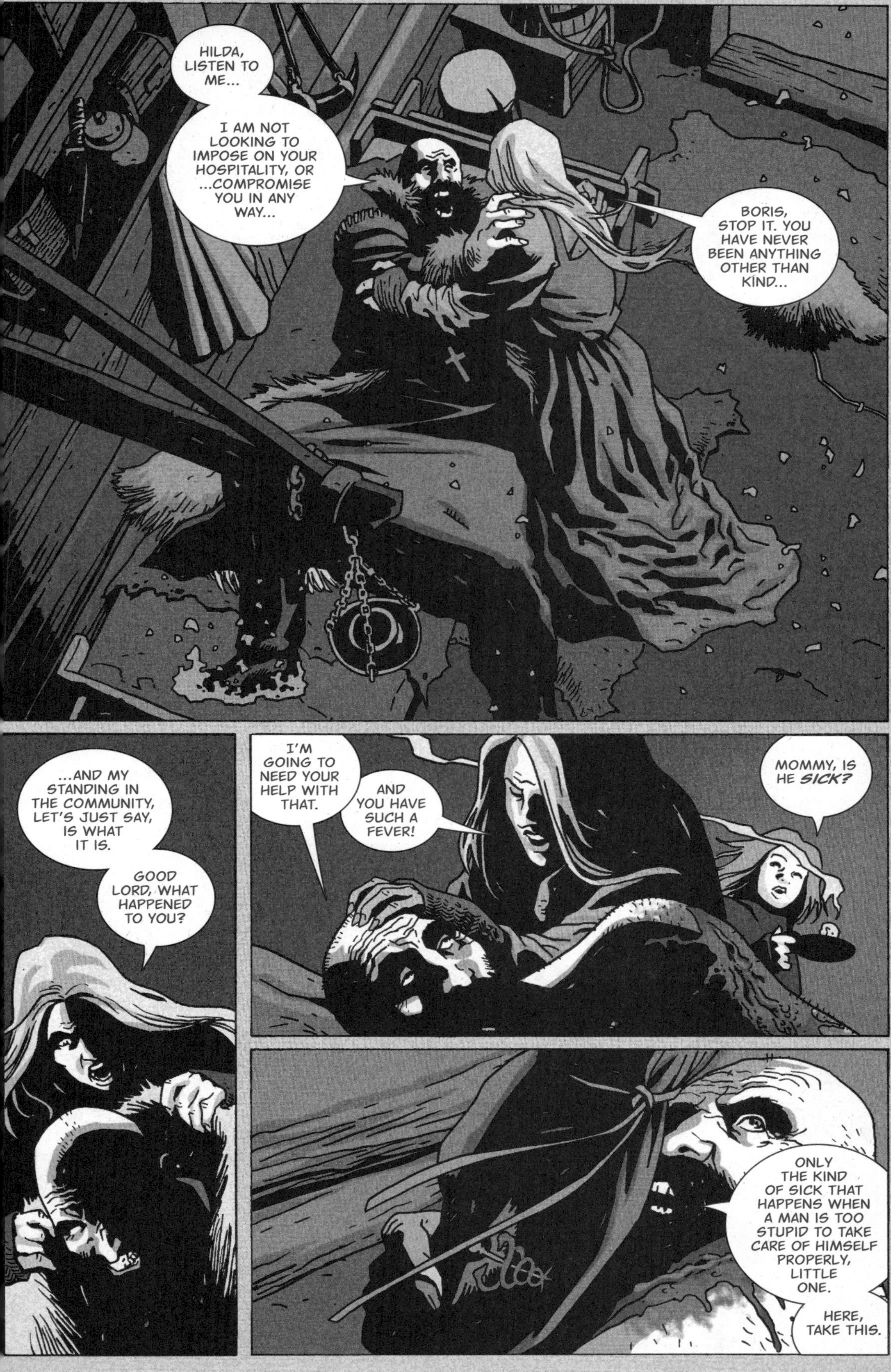
HILDA, LISTEN TO ME...
I AM NOT LOOKING TO IMPOSE ON YOUR HOSPITALITY, OR ...COMPROMISE YOU IN ANY WAY...
BORIS, STOP IT. YOU HAVE NEVER BEEN ANYTHING OTHER THAN KIND...
...AND MY STANDING IN THE COMMUNITY, LET'S JUST SAY, IS WHAT IT IS.
GOOD LORD, WHAT HAPPENED TO YOU?
I'M GOING TO NEED YOUR HELP WITH THAT.
AND YOU HAVE SUCH A FEVER!
MOMMY, IS HE SICK?
ONLY THE KIND OF SICK THAT HAPPENS WHEN A MAN IS TOO STUPID TO TAKE CARE OF HIMSELF PROPERLY, LITTLE ONE.
HERE, TAKE THIS.

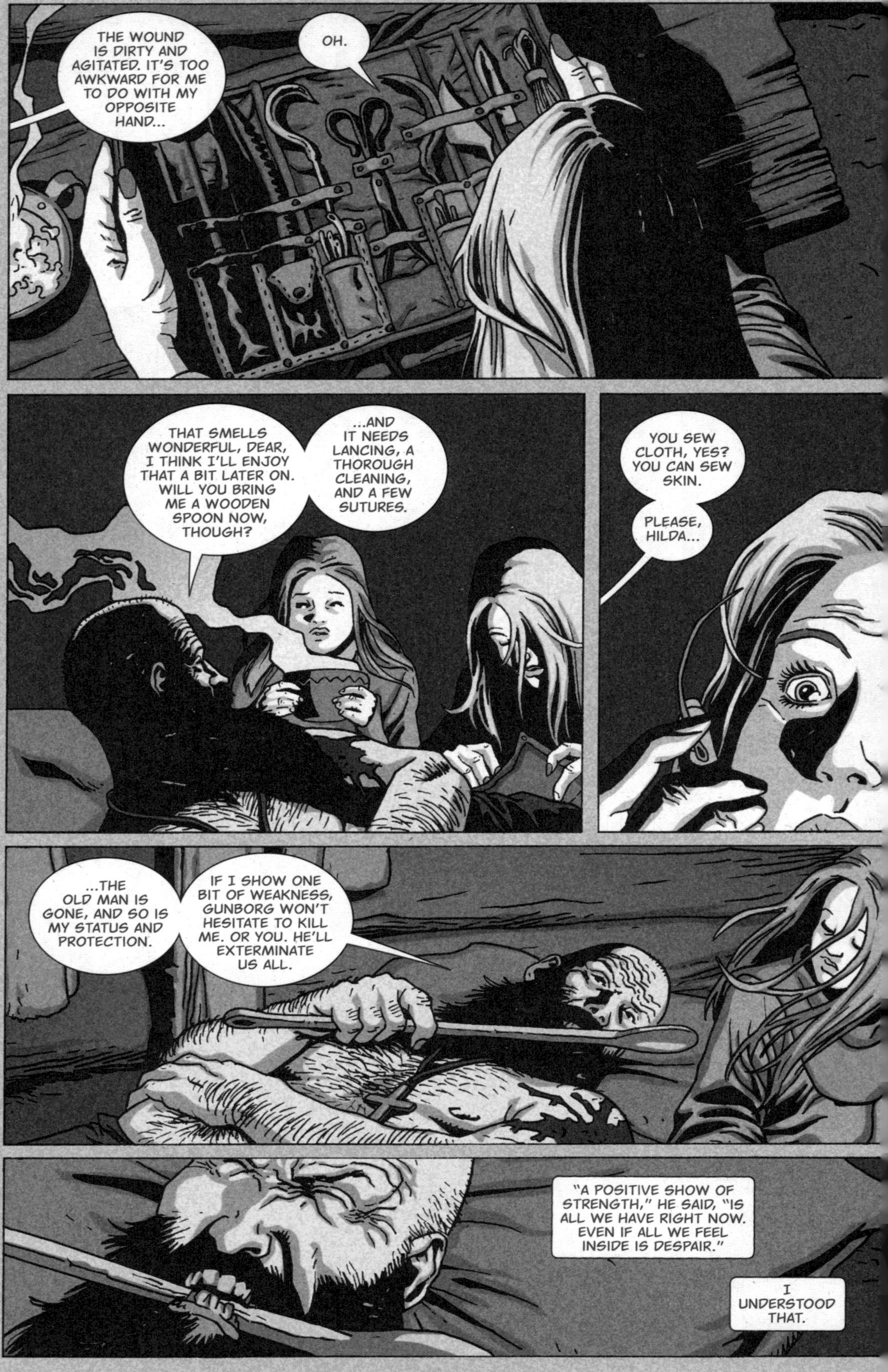
THE WOUND IS DIRTY AND AGITATED. IT'S TOO AWKWARD FOR ME TO DO WITH MY OPPOSITE HAND...
OH.
THAT SMELLS WONDERFUL, DEAR, I THINK I'LL ENJOY THAT A BIT LATER ON. WILL YOU BRING ME A WOODEN SPOON NOW, THOUGH?
...AND IT NEEDS LANCING, A THOROUGH CLEANING, AND A FEW SUTURES.
YOU SEW CLOTH, YES? YOU CAN SEW SKIN.
PLEASE, HILDA...
...THE OLD MAN IS GONE, AND SO IS MY STATUS AND PROTECTION.
IF I SHOW ONE BIT OF WEAKNESS, GUNBORG WON'T HESITATE TO KILL ME. OR YOU. HE'LL EXTERMINATE US ALL.
"A POSITIVE SHOW OF STRENGTH," HE SAID, "IS ALL WE HAVE RIGHT NOW. EVEN IF ALL WE FEEL INSIDE IS DESPAIR."
I UNDERSTOOD THAT.

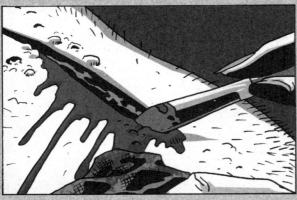

YOU, OKAY, BABY?

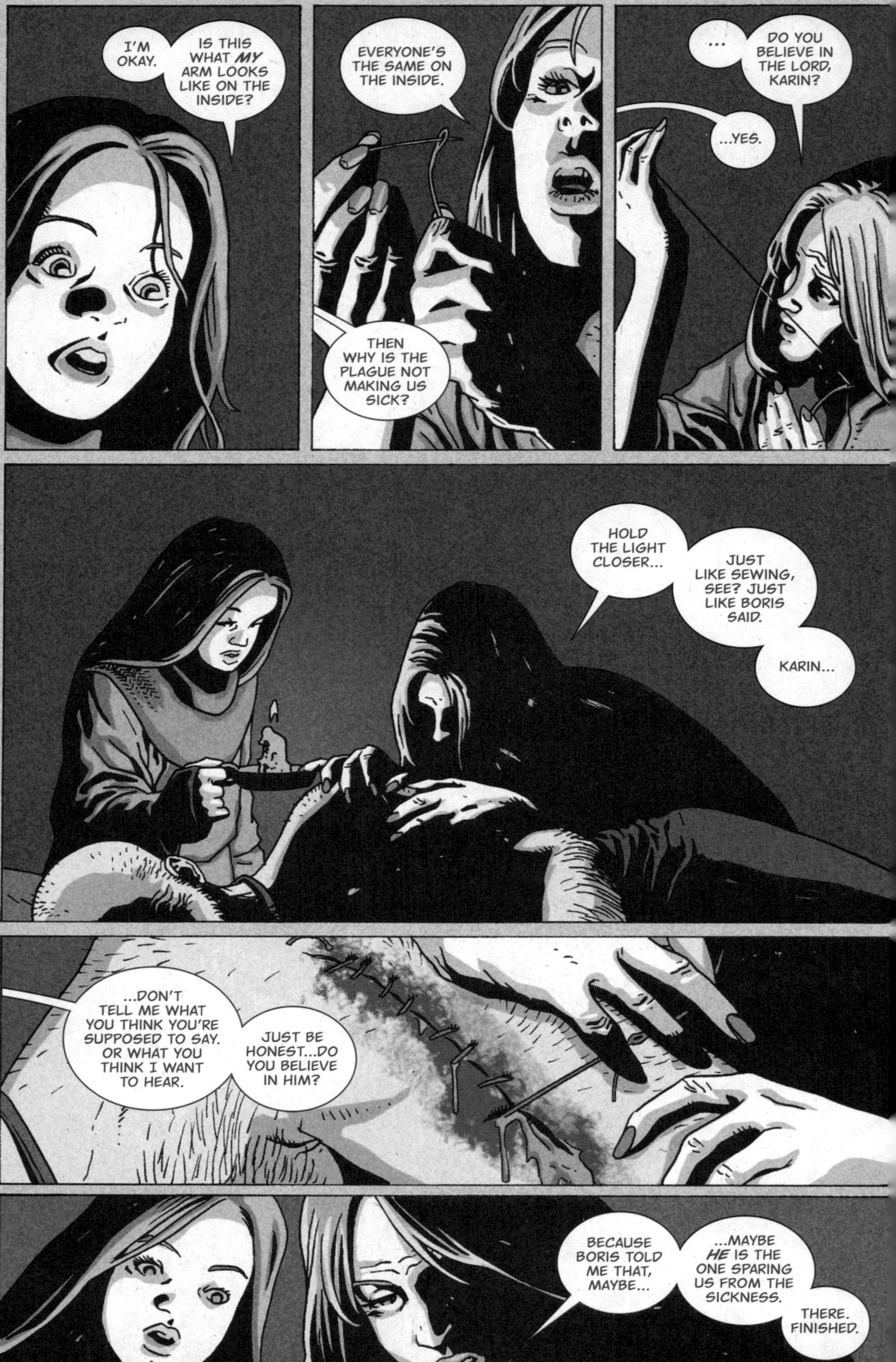
I'M OKAY.
IS THIS WHAT MY ARM LOOKS LIKE ON THE INSIDE?
EVERYONE'S THE SAME ON THE INSIDE.
THEN WHY IS THE PLAGUE NOT MAKING US SICK?
...
DO YOU BELIEVE IN THE LORD, KARIN?
...YES.
HOLD THE LIGHT CLOSER...
JUST LIKE SEWING, SEE? JUST LIKE BORIS SAID.
KARIN...
...DON'T TELL ME WHAT YOU THINK YOU'RE SUPPOSED TO SAY. OR WHAT YOU THINK I WANT TO HEAR.
JUST BE HONEST...DO YOU BELIEVE IN HIM?
BECAUSE BORIS TOLD ME THAT, MAYBE...
...MAYBE HE IS THE ONE SPARING US FROM THE SICKNESS.
THERE. FINISHED.

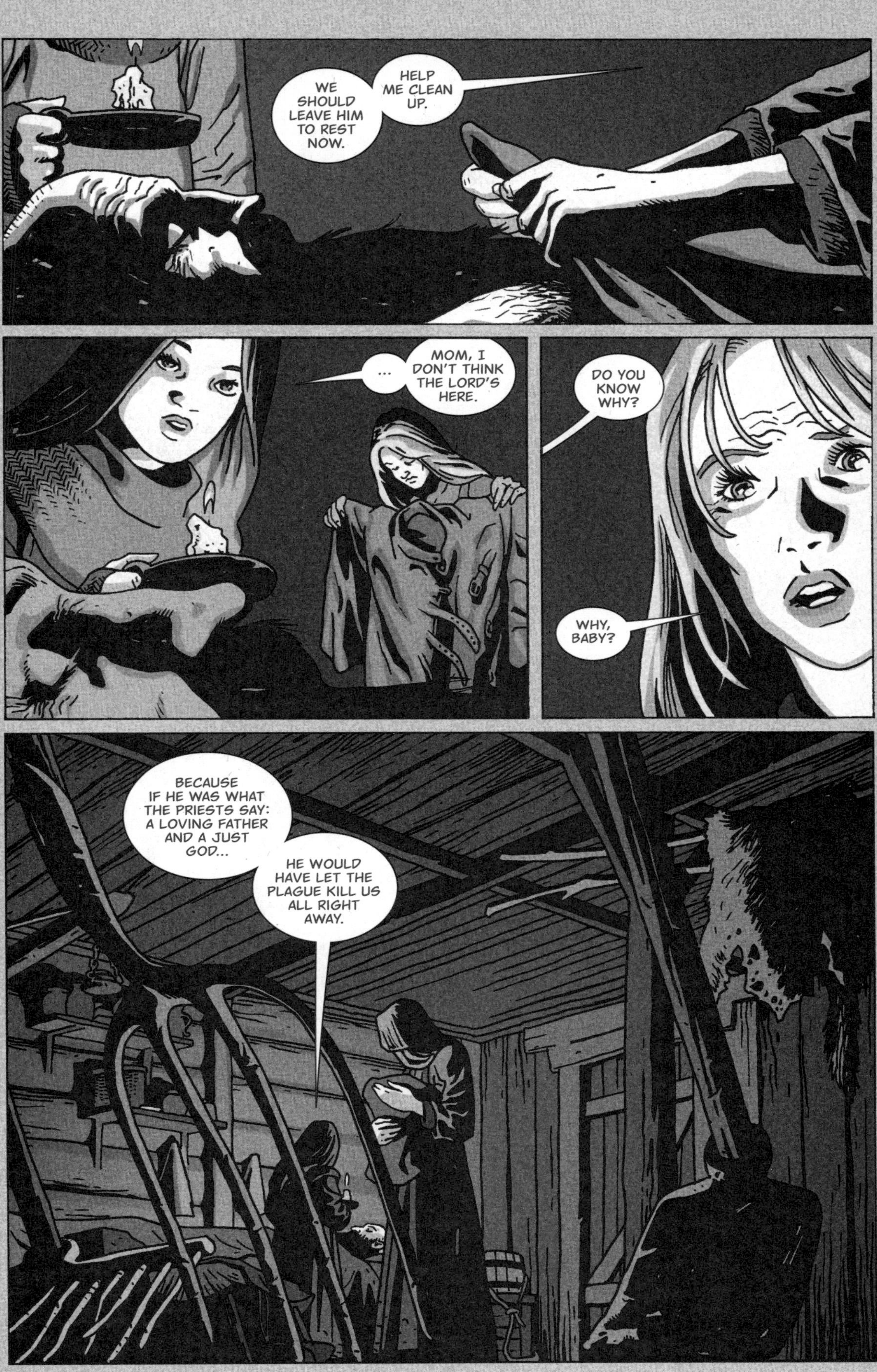
WE SHOULD LEAVE HIM TO REST NOW.
HELP ME CLEAN UP.
...
MOM, I DON'T THINK THE LORD'S HERE.
DO YOU KNOW WHY?
WHY, BABY?
BECAUSE IF HE WAS WHAT THE PRIESTS SAY: A LOVING FATHER AND A JUST GOD...
HE WOULD HAVE LET THE PLAGUE KILL US ALL RIGHT AWAY.

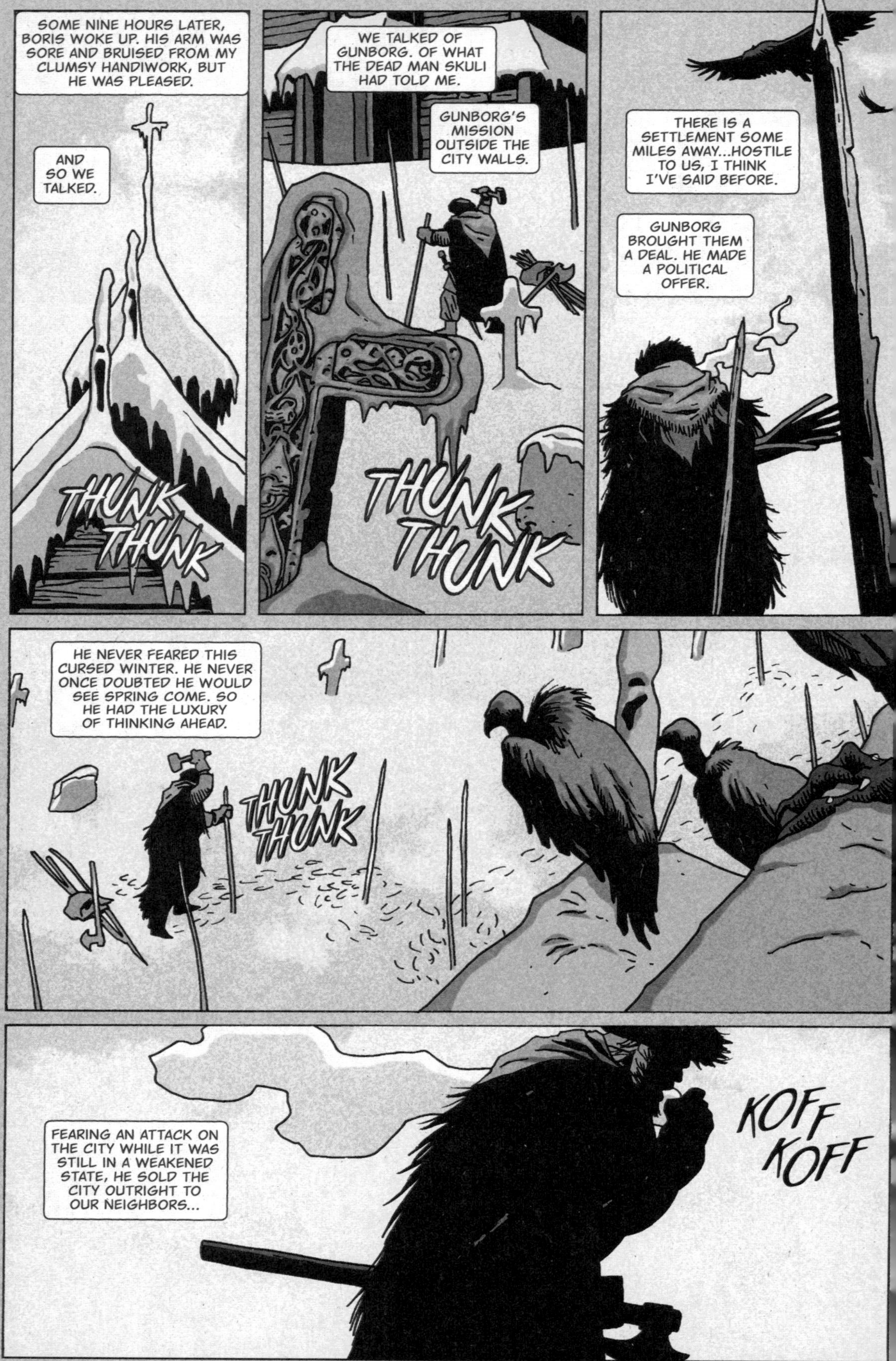
SOME NINE HOURS LATER, BORIS WOKE UP. HIS ARM WAS SORE AND BRUISED FROM MY CLUMSY HANDIWORK, BUT HE WAS PLEASED.
AND SO WE TALKED.
THUNK THUNK
WE TALKED OF GUNBORG. OF WHAT THE DEAD MAN SKULI HAD TOLD ME.
GUNBORG'S MISSION OUTSIDE THE CITY WALLS.
THUNK THUNK
THERE IS A SETTLEMENT SOME MILES AWAY...HOSTILE TO US, I THINK I'VE SAID BEFORE.
GUNBORG BROUGHT THEM A DEAL. HE MADE A POLITICAL OFFER.
HE NEVER FEARED THIS CURSED WINTER. HE NEVER ONCE DOUBTED HE WOULD SEE SPRING COME. SO HE HAD THE LUXURY OF THINKING AHEAD.
THUNK THUNK
FEARING AN ATTACK ON THE CITY WHILE IT WAS STILL IN A WEAKENED STATE, HE SOLD THE CITY OUTRIGHT TO OUR NEIGHBORS...
KOFF KOFF

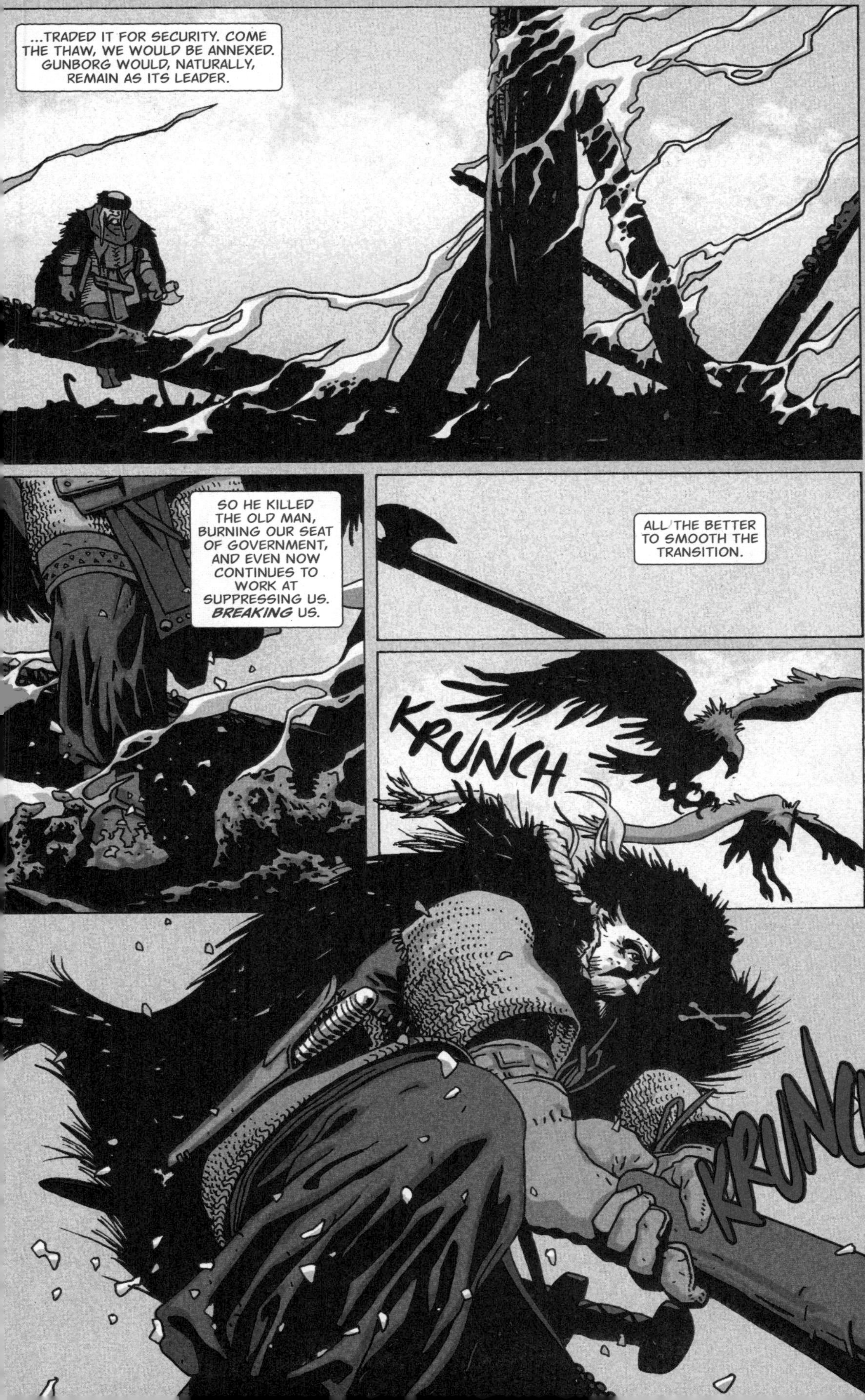
...TRADED IT FOR SECURITY. COME THE THAW, WE WOULD BE ANNEXED. GUNBORG WOULD, NATURALLY, REMAIN AS ITS LEADER.
SO HE KILLED THE OLD MAN, BURNING OUR SEAT OF GOVERNMENT, AND EVEN NOW CONTINUES TO WORK AT SUPPRESSING US. *BREAKING* US.
ALL THE BETTER TO SMOOTH THE TRANSITION.
KRUNCH
KRUNCH

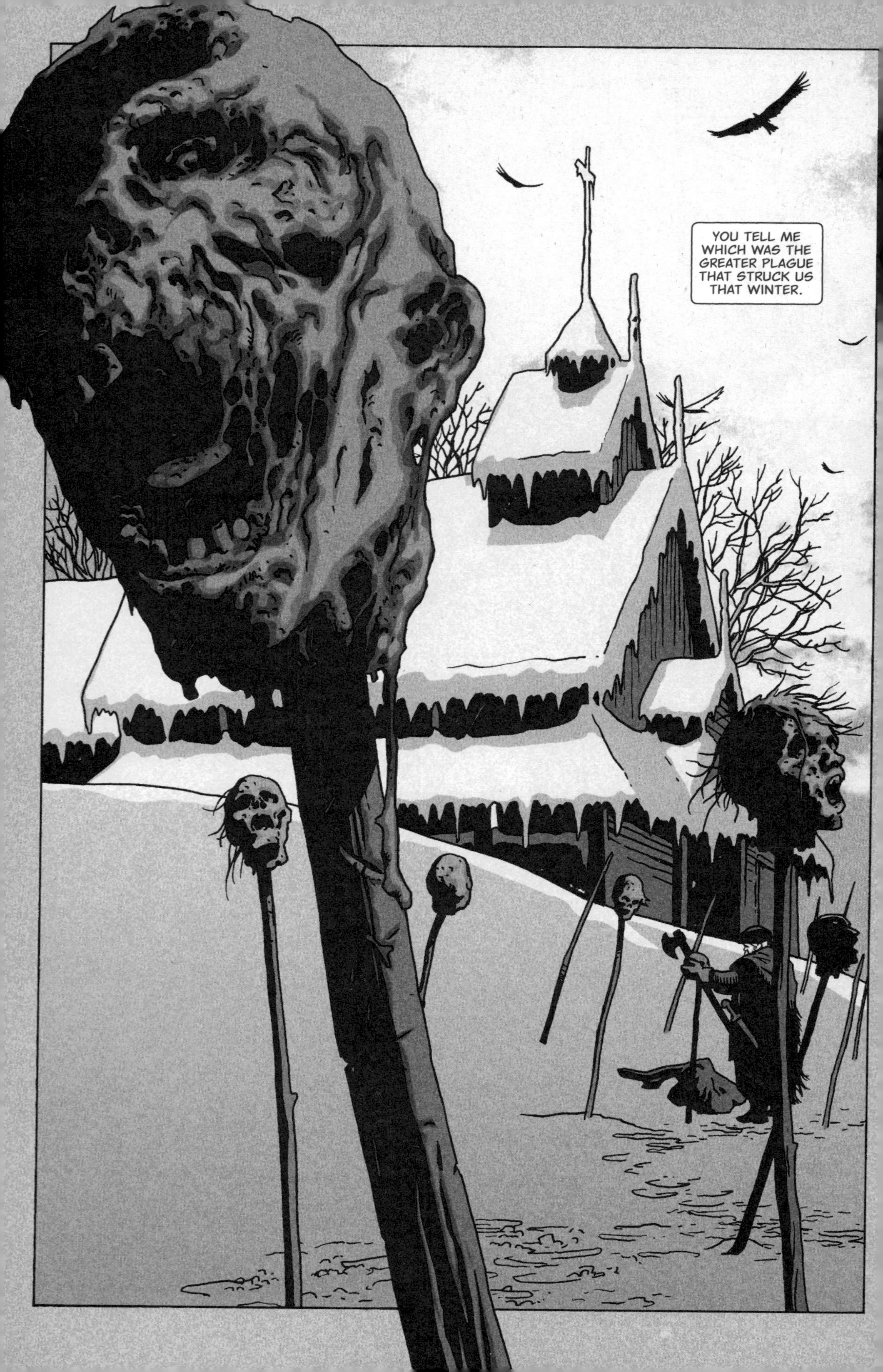
YOU TELL ME WHICH WAS THE GREATER PLAGUE THAT STRUCK US THAT WINTER.

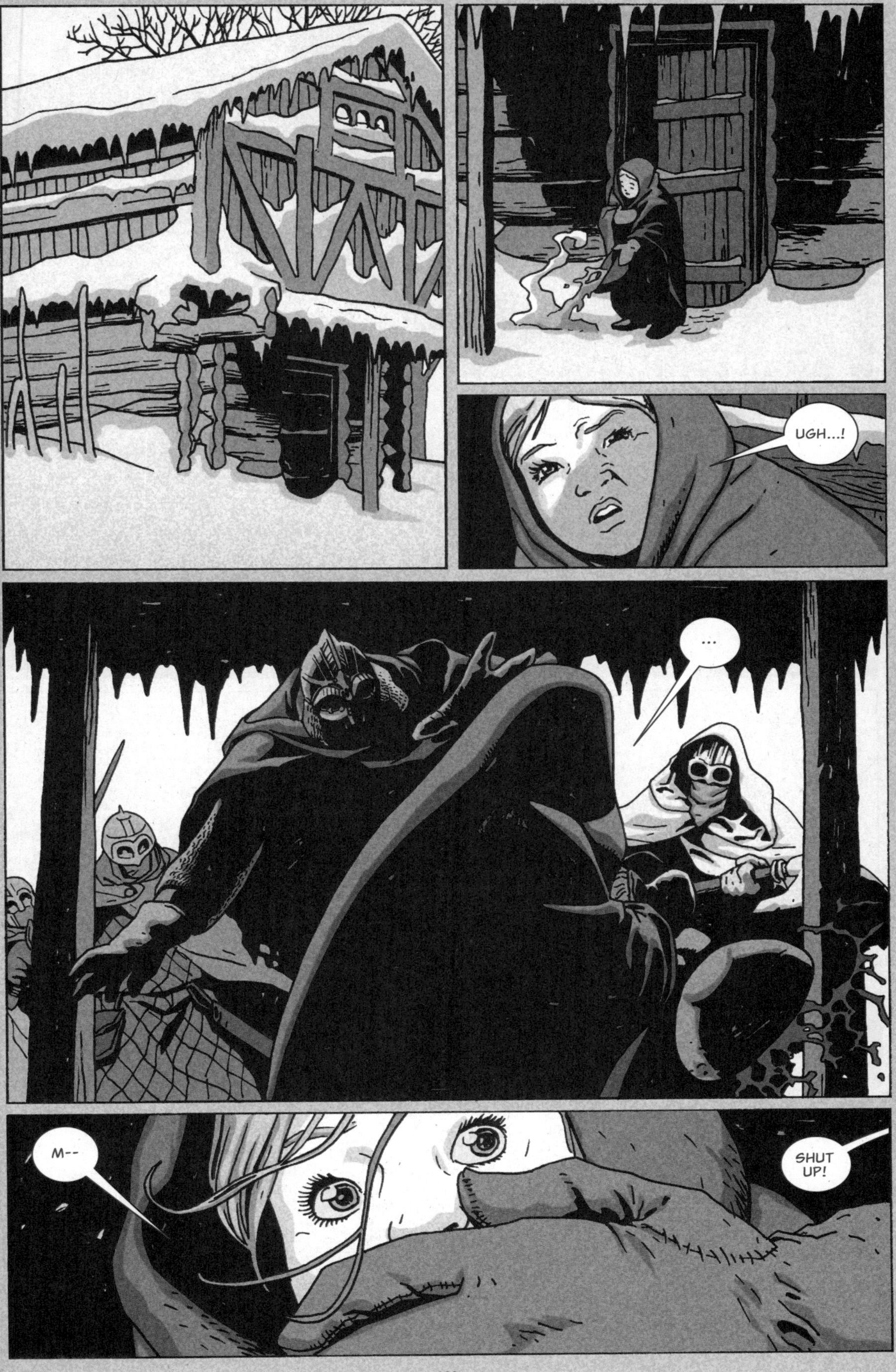
UGH...!
...
M--
SHUT UP!

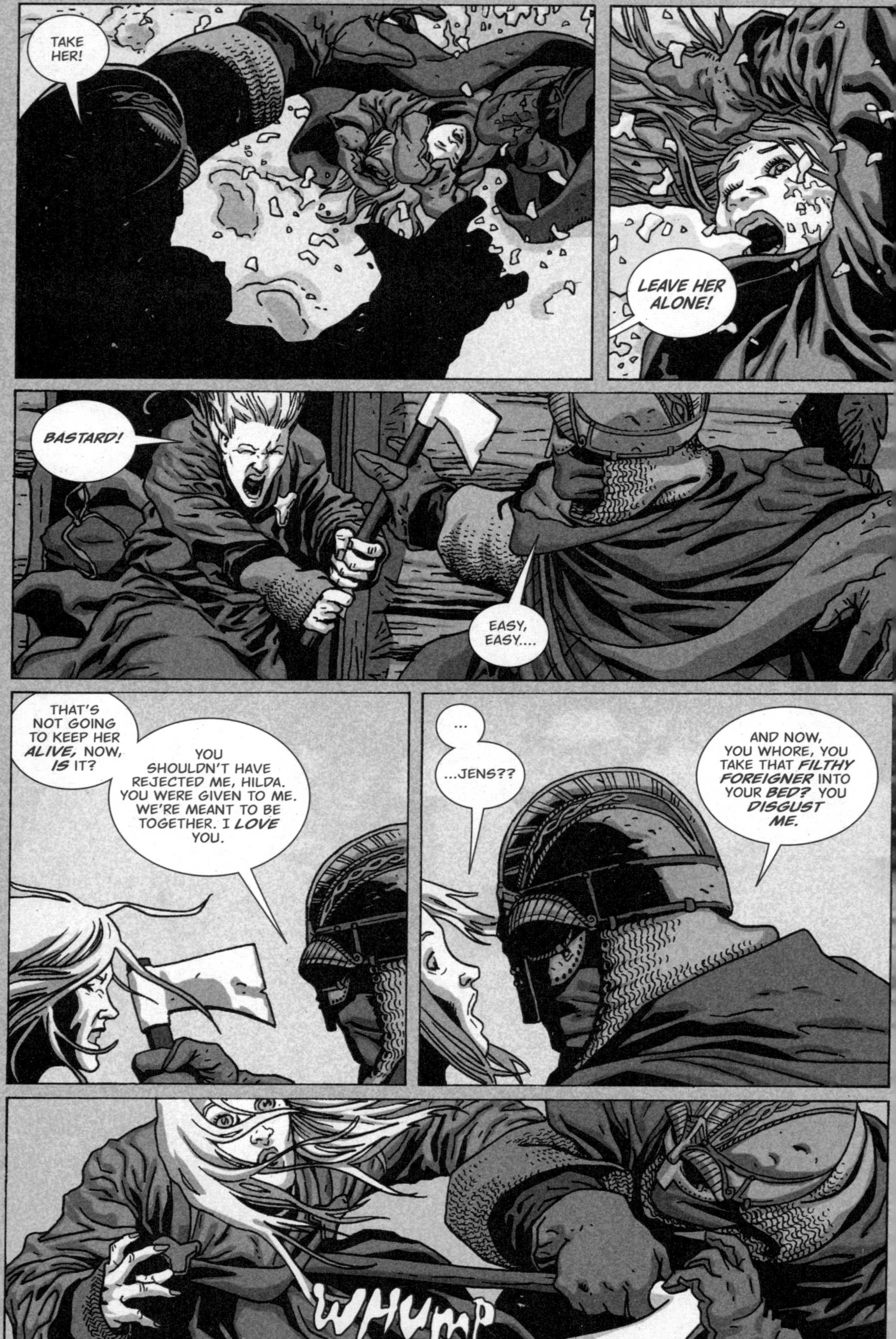
TAKE HER!
LEAVE HER ALONE!
BASTARD!
EASY, EASY....
THAT'S NOT GOING TO KEEP HER *ALIVE*, NOW, *IS* IT?
YOU SHOULDN'T HAVE REJECTED ME, HILDA. YOU WERE GIVEN TO ME. WE'RE MEANT TO BE TOGETHER. I *LOVE* YOU.
...
...JENS??
AND NOW, YOU WHORE, YOU TAKE THAT *FILTHY FOREIGNER* INTO YOUR *BED?* YOU *DISGUST ME.*
WHUMP

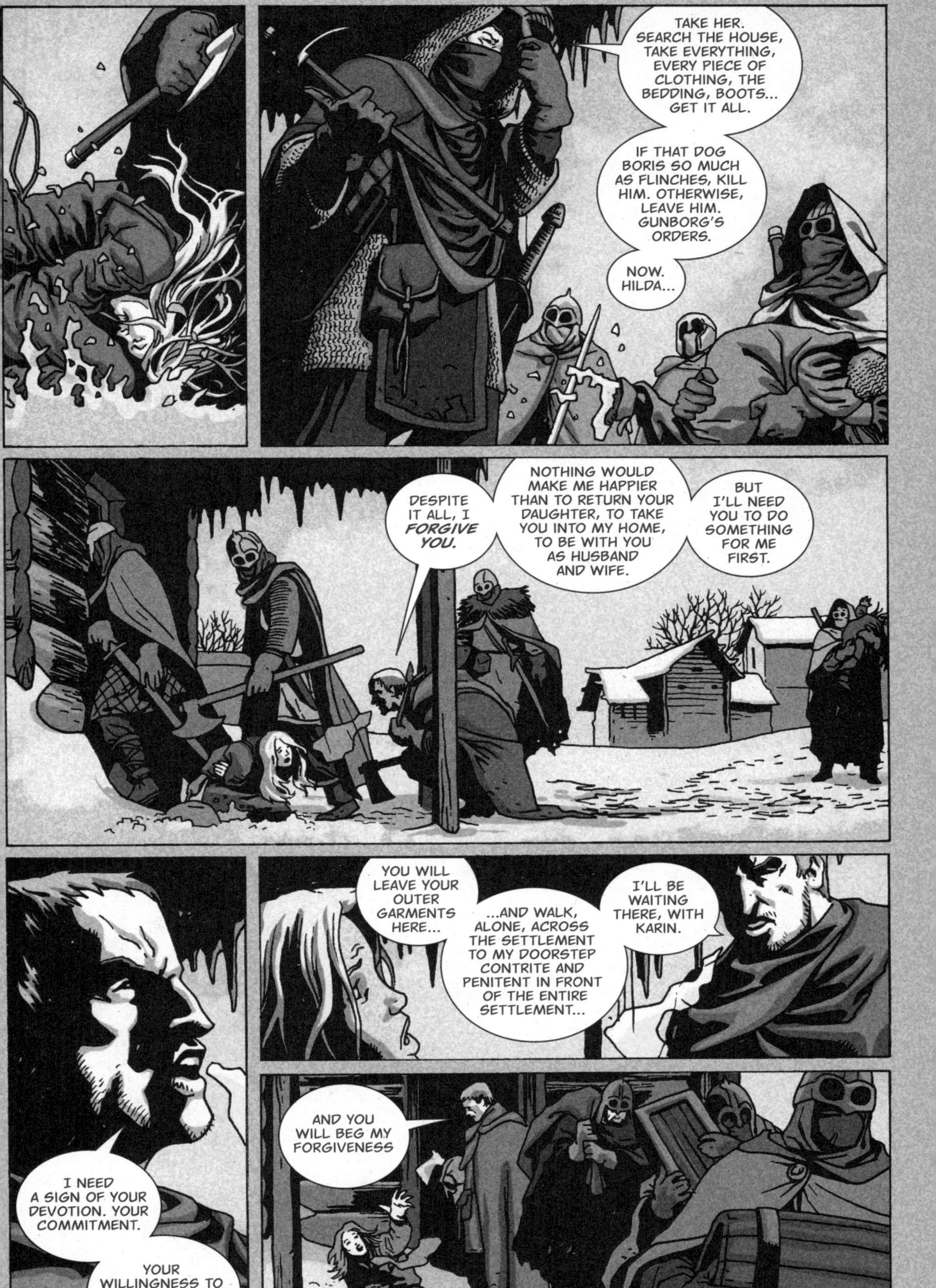

TAKE HER. SEARCH THE HOUSE, TAKE EVERYTHING, EVERY PIECE OF CLOTHING, THE BEDDING, BOOTS... GET IT ALL.
IF THAT DOG BORIS SO MUCH AS FLINCHES, KILL HIM. OTHERWISE, LEAVE HIM. GUNBORG'S ORDERS.
NOW. HILDA...
DESPITE IT ALL, I *FORGIVE YOU.*
NOTHING WOULD MAKE ME HAPPIER THAN TO RETURN YOUR DAUGHTER, TO TAKE YOU INTO MY HOME, TO BE WITH YOU AS HUSBAND AND WIFE.
BUT I'LL NEED YOU TO DO SOMETHING FOR ME FIRST.
I NEED A SIGN OF YOUR DEVOTION. YOUR COMMITMENT.
YOUR WILLINGNESS TO SUBMIT TO MY AUTHORITY.
YOU WILL LEAVE YOUR OUTER GARMENTS HERE...
...AND WALK, ALONE, ACROSS THE SETTLEMENT TO MY DOORSTEP CONTRITE AND PENITENT IN FRONT OF THE ENTIRE SETTLEMENT...
I'LL BE WAITING THERE, WITH KARIN.
AND YOU WILL BEG MY FORGIVENESS

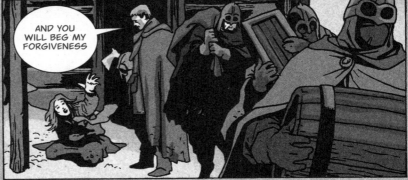

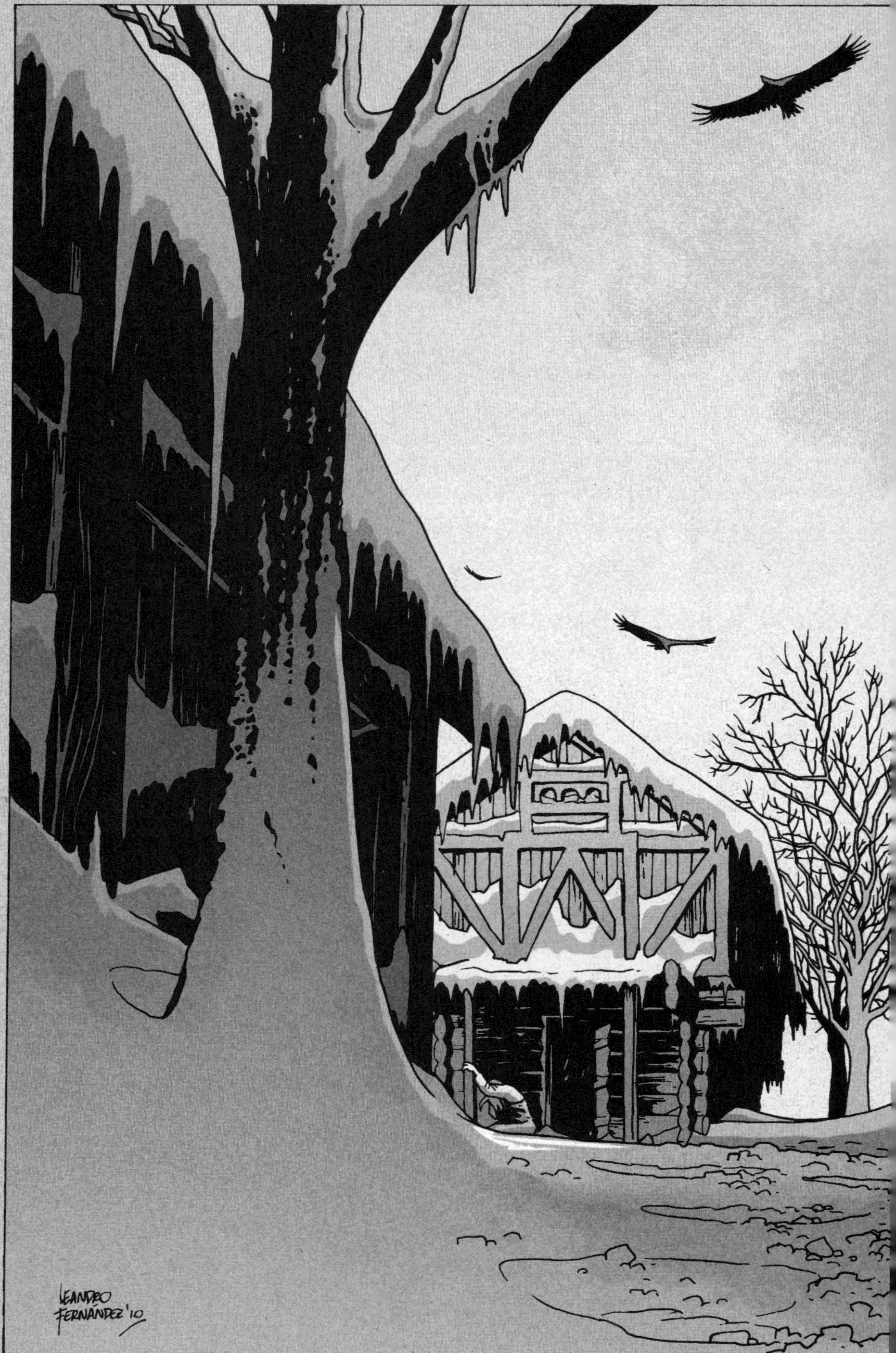
LEANDRO
FERNANDEZ '10

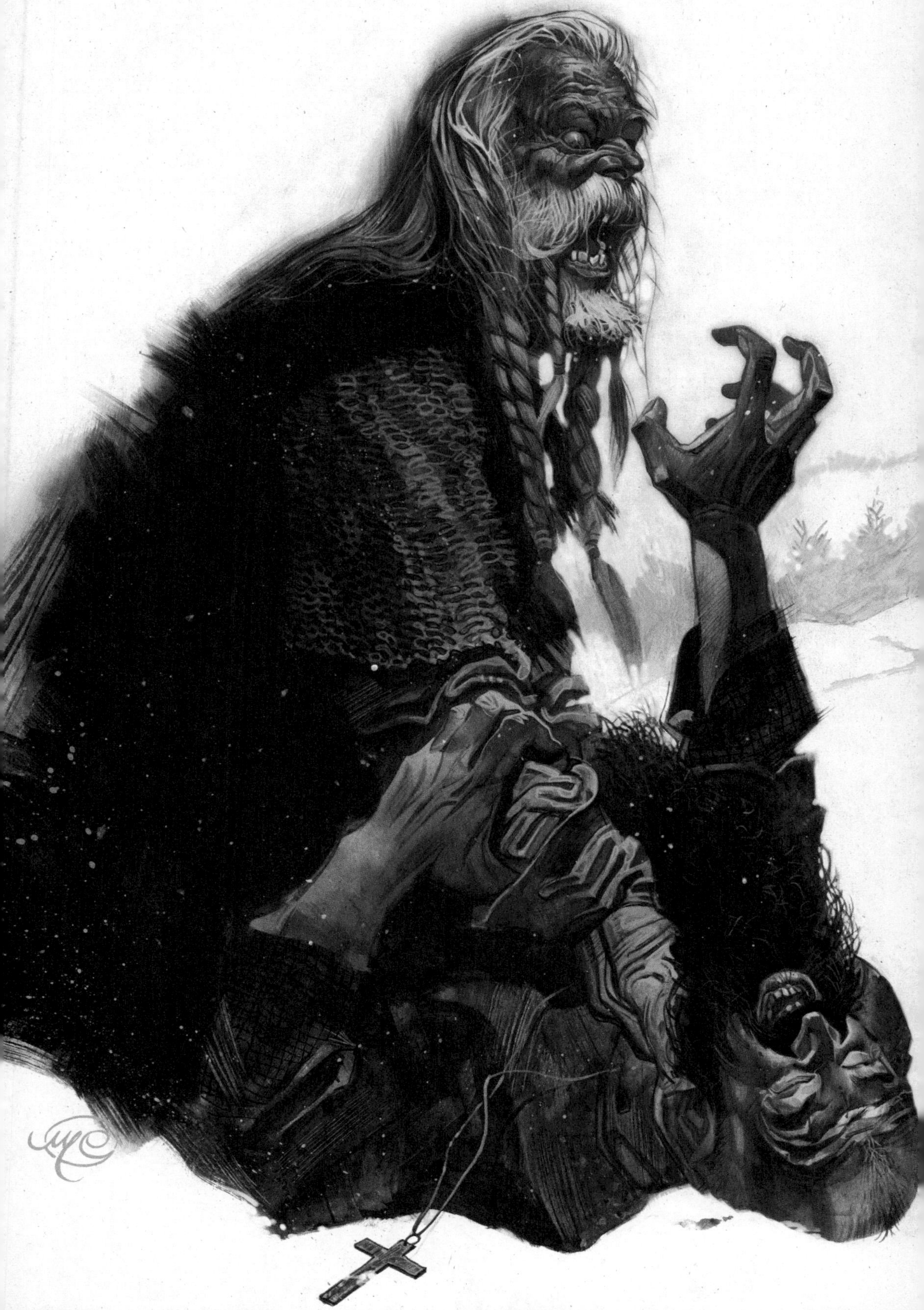

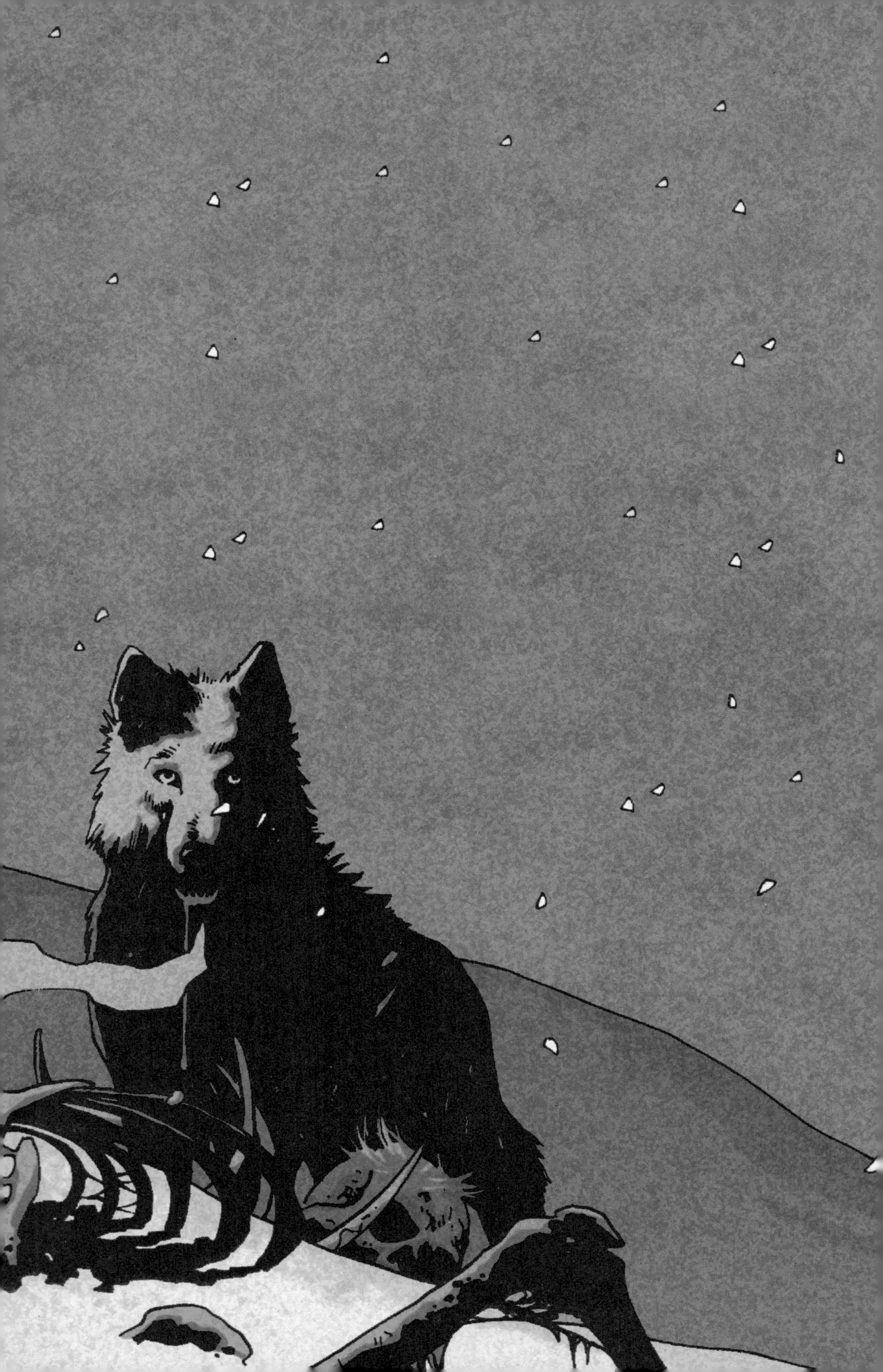

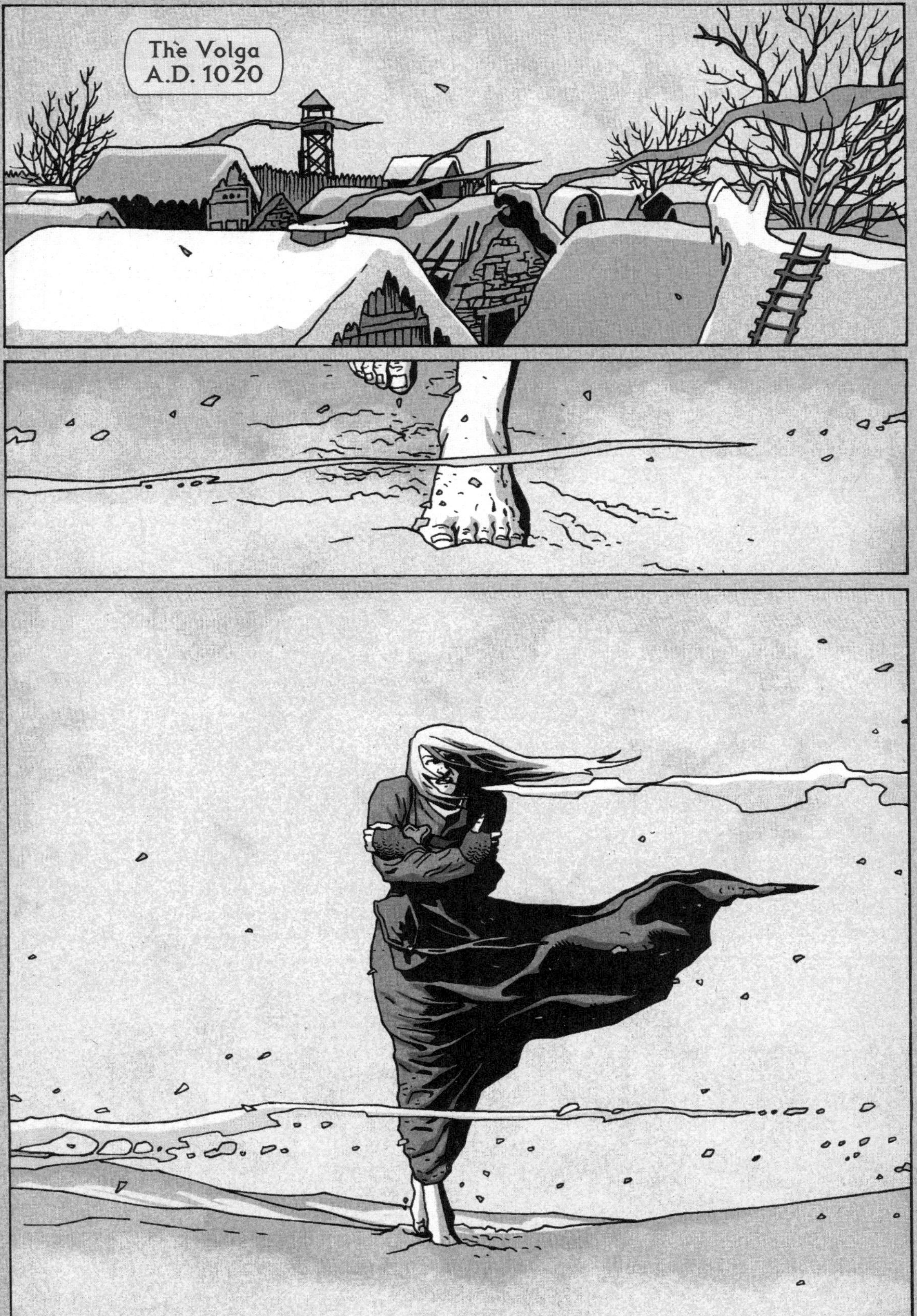
The Volga
A.D. 1020

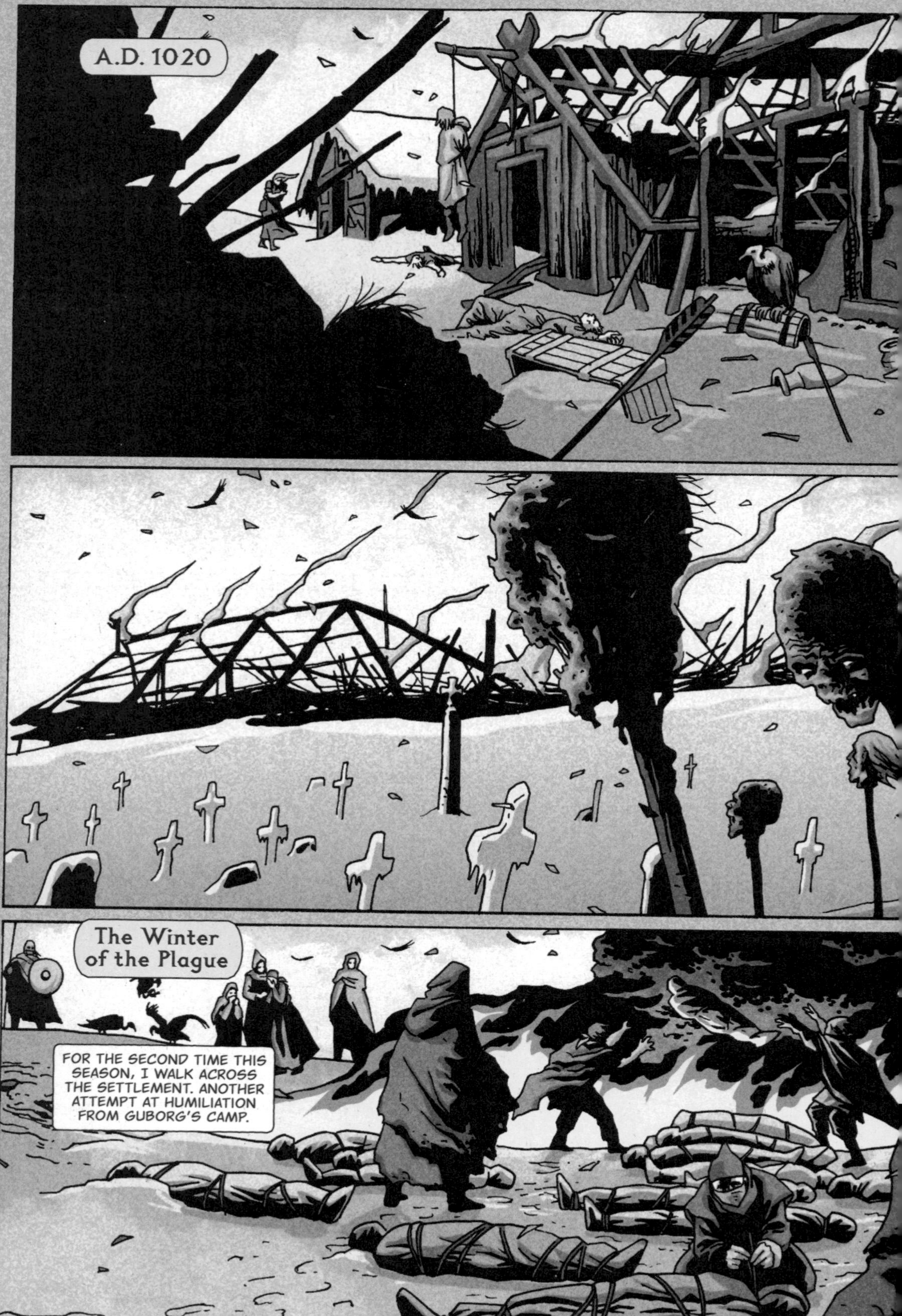
A.D. 1020
The Winter of the Plague
FOR THE SECOND TIME THIS SEASON, I WALK ACROSS THE SETTLEMENT. ANOTHER ATTEMPT AT HUMILIATION FROM GUBORG'S CAMP.

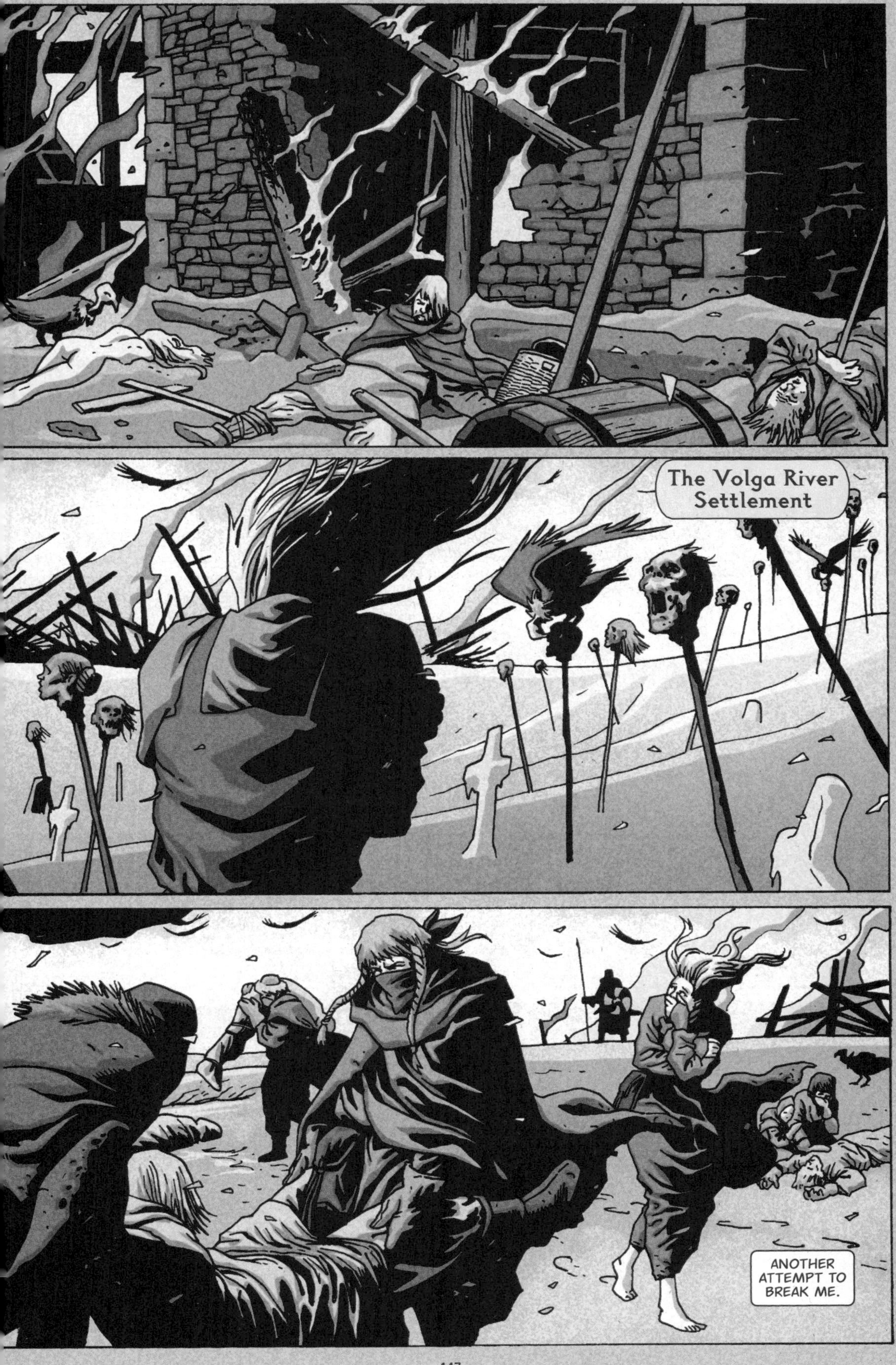
The Volga River Settlement
ANOTHER ATTEMPT TO BREAK ME.

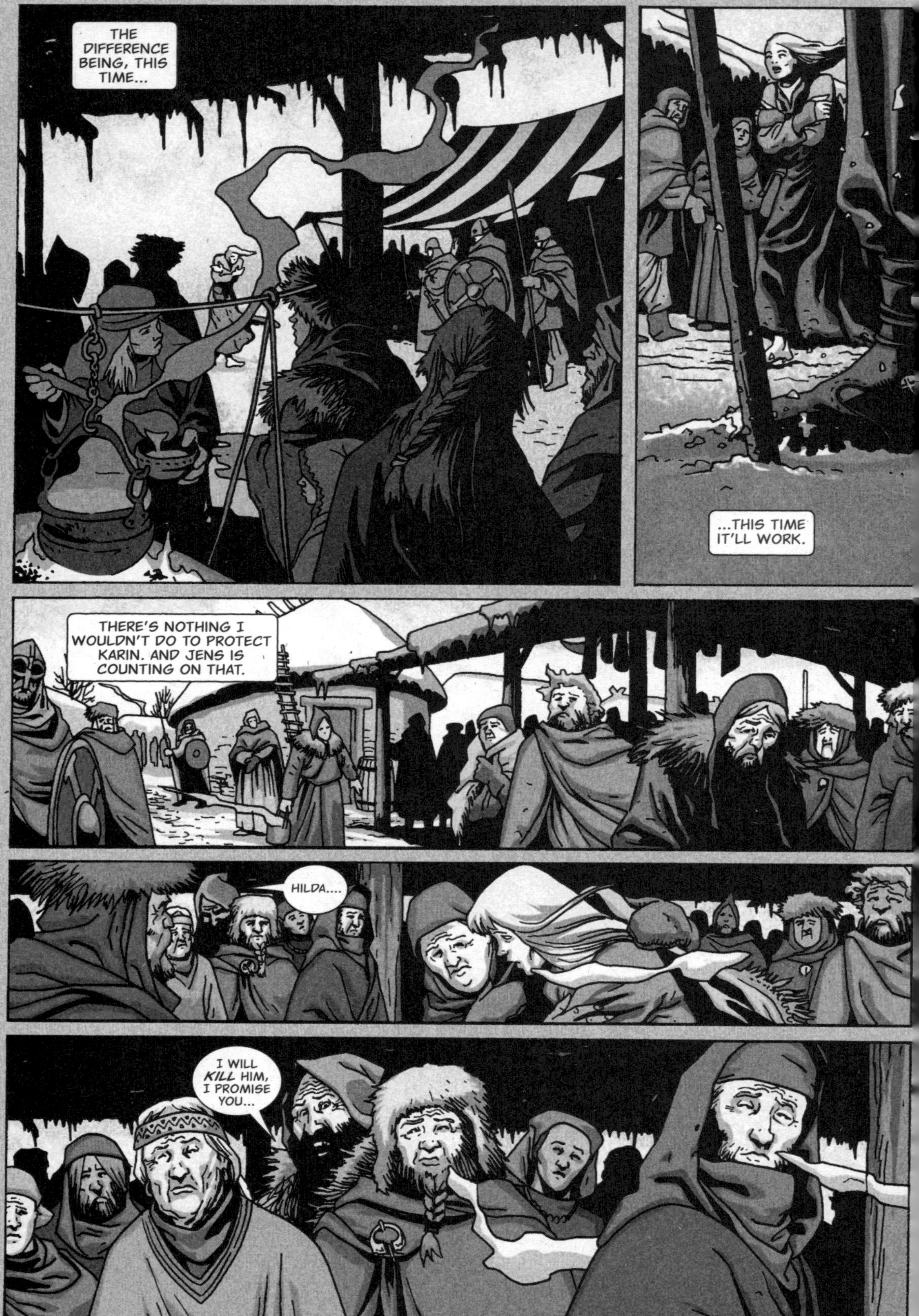
THE DIFFERENCE BEING, THIS TIME...
...THIS TIME IT'LL WORK.
THERE'S NOTHING I WOULDN'T DO TO PROTECT KARIN. AND JENS IS COUNTING ON THAT.
HILDA....
I WILL *KILL* HIM, I PROMISE YOU...

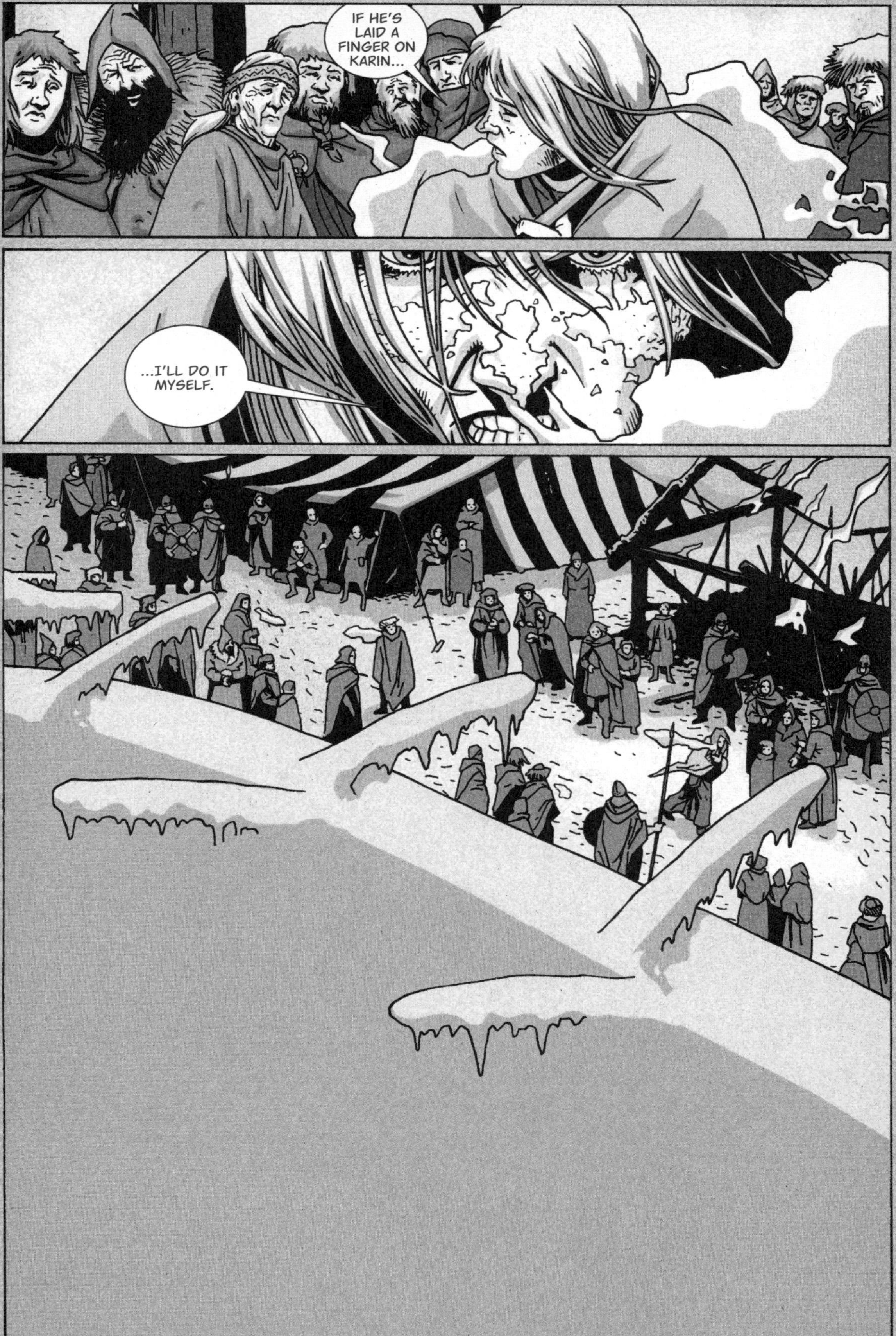
IF HE'S LAID A FINGER ON KARIN...
...I'LL DO IT MYSELF.

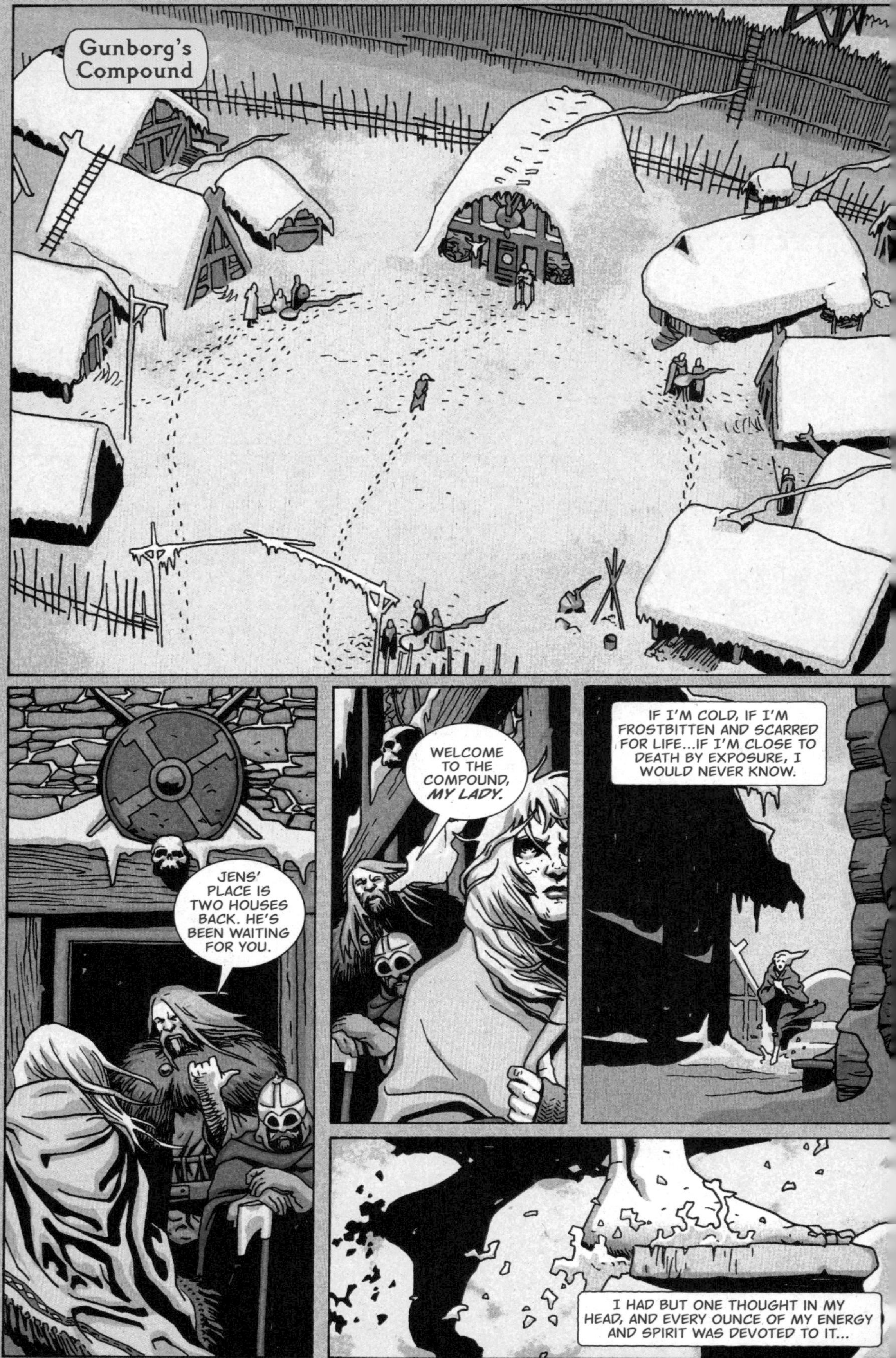
Gunborg's Compound
JENS' PLACE IS TWO HOUSES BACK. HE'S BEEN WAITING FOR YOU.
WELCOME TO THE COMPOUND, *MY LADY.*
IF I'M COLD, IF I'M FROSTBITTEN AND SCARRED FOR LIFE...IF I'M CLOSE TO DEATH BY EXPOSURE, I WOULD NEVER KNOW.
I HAD BUT ONE THOUGHT IN MY HEAD, AND EVERY OUNCE OF MY ENERGY AND SPIRIT WAS DEVOTED TO IT...

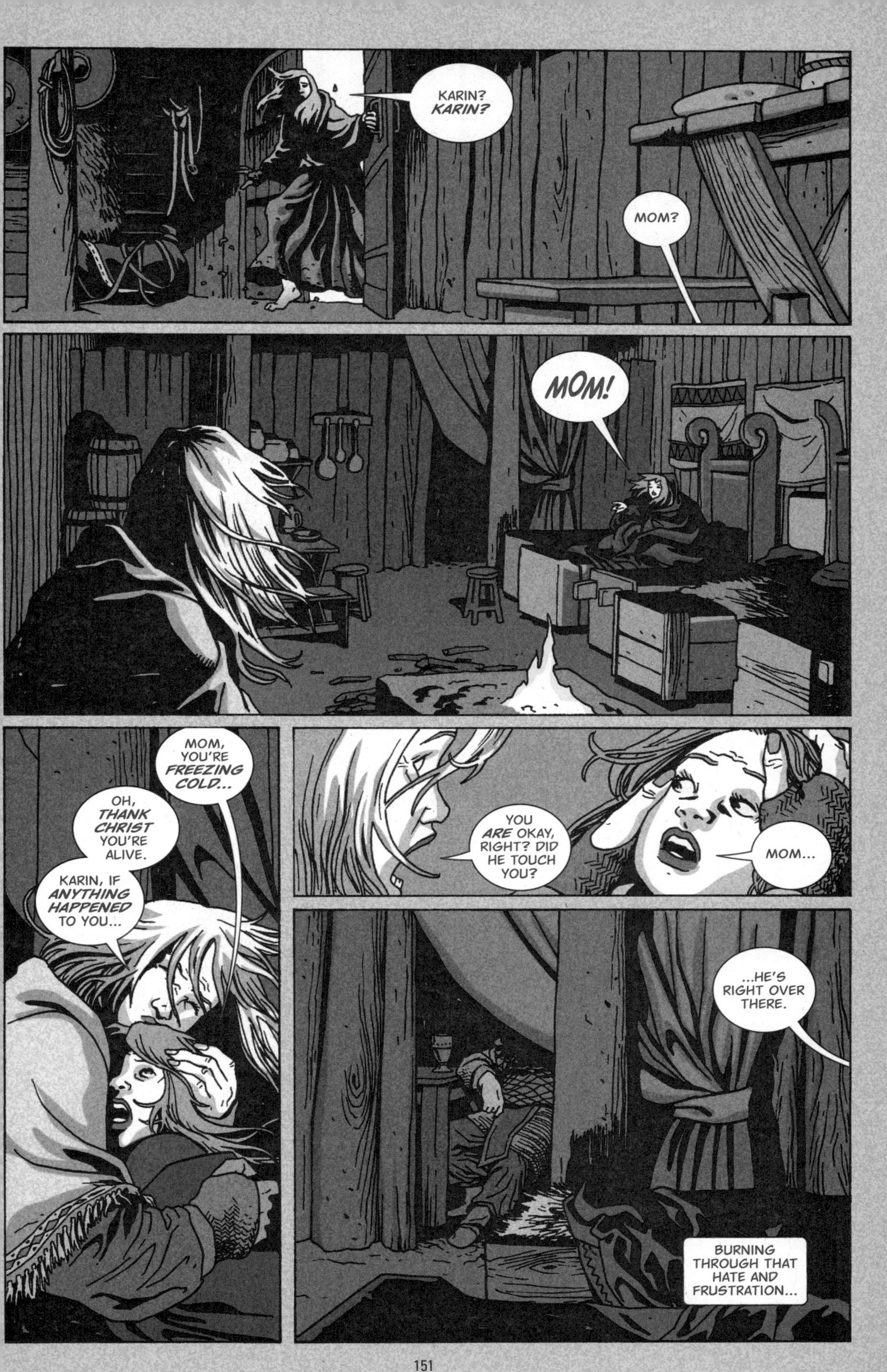
KARIN? KARIN?
MOM?
MOM!
OH, THANK CHRIST YOU'RE ALIVE.
KARIN, IF ANYTHING HAPPENED TO YOU...
MOM, YOU'RE FREEZING COLD...
YOU ARE OKAY, RIGHT? DID HE TOUCH YOU?
MOM...
...HE'S RIGHT OVER THERE.
BURNING THROUGH THAT HATE AND FRUSTRATION...

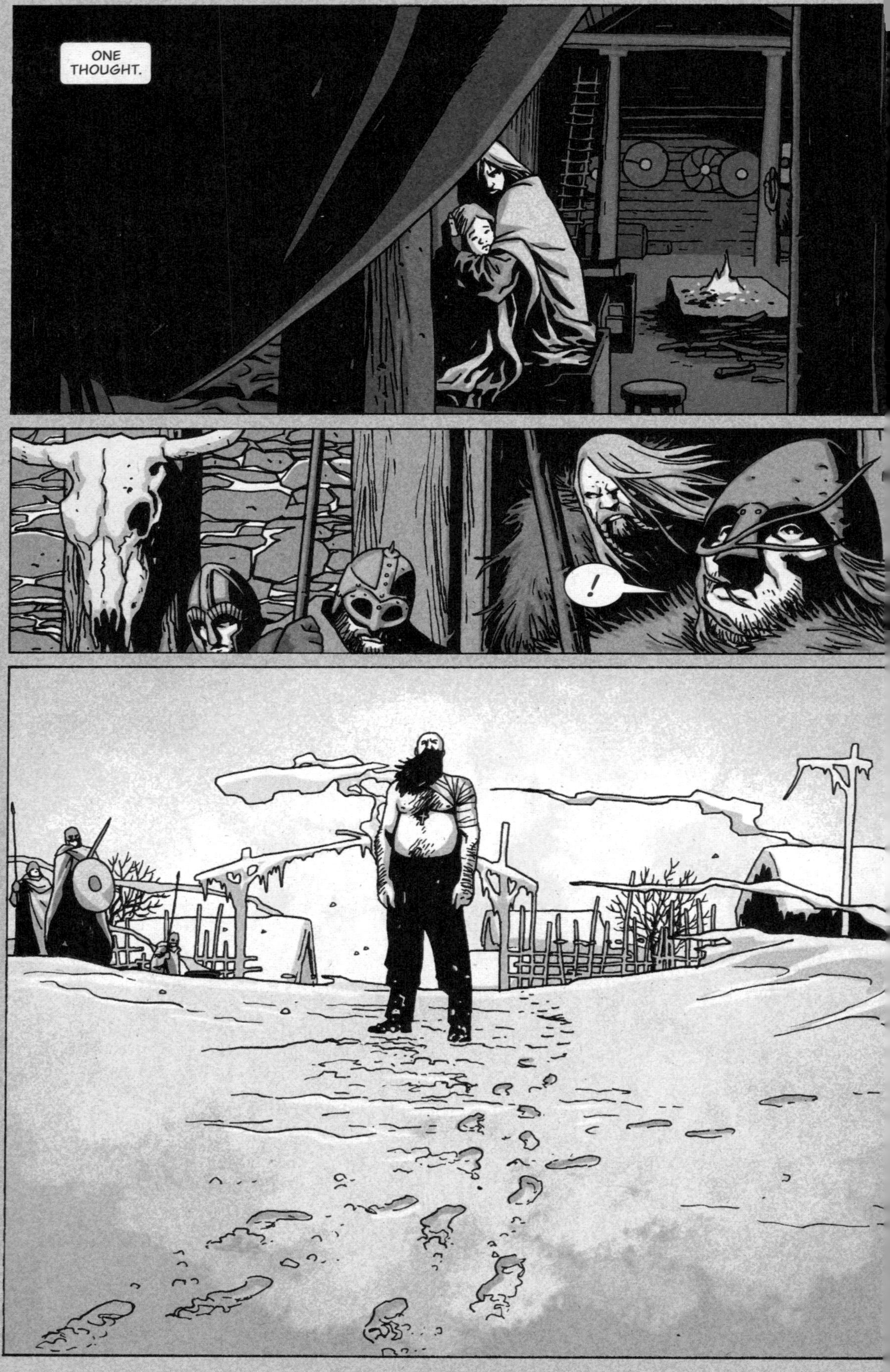
ONE THOUGHT.
!

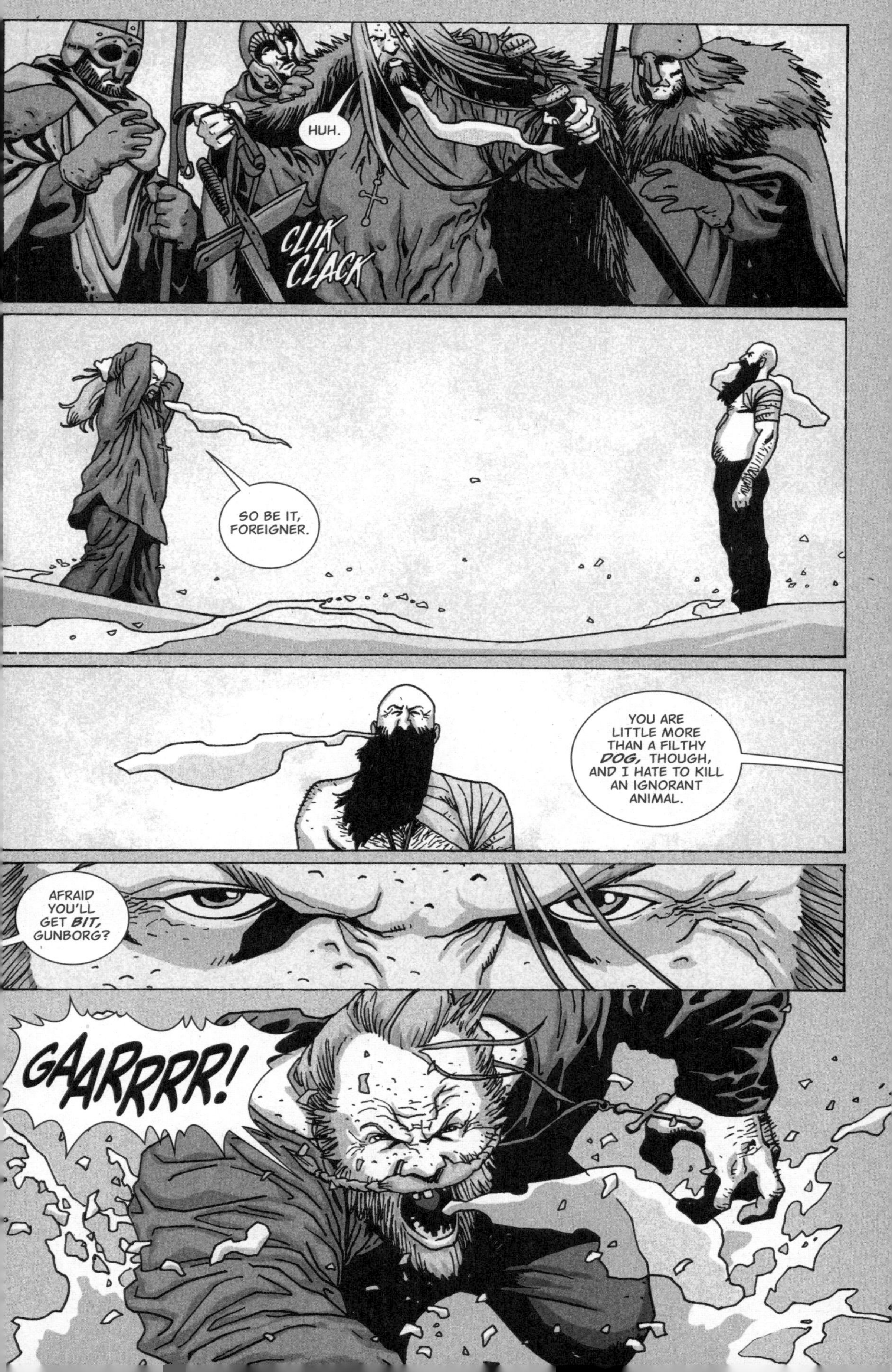
HUH.
CLIK CLACK
SO BE IT, FOREIGNER.
YOU ARE LITTLE MORE THAN A FILTHY *DOG,* THOUGH, AND I HATE TO KILL AN IGNORANT ANIMAL.
AFRAID YOU'LL GET *BIT,* GUNBORG?
GAARRRRR!

WHUNK

WSSSSSSHHH

····

KRK

THWACK

WHUMP

····

SLK

NO!

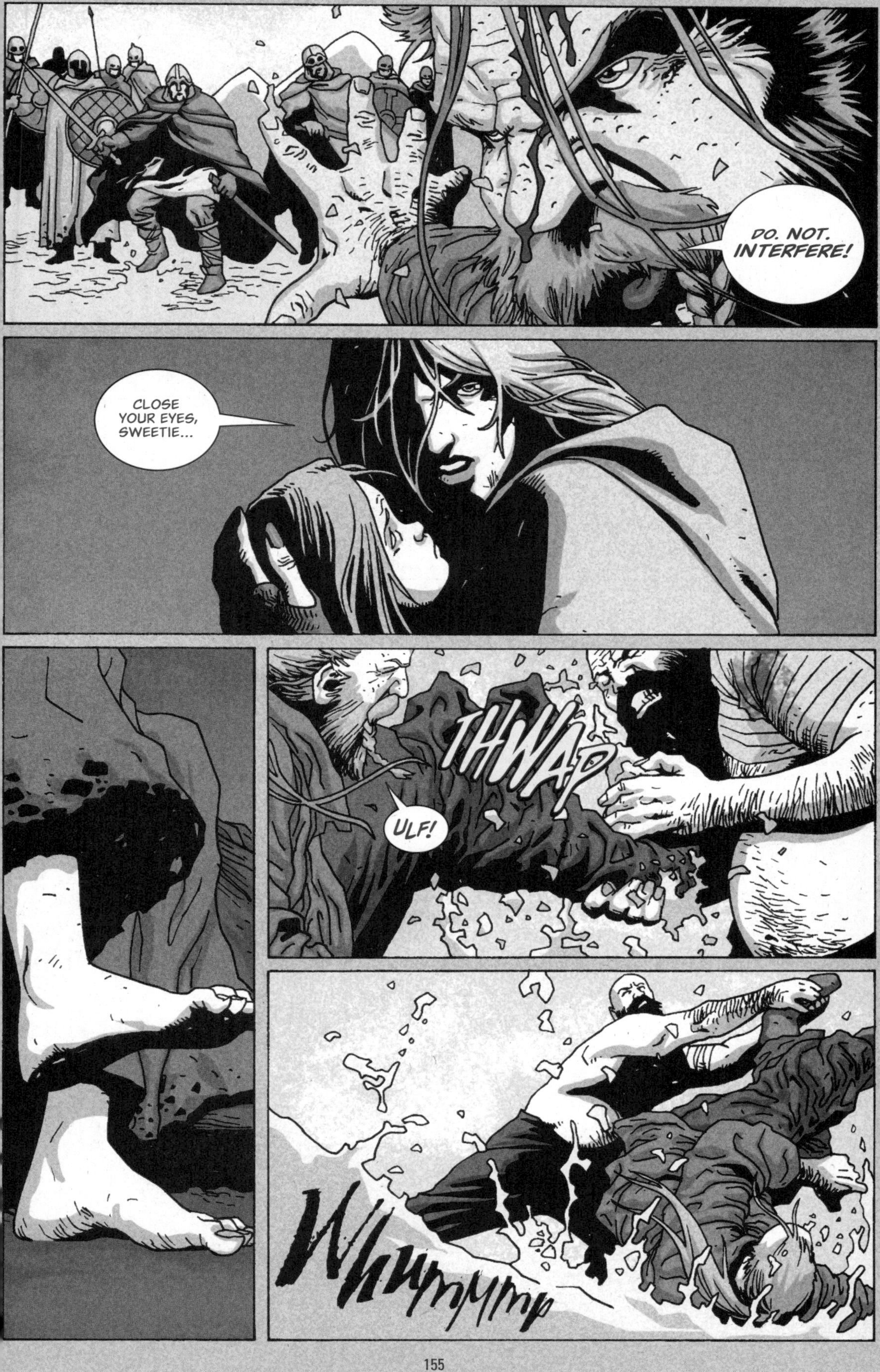
DO. NOT. INTERFERE!
CLOSE YOUR EYES, SWEETIE...
THWAP
ULF!
WHUMMMP

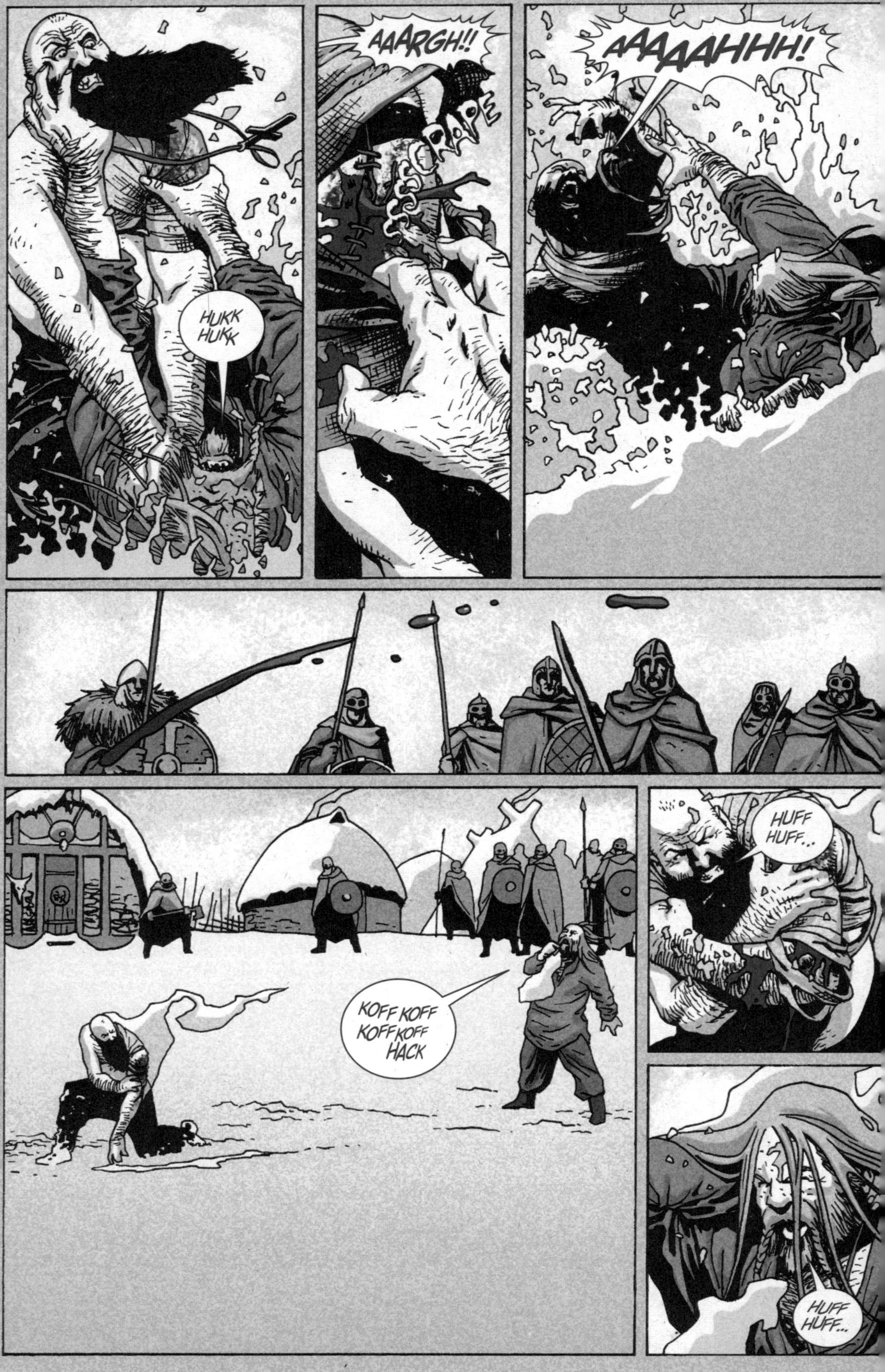
HUKK HUKK
AAARGH!!
AAAAAHHH!
HUFF HUFF...
KOFF KOFF KOFF KOFF HACK
HUFF HUFF...

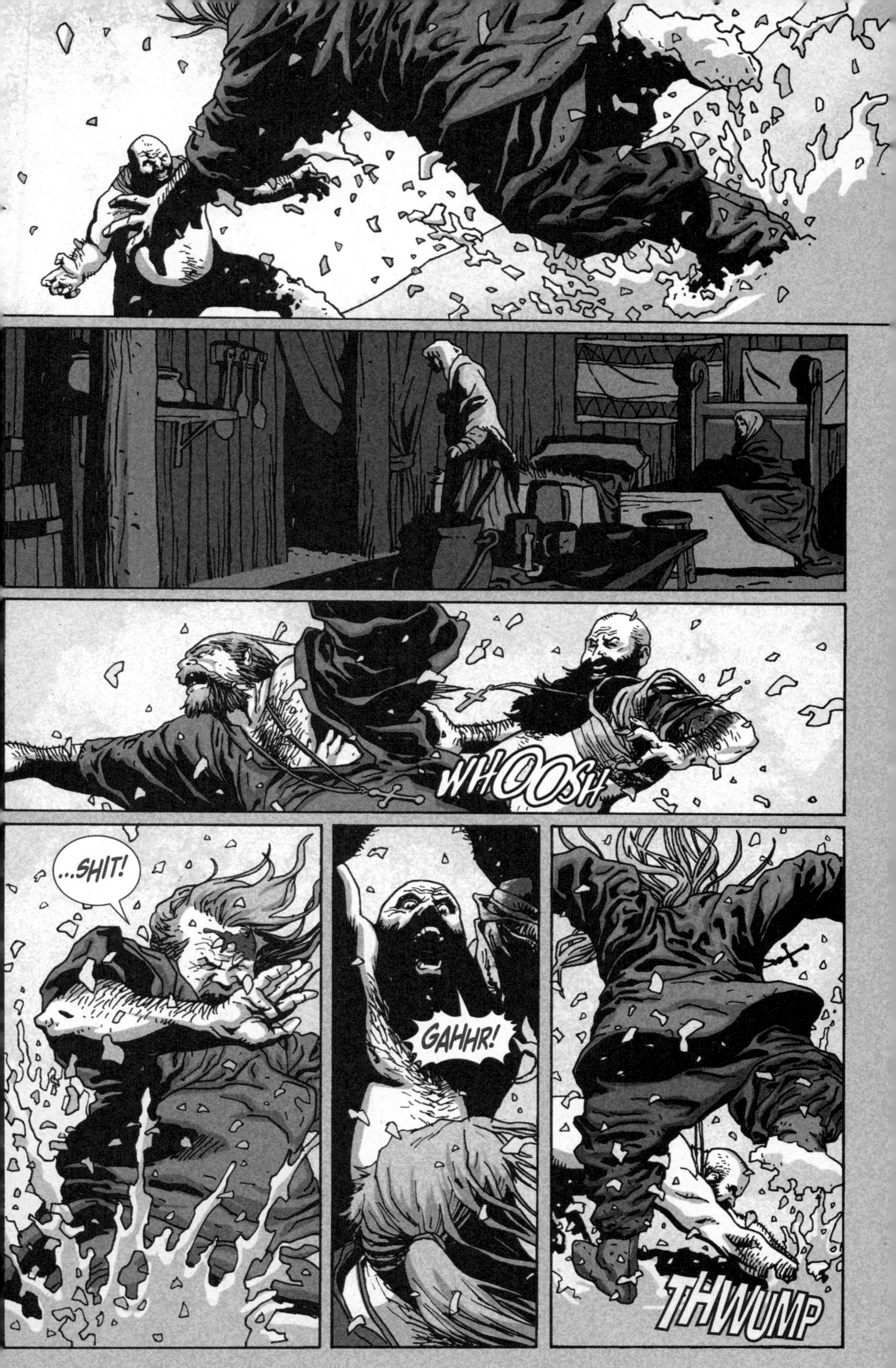
WHOOSH
...SHIT!
GAHHR!
THWUMP

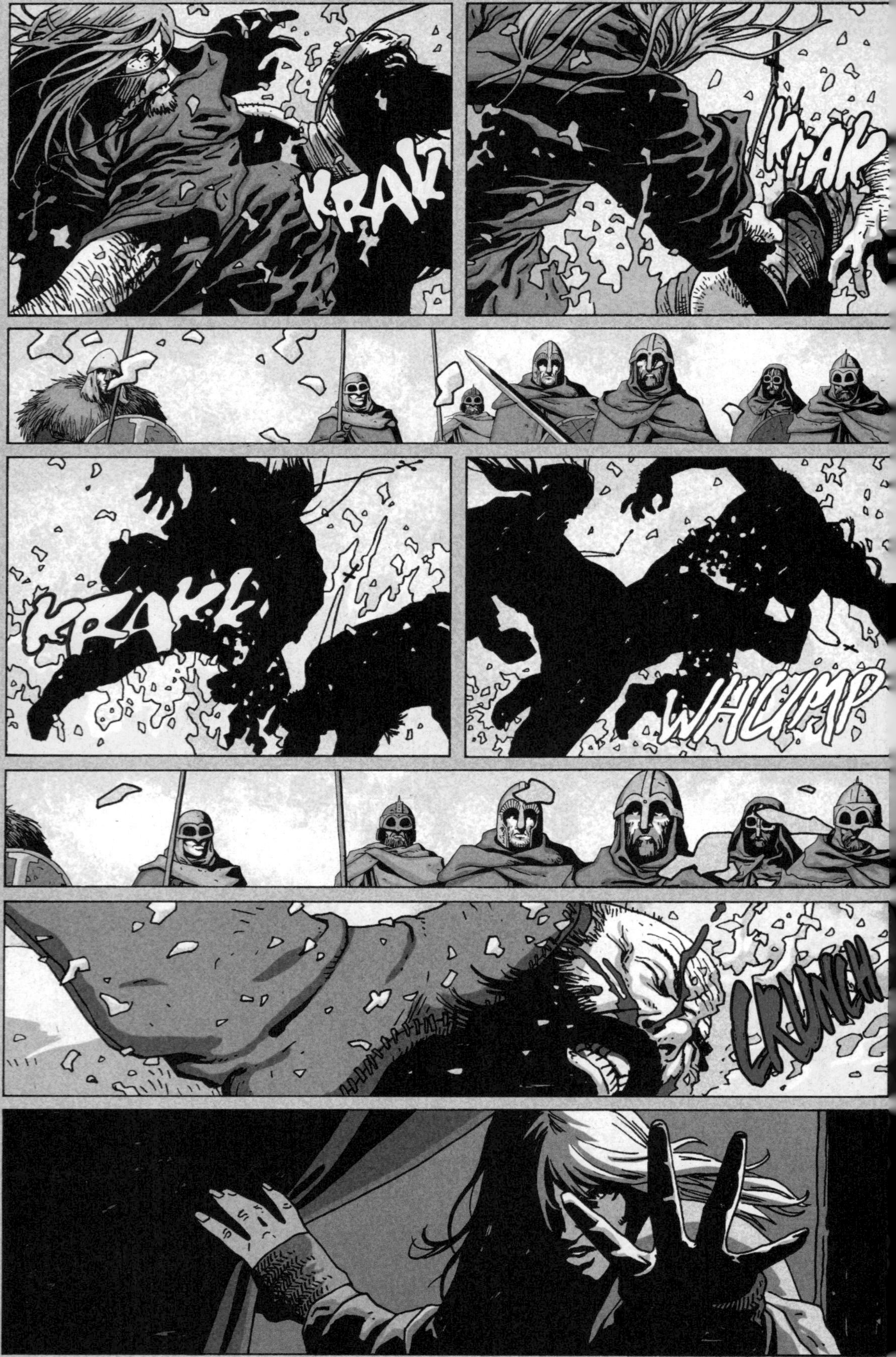
KRAK
KRAK
KRAKK
WHUMP
CRUNCH

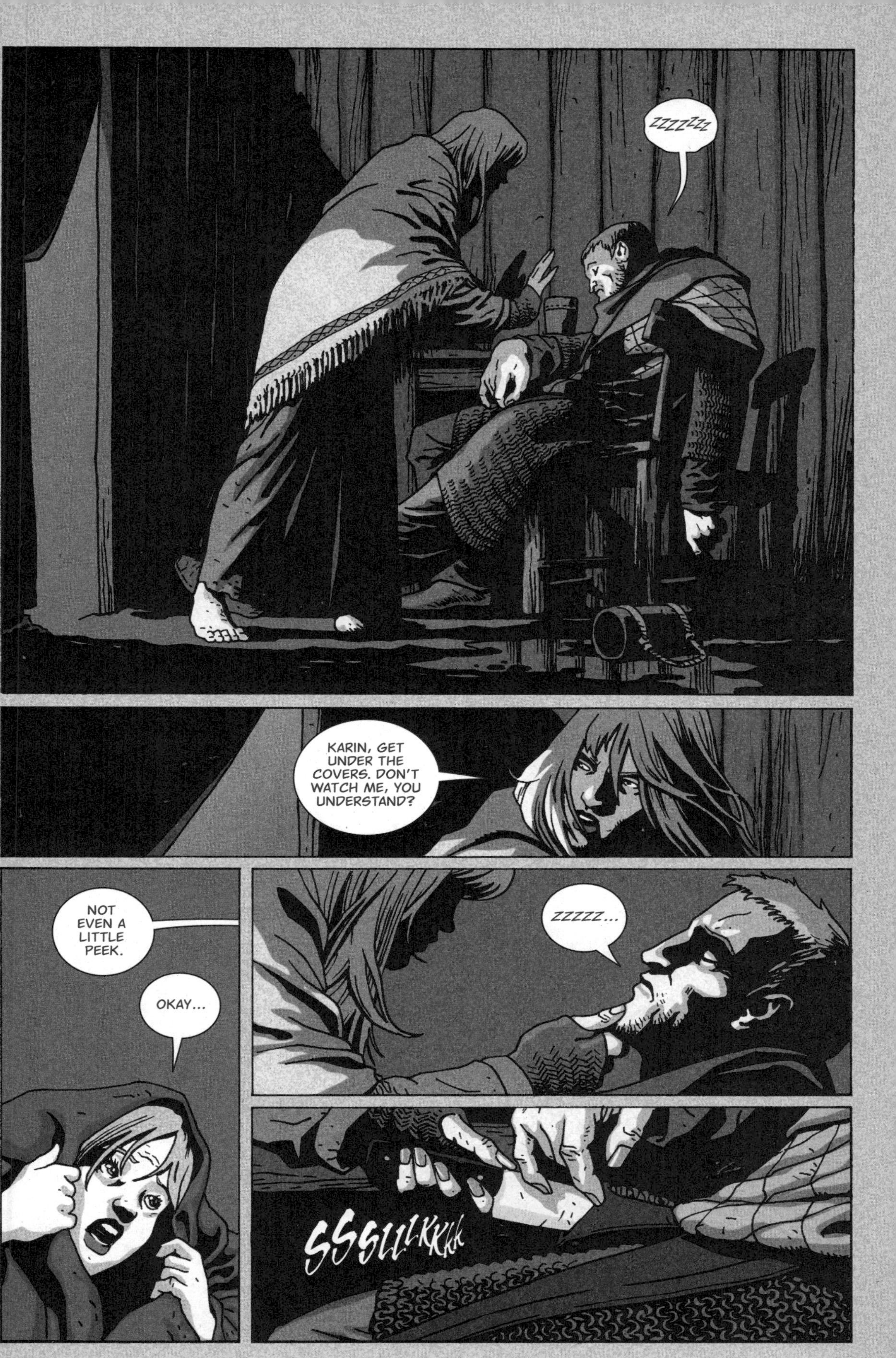
ZZZZZZZ
KARIN, GET UNDER THE COVERS. DON'T WATCH ME, YOU UNDERSTAND?
NOT EVEN A LITTLE PEEK.
OKAY...
ZZZZZ...
SSSLLLKKKK

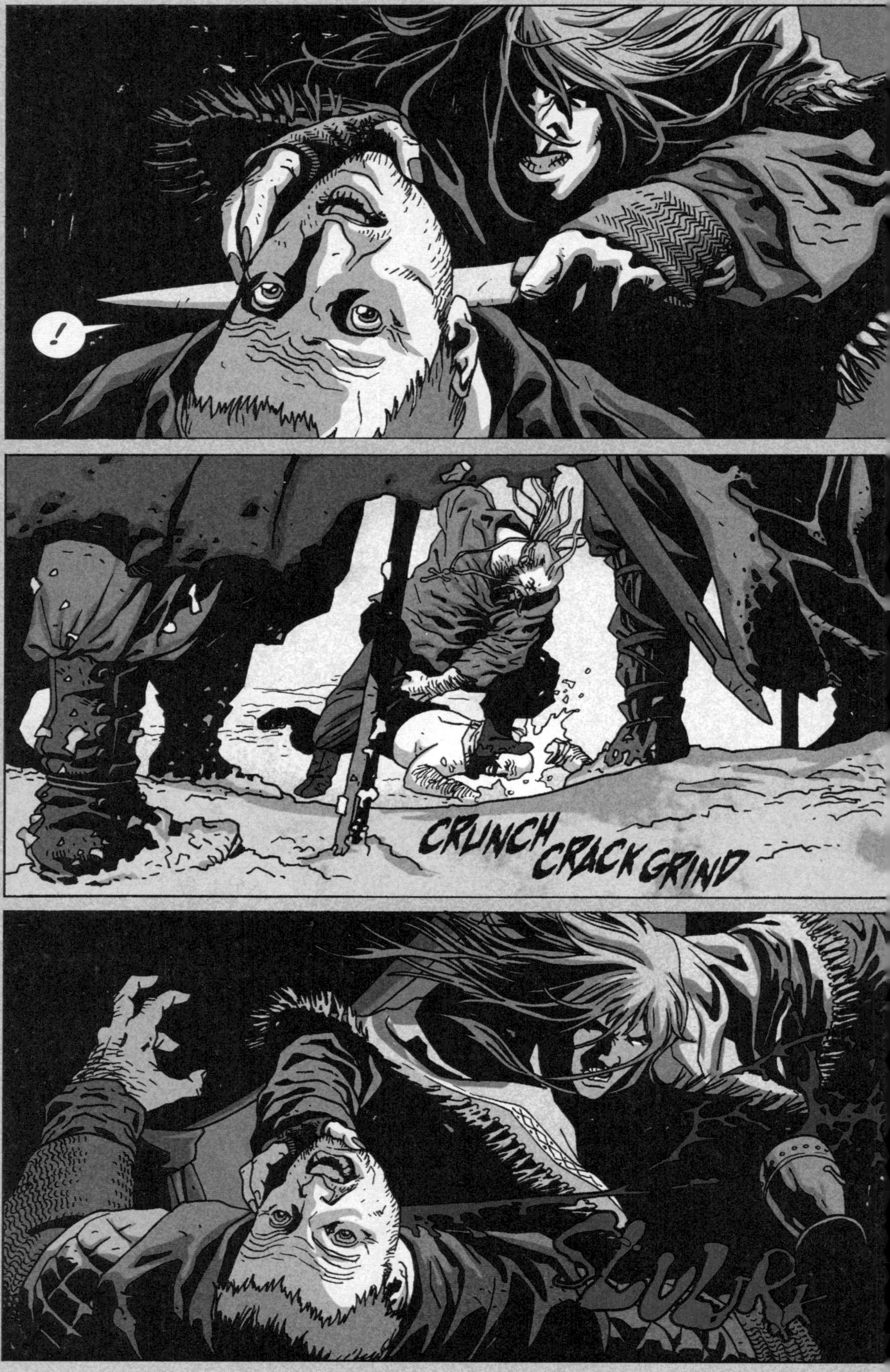
!
CRUNCH
CRACK GRIND
SLULR

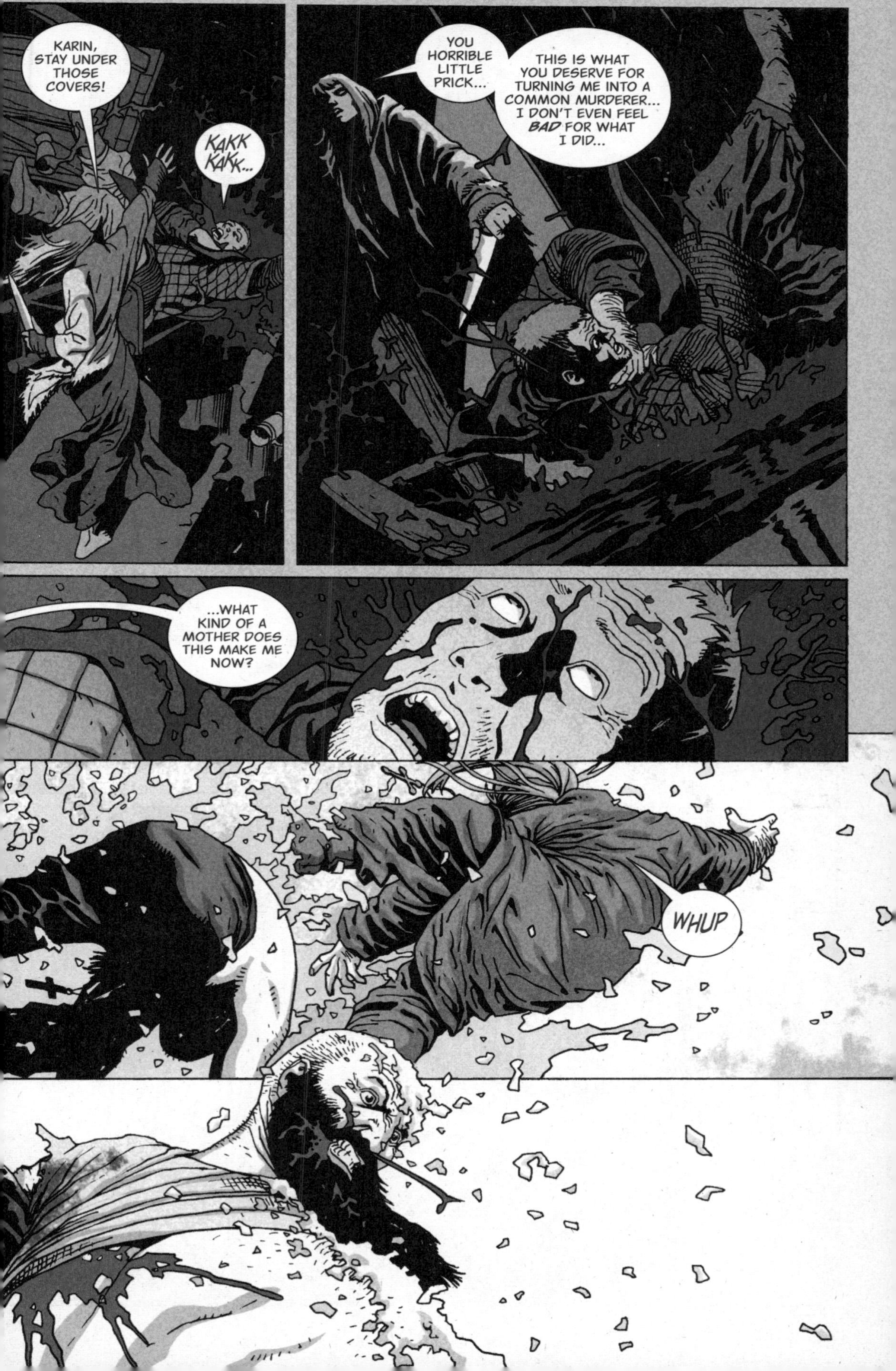
KARIN, STAY UNDER THOSE COVERS!
KAKK KAKK...
YOU HORRIBLE LITTLE PRICK...
THIS IS WHAT YOU DESERVE FOR TURNING ME INTO A COMMON MURDERER... I DON'T EVEN FEEL BAD FOR WHAT I DID...
...WHAT KIND OF A MOTHER DOES THIS MAKE ME NOW?
WHUP

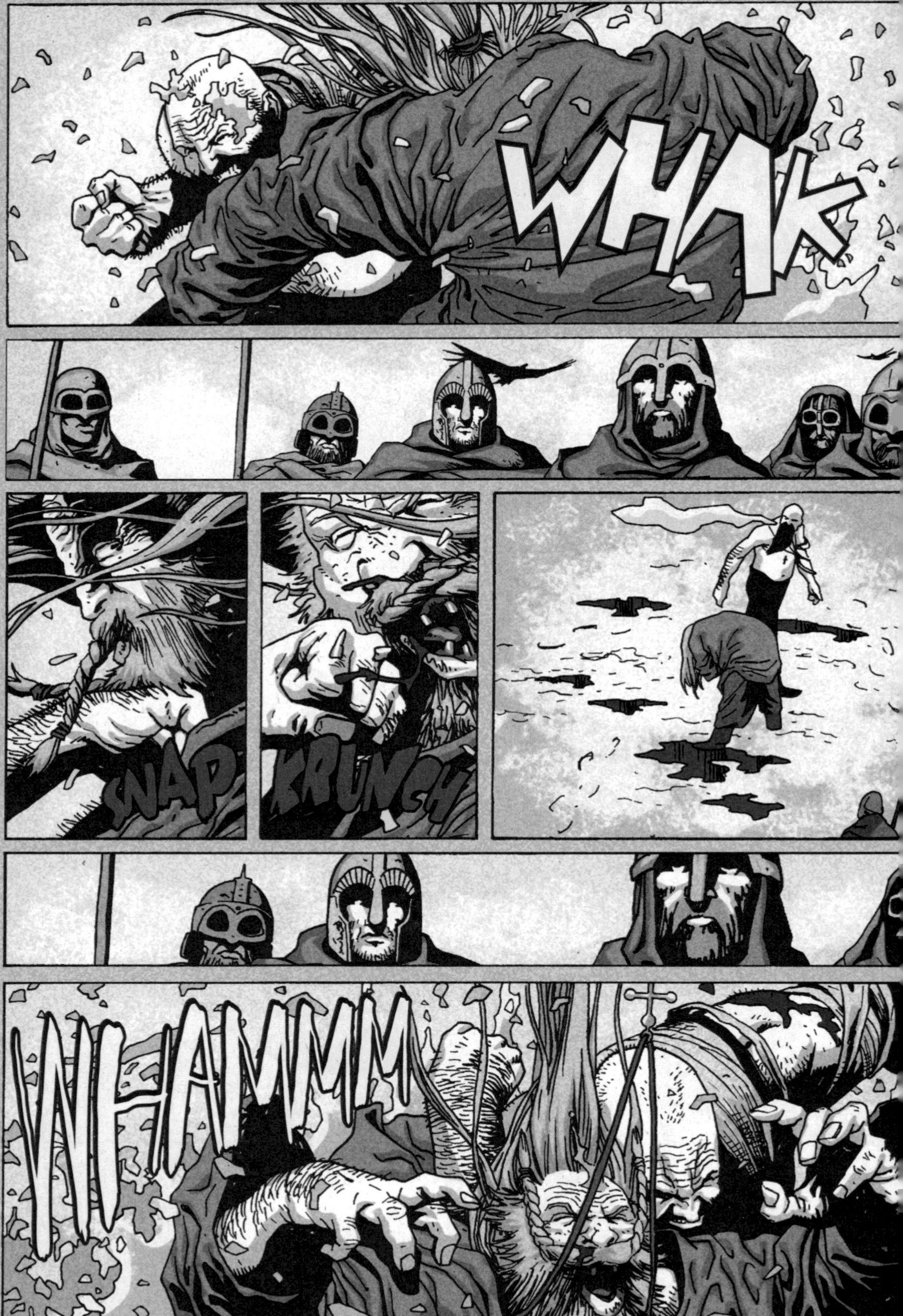
WHAK
SNAP
KRUNCH
WHAMMM

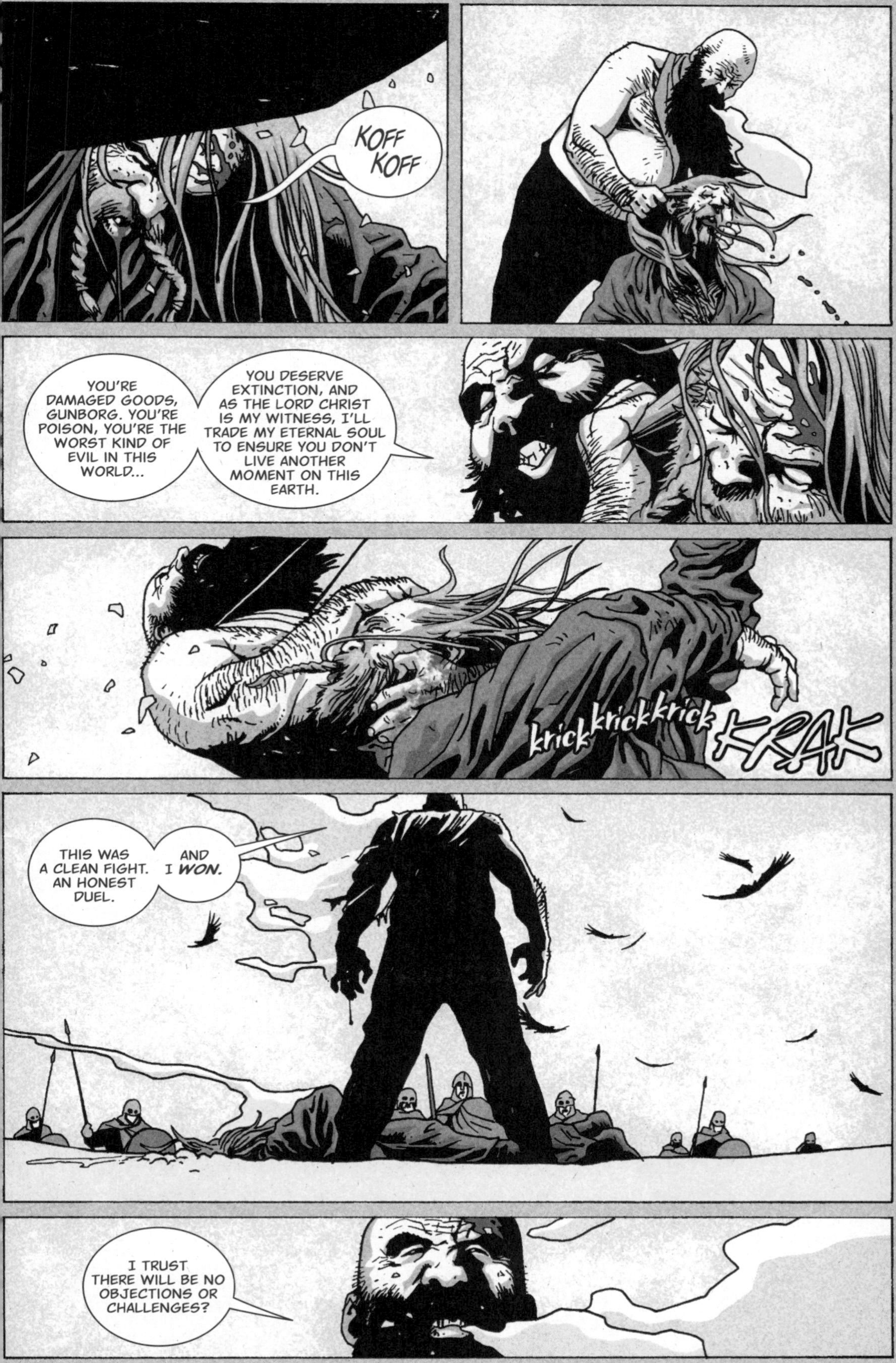
KOFF KOFF
YOU'RE DAMAGED GOODS, GUNBORG. YOU'RE POISON, YOU'RE THE WORST KIND OF EVIL IN THIS WORLD...
YOU DESERVE EXTINCTION, AND AS THE LORD CHRIST IS MY WITNESS, I'LL TRADE MY ETERNAL SOUL TO ENSURE YOU DON'T LIVE ANOTHER MOMENT ON THIS EARTH.
krickkrickkrick KRAK
THIS WAS A CLEAN FIGHT. AN HONEST DUEL.
AND I *WON.*
I TRUST THERE WILL BE NO OBJECTIONS OR CHALLENGES?

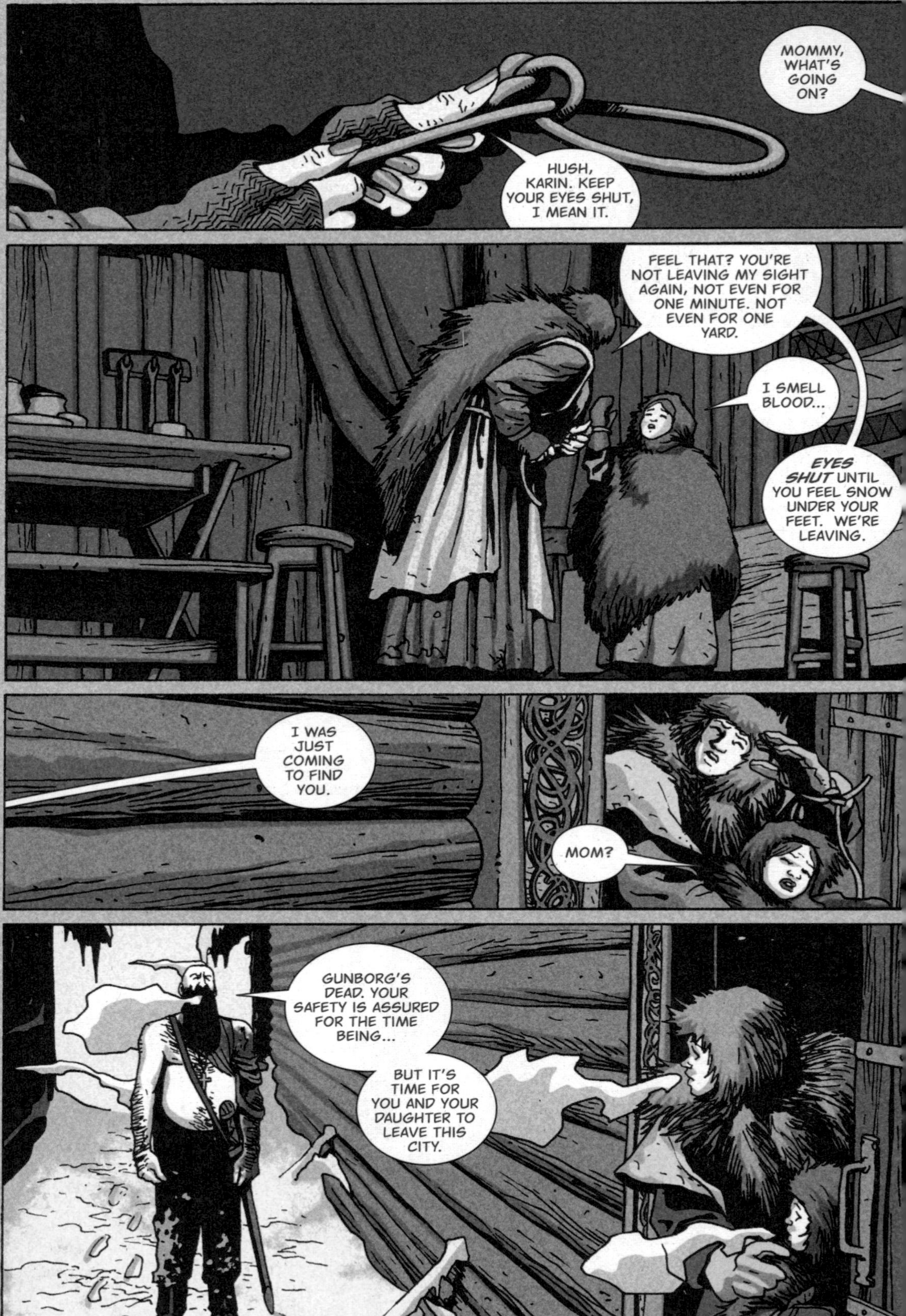
MOMMY, WHAT'S GOING ON?
HUSH, KARIN. KEEP YOUR EYES SHUT, I MEAN IT.
FEEL THAT? YOU'RE NOT LEAVING MY SIGHT AGAIN, NOT EVEN FOR ONE MINUTE. NOT EVEN FOR ONE YARD.
I SMELL BLOOD...
EYES SHUT UNTIL YOU FEEL SNOW UNDER YOUR FEET. WE'RE LEAVING.
I WAS JUST COMING TO FIND YOU.
MOM?
GUNBORG'S DEAD. YOUR SAFETY IS ASSURED FOR THE TIME BEING...
BUT IT'S TIME FOR YOU AND YOUR DAUGHTER TO LEAVE THIS CITY.

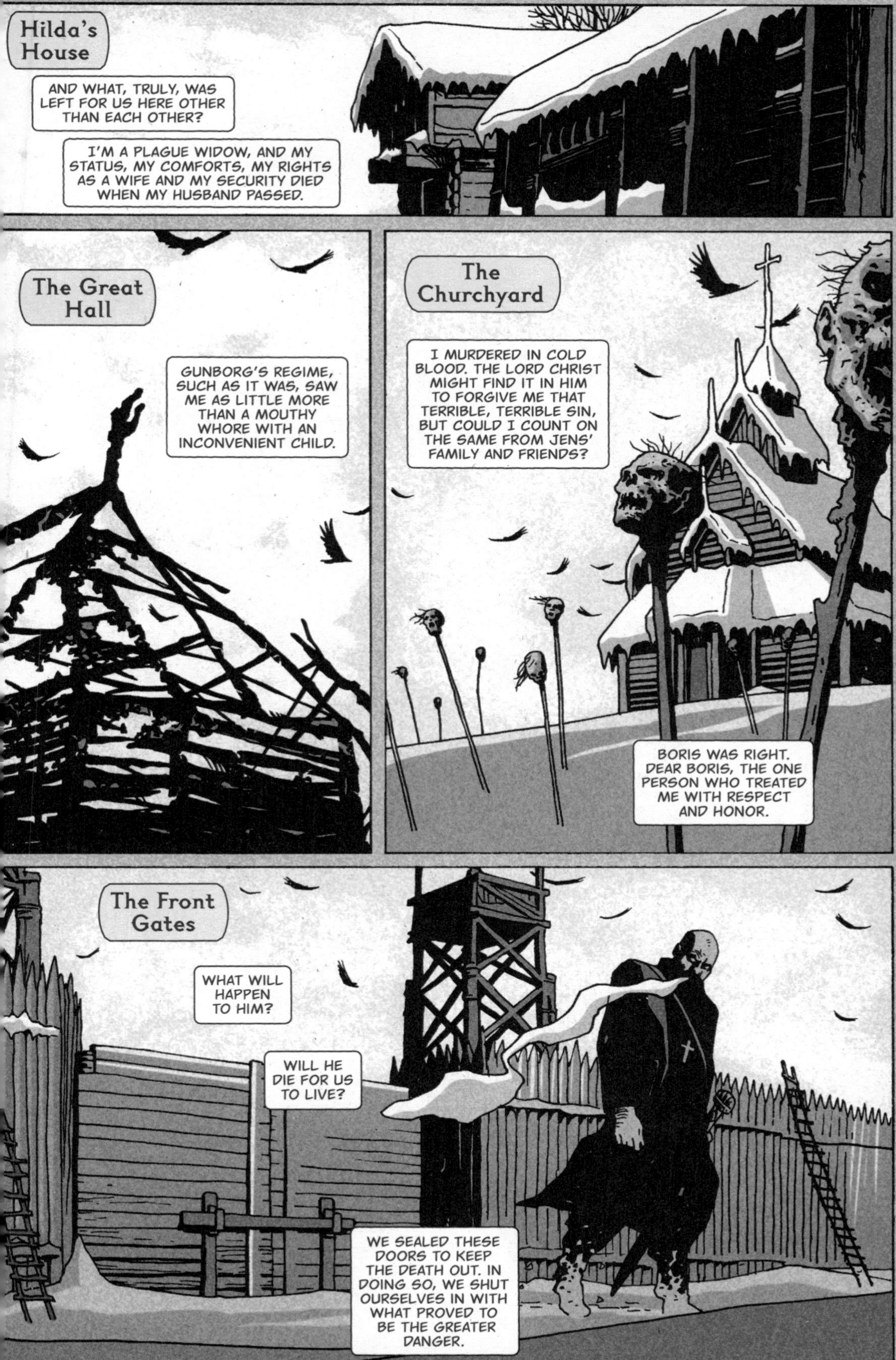

Hilda's House
AND WHAT, TRULY, WAS LEFT FOR US HERE OTHER THAN EACH OTHER?
I'M A PLAGUE WIDOW, AND MY STATUS, MY COMFORTS, MY RIGHTS AS A WIFE AND MY SECURITY DIED WHEN MY HUSBAND PASSED.
The Great Hall
GUNBORG'S REGIME, SUCH AS IT WAS, SAW ME AS LITTLE MORE THAN A MOUTHY WHORE WITH AN INCONVENIENT CHILD.
The Churchyard
I MURDERED IN COLD BLOOD. THE LORD CHRIST MIGHT FIND IT IN HIM TO FORGIVE ME THAT TERRIBLE, TERRIBLE SIN, BUT COULD I COUNT ON THE SAME FROM JENS' FAMILY AND FRIENDS?
BORIS WAS RIGHT. DEAR BORIS, THE ONE PERSON WHO TREATED ME WITH RESPECT AND HONOR.
The Front Gates
WHAT WILL HAPPEN TO HIM?
WILL HE DIE FOR US TO LIVE?
WE SEALED THESE DOORS TO KEEP THE DEATH OUT. IN DOING SO, WE SHUT OURSELVES IN WITH WHAT PROVED TO BE THE GREATER DANGER.

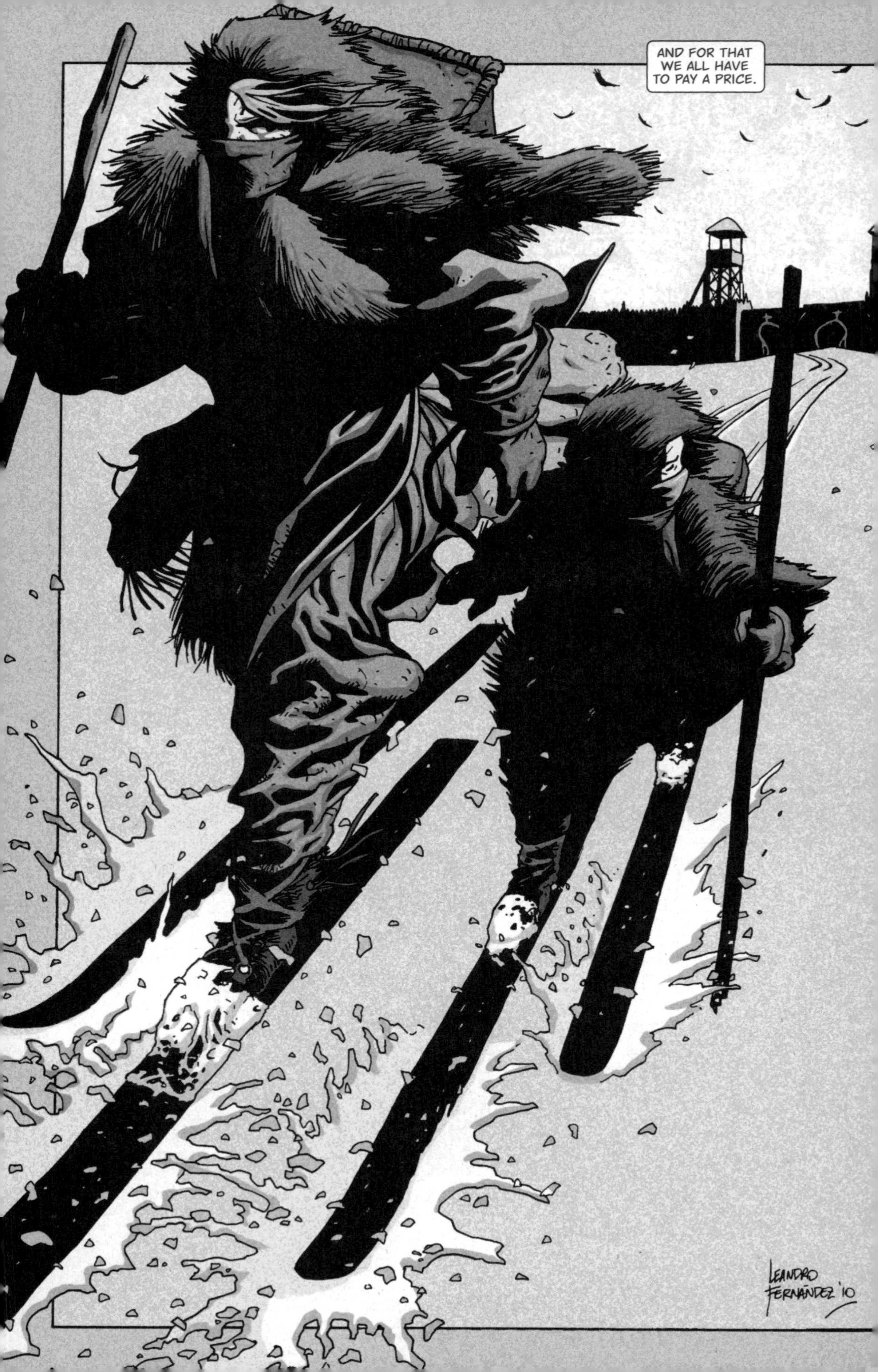
AND FOR THAT
WE ALL HAVE
TO PAY A PRICE.
LEANDRO
FERNANDEZ '10

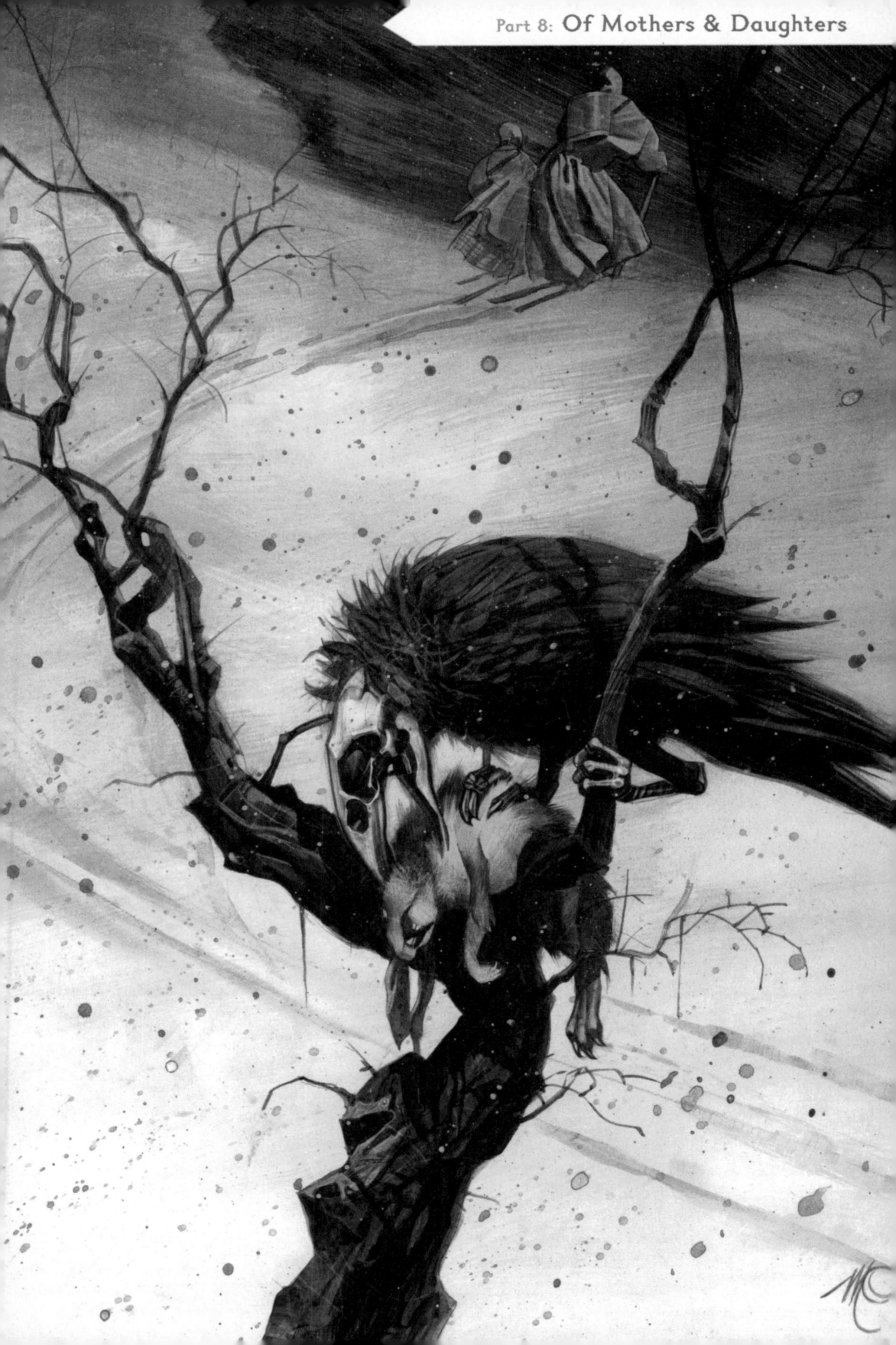

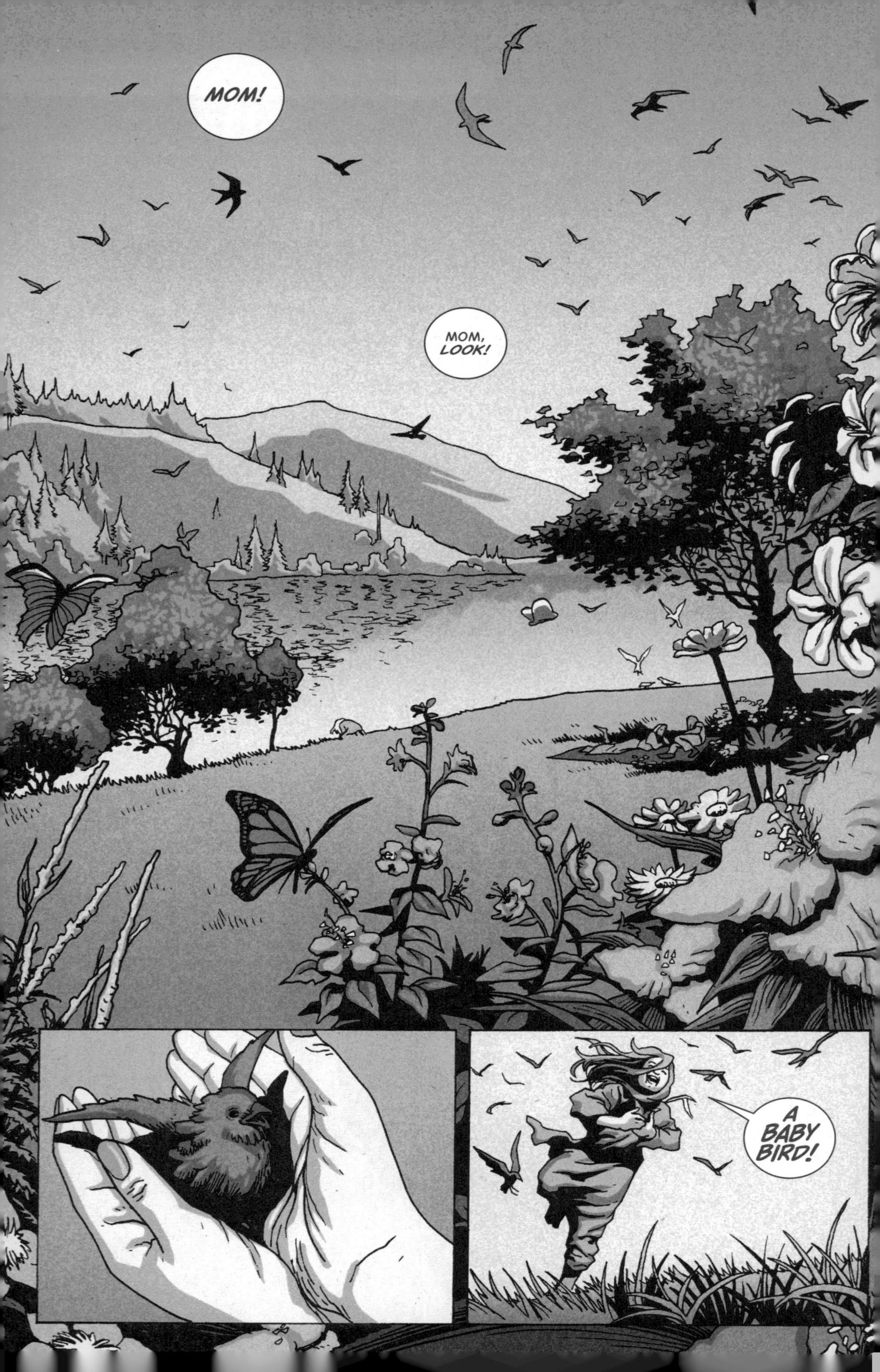
MOM!
MOM, LOOK!
A BABY BIRD!

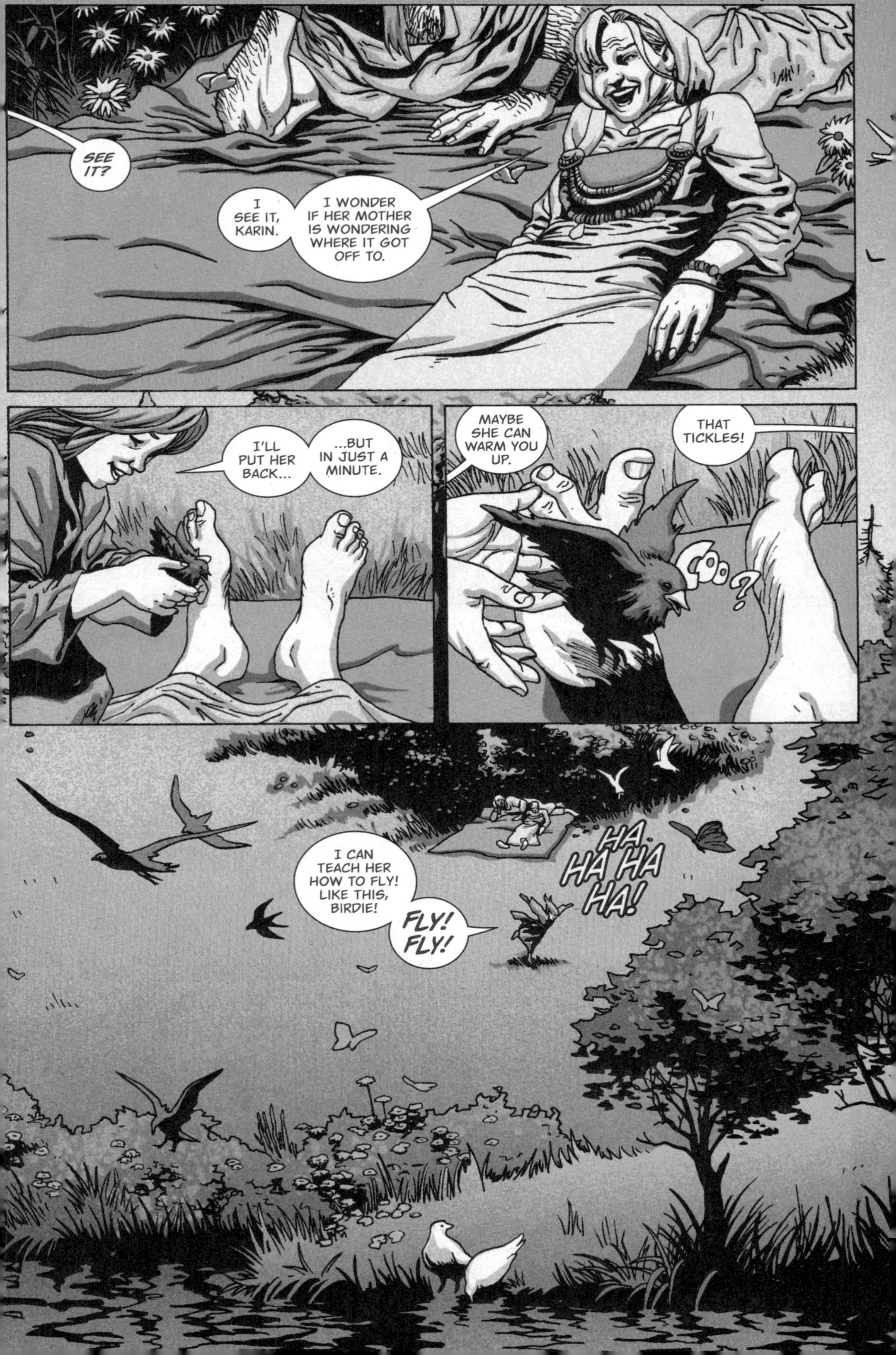
SEE IT?
I SEE IT, KARIN.
I WONDER IF HER MOTHER IS WONDERING WHERE IT GOT OFF TO.
I'LL PUT HER BACK...
...BUT IN JUST A MINUTE.
MAYBE SHE CAN WARM YOU UP.
THAT TICKLES!
COO?
I CAN TEACH HER HOW TO FLY! LIKE THIS, BIRDIE!
FLY! FLY!
HA HA HA HA HA!

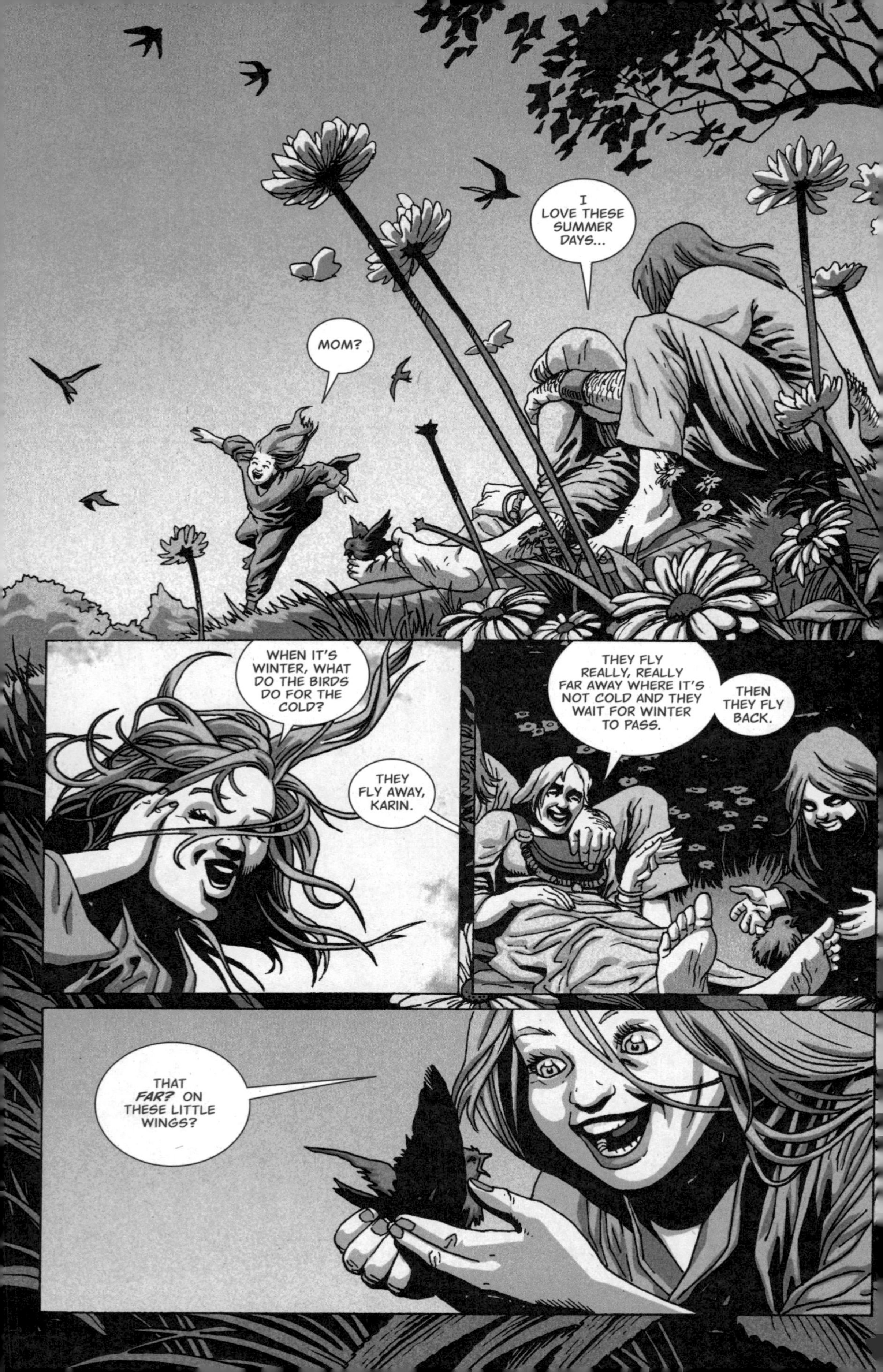
I LOVE THESE SUMMER DAYS...
MOM?
WHEN IT'S WINTER, WHAT DO THE BIRDS DO FOR THE COLD?
THEY FLY AWAY, KARIN.
THEY FLY REALLY, REALLY FAR AWAY WHERE IT'S NOT COLD AND THEY WAIT FOR WINTER TO PASS.
THEN THEY FLY BACK.
THAT *FAR?* ON THESE LITTLE WINGS?

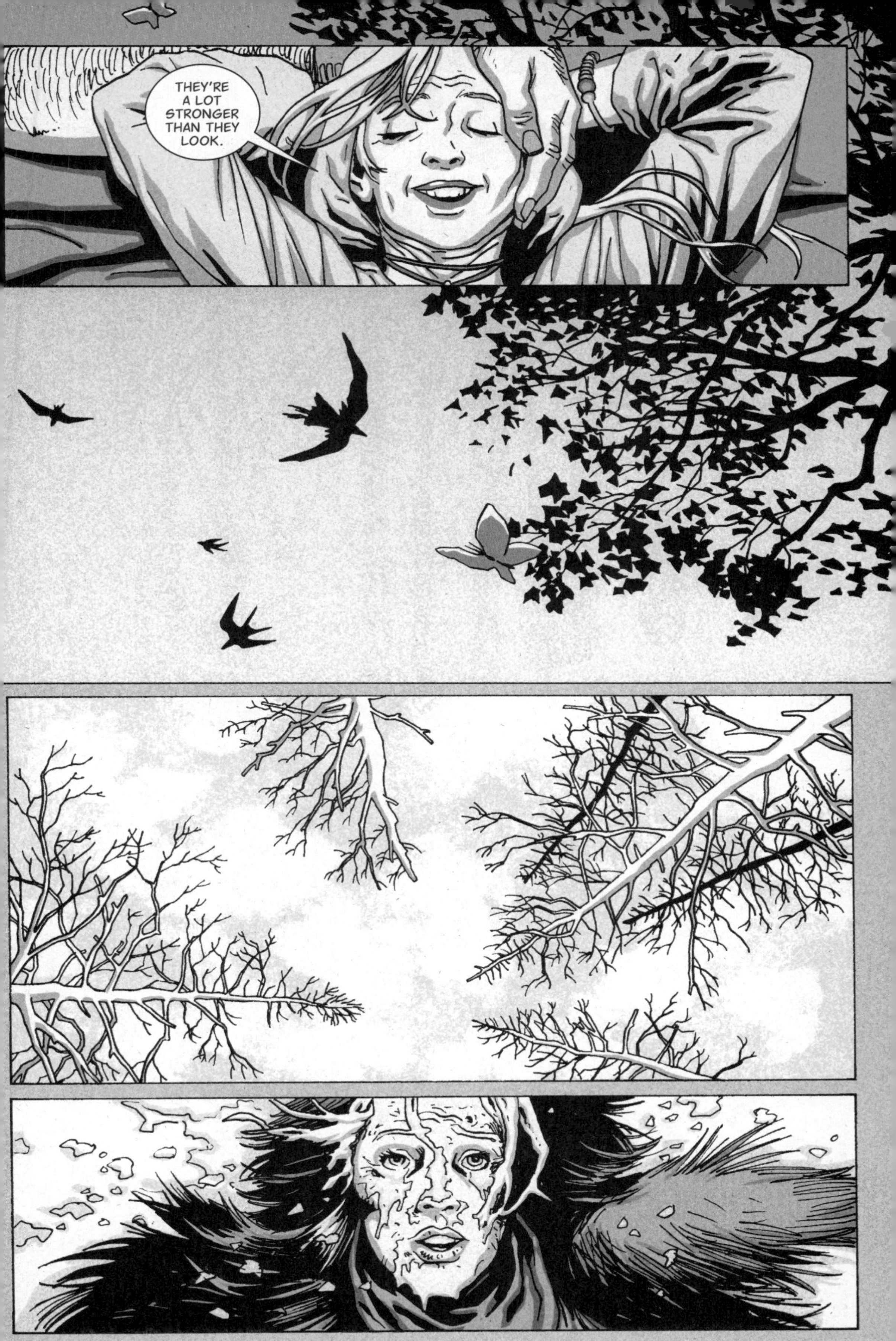
THEY'RE A LOT STRONGER THAN THEY LOOK.

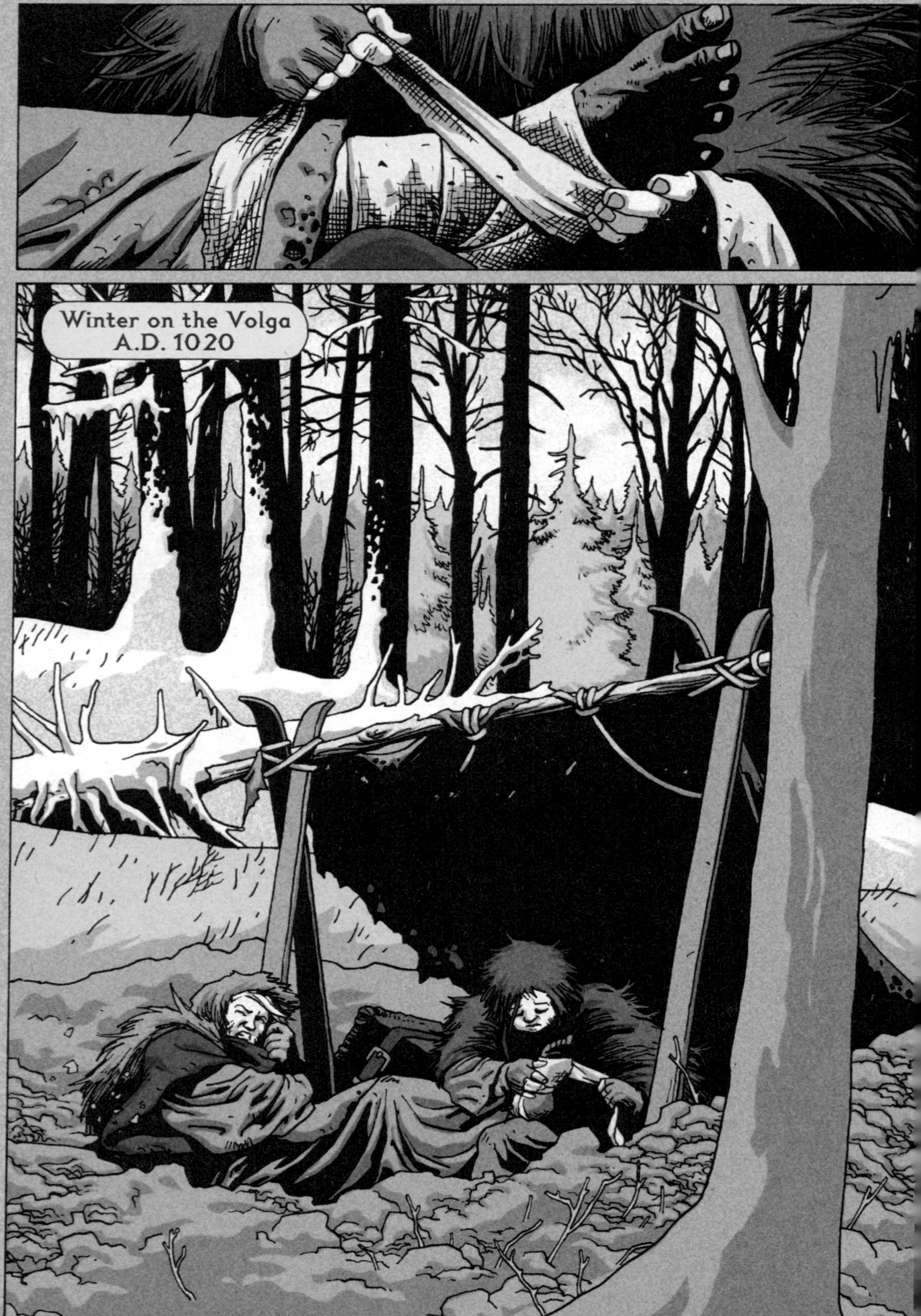
Winter on the Volga
A.D. 1020

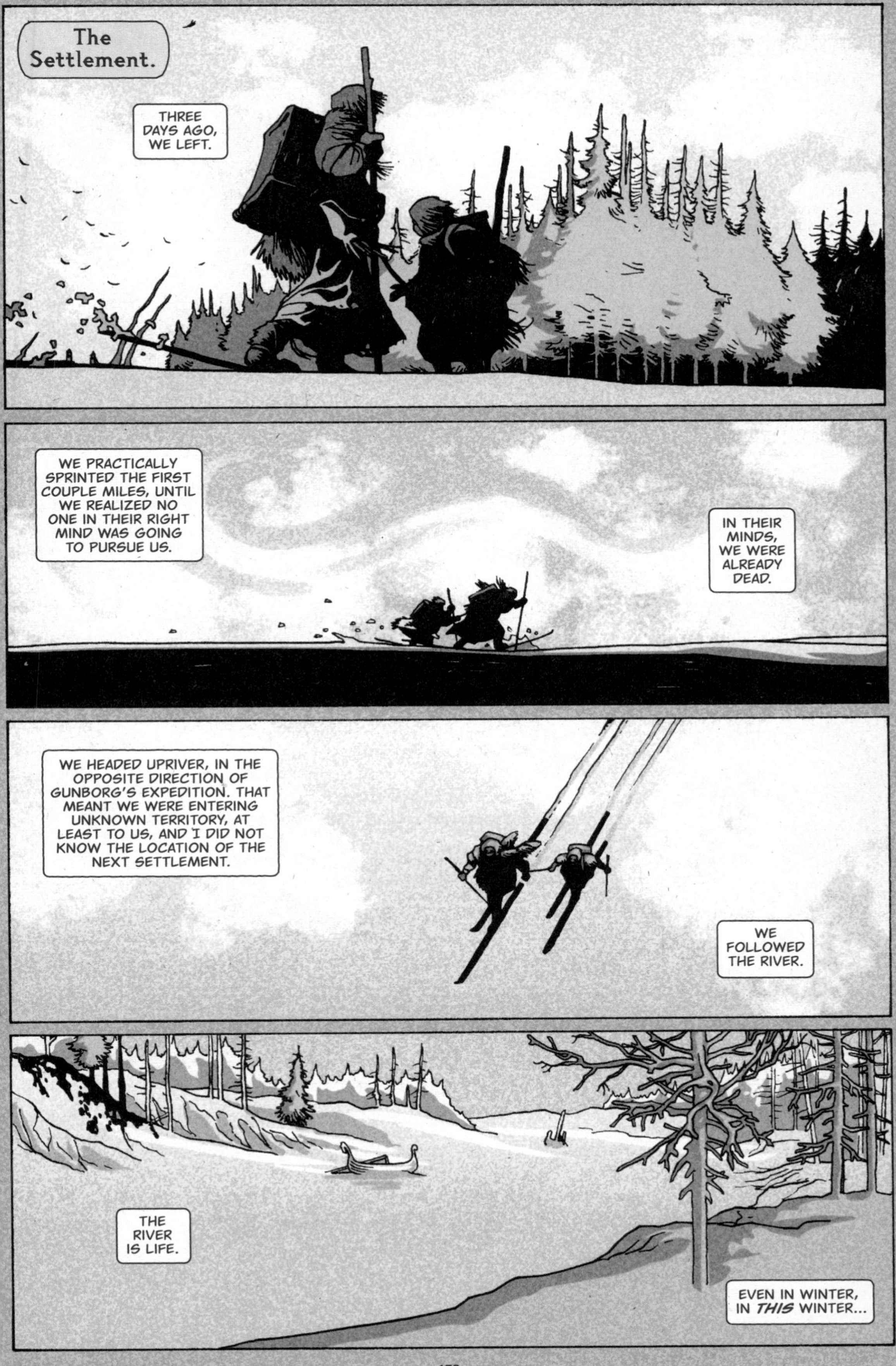
The Settlement.
THREE DAYS AGO, WE LEFT.
WE PRACTICALLY SPRINTED THE FIRST COUPLE MILES, UNTIL WE REALIZED NO ONE IN THEIR RIGHT MIND WAS GOING TO PURSUE US.
IN THEIR MINDS, WE WERE ALREADY DEAD.
WE HEADED UPRIVER, IN THE OPPOSITE DIRECTION OF GUNBORG'S EXPEDITION. THAT MEANT WE WERE ENTERING UNKNOWN TERRITORY, AT LEAST TO US, AND I DID NOT KNOW THE LOCATION OF THE NEXT SETTLEMENT.
WE FOLLOWED THE RIVER.
THE RIVER IS LIFE.
EVEN IN WINTER, IN *THIS* WINTER...

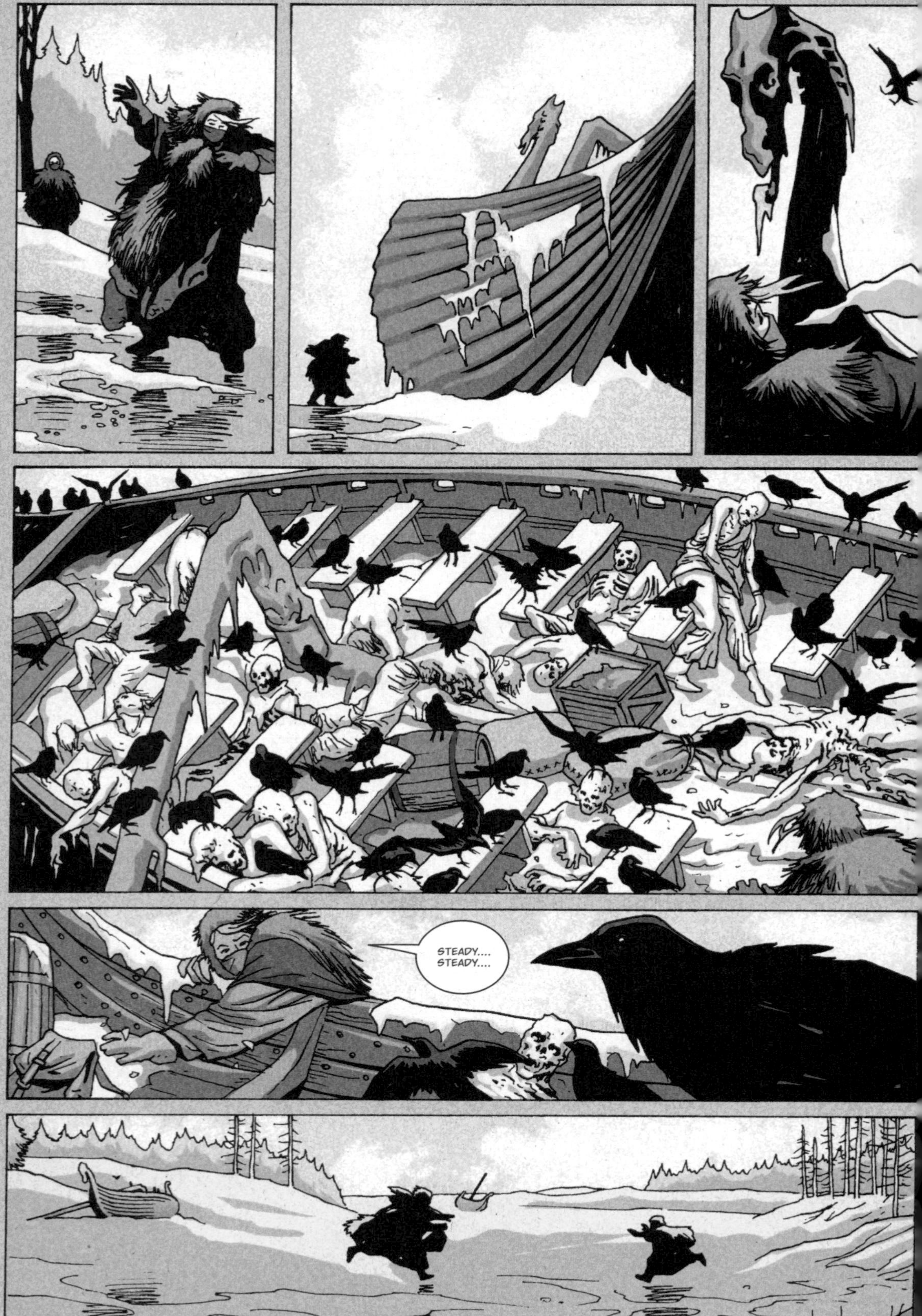
STEADY....
STEADY....
... SOMETHING CAN BE SALVAGED.

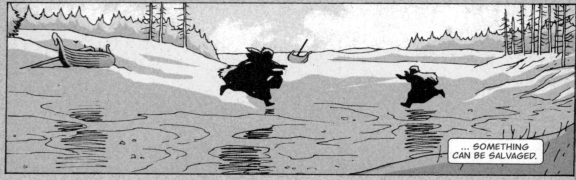

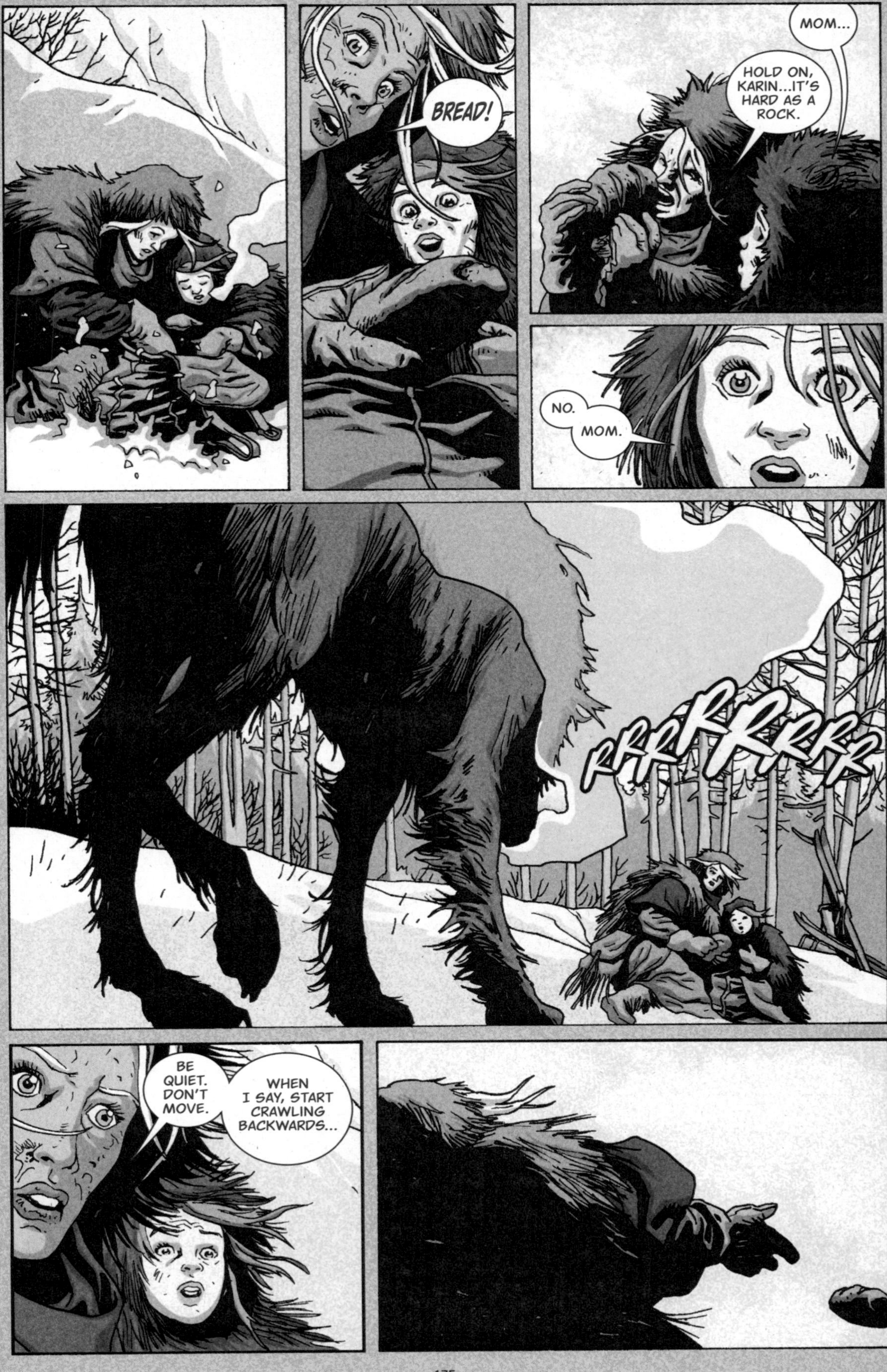
BREAD!
MOM...
HOLD ON, KARIN...IT'S HARD AS A ROCK.
NO.
MOM.
RRRRRRRRR
BE QUIET. DON'T MOVE.
WHEN I SAY, START CRAWLING BACKWARDS...

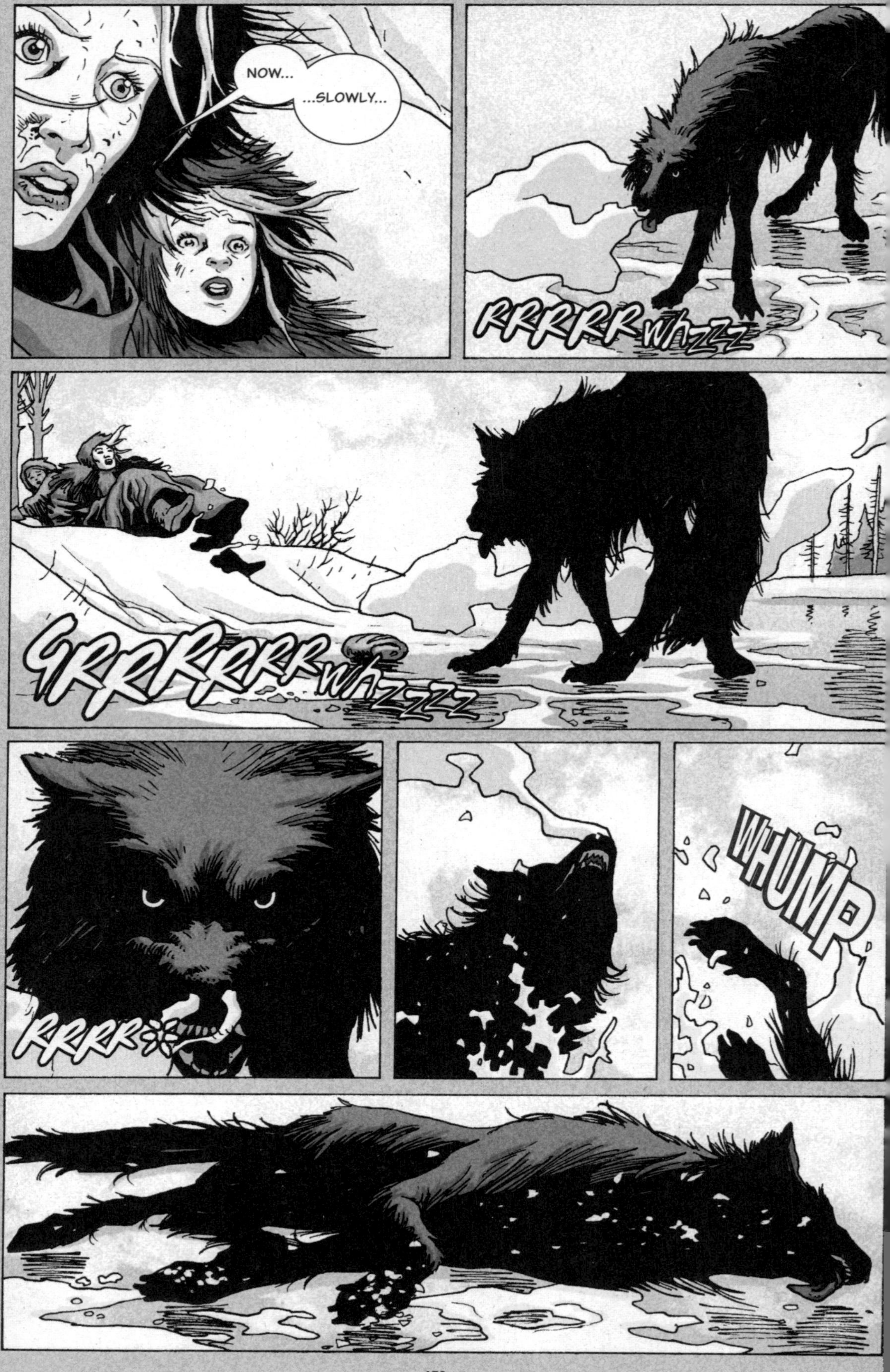
NOW...
...SLOWLY...
RRRRRRwhzzz
GRRRRRRRwhzzzz
RRRR
WHUMP

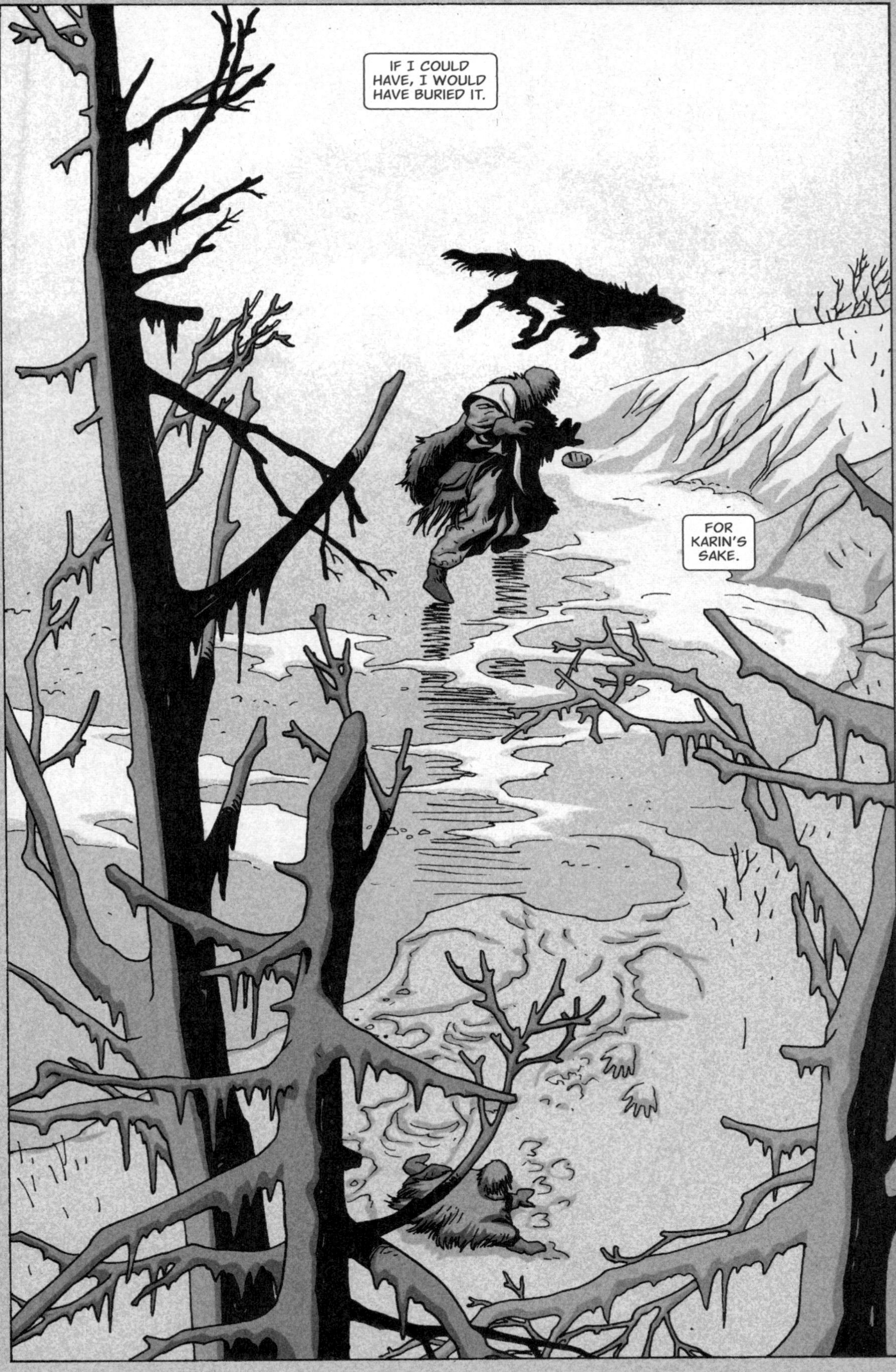
IF I COULD HAVE, I WOULD HAVE BURIED IT.
FOR KARIN'S SAKE.

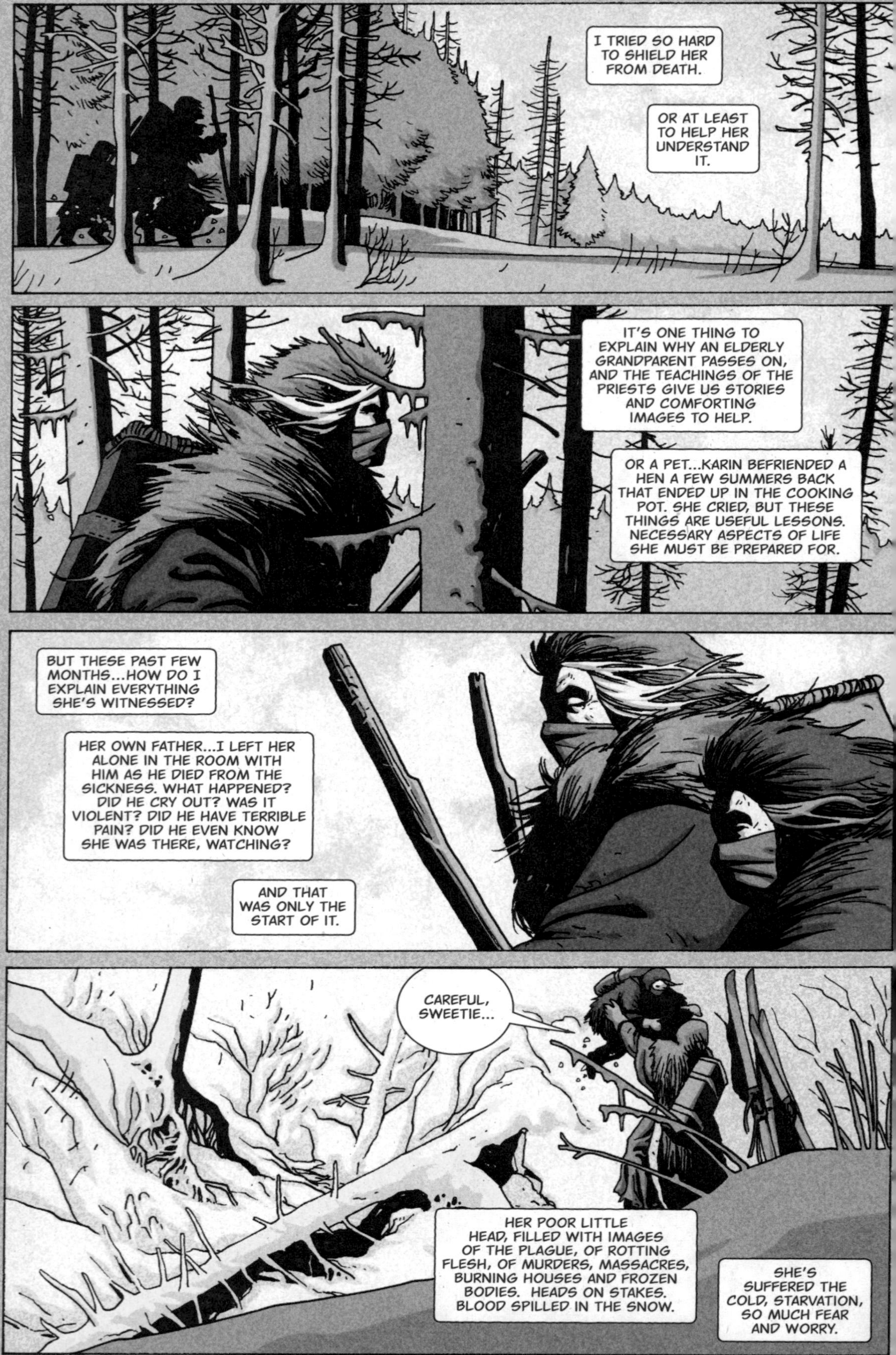
I TRIED SO HARD TO SHIELD HER FROM DEATH.
OR AT LEAST TO HELP HER UNDERSTAND IT.
IT'S ONE THING TO EXPLAIN WHY AN ELDERLY GRANDPARENT PASSES ON, AND THE TEACHINGS OF THE PRIESTS GIVE US STORIES AND COMFORTING IMAGES TO HELP.
OR A PET...KARIN BEFRIENDED A HEN A FEW SUMMERS BACK THAT ENDED UP IN THE COOKING POT. SHE CRIED, BUT THESE THINGS ARE USEFUL LESSONS. NECESSARY ASPECTS OF LIFE SHE MUST BE PREPARED FOR.
BUT THESE PAST FEW MONTHS...HOW DO I EXPLAIN EVERYTHING SHE'S WITNESSED?
HER OWN FATHER...I LEFT HER ALONE IN THE ROOM WITH HIM AS HE DIED FROM THE SICKNESS. WHAT HAPPENED? DID HE CRY OUT? WAS IT VIOLENT? DID HE HAVE TERRIBLE PAIN? DID HE EVEN KNOW SHE WAS THERE, WATCHING?
AND THAT WAS ONLY THE START OF IT.
CAREFUL, SWEETIE...
HER POOR LITTLE HEAD, FILLED WITH IMAGES OF THE PLAGUE, OF ROTTING FLESH, OF MURDERS, MASSACRES, BURNING HOUSES AND FROZEN BODIES. HEADS ON STAKES. BLOOD SPILLED IN THE SNOW.
SHE'S SUFFERED THE COLD, STARVATION, SO MUCH FEAR AND WORRY.

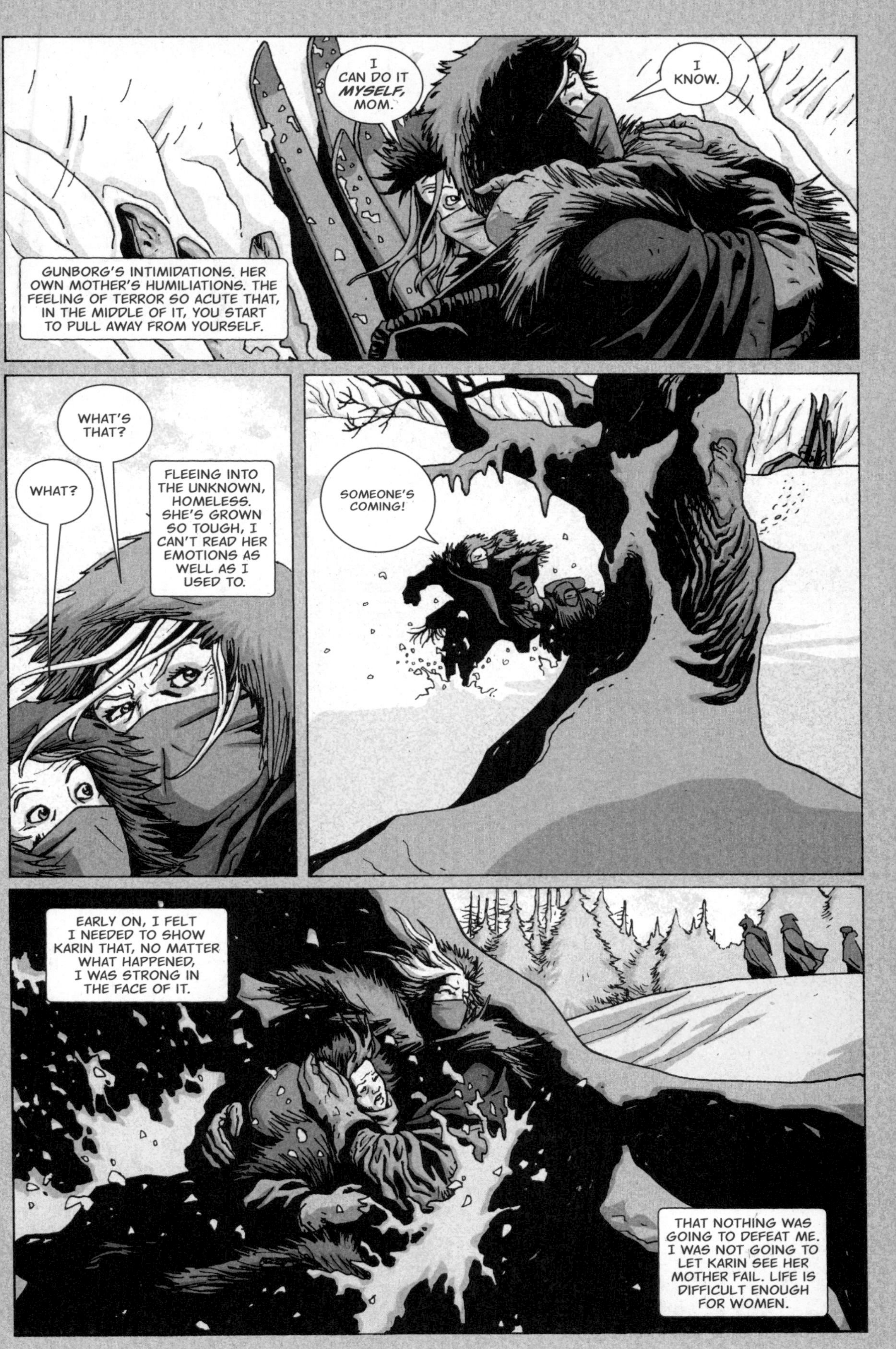
I CAN DO IT *MYSELF,* MOM.
I KNOW.
GUNBORG'S INTIMIDATIONS. HER OWN MOTHER'S HUMILIATIONS. THE FEELING OF TERROR SO ACUTE THAT, IN THE MIDDLE OF IT, YOU START TO PULL AWAY FROM YOURSELF.
WHAT'S THAT?
WHAT?
FLEEING INTO THE UNKNOWN, HOMELESS. SHE'S GROWN SO TOUGH, I CAN'T READ HER EMOTIONS AS WELL AS I USED TO.
SOMEONE'S COMING!
EARLY ON, I FELT I NEEDED TO SHOW KARIN THAT, NO MATTER WHAT HAPPENED, I WAS STRONG IN THE FACE OF IT.
THAT NOTHING WAS GOING TO DEFEAT ME. I WAS NOT GOING TO LET KARIN SEE HER MOTHER FAIL. LIFE IS DIFFICULT ENOUGH FOR WOMEN.

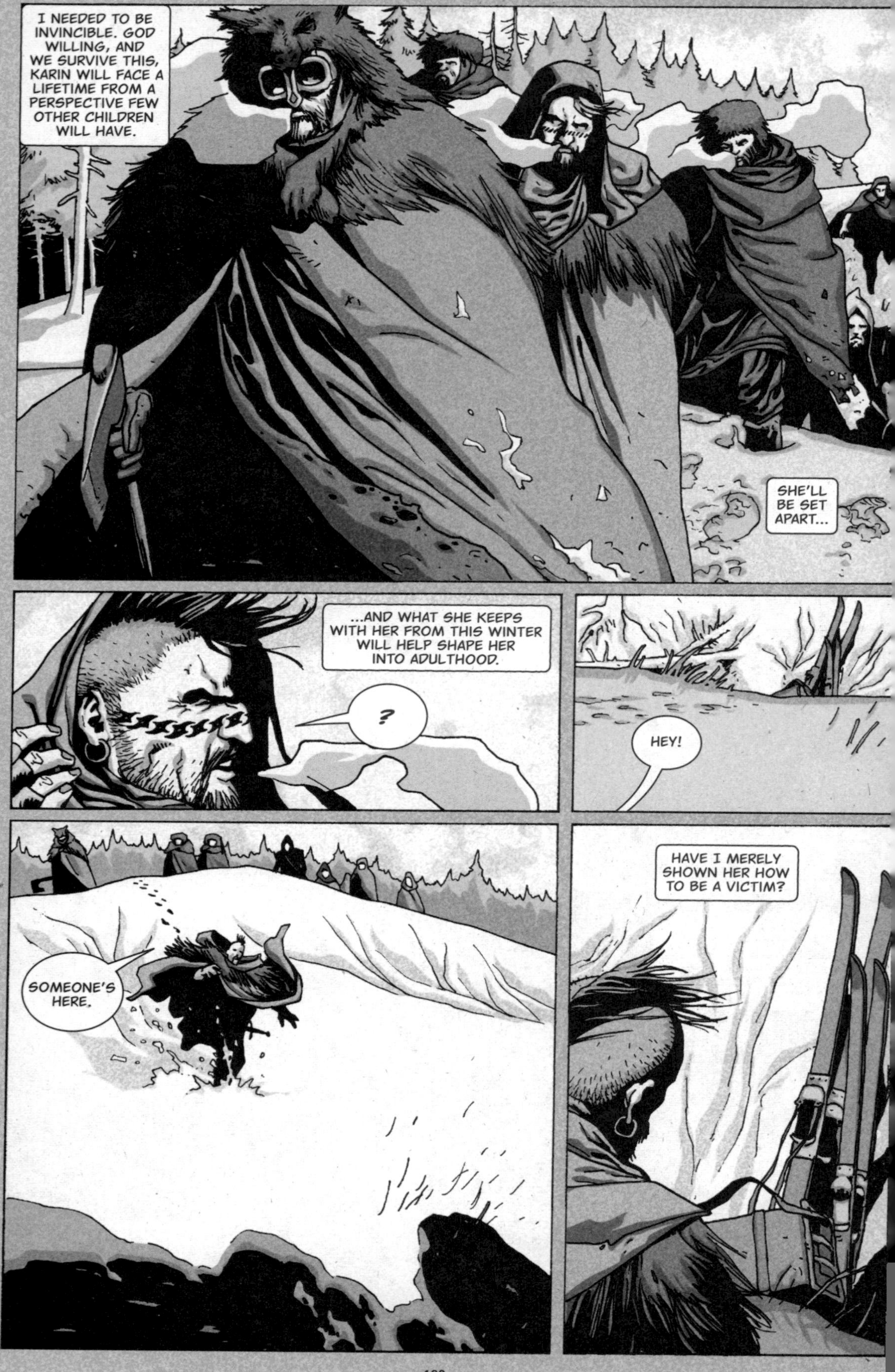
I NEEDED TO BE INVINCIBLE. GOD WILLING, AND WE SURVIVE THIS, KARIN WILL FACE A LIFETIME FROM A PERSPECTIVE FEW OTHER CHILDREN WILL HAVE.
SHE'LL BE SET APART...
...AND WHAT SHE KEEPS WITH HER FROM THIS WINTER WILL HELP SHAPE HER INTO ADULTHOOD.
?
HEY!
SOMEONE'S HERE.
HAVE I MERELY SHOWN HER HOW TO BE A VICTIM?

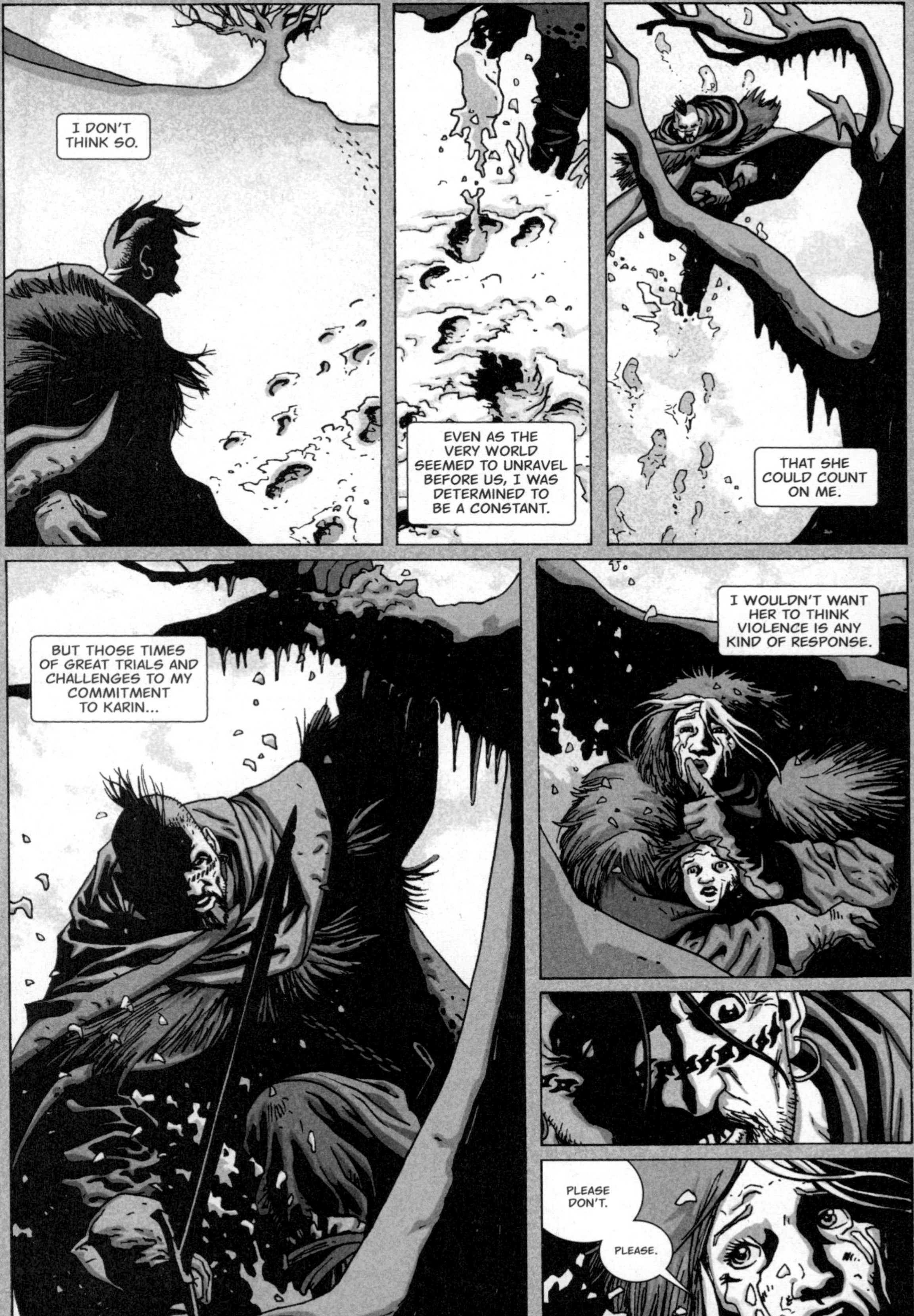

I DON'T THINK SO.
EVEN AS THE VERY WORLD SEEMED TO UNRAVEL BEFORE US, I WAS DETERMINED TO BE A CONSTANT.
THAT SHE COULD COUNT ON ME.
BUT THOSE TIMES OF GREAT TRIALS AND CHALLENGES TO MY COMMITMENT TO KARIN...
I WOULDN'T WANT HER TO THINK VIOLENCE IS ANY KIND OF RESPONSE.
PLEASE DON'T.
PLEASE.

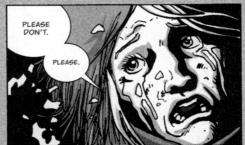

WELL? WHAT WAS IT?

NOTHING. NO ONE.

WHOEVER IT WAS, THEY FLED. LEFT NOTHING OF ANY USE.

...ALL RIGHT.

WE'D STUMBLE ON THE PATH BETWEEN CIVILIZATION AND CHAOS...

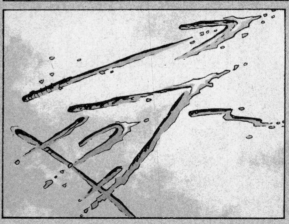

...AND SOMEHOW WE HUNG ON.

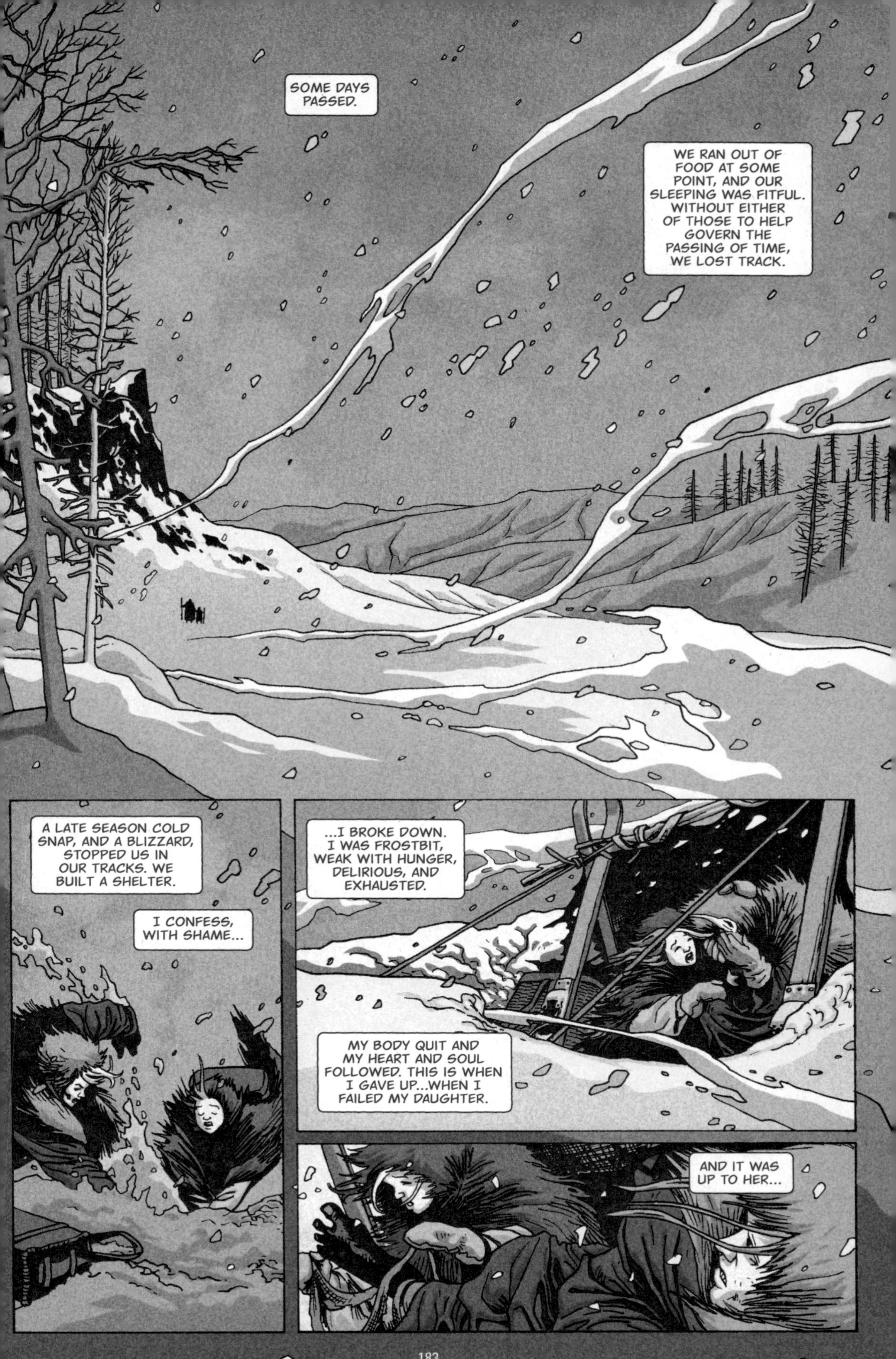
SOME DAYS PASSED.
WE RAN OUT OF FOOD AT SOME POINT, AND OUR SLEEPING WAS FITFUL. WITHOUT EITHER OF THOSE TO HELP GOVERN THE PASSING OF TIME, WE LOST TRACK.
A LATE SEASON COLD SNAP, AND A BLIZZARD, STOPPED US IN OUR TRACKS. WE BUILT A SHELTER.
I CONFESS, WITH SHAME...
...I BROKE DOWN. I WAS FROSTBIT, WEAK WITH HUNGER, DELIRIOUS, AND EXHAUSTED.
MY BODY QUIT AND MY HEART AND SOUL FOLLOWED. THIS IS WHEN I GAVE UP...WHEN I FAILED MY DAUGHTER.
AND IT WAS UP TO HER...

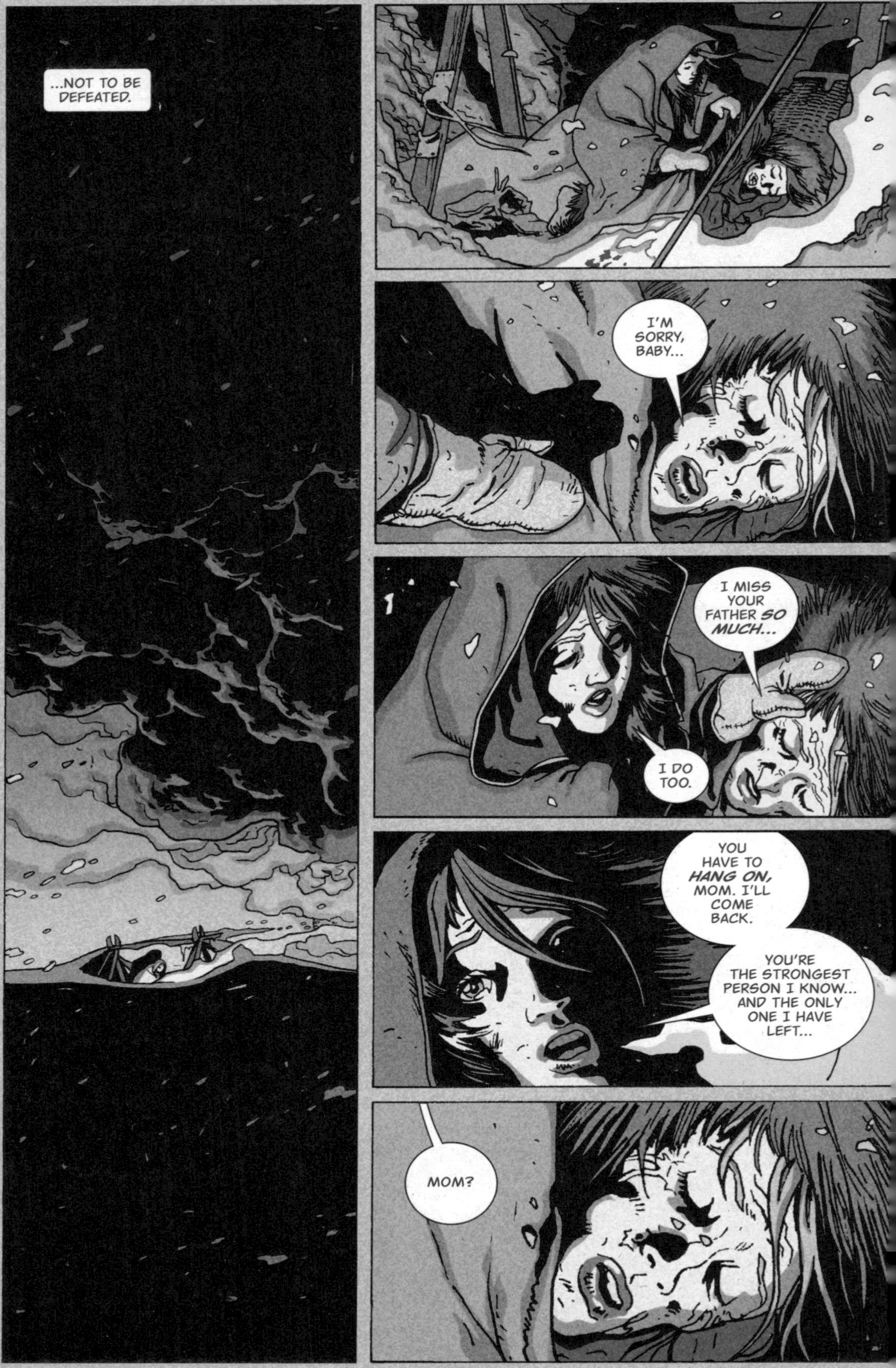
...NOT TO BE DEFEATED.
I'M SORRY, BABY...
I MISS YOUR FATHER SO MUCH...
I DO TOO.
YOU HAVE TO HANG ON, MOM. I'LL COME BACK.
YOU'RE THE STRONGEST PERSON I KNOW... AND THE ONLY ONE I HAVE LEFT...
MOM?

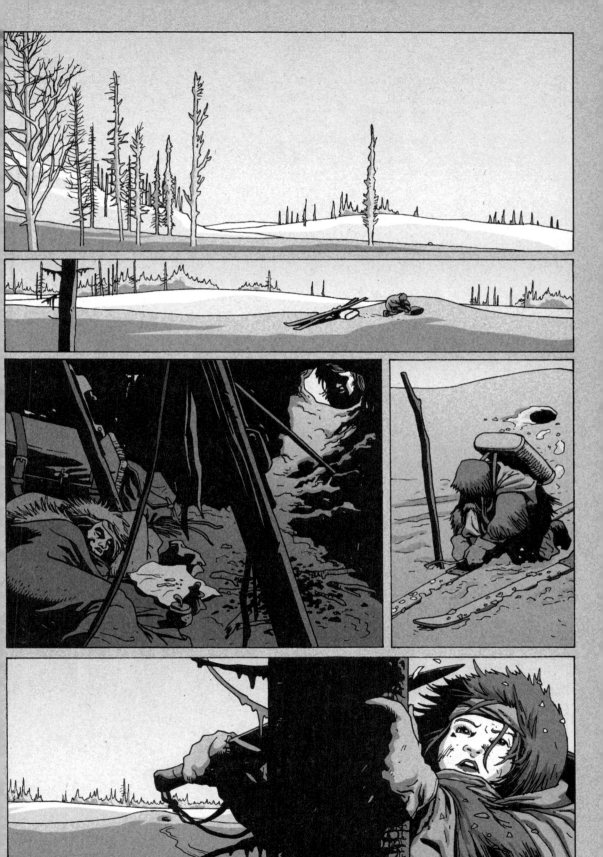

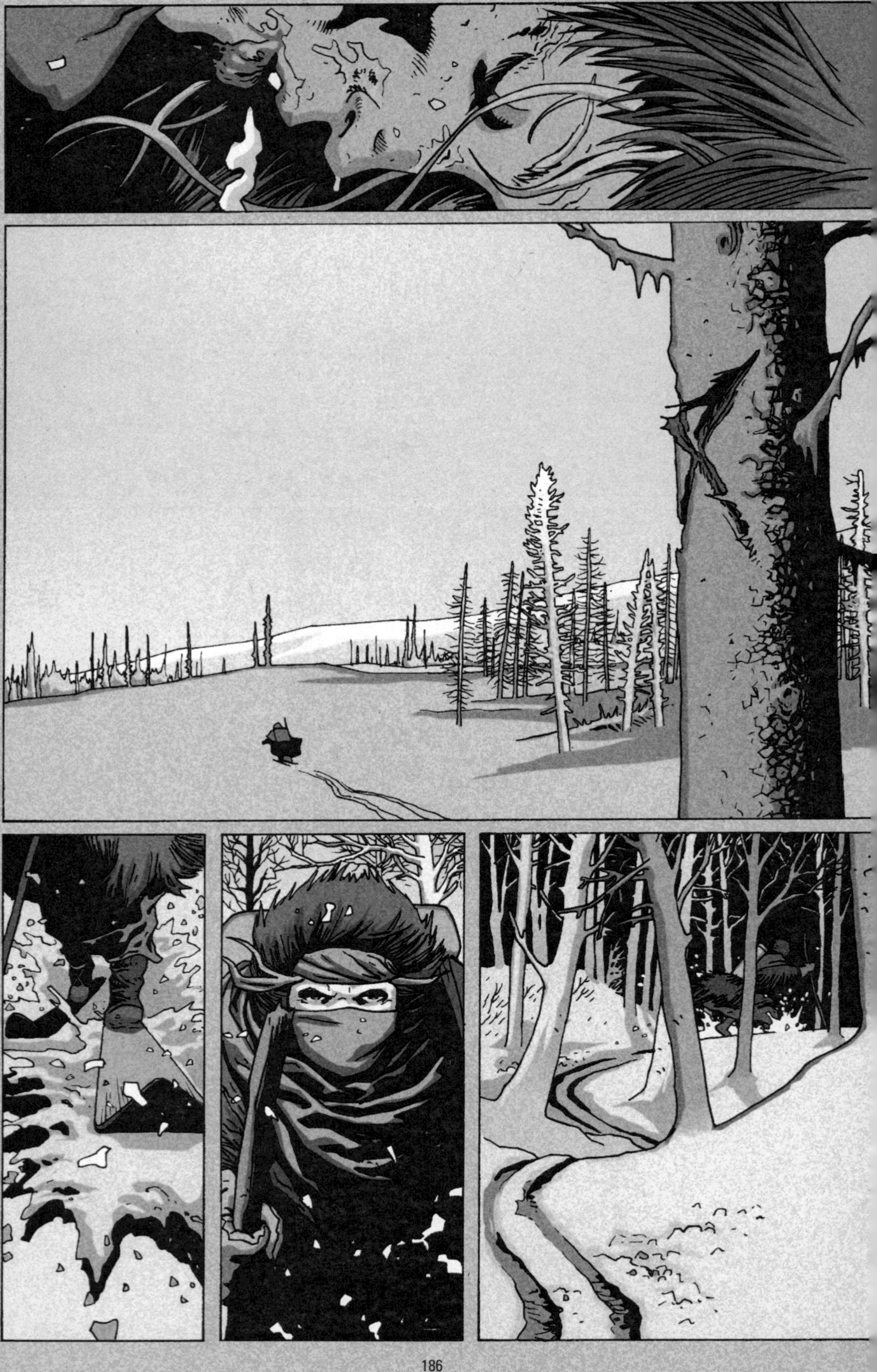

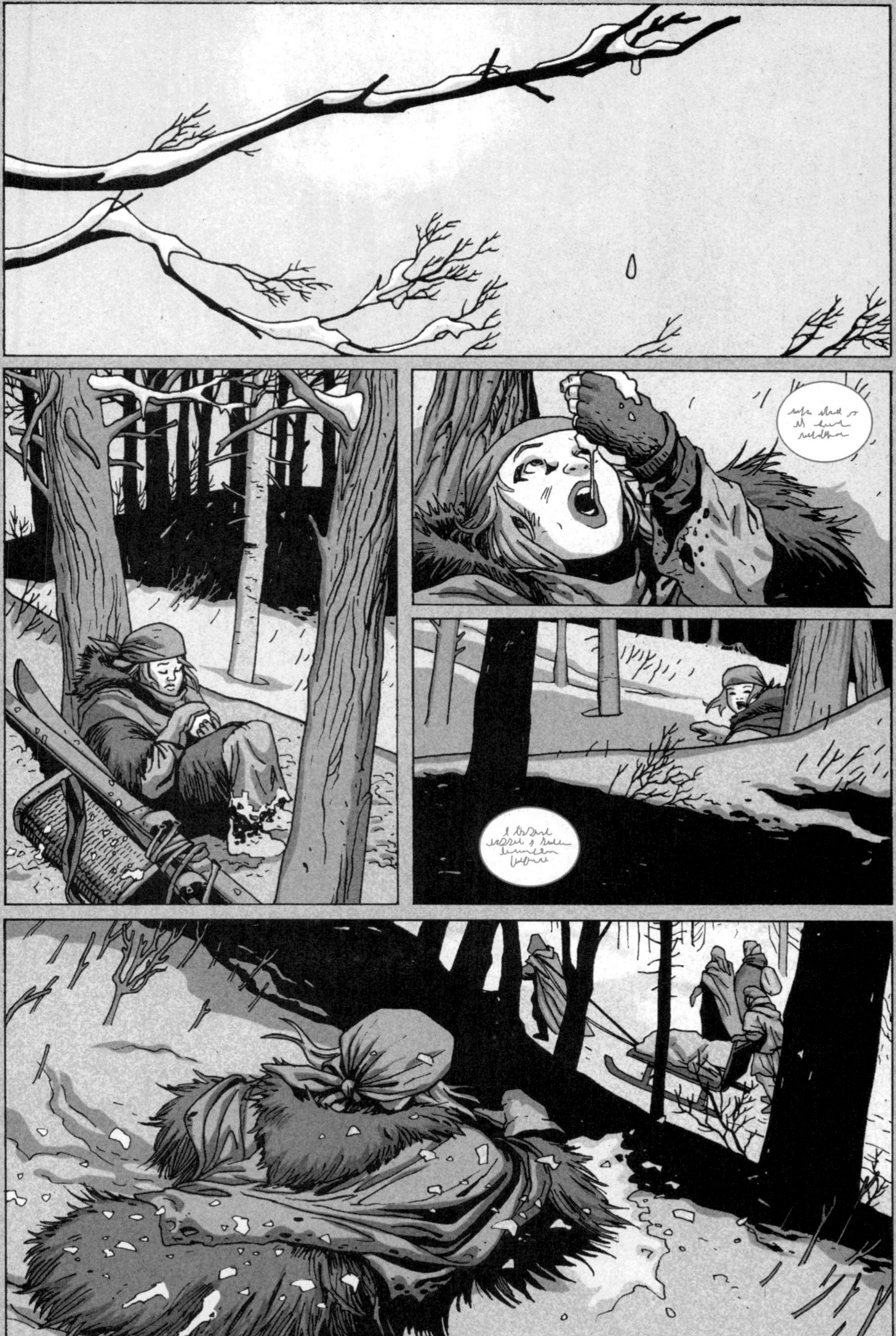

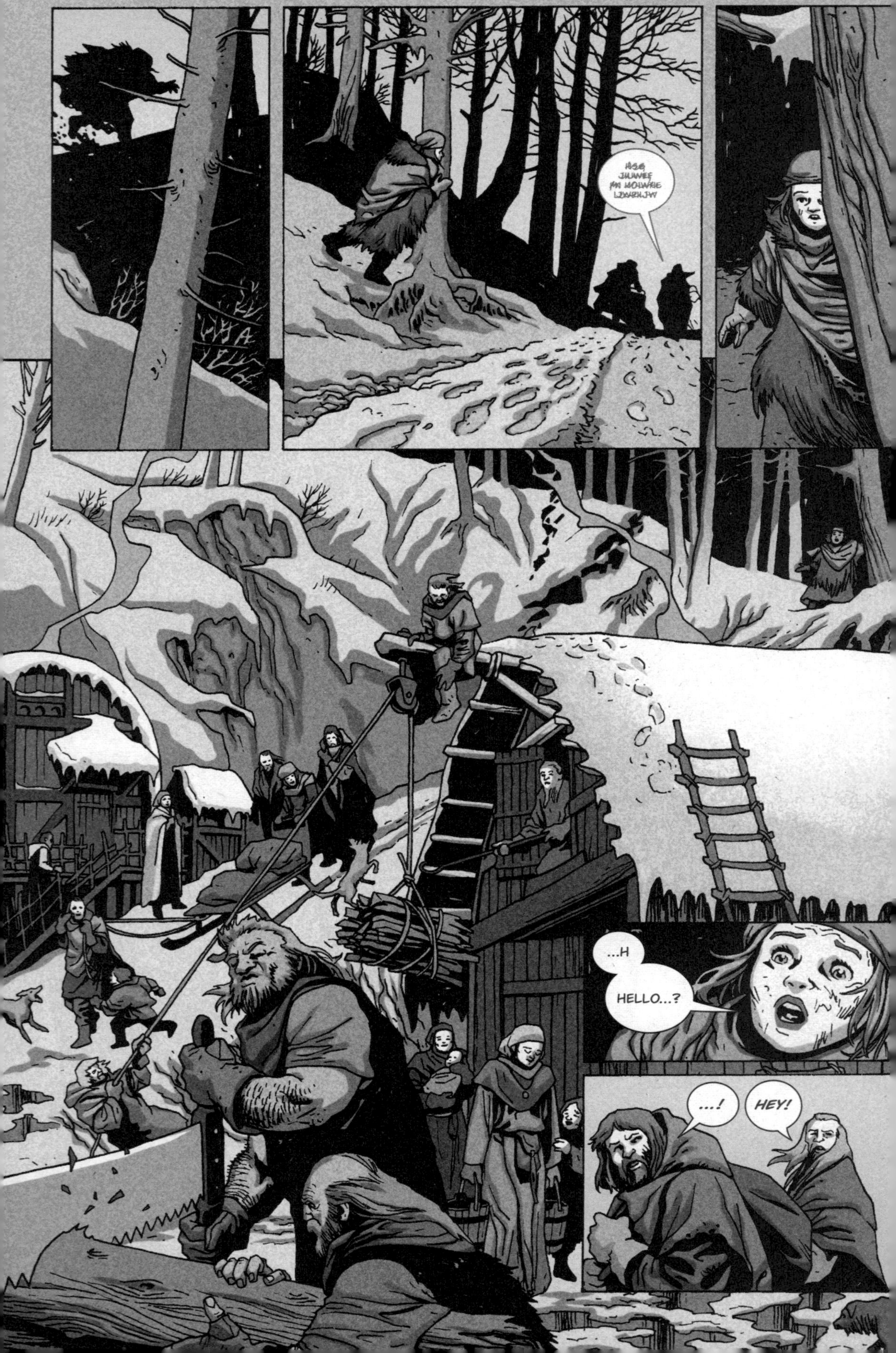
...H
HELLO...?
...!
HEY!

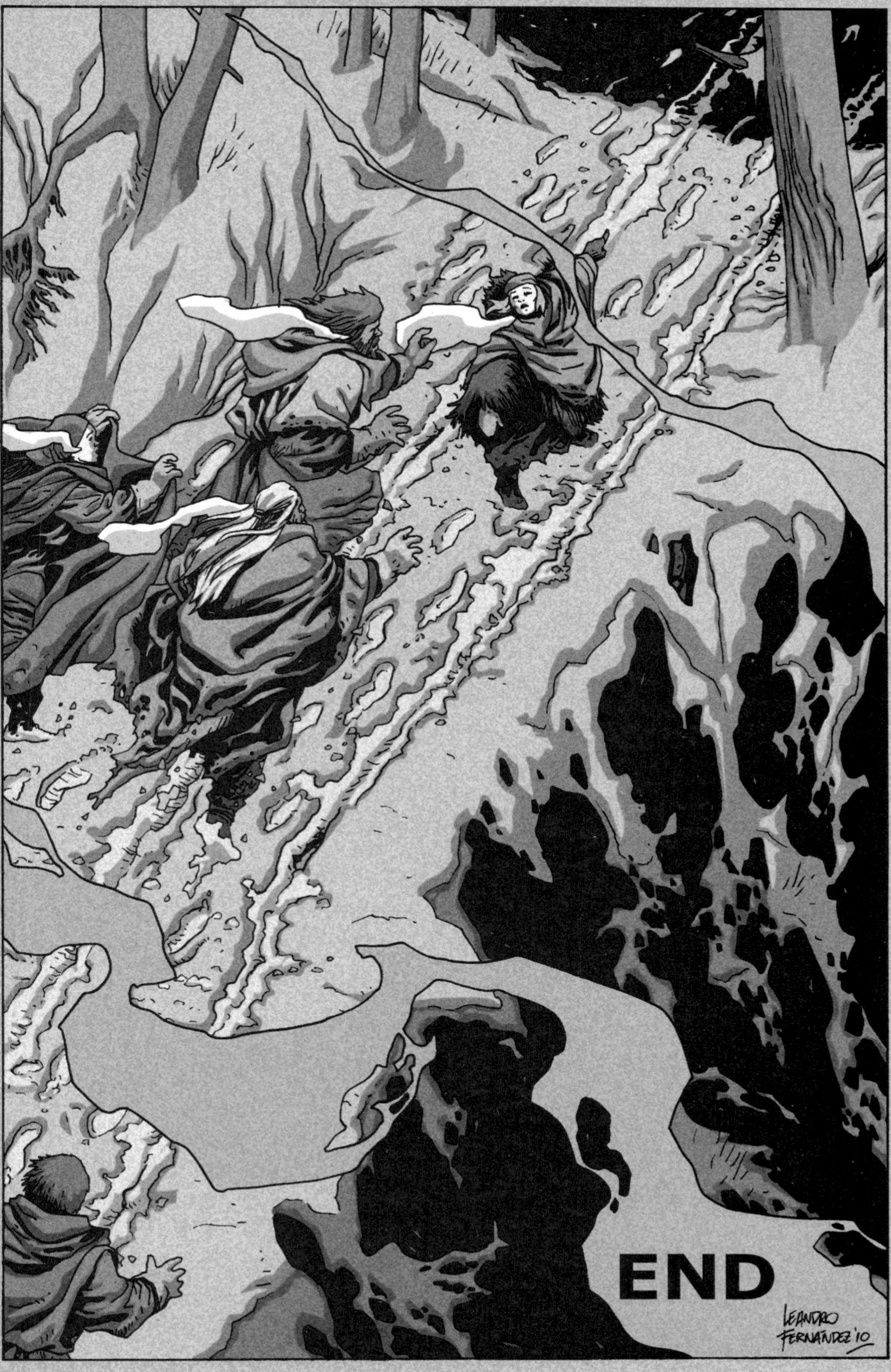
END
LEANDRO FERNÁNDEZ '10

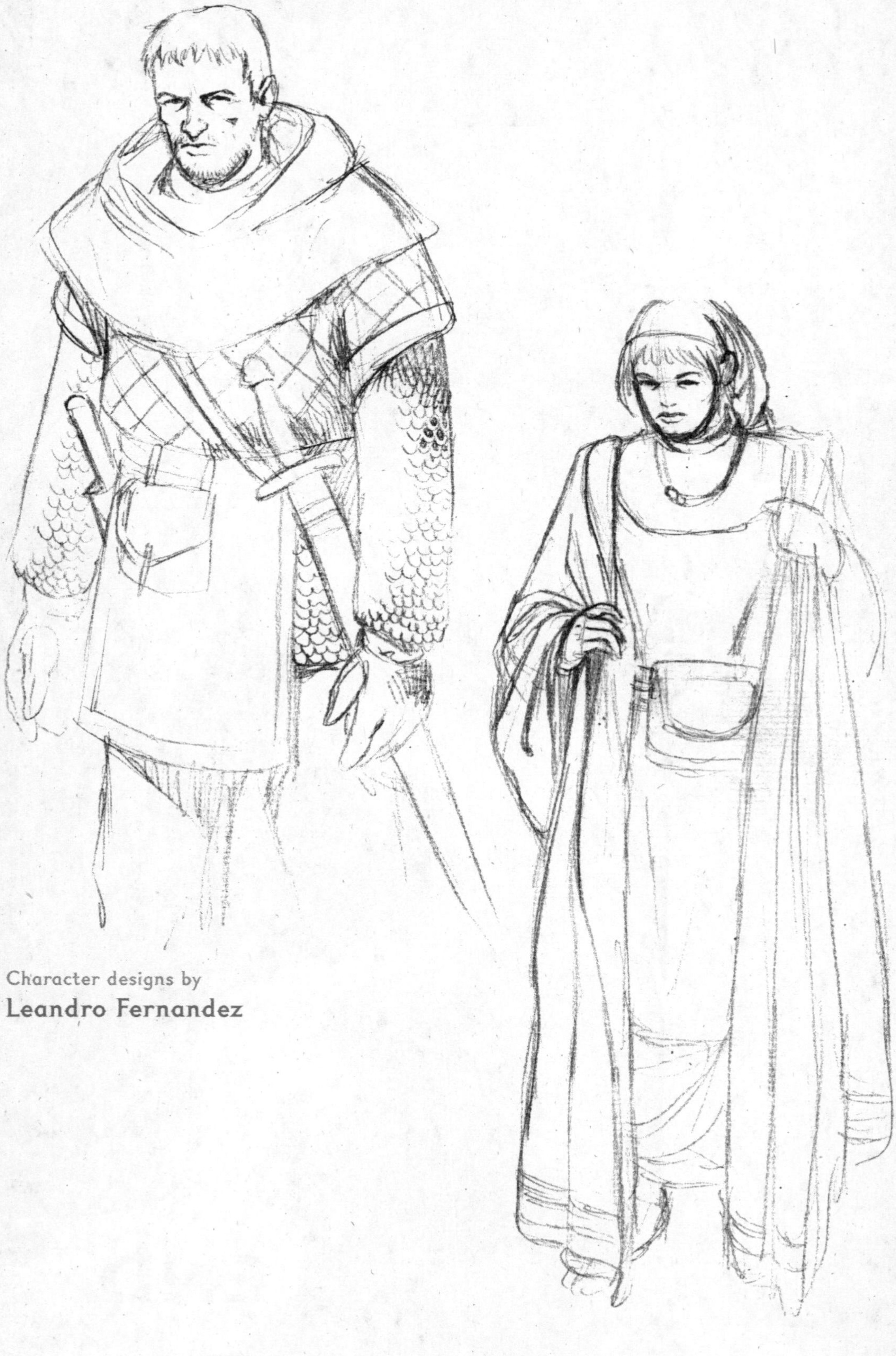

Character designs by
Leandro Fernandez

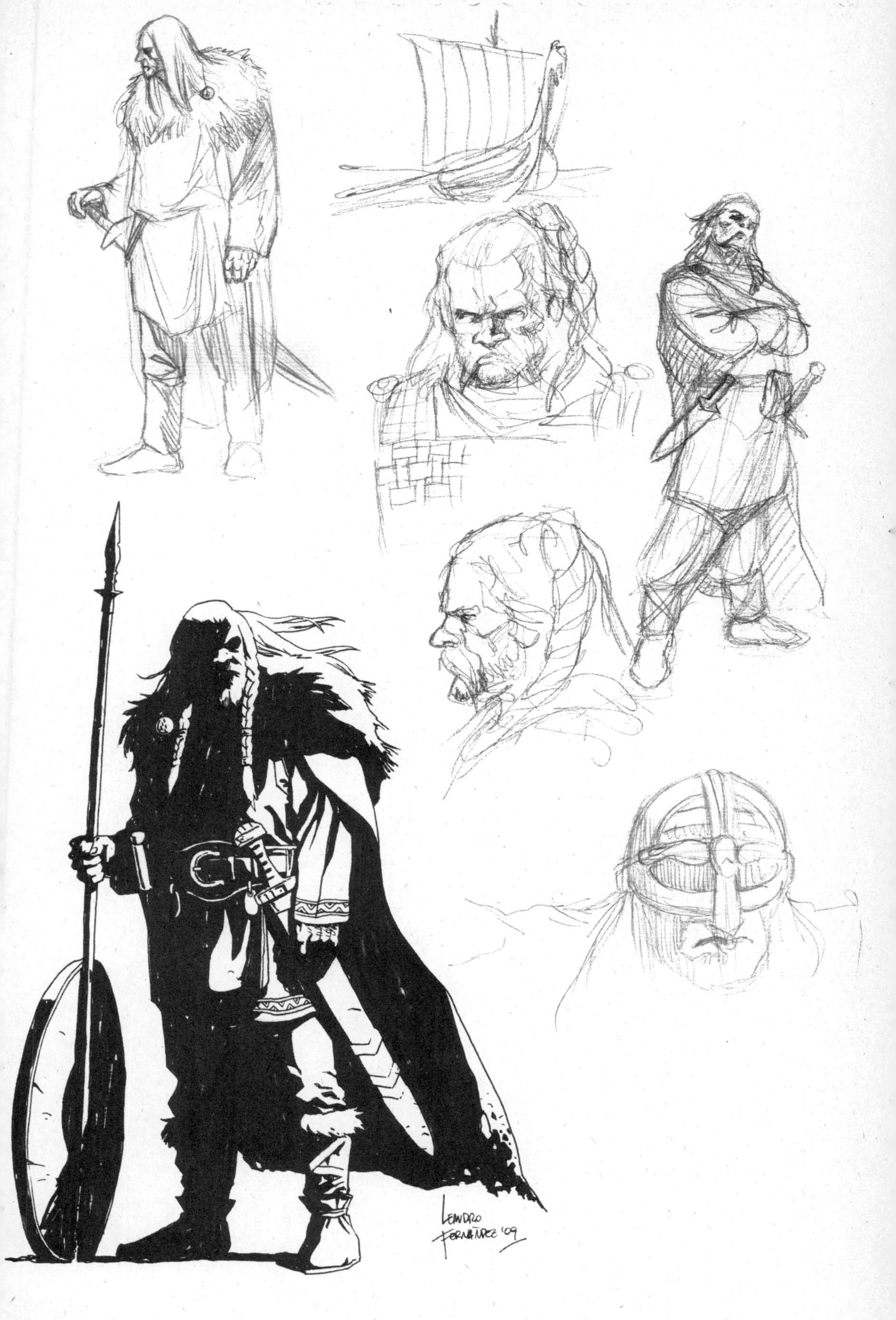
LEANDRO
FERNÁNDEZ '09

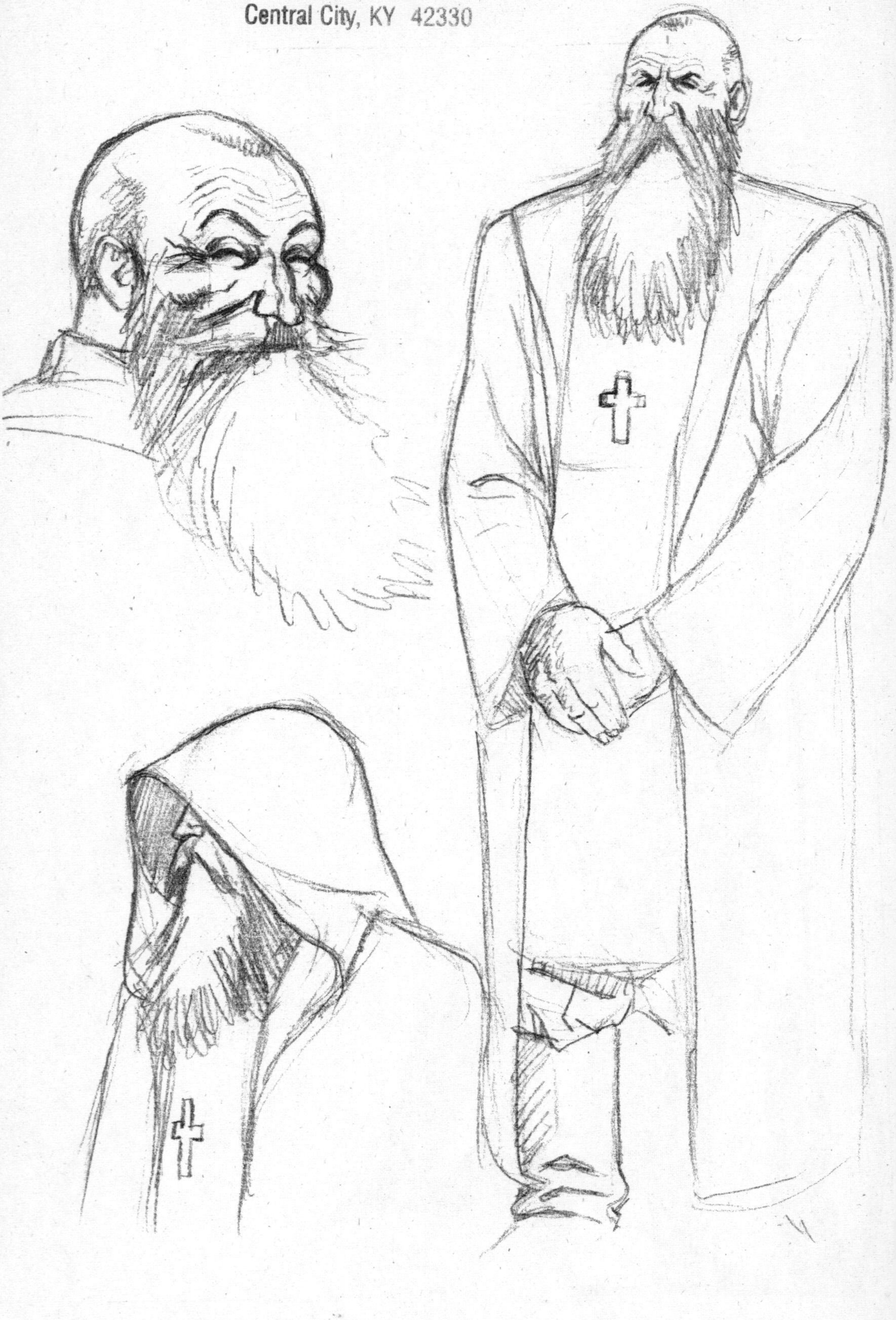